THE WHIG PARTY
1807-1812

MICHAEL ROBERTS

FRANK CASS & CO. LTD.
1965

First published by Macmillan & Co. Ltd., in 1939
and now reprinted by their kind permission.

This edition published by Frank Cass & Co. Ltd.,
10, Woburn Walk, London, W.C.1.

First edition   1939
Second edition 1965

23872

*Printed by Thomas Nelson (Printers) Ltd
London and Edinburgh*

CONTENTS

PREFATORY NOTE

I BEG leave to record my humble thanks to His Majesty the King for permission to make use of the papers of George III, Queen Charlotte, and George IV preserved in the Archives at Windsor Castle.

I have further to thank Brigadier-General W. R. N. Madocks, C.B., C.M.G., D.S.O., for having allowed me to use the papers of George Tierney which are in his possession; Professor L. B. Namier, the Editor of this series, for valuable advice and suggestions which have saved me from many errors; Professor G. S. Veitch of the University of Liverpool, and Professor W. B. Hall of Princeton University, for guidance and encouragement; Major E. B. Walker, M.B.E., M.C., for help with Chapter II; the Editor of The English Historical Review for permission to reprint Chapter I (a), Chapter IV, and Chapter V (b) (4), which have appeared already as separate articles in that journal; Mr. L. V. Sumner, who has given valuable assistance in preparing the book for the press.

The publication of this book has been facilitated by assistance from the Hiddingh-Currie publication fund of the University of South Africa. Dr. William Hiddingh and the family of Sir Donald Currie each contributed £25,000 to the University of the Cape of Good Hope. This money was utilized in the erection of the new University buildings, but when the University of South Africa became the legal successor of the University of the Cape of Good Hope and the offices were moved to Pretoria, the buildings could no longer be used for the purpose for which they were erected. They were taken over by the Union Government for £15,000, and an endowment fund was created. A portion of the interest derived from this sum has been set aside by the

PREFATORY NOTE

I BEG leave to record my humble thanks to His Majesty the King for permission to make use of the papers of George III, Queen Charlotte, and George IV preserved in the Archives at Windsor Castle.

I have further to thank Brigadier-General W. R. N. Madocks, C.B., C.M.G., D.S.O., for having allowed me to use the papers of George Tierney which are in his possession; Professor L. B. Namier, the Editor of this series, for valuable advice and suggestions which have saved me from many errors; Professor G. S. Veitch of the University of Liverpool, and Professor W. B. Hall of Princeton University, for guidance and encouragement; Major E. B. Walker, M.B.E., M.C., for help with Chapter II; the Editor of *The English Historical Review* for permission to reprint Chapter I (*a*), Chapter IV, and Chapter V (*b*) (4), which have appeared already as separate articles in that journal; Mr. L. V. Sumner, who has given valuable assistance in preparing the book for the press.

The publication of this book has been facilitated by assistance from the Hiddingh-Currie publication fund of the University of South Africa. Dr. William Hiddingh and the family of Sir Donald Currie each contributed £25,000 to the University of the Cape of Good Hope. This money was utilized in the erection of the new University buildings, but when the University of South Africa became the legal successor of the University of the Cape of Good Hope and the offices were moved to Pretoria, the buildings could no longer be used for the purpose for which they were erected. They were taken over by the Union Government for £45,000, and an endowment fund was created. A portion of the interest derived from this sum has been set aside by the

Council of the University of South Africa to commemorate the munificence of these generous benefactors by the creation of the Hiddingh-Currie publication fund and the Hiddingh-Currie Scholarship. I wish to express my gratitude to the University of South Africa for the grant made me from this fund. ˗

In order to avoid confusion with the works of the late Sir John Fortescue, the Hist. MSS. Comm. Report on the MSS. of J. B. Fortescue, Esq., is cited throughout as *Dropmore Papers*. In the Windsor Archives the Correspondence of George IV is divided into three series : Correspondence of the Prince of Wales, Correspondence of the Regent, Correspondence of George IV. As these nowhere overlap in date, but form in fact one continuous series, it seemed simplest to cite them as Windsor Archives, George IV, since the dating of the letters precludes ambiguity.

M. R.

1936

INTRODUCTION

PITT died on 23 January 1806, and the weak Ministry of which he had been the head did not long survive him. It became impossible for George III to continue his exclusion of Fox from office; and for the next year England had a coalition Government of Whigs, Grenvillites and Addingtonians, known to history as the Ministry of All the Talents. The greatest—indeed the sole—achievement of this Administration was the Abolition of the Slave Trade; but this had not by any means been the only item upon its political programme. It had hoped to put an end to the war, and it had desired to lift some of the restrictions which lay upon the Roman Catholics. But the restless ambition of Napoleon had foiled Fox's conscientious efforts to arrange a peace; and the obstinate prejudice of George III had thwarted the endeavours of Grenville and Howick to obtain Catholic Emancipation. The quarrel with the King led to the fall of the Government in March 1807; and the remnants of Pitt's party cheerfully resumed the responsibilities of office.

From 1807 to 1812 England was ruled by two Tory Governments: that of the Duke of Portland, until September 1809; and that of Perceval, until his assassination in May 1812. Neither Ministry was particularly strong. The Portland Administration was handicapped by the inefficiency of its head and by dissensions among its members, and ultimately fell as the result of the well-known quarrel between Canning and Castlereagh. Perceval, who succeeded to the Premiership, was regarded with jealousy by Wellesley and Canning; and despite his many admirable qualities, and his great influence over the Tory rank and file, he was hardly equal to the responsibilities of his post. His Government

INTRODUCTION

PITT died on 23 January 1806, and the weak Ministry of which he had been the head did not long survive him. It became impossible for George III to continue his exclusion of Fox from office ; and for the next year England had a coalition Government of Whigs, Grenvillites and Addingtonians, known to history as the Ministry of All the Talents. The greatest—indeed the sole—achievement of this Administration was the Abolition of the Slave Trade ; but this had not by any means been the only item upon its political programme. It had hoped to put an end to the war, and it had desired to lift some of the restrictions which lay upon the Roman Catholics. But the restless ambition of Napoleon had foiled Fox's conscientious efforts to arrange a peace ; and the obstinate prejudice of George III had thwarted the endeavours of Grenville and Howick to obtain Catholic Emancipation. The quarrel with the King led to the fall of the Government in March 1807 ; and the remnants of Pitt's party cheerfully resumed the responsibilities of office.

From 1807 to 1812 England was ruled by two Tory Governments : that of the Duke of Portland, until September 1809 ; and that of Perceval, until his assassination in May 1812. Neither Ministry was particularly strong. The Portland Administration was handicapped by the inefficiency of its head and by dissensions among its members, and ultimately fell as the result of the well-known quarrel between Canning and Castlereagh. Perceval, who succeeded to the Premiership, was regarded with jealousy by Wellesley and Canning; and despite his many admirable qualities, and his great influence over the Tory rank and file, he was hardly equal to the responsibilities of his post. His Government

had had the misfortune to begin life under the odium of
the Walcheren disaster, and it was further weakened by
a series of political scandals, in some of which members of
the Administration had been involved. Moreover, when the
King went mad at the end of 1810, it lost its steadiest and
most formidable supporter. The Prince of Wales, though he
was not to be trusted by any party, seemed certainly at the
beginning of his Regency to have strong Whig sympathies ;
and for the next twelve months he appeared likely to
dismiss the Tories at any moment. It was not until he
made his final decision in February 1812 that the Tory
Administration could feel secure.

It is therefore surprising that the Whigs should have
been so ineffective in Opposition. On at least four occasions
they had apparently an excellent chance of turning out
their rivals, but each time they failed. Twice they refused
office, and twice they were disappointed by the Prince.
This book attempts to explain these disappointments and
refusals, and by a survey of Whig policies to show how ill-
suited the party was to the task of ruling the country at
this crisis of her history.

After Fox's death, the leadership of the Talents had
been divided between Howick (afterwards Lord Grey) and
Grenville.　They were an ill-assorted pair—the one an
early advocate of Parliamentary Reform, the other a con-
senting party to Pitt's repressive legislation. Only mutual
forbearance upon subjects of controversy, and zealous
coöperation for Catholic Emancipation, held their alliance
together. In the years 1807–1812 Catholic Emancipation
stood first in the political programme of the Whigs, and
was consistently championed by them in Parliament. Their
enthusiasm in the cause was whetted by the bitterness they
felt at the manner of their fall in 1807 ; but their obstinate
fidelity to it alienated the sympathies of the nation, and
was one of the main reasons for their failure to obtain
office. Chapter I deals with their attitude to this question.

The circumstances of the change of Ministry in 1807 are first examined; they were to be of great importance for what followed. Next comes a consideration of the various suggestions which were put forward for granting Emancipation in exchange for some measure of governmental control over the election of Irish Catholic Bishops. The misunderstanding which arose between the Whig leaders and Dr. Milner on this point, and their persistent refusal to have anything to do with the Irish " democrats ", robbed them of the gratitude which Ireland might otherwise have felt for their disinterested efforts ; and when, in 1812, the urgency of Emancipation forced itself upon the notice of other English politicians, Tories like Canning were able to steal their thunder. Thus the Whigs' championship of Emancipation reacted unfavourably upon their chances in England, and brought them no solid support from Ireland by way of compensation.

Even more unfortunate was their attitude to the war. A considerable section of the party insisted, in the face of the clearest evidence, that an honourable peace was to be had for the asking ; and nearly all the Whigs directed a ceaseless fire of petty and ill-informed criticism at the measures of the Government and the conduct of the generals. These criticisms are analysed in Chapter II. As a rule they were singularly inept, and they were rendered still less effective by the bad military record of the Ministry of All the Talents. Thus it was that, even when the Opposition had a good case against Government—as in the matter of the Walcheren disaster—it could not press home its advantage in a division, for most of the independent members of Parliament were not prepared to trust the Whigs to carry on the war any more efficiently. Their criticisms were purely destructive ; their objections frequently cancelled out each other ; and they could not agree in championing any intelligent strategical plan. Their conduct in Parliament made them very unpopular with the nation,

whose sturdy patriotism could not understand or tolerate
their reception of the news of Wellington's victories ; and
it certainly contributed to the decision of the Prince
Regent not to admit them to office.

There was one question, however, which should have
regained for them some measure of popular support. This
was the question of Reform. In these five years the Reform
movement experienced a sudden revival. Economical
Reform first, Parliamentary Reform afterwards, became
living issues in politics once more. A great Reform agitation
swept London and the Home Counties, and spread (though
more slowly) to the Provinces. This movement forms the
link between the efforts of the 'eighties and 'nineties and
the agitation which ultimately produced the Reform Bill
of 1832 ; though it looks forward rather than backward,
and derives its inspiration from Bentham and Burdett
rather than from Burke and Price. The Whigs had
their chance to put themselves at its head, and by doing so
to save their party from intellectual stagnation. Chapter III
tells the story of the efforts of the more advanced Whigs—
in particular of Whitbread and Brand—to drag the leaders
into coöperation with the Burdettites and the extra-
Parliamentary agitation. In the matter of Economical
Reform they were able to win some successes, in spite of
passive hostility from the Grenvillite wing of the party ;
but as regards Parliamentary Reform they were sacrificed
in the end to the timidity of Grey and Ponsonby, who thus
gave the Tories another fifteen years of comparative
security. The history of their reforming activities produces,
perhaps, an impression of vagueness and confusion : it is
difficult to pin down Perry, or W. Smith, or even Whitbread, to a definite group with clear-cut opinions. Yet the
confusion is the reflection of the actual state of the party.
Grey himself was often at a loss to know what Whitbread
would do next, or how radical the Marquis of Tavistock
might be expected to be upon a given occasion. The party

was in a state of flux, and upon the reforming issue its members would drift to right or left under the influence of public scandals, or the threats of the City mob, or the hope of office. The Reformers were a disorderly corps of sharp-shooters rather than an organized army ; and hence it happened that the more advanced of them were fired on by their own heavy artillery, and did not hesitate to make immediate reply. One conclusion, however, emerges : that Whitbread, if he had persisted in 1811 and 1812 in the courses he had followed in 1809 and 1810, might have left a much greater name and reputation, and might have anticipated Brougham in radicalizing his party.

But Whitbread was an ambitious man, and the prospect of office tempted him to forsake the extremists for the moderates. He could not forget that his opinions had already been fatal to his aspirations in another direction. He had hoped to lead his party in the House of Commons, and the leadership had been denied him. He had been passed over in favour of a nonentity, and subordinated to George Ponsonby. If the leadership in the Commons had fallen to a strong man, the more serious consequences of the discords within the party might have been avoided ; but Ponsonby was a colourless person of easy-going habits and middling abilities, and quite unequal to the task of holding the hot-heads in check. Chapter IV explains the difficulties experienced by the Whigs in their search for a leader who should be objectionable to as few of them as possible, and the disastrous effects of Ponsonby's weakness upon their discipline and unity.

If the Opposition was divided, so was the Government. The successors and pupils of Pitt were struggling for his inheritance. The strong bonds of personal attachment which had held the two great parties together had loosened now that Pitt and Fox were dead, and between 1807 and 1812 politics were dominated by the intrigues of a number of relatively small groups whose leaders angled diligently for the assistance of that large body of independent members who habitually supported on principle whatever Government might be in office. Some of these groups—*e.g.* the "Saints", the Sidmouths and the Prince's party—were not sure allies either of Government or Opposition. The Canningites, too, maintained an independent position after leaving the Ministry in 1809. In such circumstances there should have been ample opportunity for the Whigs to extend the Grey-Grenville alliance to include one or other of these groups. They did make some effort to avail themselves of the more hopeful of these prospects : the first half of Chapter V shows how it happened that they were unsuccessful. Their own internal divisions, and the intractability of their leaders, made it impossible for them to compete successfully with the centripetal pull of Government, and with the efforts of their opponents to reunite the old followers of Pitt. In 1812 they were, if anything, weaker than in 1807.

The second half of Chapter V deals with the four occasions upon which the Whigs seemed to have a reasonable chance of office. Their failure to obtain it was not only the result of personal considerations—the enmity of George III, or the double-dealing of the Regent. It was the result of the impression produced upon the country, the independent members, and the sovereign, by the unpopular policies and internal squabbles of the Opposition. Their Parliamentary record was not such as to encourage any man to be a party to hazarding the safety of the country in their hands.

CHAPTER I

IRELAND AND THE CATHOLICS

(a) *The Fall of the Ministry of the Talents*

In 1806 Ireland was becoming gradually accustomed to the Union. The stream of absentee landlords was flowing steadily eastward ; Miss Edgeworth was beginning her literary career ; and Dublin was settling down, with resignation if not with contentment, into the situation of a mere provincial town. At Westminster the voice of Ireland was raised infrequently, for the difficulty of keeping Irish members at Westminster was presenting party Whips with a new problem ;[1] but in Munster and Connaught it was to be heard in the subversive whispers of the Threshers, the latest manifestation of the anti-British element. The benefits as well as the disadvantages of the Union were just beginning to be obvious. Trade was on the increase ; new canal schemes were providing at least temporary employment ; and if Ireland's agriculture was as uneconomic and as backward as ever, yet that distraction in her finances, which by 1811 had more than doubled her funded debt, was not yet become serious.[2] It was even considered by some observers that there was hope for Irish manufactures, though the less imaginative were content that Ireland's economic function should be to complement England rather than to attempt

---

[1] Wellington, *Civil Correspondence, Ireland*, p. 316 : "I know that it will end in want of the services of the Irish members at the close of the session, when no power on earth will be able to detain them in London ".

[2] Wakefield, *Statistical Account of Ireland*, ii. 38-64 (trade); i. 651-652 (canals) ; i. 580 *et seq.* (agriculture) ; ii. 272-274 (finance).

to rival her.[1] Population was estimated at about 5,000,000 ;
and of these the majority were represented by a Catholic
observer as living in moderate prosperity and rude health.[2]
There was even growing up a feeling of responsibility on
the part of the landlords ; and in 1808 an anonymous writer
was to anticipate Thomas Drummond by laying it down
that " a landlord is not a mere land merchant ; he has
duties to perform as well as rents to receive ".[3]

Still, when judged by English standards, the condition
of Ireland was undoubtedly miserable. The grievous oppression of the tithes, which even Catholic Bishops had to pay,[4]
and the iniquities of an Orange magistracy, were alone
sufficient to mar the prospect ; and there were those who
held that the Union had aggravated the condition of the
country instead of alleviating it.[5]

Such a state of affairs gave ample and obvious opportunity for controversy, and might well have provided an
Opposition with an easy line of attack and an arguable case.
Ireland, however, was not interested in party politics. In
Ireland there was neither Whig nor Tory ; only Catholic
and Protestant. In the view of some contemporary writers
even this division did not express the real truth : the line
of demarcation, they contended, was between those who
desired, and those who repudiated, the British connection.[6]
However this may be, for practical purposes of politics and

---

[1] Newenham, *View of Ireland*, pp. 309-333 ; against him Wakefield,
i. 758-62.

[2] M'Kenna, *Views of the Catholic Question*, p. 3 (for population) ;
Milner, *Letters from Ireland*, p. 203. For a criticism of Milner see Ryan,
Dr. Milner's Tour.

[3] *A Sketch of the State of Ireland, Past and Present*, p. 42.

[4] Ward, *The Eve of Catholic Emancipation*, i. 13-14.

[5] Bridge, *Two Centuries of Irish History*, p. 223 (magistracy) ;
Grattan, *Life of Grattan*, v. 401-402 ; *Memoirs of Edward Fitzgerald*,
p. 482 (Curran's view).

[6] Wakefield, ii. 319 ; *A Sketch of the State of Ireland, Past and Present*,
p. 49 ; Lord Kenyon, *Observations on the Roman Catholics*, p. 63.

jobbery the Catholic and Protestant parties between them comprehended the Irish nation. Here and there a particularly saintly or a particularly irreligious man might stand outside either camp, but such men were rare ; and though Bishop Jebb (who was of the former sort) could carry on a correspondence upon episcopal and ecclesiastical topics for thirty years without allowing it to appear that he was conscious of the existence of Roman Catholicism in the country, there were few on either side who could emulate his detachment.[1] The Irish voter was even more ignorant and bestial than his brother of England, though he had little chance of enjoying the pleasures and perquisites of an English election.[2] His political life lay therefore not in the exercise of a privilege which he was made to use at the discretion of his superiors, but in a constant struggle against the inferior status to which his religion condemned him. If he were a respectable tradesman, he supported a Catholic Committee to petition Parliament ; if he were a peasant of the west country, he enlisted with the Threshers and burnt the corn of the tithe-owners. And if all other ways of venting his political exuberance were stopped up, he indulged in faction fights with his neighbour, and became a Shanavest or a Caravat.[3] But when Whig and Tory politics for the moment coincided with the Catholic and Protestant controversy, then it was seen that Ireland had a public opinion which could speak decisively, and which paid but little attention to its official leaders.

At this time the leadership of the Catholic party in Ireland was in a state of transition. The former leader of

---

[1] *Correspondence of John Jebb, passim.*

[2] " We have seen, in some counties, the majority of constituents driven, like cattle, to the hustings. We have seen them—unable even to speak English—attempt to poll in Irish. We know that these miserable creatures are weapons wielded by the gentry against each other at elections . . . " (*A Sketch of the State of Ireland, Past and Present*, p. 38).

[3] Plowden, *History of Ireland*, iii. 608-609 ; Wellington, *Civil Corr.* pp. 332-333, for origin of the names.

the laity, John Keogh of Mount Jerome, " the first plebeian
leader of the Irish Catholics ", was growing old, and was
losing control of affairs. In his place James Ryan, a
rich young Catholic merchant, was endeavouring, by the
formation of a private junto which met at his house, to
bring the management of Catholic affairs into his own
hands.[1] Opposed to the Ryan faction were, besides the
old supporters of Keogh, the great Catholic nobles, and
particularly Lord Ffrench, who, with Lords Fingall,
Gormanstown, and Trimleston, formed the nucleus of an
" aristocratic " Catholic party. In general Keogh and the
aristocrats were in favour of a cautious line of conduct,
while Ryan and his friends were anxious to press the
demand for Emancipation. At first Ryan's policy prevailed,
and in 1805 led to the presentation to Parliament of the
first of many petitions for Catholic Emancipation.

Of the numerous Irish Catholic Bishops the most
important were Archbishop Troy of Dublin and Bishop
Moylan of Cork. They endeavoured to maintain a conciliatory bearing towards the Government, and were considered by the more extreme of their brethren, and by
many of their flock, as " Castle " men. The Primate,
O'Reilly of Armagh, was old, weak, and unimportant.[2]

Such was the situation which Ireland presented to the
Talents when they came into office. Their accession to power
was received with satisfaction and hope in Ireland ; their fall
from it was viewed with contemptuous indifference. How
was it that men so well-meaning and, on the whole, so
friendly to Ireland came to be distrusted by the people they
had intended to serve ?

From the outset the Talents were unfortunate in their
treatment of the Irish problem. They had hardly been in

---

[1] Falkiner, *Studies in Irish History*, p. 212; *O'Connell*, Dunlop, p. 28;
Plowden, ii. 293 ; Wyse, *Historical Sketch of the late Catholic Association*,
i. 123-127, 138-140.

[2] Ward, i. 16-17.

office a month before they gave a severe blow to the
confidence which the Catholic party had previously felt in
them. The new progressive Catholic party in Ireland,
headed by James Ryan, entered into unofficial communication with Fox, and announced their intention of
petitioning Parliament, in the full expectation of receiving
his support. But Fox judged, quite rightly, that the situation
of the country demanded that he should not wreck his
Ministry by wilfully bringing forward this question; and he
wisely suggested that the petition should be abandoned. In
exchange, he promised to do his best for them. They should
have better magistrates, quicker promotions in the Army,
and no more emergency legislation. Ryan accepted these
terms, and at once laid himself open to a damaging attack
from his rivals. An aggregate meeting on 13 March 1806
reversed his decision, broke up the Ryan domination, and
led to the forming of a Catholic association in which was to
be comprised "the full respectability of the Catholic body".[1]

The Whigs were not fortunate in their choice of an
Irish Administration. The Duke of Bedford was amiable
and well-intentioned; but his Lord Chancellor, George
Ponsonby, and his Chief Secretary, William Elliot, were
not popular. Ponsonby's services to Ireland dated from as
early as 1782, when he had assisted Grattan, and he was,
of course, a member of the well-known Irish family of that
name. As Lord Chancellor, however, he was not a success.
Elliot was regarded by many as little better than an
Orangeman.[2] The old champions of the Irish cause were
slighted. Grattan, who had no desire for office, was not

---

[1] Wyse, *Historical Sketch of the late Catholic Association*, i. 138-141;
Grattan, *Life of Grattan*, v. 295.

[2] Falkiner, *Studies in Irish History*, p. 210; Holland, *Memoirs of
the Whig Party*, ii. 162; Plowden, *History of Ireland*, ii. 291; *A Vindication of the Conduct of the Irish Catholics*, by a Protestant barrister,
p. 22 (where Ponsonby is described as " collecting during one half of
the day the equity he was to detail in the other "). But see O'Flanagan,
Lives of the Lord Chancellors of Ireland, art. " Ponsonby ".

even consulted ; and Curran, whose claims to the office of
Attorney-General were of long standing, was fobbed off
with the unsuitable post of Master of the Rolls, an appointment which actually involved him in pecuniary loss.[1]
More serious than the wounded feelings of individuals was
the indignation of the country at the continuance in office
of many of the men who were associated in the popular
mind with the worst and most bigoted elements of the
Castle system :

The friends and co-operators of Lord Redesdale, the Attorney-
and Solicitor-General, retained their situations and confidence :
Mr. Alexander Marsden, the secret adviser and machinist to the late
administration, was not displaced. The whole of the Orange magistracy
remained undisturbed in the commission of the peace. Even Major
Sirr was still seen, as the tutelary guardian of the Castle-yard.[2]

The failure to remove the more glaring offenders among the
Protestant magistracy, or to put leading Catholics into the
Commission, was indeed the heaviest charge against the
Bedford Administration ; and the matter came to a head
when Mr. Wilson, a Protestant magistrate of Armagh, was
unable to secure a proper investigation of grave charges
against two of his colleagues on the bench, and in consequence published his correspondence with the Government.[3] Some attempt was indeed made towards the end of
the Administration to remodel the notorious Commission
of Co. Wexford ; but in general so little was done that even
Whigs suspected that Ponsonby was acting with an eye
rather to electoral influence than to the dispensation of
justice.[4] When to these errors are added the personal
indiscretions of which Ponsonby was guilty, and the aloof-

---

[1] Phillips, *Recollections of Curran*, pp. 357-360 ; Grattan, v. 291 ; Fitzpatrick, *Life and Times of Lord Cloncurry*, pp. 170-171 ; *Vindication of
the Irish Catholics*, pp. 12-15.

[2] Plowden, ii. 291 ; *Vindication*, pp. 9-11.

[3] *Correspondence between Wilson . . . Elliot and . . . Ponsonby*
(especially pp. 52-57) ; *Vindication*, pp. 18-19.

[4] Plowden, ii. 370-372 ; Holland, ii. 168.

ness of manner both of himself and of Elliot, it is not
surprising that the Government was unpopular. The
Protestants were hostile, the Catholics disappointed ; and,
in short, under the " cold-blooded, temporizing, timid,
left-handed policy of Mr. Ponsonby . . . all were disaffected and dissatisfied ".[1] It was partly to allay this
dissatisfaction, at all events among the Catholics, and
partly perhaps from honest conviction, that in February
1807 the Talents embarked upon the enterprise which
brought them to the ground.

From the beginning of the year all sections of the Irish
Catholics had concurred in renewing agitation, and in preparing a petition. Moreover, fresh disturbances had broken
out in Sligo, where the Threshers were again active ; and in
the opinion of the Government these would necessitate the
proclaiming of the county, unless measures were quickly
taken to conciliate public opinion. The more responsible
Irish leaders approached the Administration to ascertain
their views on the advisability of petitioning, and made it
clear that they expected some declaration of policy from
the Castle.[2] On 4 February, therefore, Bedford wrote to
Lord Spencer, and expressed the opinion that the Catholics
might be bought off by the concession of the right to serve
in the Army, Navy, and Corporations.[3] The Whigs were
suddenly stung into activity. On 9 February they drew up
a reply to Bedford, outlining a measure in general con-
formity with his suggestion ; and on the following day they

---

[1] See Wellington, *Civil Correspondence, Ireland*, p. 546. Ponsonby disclosed a confidential opinion which had been written at his request ;
the writer was sued for libel, and the next Government paid his costs.
Holland, ii. 162 ; *Vindication*, p. 20 ; *A Sketch of the State of Ireland*,
p. 23. For the Protestant view, *All the Talents in Ireland*.

[2] Holland, ii. 160 ; *Dropmore Papers*, ix. 101 (Bedford to Spencer);
Buckingham, *Court and Cabinets of George III*, iv. 117. " They have
put it definitively to us to say what we will do " (Grenville to
Buckingham).

[3] *Dropmore Papers*, ix. 101.

laid their draft before the King. At first the King would not hear of it ; and Grenville expected the Government to fall. By degrees, however, he yielded to the representations of Grenville and Sidmouth, and on 12 February consented to the sending of the dispatch to Ireland.[1] The dispatch displayed a good deal of anxiety to prevent the embarrassment of a Catholic petition, and was at pains to point out that the projected Bill was not to be considered as a *quid pro quo*, but rather as a measure previously contemplated by the Government, and now in a happy hour come to birth. It is, of course, true that something of the sort had been adumbrated by Fox ; but there is no reason to suppose that there would have been any prospect of its taking shape, if the Lord Lieutenant's dispatches had not borne in upon the Ministers the desirability of forestalling the major evil of a Catholic petition.[2] It soon appeared, moreover, that the Irish Catholics were resolved to continue their preparations ; and at a meeting at the Dublin Rotunda, on 17 February, the draft of a petition was read and adopted. Keogh was absent, but so steady-going a man as Lord Fingall was in the chair. This persistence was a source of much annoyance to the Whigs : as Grenville complained,

they know their petition cannot be carried — they continue to embarrass the only public men who are friendly to their cause, and put upon us the necessity of either breaking up the Government for their sake . . . or of ranging ourselves also in opposition, not to the cause itself, but to the time, and still more to the manner, in which it is brought forward.

Grattan, who was appealed to, was clear that the petition

---

[1] Windsor Arch., George III, King to Grenville, 10, 12 Feb. ; Grenville to King, 11 [*sic*, *i.e.* 10] Feb. ; Pellew, *Life of Sidmouth*, ii. 457.

[2] Nearly all the documents dealing with this crisis have been printed, some of them many times. References are, therefore, usually to printed sources ; but these have been checked where possible by reference to the originals at Windsor. Holland, ii. 161 (Ponsonby's views on the necessity of proclaiming the disturbed counties).

ought to be suspended ; and it was decided to send over
Lord Ponsonby (nephew to the Chancellor) to dissuade the
Irish from going on with it.[1]

No doubt one reason for the intractability of the Irish
was their uncertainty of the value of the proposed Bill. No
sooner had news of the project arrived in Ireland than
Elliot was closely questioned as to the extent of the proposed concession. Was it to extend to *all* military commissions, or were staff appointments to be reserved ?
Elliot was not quite sure. He gave a vaguely reassuring
answer, and wrote home for further information. A Cabinet
was held to settle on a reply ; and it appeared that there
was grave disharmony in it, for Lord Sidmouth, with his
friends Erskine and Ellenborough, were taken aback by
this new development. However, in spite of their dissent,
a reply was drafted clearly confirming Elliot's answer in its
widest implications. This was sent to the King, and returned without comment on 2 March; and on the following
day it was sent off to Ireland. On 4 March there was
a Levee : both Howick and Grenville saw the King,
discussed the Catholic Bill with him, and returned with
the clear impression that George III, though reluctantly,
had brought himself to consent to it. The scheme had
already been introduced on 20 February, in the shape of
additional clauses to the Mutiny Bill, but on 4 March
Howick brought it forward as a separate measure.[2]

The Catholic Militia Bill was based on the similar Bill
which had passed the Irish Parliament in 1793. But
whereas that Act had applied only to Irish Catholics, and
to appointments other than to the staff, this Bill was to
throw open " any military commission whatever " to " any

[1] Plowden, ii. 435-436 ; *Court and Cabinets*, iv. 120 ; Grattan, v. 335 ;
Dropmore Papers, ix. 60-61, 68 ; Butler, *Historical Memoirs of the . . .
Catholics*, ii. 210-211 ; Grey, *Life and Opinions of Earl Grey*, pp. 143-148.

[2] *Dropmore Papers*, ix. 112-113 ; Cobbett's *Parliamentary Debates*,
ix. 266 *seq.* (Howick's explanation) ; *ibid.* viii. 931, 1073.

of His [Majesty's] liege subjects, without exception ",
provided that they took the oath contained in the Bill.
The effect was thus to admit Dissenters, equally with
Catholics ; and to legalize the position of the Irish soldier
who found himself in England, to which the Irish Act had
not, of course, applied. There was a clause extending the
Act to the Navy, and another giving security for the undisturbed exercise of their religion to men who enlisted.[1]

It was on 11 March, six days after the introduction of
the Bill, that the Government first learned of the King's
hostility to the measure.[2] On that day Grenville was told
by the King that he should allow his opposition to be
publicly known. George was prepared to accept the application of the Act of 1793 to England, but he would not go
one step further ; and he referred to the objections which
he said he had stated to Howick at the Levee just a week
previously. The Whigs were taken by surprise at what
seemed to them a sudden change of front. From 11 March
to 14 March they tried to save both themselves and their
measure by compromising. But they found Lord Sidmouth,
" together with all Pitt's party, whom we naturally considered as friends to Catholic Emancipation ", definitely on
the King's side ; indeed, Sidmouth attempted to resign on
the 11th. They knew, too, that the Bill was now bound to
fail when it reached the Lords. At first they proposed the
Bill of 1793, extended only to the Dissenters and applied only
to the Navy ; but George declined that also. At last, that
section of the Cabinet which had the interests of the
Catholics most at heart[3] decided that they could best
serve them by a total abandonment of the measure. But

---

[1] Holland, ii. 307–311, gives the text of clauses P–T, the most important of the Bill.

[2] Windsor Arch., George III, No. 9 in the numbered series, Grenville
to King, 12 March.

[3] *I.e.* Holland, Moira, Petty, Grenville, Windham, T. Grenville.
Lord Spencer was absent, ill.

they added that, in view of the fact that a Catholic petition was now to be expected, they must be free to express their opinions, and to submit the subject to the King for his decision from time to time in the future.[1] The King was not content with this surrender. On 17 March he demanded " a positive assurance from them, which shall effectually relieve his mind from all future apprehension ". On the following day they returned a flat refusal :

It would be deeply criminal in them, with the general opinion which they entertain on this subject, to bind themselves to withhold from your Majesty under all the various circumstances which may arise, those councils which may eventually appear to them indispensably necessary for the peace and tranquillity of Ireland, and for defeating the enterprizes of the enemy against the very existence of your Majesty's empire.[2]

A curious situation now arose. Ministers did not know whether they were out or in. On 17 March they seem to have contemplated resignation ; on the next day they thought better of it. They would throw the odium of dismissing them upon the King, who, they concluded, was at that moment looking out for a new Government. As late as 23 March there was some uncertainty ; but on that day the King informed Lord Howick " that in consequence of what had passed upon Wednesday last, the King had sent for persons not in the number of his present Ministers. But Lord Howick must be aware that the arrangements must take some days as yet." However, the Whigs went down

---

[1] *Parl. Deb.* ix. 266 *seq.*; *Dropmore Papers*, ix., 81-82, 112-113 ; *Court and Cabinets*, iv. 134-138 ; Pellew, ii. 461-464 ; Cabinet Minute of 15 March, *Dropmore Papers*, ix. 117 ; Windsor Arch., George III, No. 12. "They have thought this course of proceeding would be both more respectful to your Majesty, and more advantageous to the public interests, than any attempt to alter the Bill so as to bring it nearer to the strict letter of the Irish Act. The points of difference which exist between that law and the present Bill relate to matters the consideration of which . . . it is almost impossible to separate from the measure itself."

[2] *Dropmore Papers*, ix. 120.

to Windsor the next day and delivered up the seals ;
though Erskine stayed in until 1 April in order to finish off
the outstanding Chancery business.[1]

So fell the Ministry of the Talents. Whose fault was it ?
Did the King jockey them out by mendacity and sharp
practice ? Did they take insufficient measures to apprise him
of the true scope of their Bill ? Were they right to abandon
it ? Can the King's demand for a pledge be excused, even
though it cannot be justified ? And lastly, was the Bill
calculated to satisfy the classes it was designed to relieve ?

There can be little doubt that at first there was a
genuine misunderstanding as to the precise scope of the
Bill. The reply which was sent to Bedford on 12 February
was sufficiently ambiguous to oblige Elliot to ask for an
explanation of it. The all-important point—whether the
Bill was a mere extension of the 1793 Act to England, and
to the Dissenters, or whether it contained the new principle
of throwing open *all* military and naval appointments—
was not made clear. The King seems to have conceived the
former interpretation to be the true one. Grenville's remonstrance of 11 February indeed gave him good reason
for such an opinion.

> The measure in question, [he wrote] so far from being in opposi-
> tion to any known or expressed opinion of Your Majesty, is perfectly
> conformable in its principle to that concession to which Your
> Majesty had long ago been pleased most graciously to consent.[2]

---

[1] The Whigs maintained to the end that they were dismissed : the
King to the end tried to put them in the position of resigning. Windsor
Arch., George III, 24 March 1807, King to Grenville : " he is now prepared to receive the *resignations* ". Grenville to King : at the King's
" *command* ", they will deliver up the Seals. (The italics are mine.)
Court and Cabinets, iv. 142-148 ; *Morning Chronicle*, 23 March 1807;
Dropmore Papers, ix. 125 (Buckingham to Grenville, under the impression that they were resigning) ; *Sunday Review*, 29 March, 1807,
ap. Add. MS. 27838. See also Grenville's letter to Auckland on
resignation in Add. MS. 34457, ff. 247-248.

[2] Windsor Arch., George III, 11 Feb. ; *Dropmore Papers*, ix. 107.

Now Grenville must have known perfectly well that the King objected to Catholics on the staff; hence the limitation in the Act of 1793. Similar language, but even more misleading, was used in the Cabinet minute of 10 February :

They had persuaded themselves that in the clauses to be proposed for the *Mutiny Bill*, your Majesty would be of opinion that they are only fulfilling the engagements which had been formerly entered into under your Majesty's authority, and carrying into effect a *principle* which has already received the fullest and most formal sanction by the Act [of 1793]. . . . That Act enables your Majesty's Catholic subjects in Ireland to hold commissions in your Majesty's army, with no other restrictions than is there pointed out ; and if a similar provision be refused to this part of the now united Kingdom it appears obvious that the grace thus conferred by your Majesty on that large body of your people must be rendered wholly illusory.[1]

And George's reply on the following day made it obvious what was his interpretation of the proposal :

. . . He will not under the circumstances in which it is so earnestly pressed, and adverting particularly to what took place in 1791 [*sic* : *i.e.* 1793] prevent his Ministers from submitting for the consideration of Parliament the propriety of inserting the proposed clause in the Mutiny Bill. Whilst however the King so far reluctantly concedes, he considers it necessary to declare that he cannot go one step farther ; and he trusts that this proof of his forbearance will secure him from being at a future period distressed by any further proposal connected with this question.[2]

Either Grenville was keeping back the proposed extension to the staff, or he did not at that time intend it. The latter explanation seems almost incredible. Of what value as a measure of conciliation to Ireland was an Act which merely brought to the English Catholics and Dissenters privileges already enjoyed by the Catholics of Ireland ? Moreover, the dispatch to Bedford, which Elliot

[1] *Dropmore Papers*, ix. 109.
[2] *Ibid.* 110. In the Windsor Archives copy the date is over-written 1793.

found ambiguous, does in fact propose to confer " any military commission whatever ".[1] Yet on the other hand it is abundantly clear that at the Cabinet of 10 February Sidmouth and Ellenborough supported the clauses as a *corollary* to 1793 ; and, moreover, that Sidmouth exerted a great deal of influence on the King, and induced him to consent at last, by arguments based entirely on this ground.[2] It seems plain that when the point was raised at the Cabinet of 1 March by Elliot's enquiry, Sidmouth and his friends were startled, and at once opposed Grenville's interpretation, as though its significance were now borne in upon them for the first time.[3] The Cabinet of 10 February is known to have been divided ; Windham was openly sulking ; Erskine feigned sleep so as not to commit himself ; and it seems likely that Grenville and Howick allowed Sidmouth and Ellenborough, as they later allowed the King, to misinterpret the meaning of the concession. They hoped, no doubt, that the Castle Government would give it the wider interpretation, and thus conciliate the Irish ; and they were probably much annoyed when Elliot again raised the question.

However, the new dispatch to Bedford was sent to the King on 2 March. It made it incontrovertibly clear that the limits of 1793 were to be exceeded. Both Howick and Grenville agreed that at the Levee of 4 March the King made no reference to this new development. The King's account of what happened appears irreconcilable with that of the Whigs. If the King was taken by surprise by the terms of the Bill which Howick introduced on 5 March, he might well, after a day or two to look round for support, have given vent to his indignation on 11 March, and attempted to

---

[1] *Dropmore Papers*, ix. 103. Windham's copy of the draft Bill is in the same terms. Add. MS. 37889, ff. 215-216.

[2] Pellew, ii. 455 ; Holland, ii. 181-187.

[3] *Parl. Deb.* ix. 266 *seq.* ; Pellew, ii. 459. Sidmouth communicated his hostility to further concession to the Speaker on 1 March.

strengthen his case by a false reference to his conversation
at the Levee ; or he might simply have forgotten what he
said on that occasion. But from the Whig point of view
it seemed that he had lured on Ministers to introduce the
Bill, with the intention of overthrowing the Government
by a declaration of his hostility, the moment its terms
became public. For (they argued) the King's opposition
must either lead to the fall of the Government, or to the
fatal compromising of its reputation with the Catholics.
Moreover, the dispatch of 2 March must have revealed to
the King what the proposals really involved. But did the
King read it ? Palmerston made the interesting suggestion
that the box containing it may have been sent down to
Windsor without any note drawing attention to the vital
point in it, and that therefore the King, weary of the whole
matter, and assuming the Bill to be in accordance with his
concession of 12 February, sent it back without ever
reading it.[1] This is not very plausible ; for he is known to
have kept a sharp eye on the progress of this affair. When
Lord Spencer sent a dispatch to the King on 20 February
without observation on its contents, it was nevertheless carefully read. This was the dispatch which transmitted the all-important enquiry of Elliot, and the fact
that Spencer refrained from drawing attention to this new
development was duly noted by George.[2] But in fact
Palmerston's theory is exploded by the presence in the
archives at Windsor of the note which Howick actually
sent with the crucial dispatch. It ran as follows :

In the absence of Earl Spencer who left London this morning [ill]
. . . . Lord Howick has the honour of transmitting to your Majesty

---

[1] Bulwer, *Life of Palmerston*, i. 73.

[2] Windsor Arch., George III, Spencer to King, 20 Feb. 1807 ; Heads
of Dispatches (No. 17 in the numbered series of copies of papers and
correspondence between the King and his Ministers " upon the Admission
of Catholics and other Dissenters into the Army and Navy ", 9 Feb. to
18 March, 1807).

the draft of a dispatch to his Grace the Lord Lieutenant of Ireland enclosing copies of the clauses intended to be submitted to Parliament for the purpose of enabling your Majesty's Catholic subjects to hold military commissions, and securing to them the free exercise of their religion when serving in the army.[1]

This is a most disingenuous document, at least in appearance. It was not easy to gather from it that the proposed clauses were to affect the Navy, the Dissenters, and staff appointments. But it was very easy to suppose that the clauses in question did no more than extend the 1793 Act to England, and give security for free exercise of religion to Catholic soldiers ; in short, that they merely represented the King's concessions of 12 February. It might have been contended that Howick believed that George had then consented to the wider interpretation; but apparently Sidmouth at the Cabinet meeting of 1 March told his colleagues that the King did not realize what the new clauses involved, and urged that someone ought to make the point clear to him. Grenville refused ; and Howick resorted to subterfuge.[2] To George, who was wide awake, it appeared as though his Ministers were trying to smuggle the new clauses past him, which was indeed the case. Lord Spencer had tried the same trick on 20 February, and had been found out. Is it surprising that the King's hostility and suspicion were still further aroused by Howick's too innocent note ? A document at Windsor, entitled " Heads of the Dispatches from Ireland ", drawn in the handwriting of the King's secretary, Colonel Taylor, gives an account of the King's conduct which practically exculpates him from the charges of the Whigs :

On the 3rd of March,[3] the King received from Lord Howick (in the absence of Lord Spencer) a copy of the proposed clauses, together with the draft of a dispatch . . . transmitting them. They were unaccompanied by any observation, although upon reading them

[1] Windsor Arch., George III, Howick to King, 2 March 1807.
[2] Pellew, ii. 459. [3] Sic : i.e. 2 March.

they proved materially to differ from those originally submitted to the King, inasmuch, as they admitted of the employment of Dissenters of all descriptions, including Catholics, in all ranks of the Army and Navy. His Majesty returned them without any observation, considering that to be superfluous, after having declared so positively in his letter of the 12th of February to Lord Grenville that he would not go one step farther, etc.

The King, however, repeated that declaration verbally to Lord Howick on the following day the 4th, when it appeared that Lord Howick had in the intermediate time sent the dispatches.[1]

This explains why Howick and George III were able to give such different versions of the interview at the Levee. George was in fact turning his enemy's weapons against him. If they could be silent, so too could he. They knew his opinions ; there was no need to repeat them ; he, at least, was not proceeding to new demands. It was clear to him that the Whigs were not to be trusted, and he was determined to get rid of them if possible. So he waited until the Bill was fairly introduced, and then unmasked his batteries. Who can blame him ?

One of the topics upon which there was discussion at the Levee between Howick and the King, was the alteration in the form of the Bill. Instead of being a tack to the Mutiny Bill, it was to be brought in on its own. It was some half-knowledge of this fact that led Lord Malmesbury to write his most inaccurate account of the quarrel, an account which is a warning against the most plausible contemporary evidence. Malmesbury asserts that the Bill contained objectionable principles not to be found in the tacked clauses ; and he continues :

On Wednesday the 11th Lord Howick, as I before said, brings the Bill to the King. The King refuses to assent to it. Lord Howick withdraws from the closet, and either does, or affects to, misunderstand the King, and brings in the Bill.[2]

[1] Windsor Arch., George III, No. 17 in the numbered series.
[2] Pellew, ii. 460 ; Malmesbury, *Diaries*, iv. 358, 371.

Malmesbury had his information direct from men who
had seen the King's collection of documents ; but it is
plain that he had got his dates a week wrong, and his facts
a little distorted. No doubt the Bill was more explicit than
the clauses in the Mutiny Bill ; but it was not sprung as a
surprise on the King, who had indeed been expecting
something of the sort since 20 February ; and it was the
sending of the obnoxious clauses back to Ireland that the
King complained of : when that was done, it was too late
to stop the introduction of the Bill.

However, the King waited until 11 March before he
took measures to defeat the project. And here another
difficulty presents itself. Did he get any encouragement to
dismiss his Ministers, either from the Tory or the Whig
side ? The Whigs, of course, suggested Lord Eldon, who
undoubtedly saw the King on " private business " at this
time.[1] But Eldon's explanation is satisfactory ; for though
he saw the King " on the Saturday before the demand for
a pledge ", yet the only business they discussed, according
to Eldon's account, was the "Delicate Investigation " ;
and, moreover, Eldon asserted, and it was not denied, that
he had told Lord Grenville that he was going to Windsor,
and promised him to keep clear of politics.[2] And this
Saturday was 14 March, three days after the King had
announced his intentions.

Still less was Lord Hardwicke responsible, though there
have been some who have thought so.[3] He did visit
the King on 21 March, but it was with precisely the
opposite object : for he was urging him to retain his
Ministers, not to dismiss them.[4]

It is not so easy, however, to exculpate the Duke of
Portland and Lord Hawkesbury. Holland was certain that

[1] Holland, ii. 194. See, too, the hint in *Edinburgh Review*, xi. 116.
[2] Twiss, *Life of Lord Eldon*, ii. 36–39.
[3] Grattan, *op. cit.* v. 350 n.
[4] Malmesbury, iv. 375 ; *Morning Chronicle*, 23 March 1807.

the Tories knew before 11 March of the King's objection
and his intention to break with the Whigs.[1] Lord Liverpool,
indeed, in a letter to Lord Auckland, asserted that his son
knew nothing of the matter until he was summoned to
Windsor on 18 March, and this although he was a great
favourite with the King.[2] Malmesbury, who was much in
the Duke's confidence, seems to make it clear that until
12 March, at all events, no definite information of the
King's feelings had been received. The Duke suspected the
true state of affairs, but could not be certain.[3] Malmesbury,
however, only returned to London from the country on
9 March, and in the meanwhile Portland had written the
following letter to Hawkesbury on 8 March :

My dear Lord,

   I am very sorry to intrude upon you in the country, but as I
find that it is very doubtful whether you will be in Town tomorrow,
considering how much the Catholick question presses upon us, and
knowing as I now do, the extreme importance of its being rejected,
I can not but entreat you to come to Town tomorrow as early as
possible in order to consult on the best means of defeating that
measure.[4]

What do these italics mean ? Had Portland seen the
King ? Had he been told of the King's objections through
someone else ? Or was he merely referring to the fact that
the provisions of the Bill were now known to him in their
full extent, since it had been introduced on 5 March ? If
the latter, surely Portland would have said so without
circumlocution ? It is known, however, that he had not
seen the King, and that he was in the dark as to the
King's intentions, though he guessed at his sentiments.
Malmesbury and Portland were, in fact, hesitating what to
do. At last they decided to take the highly irregular step of
addressing a letter to the King, offering assistance to turn
out his Ministers. It seems probable, therefore, that when

[1] Holland, ii. 200.   [2] Add. MS. 34457, ff. 279-280.
[3] Malmesbury, iv. 359.   [4] Add. MS. 38191, f. 246.

Portland summoned Hawkesbury to London he meant no
more than to refer to the new Bill ; and that he had no
more certain ground than mere suspicion for presuming
the King to be against it.[1]

Portland's letter to the King was certainly most improper ; but it was not the deciding factor in the King's
treatment of his Ministers. For before Portland sent it, on
12 March, he heard that two of his nephews had been
ordered to vote against the Bill, which proved that the
King had taken his decision.[2] Nevertheless, the letter is
very remarkable, urging as it does the bold use of the
veto if necessary, and an appeal to the nation against the
Ministers.[3] A message which came to Malmesbury from a

---

[1] Malmesbury, iv. 358-362.   [2] *Ibid.* 363.
[3] Windsor Arch., George III, Portland to King, 12 March 1807.
This differs considerably from the draft given in Malmesbury, iv. 360.
The passage on the veto is as follows : " Should however the belief I
wish to entertain be well founded, and that your Majesty shall not
have given your consent to the measure in its present shape, I have
little apprehension of disappointing your Majesty when I venture to
express my opinion that it may be ultimately defeated, though not
sooner, I fear, than in the course of its progress through the House of
Lords, but for that purpose, I must take the liberty of saying that it
will be absolutely necessary that your Majesty's wishes should be so
distinctly intimated that no doubt may exist respecting them, that
your Majesty's Ministers must not have any pretext for equivocating
upon the subject, or any ground left them for pretending ignorance of
your Majesty's sentiments, or of your Majesty's determination, not
only to withhold your sanction from the measure, but if necessary, which
God forbid, to put those means into force, with which the constitution
has vested your Majesty, to prevent its becoming a law. The effects of
such a proceeding as this on the part of your Majesty (though it may,
& is to be hoped that it will stop far short of the length to which I
have pointed) may possibly prevent any material change among the
persons who at present administer your Majesty's affairs, if it shall be
your Majesty's pleasure to retain them in their present situations. But
as it is more natural to expect that they will desire your Majesty's
permission to quit your service I can not but suppose that your Majesty
is prepared in case of such an event, & there seems no reason to apprehend that your Majesty can be seriously at a loss to meet with persons

friend in the Queen's House on the 13th shows that
Ministers on their side had not failed to put out stories
representing the King as indifferent on the subject, or
weary of it; and the King resented this strongly.[1] Perhaps
it made him more ready to listen to Portland's advice;
but it would seem that he had already determined to
risk a breach with his Ministers. It appears probable that
the attitude of Sidmouth was responsible for this confidence in the future. Indeed, it is just possible that knowledge of the King's feelings leaked out through him to the
Tories. The part he played throughout the crisis was a
consistent one, and not dishonourable to him. He might in
fact feel aggrieved that he had been enticed into a false
position by his colleagues, and that he had been made the
instrument for enticing the King.[2] After the arguments
Sidmouth had used to persuade the King, there was no
other course open to him but to oppose the new Bill to the
uttermost. The Whigs, however, suspected him of treachery.
Lord Temple wrote to his father : " Lord Sidmouth has
played his tricks with the King " ; and this belief was held
by many, particularly by the Grenvilles, with whom he
was on bad terms, and who were scheming to replace him
in the Cabinet by Canning.[3] Sidmouth's reputation seems
to have suffered ; he began to be considered a dangerous
ally ; hence perhaps the rejection of his overtures by the

of sufficient abilities & experience to undertake & perform the duties
of the respective stations which your Majesty may think fit to assign
to them in consequence of the event I have alluded to. In such a case
it will be obvious to your Majesty of what importance it must be &
what advantage it must afford to those to whom your Majesty shall
think fit to intrust the management of your affairs, that the necessity
you have been under to part with your present servants should be
generally made known."

[1] Malmesbury, iv. 365.

[2] See a significant letter of Hatsell (one of Sidmouth's party) dated
25 March, expressing the opinion that Grenville had behaved dishonour-
ably. Add. MS. 34457, ff. 266-267.

[3] *Court and Cabinets*, iv. 140.

Tories at this time.[1] As the Queen remarked to Lady Harcourt, " He verifies the proverb that every body's friend is nobodies friend ".[2] That saying was, perhaps, not strictly true, for certainly he earned the gratitude of the King, who wrote to him on the day he left office :

Although the King is deprived of the services of Lord Sidmouth in the arrangement which he has made for the formation of a new administration, H.M. cannot release him from his situation without expressing to him the satisfaction which he has derived from the support which Lord Sidmouth has given to him throughout the progress of a transaction in which his dearest principles and his feelings were at stake.[3]

The reason for the shade of odium which lay on his conduct at this time was undoubtedly his interview with the King on 4 March, just before the famous Levee, at which he warned the King of the undesirable nature of the new clauses.[4] But against these he had already protested most emphatically to his colleagues on 1 March ; he had then urged that the King should be made acquainted with the true scope of the Bill; and he had certainly not told the King anything of which he was not quite well aware already.

To sum up : George was taken by surprise first by the dispatches of 20 February which Spencer sent to him. He judged, correctly, that the Whigs were trying to inveigle him into a concession which he had never intended to make. He allowed them to proceed on the assumption that they had been successful, most probably because he felt that in Sidmouth he had an ally on whom he could rely in a crisis. Portland's letter of 12 March made him nearly sure of victory ; he therefore proceeded to consolidate his position and use his advantage to drive the Talents from office and terminate the Catholic question for good, by

[1] Pellew, ii. 464, 470. [2] *Harcourt Papers*, vi. 91.
[3] Windsor Arch., George III, 25 March 1807.
[4] Pellew, ii. 459-460.

presenting a pledge they could not take. Though the King
cannot entirely be acquitted of blame, some excuse can be
made for him : even the pledge was a measure of security
which the conduct of the Whigs made comprehensible.
It was, however, a blunder. The feeling that he was fighting
for his throne blinded his usually acute tactical vision.[1]
When the Whigs consented to abandon the Bill they
delivered themselves into their enemies' hands. They had
deserted the Catholics at the threats of the fanatics ; and
Holland, Buckingham, Spencer, Horner, and Bedford all
felt that they were behaving shabbily, and were much
relieved when the King took the odium off their shoulders,
and placed it upon his own.[2]

The fall of the Government, however, was not unpopular
in the country. Even before the factitious excitement of
Perceval's general election, congratulatory addresses to the
King on the firm exercise of his prerogative were pouring
in.[3] The reputation of the Whigs was saved, however ; and
they appeared by accident on the side of constitutional
progress, martyrs to the King's rancour. Grenville put their
point of view very well when he wrote to his brother :

> We have heard much on this Catholic question of his coronation
> oath. He appears to have forgot that our oath, as Privy Councillors,
> as well as our manifest duty, obliges us to give him true counsel to
> the best of our judgment.[4]

And it was, of course, a great grievance to the Whigs that
the new men were not asked for a pledge.[5]

---

[1] Twiss, *Eldon*, ii. 34.

[2] *Dropmore Papers*, ix. 125 ; *Court and Cabinets*, iv. 140 ; Horner,
i. 397 ; Holland, ii. 200 ; *Morning Chronicle*, 18 March 1807. Mr. Fremantle (*England in the Nineteenth Century*, ii. 188) mistakes the real
reason for Holland's uneasiness.

[3] Plowden (*op. cit.* iii. 554, n.) admits to 36 counties. Windsor Arch.,
George III, Lord Hawkesbury to King, 11 April 1807, for those of Oxford,
Cambridge, and the City.   [4] *Court and Cabinets*, iv. 143.

[5] *Morning Chronicle*, 23 March 1807 ; Grenville, *Substance of a
Speech* (1807), p. 53.

The more moderate Catholics in Ireland were conciliated by the eventual self-sacrifice of the Ministers, and at last consented to suspend the fatal petition.[1] In England, the Whigs made the best of their case. To the casual reader, John Allen's excellent defence of their conduct is completely convincing : the Whigs appear as upright champions of the constitution, the King (by implication) as a violent and mendacious intriguer.[2] And when the heats of the election drew on, Sydney Smith made great play with those *Letters of Peter Plymley* which have always been considered the last word on the subject. Brilliant as they were, they were not free from vulgarity in their gibes at Perceval, and they were, of course, quite irrelevant. On the issue of Bigotry *versus* Toleration, *Peter Plymley* was decisive; but that was not the issue in 1807. It was useless to bring forward examples of concessions already made by the King, and to observe that 1807 seemed to be "fruitful in moral and religious scruples (as some years are fruitful in apples, some in hops)".[3] The Whigs fell, not because of George's scruples, but because of his indignation at sharp practice.

The official Whig view of the measure for which they gave up office was that it was a " commencement of wise and moderate justice to the Catholics " ;[4] but the only class which really seems to have appreciated it was that of the Protestant Dissenters, who noted with gratification that the Whigs had only abandoned the Bill when the King refused to extend the privileges of 1793 to them.[5] Yet for some time the Whigs thought that they had the country behind them ; and they were not undeceived until the general election, in which Protestant bigotry was

[1] Plowden, ii. 537 ; Grattan, v. 347. This was on 17 April 1807.
[2] *The Letters of Scaevola* (1807).
[3] *Peter Plymley*, pp. 4, 5.   [4] Horner, i. 394.
[5] *A Letter stating the connection which Presbyterians [etc.] . . . had with the recent event, which has agitated . . . the British Empire*, p. 12 ; *Letters of Scaevola*, ii. 32 *.

certainly mobilized on the Tory side. It then became clear
that Ponsonby's rash assertion that " No Popery was dead "
was very wide of the mark.[1] Apart from High Tory attacks
on the Bill, few of which are of any value,[2] the most
damaging criticism came from Ireland. The Aristocratic
party might be gratified by the Whigs' stand for principle ;
the Democrats were not so easily taken in. The party of
O'Connell and the younger (Cornelius) Keogh was very
scornful of the proffered sop. As one of them wrote, " its
object was to buy the Catholic cheaply, to deceive the
King safely, to establish themselves permanently " : not
very far from the truth. " In Dublin, it was a triumph
to Ireland ; at Windsor, it was justice to England."
And Cornelius Keogh called it " a curious instance of
cunning overreaching itself ". Dr. Duigenan, the Protestant
champion in the House of Commons, did not fail to draw
attention to these things.[3] The Bill was, in fact, even in
its most extended interpretation, a very poor measure of
relief. Appointments to the staff were not within the
reach of many Irishmen ; and the only other point in
which Ireland was particularly affected—namely that by
the extension of the law to England Irish Catholic officers

---

[1] *Court and Cabinets*, iv. 147 : Temple to Buckingham, 23 March :
" The country gentlemen and the saints are now with us, and if pledged
now will continue so ; but if Easter is suffered to intervene, their anger
will cool " ; *Jackson Diaries*, F. J. Jackson to G. Jackson, 20 April :
" the country is unequivocally pronounced against them, which, when
the present Parliament is dissolved, will be seen still more clearly " ;
Nat. Lib. of Wales MS. 4812, f. 196, Southey to C. W. Wynn, for the
strictures of a moderate on Perceval's tactics ; Add. MS. 34457, f. 287,
for example of difficulty with "No Popery" constituents of Woodstock ;
Add MS. 37887, f. 11, Routh of Magdalen to Windham, refusing support
to Herbert on this ground. Even so good a friend to Grenville as the
Bishop of Carlisle wavered in his support : *Harcourt Papers*, xii. 138 ;
Falkiner, *op. cit.* p. 209, for Ponsonby's remark.

[2] *Observations on the Catholic Bill* is the best of them.

[3] *A Sketch of the State of Ireland*, p. 24 ; Keogh, *The Veto*, p. 16 ;
Add. MS. 35646, f. 263 ; *Parl. Deb.* ix. 322-325.

landing there ceased to be in an illegal position—was a
purely technical one. It is true indeed that all Catholic
soldiers would have been affected by the clause which
protected them in the exercise of their religion. But in
spite of occasional cases of hardship, this was not a serious
matter. Wellington in the Peninsula found no great
religious zeal among his numerous Catholic soldiers—
quite the contrary, in fact—but they were perfectly free
to go to mass if they chose.[1]

In short, the Whigs propounded a Bill, hastily got up
to meet an awkward agitation, which offered no attractions
to the agitators, but which did something to conciliate the
peaceful English Dissenters, and the still more peaceful
English Catholics.[2] By a sort of juggle they hoped to turn
it into something which would at least give the Irish a
privilege they had not already got. They failed in their
game, because the King saw through it. They fell back
on their first project ; he refused it ; and they fell with
an air of nobility wholly fictitious, having engendered a
storm of religious bigotry in England, having made Whig
coöperation with the King for the future impossible,
having connected the Catholic question with an attack
on the monarchy, and having alienated that dangerous
class of Irish agitators which their Bill had been designed
to conciliate.

The best arguments for the measure are, that it was
as much as the Government could hope to obtain, and

----

[1] *E.g.* the bad case of Patrick Spence, Plowden, iii. 778-780 ; Wellington, *Despatches*, v. 133, 8 Sept. 1809 : " The thing now stands exactly
as it ought: any man may go to mass who chooses, and nobody
makes any inquiry about it. The consequence is that nobody goes to
mass . . . " ; also Wellington, *Civil Corr.* p. 443 (his orders for safeguard-
ing attendance at mass to soldiers in Ireland).

[2] Add. MS. 35646, f. 217. Bishop of Kildare to Hardwicke, 1 April :
" The Roman Catholics here indeed cared very little for the subject of
disagreement,—and were rather offended than otherwise by the intended military relaxations ".

that it was a pledge of sympathy and good-will which the state of Ireland rendered it imperative to give. Moreover, it had been intended to follow it with a Tithe Bill, on which the Whigs had been working for some time, and of the necessity of which the more enlightened of them were fully persuaded. It is not quite fair, therefore, to accuse them of supplying a political remedy for a social evil.[1] It seems unlikely that those who imagined that the Militia Bill would lead to increased recruiting from Ireland were justified in their opinion ; [2] but there is more to be said for the view that any measure which tended to conciliate Ireland tended also to reinforce a dangerous joint in the country's defensive armour. The fear of rebellion was not by any means the Whig fantasy which it has been thought to be by some historians. The Whigs, it is true, and particularly the Grenvilles, were extremely gloomy about the Irish situation ; but their gloom was shared by many Irish patriots, not least by Grattan, and was even exceeded by the Tory Irish Secretary, Arthur Wellesley.[3] There were

---

[1] As Mr. Fremantle does, *op. cit.* ii. 185; *Dropmore Papers*, ix. 68, 82-97, for this project ; *Plymley*, p. 29 : " There is no disguising the horrid truth ; *there must be some relaxation with respect to tithe :* this is the cruel and heart-rending price which must be paid for national preservation ". See, too, Grenville in Add. MS. 34457, f. 319 ; and *Court and Cabinets*, iv. 215.

[2] *E.g.* Wynn to Southey, 25 March 1807, Nat. Lib. of Wales MS. 4814, f. 25 : " The one great desideratum at present is the augmentation of our regular army. In Ireland you have a superabundant population which wants such a drain. Till you give professions to the middle ranks of Catholics . . . they never can *bona fide* assist recruiting."

[3] Mr. Fremantle seems to think that the Whigs were alone in their fears (*op. cit.* ii. 186). Add. MS. 34457, ff. 317 *et. seq.*, for examples of Grenville's endlessly reiterated apprehensions ; also Grattan, v. 364 ; *Plymley*, p. 17. Against this view, Plowden, iii. 611. For Wellington's views, *Civil Corr.* pp. 33, 30 : " I am positively convinced that no political measure which you could adopt would alter the temper of the people of this country. They are disaffected to the British Government ; they don't feel the benefits of their situation, attempts to render it better either do not reach their minds, or are represented to them as additional

Irish traitors still in Paris, and there were said to be Irishmen in communication with them; for after all it was only four years since Emmett's rebellion. The growth of a party bitterly hostile to the Union, which was already noted by some keen observers to involve also the growth of a small section desirous of breaking away altogether, was a sign of the times. The power of Napoleon had never stood higher; the energy of Napoleon was incalculable. Decidedly there was ground for alarm.[1]

But when all has been conceded, the Bill of 1807 was a pitiful expedient, produced in haste, and certainly repented of at leisure. If the Whigs were to make constitutional martyrs of themselves, if George III was to be held up to the execration of posterity, it was unfortunate that the squabble did not concern a more worthy measure, and a more substantial concession.

(b) *The Veto*

The Whigs were now in Opposition, and they looked at the Irish problem with rather different eyes. In their treatment of it they were no longer restrained by considerations of expediency and practicability. On the contrary, they could without reserve act upon the principles which had led them to lay down their offices. Henceforth the Whigs were above all the party favouring the Catholics. As Reformers, they had their doubts; in the sphere of foreign policy their notions were mere notions, hurting none but themselves. But for two or three years, at any rate,

injuries; and in fact we have no strength here but our army.... Ireland, in a view to military operations, must be considered as an enemy's country." See also *Dropmore Papers*, ix. 165.

[1] Wellington, *Civil Corr.* p. 12 : " Lord Fingall was with me yesterday. The object of his visit was to acquaint me that there was a person in Dublin who he believed communicated with Arthur O'Connor at Paris." Also *Civil Corr.* pp. 119-121, 139-141, 193; *Plymley*, p. 26 ; *Dropmore Papers*, ix. 161-162.

the Whigs peculiarly identified themselves with the Catholic cause. They made reservations, of course. They were not prepared to countenance those Catholics who attacked the Union, still less those who went further. They looked with suspicion and hostility on the Democratic party in Ireland. They were quite determined that they would promote Catholic interests in the way which seemed best to themselves, rather than in that which seemed most desirable to the Catholics. By this attitude they laid up for themselves many of the difficulties which harassed them later on, and particularly those which arose from the unfortunate dispute over the veto. For the Democratic party in Ireland was strong, and was getting stronger. Early in 1808 the elder Keogh was definitely deposed from the leadership of the Catholic Association and was succeeded by O'Connell. And about the same time there was presented a petition from the skinners of Dublin demanding the repeal of the Union.[1] The Whigs might intend to make party capital out of Ireland, but at least one section of the Irish nation had other views.[2]

Moreover, there were difficulties for some time after the change of Government, which tied the hands of the Opposition and embarrassed them not a little. There was the legislation they had left behind them when they went out, and which was in a sufficiently forward state to be adopted without alteration by Perceval. It comprised a renewal of the Insurrection Act, and a very stringent Arms Bill. How could the Whigs oppose these measures ? The Tories—and the Irish Patriots—did not fail to point out that these were

[1] Grattan, v. 367 ; Dunlop, *O'Connell*, p. 29 ; Wyse (*op. cit.* i. 142) considers that the change made no difference, and that the Association remained the same ; but the Government certainly regarded it as a new Association. Add. MS. 38242, ff. 195-196.

[2] *Jackson Diaries*, ii. 236-237 : " The Opposition must have something to operate with, and unfortunately, they are going to take up the cause of the Irish Catholics, which may and indeed must be, provocative of mischief ".

Whig Bills. Yet as seen from the Opposition benches there was a great deal that was objectionable in them, and perhaps a little that was intolerable. The Whigs split upon the question. The leaders stuck to their guns, and under Grattan's command contended for the Bills as the only defence against the rising menace of a " French party " in Ireland ; the irresponsibles, and the more liberal of the party, bitterly opposed them. They were of course carried ; and they seem to have been applied by Wellesley with discretion. But they did not enhance the reputation of the Whigs with the Democratic party in Ireland.[1]

Sheridan, however, was always a true friend to Ireland ; and in a motion which he made on 13 August 1807 to enquire into the state of Ireland he marshalled all the arguments for a conciliatory policy, and adduced a good deal of evidence to show that extraordinary measures were unnecessary. The Whigs had been afraid of some such indiscretion on Sheridan's part ;[2] and certainly he bore very hardly upon his party. He rejoiced that their Militia Bill had failed ; and he compared it to a decorating of the topsails with ten feet of water in the hold. The speech was one of his best ; and demonstrated Sheridan's ability to rise above petty considerations of party to enlightened patriotism and humane statesmanship—an ability which to the very end of his life appeared in occasional flashes, and which always raised him a little above the Greys and the Grenvilles. On this occasion he obtained 33 votes in a thin House.[3] The Whigs, in fact, were at first rather shy of the Catholics. They would have preferred the subject of

[1] *Parl. Deb.* ix. 751*, 911, 1057-1067 ; *Morning Chronicle*, 28 July 1807 ; Romilly, ii. 214 ; Plowden, iii. 568 ; Grattan, v. 362.

[2] *Tierney MSS.* Tierney to Whitbread, 28 Dec. 1807 : " This will cause a world of trouble afterwards for it will probably make it impossible to bring forward anything relating to Ireland with the least chance of success for the remainder of the session. One fine speech will thus do poor Pat's business effectually."

[3] *Parl. Deb.* ix. 1185 *et seq.*

Catholic Emancipation to remain in the background for some little time. Grey wrote to Tierney in November 1807 :

I believe your information to be right as to the intention of the Catholics to petition. Whenever I have had an opportunity of doing so I have stated how prejudicial I think such a measure to be to their own interests. If the petition comes however I must support it. I do not see that it makes much difference to our hope of office, for after what has happened this is a question which can no longer be avoided. . . . The truth is that the Catholics have now been taught to consider the whole English nation as so hostile to them that they feel comparatively very little interest in the different changes of administration that may take place ; and believing that those who have the inclination will never have the power to grant them redress ; and being convinced that their only chance of justice is in the wars and in the distresses of England, they are naturally led to press the question without reference to the state of politics as it affects the different parties in Parliament. But I must repeat that I do not think this a matter of much moment to *us*.[1]

Nevertheless the Whigs began to consider the possibility of other remedies than Emancipation, for the ills of Ireland, particularly as the Tory Government adopted a policy of " vigour " which offered them a good line of attack ; and there was much discussion of social and economic questions among the Whig leaders. The only perceptible result was an increased ardour in the attacks on the policy of the Lord Lieutenant and his Chief Secretary. But the Tories do not seem to have done anything very terrible, or to have revived any very great abuse. They eventually reduced the Maynooth grant by £4000 to a figure rather higher than the original grant of £8000 (which annoyed the Whigs a great deal) ; they made Dr. Duigenan a Privy Counsellor (which no one in Ireland minded at all) ; and they sent over Lord Manners as Chancellor (who at least cannot have been worse than

[1] *Tierney MSS.* Grey to Tierney, 8 Nov. 1807 ; Grey, *Life and Opinions*, pp. 158-160.

Ponsonby).[1] No doubt some Orangemen got into place again ; but on the other hand a determined, though vain, effort was made to retain Plunket as Attorney-General, and Wellesley seems to have been on friendly terms with Lord Fingall.[2] The Government made some effort to investigate deficiencies in the facilities for education ; and Lord Manners set himself to improve the magistracy. Still, the Tories concerned themselves more with the needs of the Established Church than with those of the country at large.[3] Sir Arthur Wellesley had no very sanguine expectations of reform. " Ireland " he wrote, " is not a country on which the experiment of sudden and rapid reforms of abuses can be tried. However enormous the latter may be, they are too inveterate and of too long standing to bear the sudden application of the former. . . ." [4] Nevertheless, the problem of tithes was becoming more acute ; and though the Government professed to believe that the real evil was the exorbitance of the rents, there were meetings of undeniable respectability which testified to a contrary opinion. And the Whigs were beginning to realize the difficulties and the urgency of the problem.[5]

It was thus under peculiar circumstances that the Irish Catholic agitation was revived in 1808. The cry against the Union was growing daily stronger ; [6] the cry against tithes was already very loud. In the Castle was a Government which, if not paternal, was not remarkably

[1] *Morning Chronicle*, 6 Nov., 12 Dec. 1807 ; Grattan, v. 358 ; *Parl. Deb.* ix. 817-829, xi. 89-98, 145 *et seq.* ; *Morning Chronicle*, 14 May 1808, for Duigenan.

[2] Add. MS. 35647, f. 182; Plunket, *Life and Speeches*, i. 225; Wellington, *Civil Corr.* p. 15.

[3] Wellington, *Civil Corr.* pp. 242, 150 ; *Parl. Deb.* ix. 497 (grants for repairing churches and glebehouses) ; Add. MS. 36650, f. 27 (Manners to Redesdale) ; *Dropmore Papers*, ix. 195-197.

[4] Wellington, *Civil Corr.* p. 247, 25 Dec. 1807.

[5] *Ibid.* pp. 146, 164 ; Plowden, iii. 611 ; *Dropmore Papers*, ix. 154.

[6] Wellington, *Civil Corr.* p. 403 ; M'Kenna, pp. 102, 120.

odious ; and at Westminster was an Opposition in regard
to which there was a well-marked division of Irish opinion.
When, therefore, the Catholic Association met early in the
year to consider the expediency of a petition, they hesitated
as to the line to be adopted. They even offered the charge
of the projected petition to the Duke of Portland ; but
when he refused it, they turned once more to Lord
Grenville.[1] It was felt, however, that something should
be done to make the Catholic claims more palatable to the
English nation ; for the fury of religious bigotry in the
election of 1807 had shown the necessity for some step
of this nature. Discussions were accordingly initiated as
to the possibility of conceding to the Crown some control
over the election to Irish Roman Catholic Bishoprics, and
thus affording a guarantee of the loyalty of the hierarchy.

In the torrent of recriminations which followed the
breakdown of this scheme later in the year, it is not easy
to arrive at a just view of its early history : each party
was anxious to father it on the other. But in essential
outline it appears to be as follows. In 1791 the Board of
English Catholics made an attempt to win Emancipation
by offering to take a special oath in place of the Oath of
Supremacy, and by adopting the comprehensive title of
" Protestant Catholic Dissenters ". Nothing came of the
scheme (except a good deal of bad feeling) ; but Sir John
Coxe Hippisley, a Protestant busybody well liked at the
Papal Court, conceived the idea of expanding this principle
into the concession to the Crown of a veto on the appointment of Catholic Bishops. When Pitt was negotiating for
the Union he availed himself of the existence of these
projects to come to an agreement with some of the leaders
of the Irish Catholic hierarchy. It appeared just probable
that he might succeed in making the Catholic Church of
Ireland a Government Establishment : the Maynooth grant
had shown the way. At all events, in the expectation

[1] *Dropmore Papers*, ix. 167 ; Grattan, v. 367.

of Catholic Emancipation at the Union, and perhaps of
further financial assistance, ten leading Catholic prelates
signed the resolutions of 1799, committing themselves to
support of the veto. When the Union was carried without
concessions to the Catholics the bargain terminated, and
the whole affair remained a profound secret.[1]

The idea, however, remained in the air. Sir John
Throckmorton, a leading English Catholic, entertained it ;
and Sir John Hippisley could not easily be brought to
abandon his scheme. In 1805, therefore, he came forward
with a suggestion for a veto in his speech upon the Catholic
question, on 13 May of that year, and he received the
support of Bishops Troy, Moylan, and Milner, and also (if
Charles Butler is to be believed) of that same J. Bernard
Clinch who was later to be so hostile to the Vetoists.[2] It
was not until the beginning of 1808 that the subject was
again brought forward, though a significant passage in
Peter Plymley seems to show that Whig opinion was
already moving in that direction.[3] When the Association
began to discuss the presentation of a new petition Lord
Fingall drew out a proposal (of which no trace seems to
remain) for a concordat upon the continental model.[4]

---

[1] Wyse, i. 166-167 and notes ; Plowden, iii. 787 ; Grattan, v. 57-58 ;
Ward, *Eve of Catholic Emancipation*, i. 49-50 ; Ward, *Catholic London*,
pp. 14-17 ; Clinch (*op. cit.* p. 31) asserts that the Government's proposal
was " little less than a menace ; if not a menace, was palpably an
insult ", but Ward (*Eve of C.E.*, *loc. cit.*) denies this, and (i. 55) enters
into the vexed question as to whether the ten Bishops were really
representative : see *Dropmore Papers*, ix. 233, for Archbishop Troy's
view ; also Keogh, p. 23 ; *Royal Veto*, p. 23.

[2] Butler, *Historical Memoirs*, ii. 170 *et seq.*; Hippisley, *Substance of
Observations* (1805), p. 115.

[3] *Plymley*, p. 9 : " Everybody who knows Ireland, knows perfectly
well, that nothing would be easier, with the expenditure of a little
money, than to preserve enough of the ostensible appointment in the
hands of the Pope to satisfy the scruples of the Catholics, while the real
nomination remained with the Crown ".

[4] Wellington, *Civil Corr.* pp. 292-294.

About the same time Sir Jerome Fitzpatrick produced a similar scheme,[1] and it was one or both of these which they thrashed out at a meeting held some time in February 1808.[2] Apparently the Bishops could not view such a scheme with any great favour ; and it appears that it was suspect as being a move of the *laity*, who were supposed to be improperly anxious to enjoy the fruits of Emancipation. The suspicion and lack of coöperation between the clergy and laity (particularly the upper-class laity) was, both in Ireland and in England, to be a fruitful source of trouble for the future. However, it seems that Fingall's plan was not specifically condemned, for when he went to England with the petition in the spring he got into touch with Ponsonby and asked him to see Dr. Milner about it.[3]

Dr. Milner was a very learned and very zealous man, celebrated already as a controversialist, and having perhaps the ethics of a controversialist rather than of a Bishop. For Milner was Vicar Apostolic of the Midland District of England, and Bishop *in partibus* of Castabala. Moreover, he was the accredited agent of the Irish Catholics and represented their interests in England. As Cornelius Keogh bitterly put it :

A political adventurer, the right reverend Dr. Milner, whose erudition and persuasive powers would do credit to a purer character, made a tour of Ireland in 1807 to win the unwary . . . bepraising all he found in his way :—if he met but an Irish hen, she unquestionably laid the freshest eggs of all the gallinaceous tribe. . . . During the tour, he was named, in the Castle-hack episcopal Junta, in the Maynooth Convocation, and by the Lord-Knows-What authority, agent of the Irish prelacy near the English Government.[4]

[1] *Ibid.* p. 321, 31 Jan. 1808.

[2] Add. MS. 38242, f. 195, where the Concordat is reported as having been supported by " Counsellor Connell ". Can this be O'Connell ?

[3] Grattan, v. 376.

[4] Keogh, pp. 23-24 ; Milner, *Letters to a Parish Priest, ap.* " A.B.", *Six Letters on the Subject of Dr. Milner's Explanation* ; the " Castle-hack Junta ", it is fair to note, included four Metropolitans. One of Milner's

By whatever authority named, Milner was regarded by
responsible persons in England and Ireland as a proper
person to carry on conversations of this nature ; and
Ponsonby had no hesitation in acceding to Fingall's
suggestion. The three met on 3 May, and as a result of
discussions on that day Ponsonby felt himself justified in
making a statement in Parliament when the Catholic
petition should come up for discussion.[1] This did not happen
until 25 May, and the delay was really the fault of Grey,
who could not be induced to come up for the occasion. The
remonstrances of his colleagues made no impression, for
Grey felt, even more strongly than they did, that the time
was inopportune for a reopening of the question. The Duke
of Bedford and others were alarmed at the unfavourable
opinion of Grey's conduct which the Irish Catholics in
consequence entertained, and made a strong effort to secure
his attendance. But, as usual, Grey put personal con-
venience before the welfare of his party, and stayed away.[2]

On 25 May Grattan moved to take the Catholic petition
into consideration. His eloquence was as lucid, his arguments
as convincing, as ever ; but it was not until he propounded
the veto that the interest of the House was really aroused.

I have a proposition to make [he said], a proposition which
indeed the Catholics have authorized me to name. It is this : " That
in the future nomination of Bishops, His Majesty may interfere and
exercise his Royal privilege, by putting a negative upon such
nomination ; that is in other words to say : that no Catholic Bishop
shall be appointed without the entire approbation of His Majesty ".[3]

Ponsonby elucidated and elaborated the proposal in an
excellent speech, and in further explanation avowed that

friends wrote : " Dr. M. is perhaps the ablest and deepest-read Roman
Catholic divine in the British Empire ; and it is notorious that none is
more zealous or less complying " (*Answer to Dr. Duigenan*, p. 18).

[1] *Parl. Deb.* xvii. 217 *seq.*
[2] *Dropmore Papers*, ix. 197-199 ; *Parl. Deb.* xi. 643.
[3] *Ibid.* 556.

Milner had authorized him to make the proposal.[1] The
Whigs as a party supported their leaders ;[2] but even this
new concession failed to move the impregnable Protestants
of the Government benches, and the motion was beaten
by 281–128, the minority including no less than 40 Irish
members.[3] Grattan thought the debate had gone off
excellently from the Catholic point of view.[4] Two days
later Grenville made the same motion and the same
proposition in the House of Lords, and secured 74 votes,
among them that of the generous and enlightened Bishop
of Norwich.[5]

At first the reaction in Ireland was favourable. The
Catholic hierarchy—or a considerable section of it—
actively approved the proposition ; and to the Aristocratic
party it was naturally acceptable. Archbishops Dillon and
Troy, Bishops Caulfield, Delany, and Lanigan, all assured
Grenville in the course of June that they had no doubt
of a resolution in support of it passing the general Convocation of prelates.[6] The Duke of Richmond, the Lord
Lieutenant, wrote to Sir Arthur Wellesley, on the strength
of Grattan's speech, suggesting a revival of Pitt's project
for the payment of priests. In short, in the months of June
and July all was harmonious speculation. But at the end of
July the opposition, which had, unnoticed, been growing
rapidly, became apparent. It was headed in the main by
the Democrats, who exploited the religious fears of the
ignorant masses in order to defeat an essentially Aristocratic
scheme ; it was joined from conviction by some of the
younger Bishops ;[7] and it had a great deal of not very

---

[1] *Ibid.* 608, 619.

[2] Though some (*e.g.* Petty) would have preferred that the petition
had not been brought forward. *Parl. Deb.* xi. 592.

[3] *Ibid.* 638 ; *Morning Chronicle,* 28 May 1808.

[4] Grattan, v. 381.   [5] *Parl. Deb.* xi. 643-694.

[6] *Dropmore Papers,* ix. 203-204 ; Ward, i. 67, citing Westminster
Archives.

[7] *E.g.* Coppinger of Cloyne. Ward, i. 68.

scrupulous press support. There was resentment among Irishmen at being thus disposed of by an English Vicar Apostolic ; there was suspicion of the Maynooth influence among the Catholic Bishops ; and there was indignation that even the veto, preposterous in itself as it seemed to them, could not extort acquiescence from the English Parliament. The Irish have always been inclined to be self-willed in their devotion to the Church of Rome, and they had now no hesitation in attacking their Bishops. Passionate and pathetic letters appeared in the Dublin papers with such pseudonyms as " Sarsfield ", " Laicus ", " Inimicus Veto ", appended to them. A spate of pamphlets of very varying merit accompanied them.[1] Of all these writers perhaps the best and most influential was J. Bernard Clinch, a barrister of talent and a member of the Democratic group. His pamphlet, entitled *An Inquiry, Legal and Political, into the Consequences of giving His Majesty a Negative*, appeared at the beginning of August. It warned the Bishops that the eye of the Irish nation was upon them : " their place, their honour, their innocence, demand a loud vindication. It is impatiently expected now. In a month hence it may be a posthumous apology."[2] " . . . Emancipation, upon this plan, will, in plain honest English, be neither more nor less, than an *act for discontinuing the Roman Catholic system, by making compensation for its abolition, to the present holders of that faith*."[3] And in the streets of Dublin appeared a placard to this effect :

To be sold to the highest bidder, an Antient Hierarchy, very little the worse for the wear, which has stood many storms, but cannot endure fair weather. Apply to Messrs. Troy, Moylan, & Co., on the premises ; to Randall McDonnell, broker to the concern ; or to Dr. Milner, travelling agent.[4]

[1] Hippisley, *Speech* (1810), p. 13.
[2] Clinch, p. xix. See *Dropmore Papers*, ix. 256-260, for Hippisley's opinion of Clinch's pamphlet.
[3] Clinch, p. 66.   [4] Ward, i. 68.

The Irish Bishops grew fearful in the face of so strong an agitation. They met in synod at Dublin on 14 and 15 September, and in a series of resolutions condemned the veto as "inexpedient". They did not condemn it as totally inadmissible, or as being at variance with the essential tenets of the Roman Catholic Church. How could they do so, when the archives of the deserted Vatican were littered with analogous Concordats with half the countries of Europe ?[1] How could they do so, when ten of their number had signed the resolutions of 1799 ? Three of the ten, more courageous and consistent than the rest, stuck to their opinion. The other seven went to swell the majority of twenty-three. By way of a friendly gesture to the rear, they voted their thanks and confidence to the unfortunate Milner.[2]

Milner was now in a most unpleasant situation. He found himself execrated in Ireland by the vast majority of Catholics, and regarded with suspicion by the Whigs with whom he had discussed the proposition.[3] At the beginning of August he had written a series of letters, which got into print, as he asserted, contrary to his intention, in which the case for the veto was argued with the utmost persuasiveness. These were the *Letters to a Parish Priest*.[4] Milner himself had arrived in Ireland in the middle of August and had been astonished at the virulence of the newspaper attacks on his conduct. He had not been admitted to the synod of Bishops which declared against the veto on 14 September. Thus he

---

[1] " There is perhaps ", wrote Milner, " no *civilized* Christian country in which the Government does not interfere in the appointment of the prelates . . . and *it is judged that there is no country in which this interference is so necessary as in Ireland* " (*Letters to a Parish Priest*, *ap.* " A.B." p. viii).

[2] Keogh, p. 26; *Morning Chronicle*, 19 Nov. 1808; Milner, *Appeal*, p. 14.

[3] *Ibid.* p. 4. He was called Judas Iscariot, and burned in effigy in Dublin. *Morning Chronicle*, 19 Nov. 1808.

[4] Milner, *Appeal*, p. 61.

found himself, after that date, in the awkward position of having openly supported (in the *Letters to a Parish Priest*) a course of action which the hierarchy, whose agent he was, had declared to be inexpedient. He therefore embarked, with a recklessness which appalled his colleagues and disgusted his Whig associates, upon a long controversy. His hope was to clear himself from responsibility for the veto, and to lay the blame on the Whigs.[1]

The agitation in Ireland which coerced the Bishops into rejecting the veto was very largely the result of perverted reports of what had been said in Parliament. Milner himself, before the fateful 14 September, had been loud in his complaints on this score.[2] Ponsonby was widely reported in the Irish press as having said that, as a result of the concession of the veto, the King would become virtually head of the Catholic Church in Ireland.[3] If Ponsonby really said this, he was guilty of an egregious blunder. But in fact no such words are attributed to him in the *Parliamentary Debates*, or in the *Morning Chronicle*. The utmost limit of his verbal expansiveness was reached when in explanation, at the end of the debate, he remarked that if the veto were conceded " the appointment should finally rest with the King ".[4] Grattan, however, was much less discreet, for he plainly said, " The proposition will make a double connection : the two churches will be one, and the King at the head ".[5] It is obvious that the Irish press fathered this remark on to Ponsonby in order to avoid the ungraciousness of an attack on Grattan. Still, Ponsonby was not free from blame in this matter.

[1] Ward, i. 74-80, 244, and 82, for Milner's pathetic letter to Bishop Collingridge, complaining that he is vilified by both sides.

[2] " It is evident that the writers give implicit faith to the accounts of negligent, drowsy, tippling, and ignorant reporters."—" A.B." App. p. xxxiii ; and see *Appeal*, p. 31.

[3] *Dropmore Papers*, ix. 233-234 ; Milner, *ap. Morning Chronicle*, 19 Nov.

[4] *Parl. Deb.* xi. 619.   [5] *Ibid.* pp. 556 *et seq.*

It was not mere spite that led Milner later to accuse him of lack of discretion ; for before the Irish Bishops had rejected the veto, Milner had written to the *Dublin Herald* insisting that, although Ponsonby and Grenville had not gone so far as was reported in the papers, they had indeed gone further than they were entitled to do.[1] (It is true that in his *Letters to a Roman Catholic Prelate* of 1811 he puts Grattan's remark into Ponsonby's mouth ; but this was a typical Milnerism, to be attributed to carelessness or unblushing falsehood, according to the view taken of Milner's character.[2]) Lord Holland, moreover, thought that Ponsonby had gone too far.[3] And Ponsonby himself, in his exculpatory speech two years later, stated that on the day after his speech of 1808, when Milner had called upon him to protest, he, Ponsonby, had denied that he had ever said that the veto would make the King head of the Church of Ireland.[4] It is clear, then, that Milner's apprehensions had been immediately aroused, and that Ponsonby's speech must have been, to say the least, ambiguous. Moreover, it becomes apparent that Ponsonby in this, as in so many other things, showed a reprehensible slackness and lack of care for the reputation of his party. It seems that Hippisley pointed out to him that incorrect versions of his speech were being circulated, and suggested that he should correct them : to which—

[1] " A.B." p. xxxiv. " I may add, in justice to them as well as to myself, that after the debate was over, they acknowledged themselves to have advanced certain positions, the most alarming of all that were made, for which they had no warrant but their own way of viewing the subject " (Milner to the Parish Priest).

[2] *Letters to a Roman Catholic Prelate*, pp. 23-24. But perhaps it ought to be mentioned that the Duke of Buckingham later said (on what authority ?) that Ponsonby had used the phrase " in explanation ". *Dropmore Papers*, ix. 368.

[3] Holland, *Memoirs of the Whig Party*, pp. 252-253. Not contemporary evidence.

[4] *Parl. Deb.* xvii. 218-220, 25 May 1810.

Mr. Ponsonby told me he had never corrected any speech for publication ; but added that I might correct it. This, on a point of so much delicacy, I declined to do ; but I anticipated the ill consequences of this over-statement.[1]

It is hardly surprising that so lofty a contempt for public opinion should have afforded scope for calumny. Ponsonby considered himself ill-used ; and indeed Milner's behaviour to him was hardly straightforward, for when the resolutions of the Bishops were known, Milner wrote a smooth and flattering note to him, and simultaneously attacked him violently in the Cork and Waterford papers.[2] And there were enemies of Milner who, from mere dislike of him, were prepared to believe that Ponsonby had been duped.[3] But upon the whole it cannot be denied that Ponsonby overshot the mark ; and the occasion of his erring was not the headship of the Catholic Church, but the vital question whether the projected veto should be in practice a positive, or only a negative, power.

The method of election to an Irish Roman Catholic Bishopric was as follows. The chapter of the vacant see selected three persons, styled respectively *Dignus, Dignior, Dignissimus* ; these three names, after approval by the Bishops of the province, were then sent to the Pope, whose selection nearly always fell on *Dignissimus.* As Ponsonby had proposed it in Parliament, the veto would have operated in the following manner. The names of the three were to be sent to the Lord Lieutenant, " and if he should object to all the three, they [the Irish Bishops] strike them out, and send other three in their stead, until the King's approbation of some one of them be received. Even then, they send that name to Rome to receive the approbation of the Pope."[4]

---

[1] *Dropmore Papers*, ix. 260. To Grenville, 5 Jan. 1809.
[2] *Ibid.* 226, 231-232.   [3] *The Royal Veto*, pp. 73-74.
[4] *Parl. Deb.* xi. 608-609. It is only fair to Ponsonby to notice that in his later explanation (xi. 619) candidates were to be presented one by one. See also Newenham, *View of Ireland*, App. p. xxix, for method of election.

Now this gives the Crown a measure of positive power ; for, first, it can choose among the three, and, secondly, it can, by rejecting a large number of candidates, arrive at any particular person by a process of exhaustion. In other words the Crown was to have both a limited right of selection and an unlimited right of rejection. The controversy between Milner and Ponsonby turned on whether Ponsonby had ever been given any ground to propose concessions to this extent. Milner seems to have taken alarm on the very day after Ponsonby's speech, and to have maintained upon the whole a consistent attitude thereafter. On 26 May 1808 he wrote and printed a Protest against the misrepresentations of his conversation of which (as he alleged) Ponsonby had been guilty in his speech of the previous day. This Protest, which was the foundation of Milner's charge against Ponsonby, was believed to be a figment of Milner's imagination by many of his enemies, for Milner suppressed it at the request of Lord Fingall and others, in order that its publication should not detract from the favourable impression produced by Ponsonby's speech.[1] It was real enough, however. In it he denied that he had ever given Ponsonby reason to propose the selective power : the candidates should be presented one by one.[2] And in a letter to Lord Grenville of the same date he made his position more definite :

. . . the Catholic prelates, when they have made choice of a proper person to succeed to the vacant see, will send up the name to His Majesty's Ministers, and, if it is objected to, will send up another and another in succession *to a reasonable number* until one of them is approved of.[3]

So that the unlimited right of rejection is not conceded either. Now this is the view of the veto that Milner adopts

---

[1] " A.B." pp. 58-59 ; Milner, *Letters*, pp. 1-3, 10, 53 ; Milner, *Elucidation of the Veto*, p. 8.

[2] Ward, i. App. B, p. 234, prints this Protest.

[3] *Dropmore Papers*, ix. 202. The italics are mine.

in all his subsequent publications, whether he is still in favour of the veto (as in the *Letters to a Parish Priest*), or whether he has accepted the decision of the Irish Bishops as to its inexpediency (as in the *Appeal* and the *Elucidation*). His opinions changed as to the desirability of treating with the vetoists, but his views as to the theological inoffensiveness of such a veto remained constant ; and his account of the scheme he had countenanced remained consistent, from the Protest of 1808 to the *Letters to a Roman Catholic Prelate* of 1811.[1]

It is possible to vindicate Milner's consistency after the debate (though it has been much called in question) ; but it is rather his remarks before it that are the crux of the matter. What exactly did he say to Ponsonby ? There has unfortunately been some confusion of dates as to the interviews between them. It seems likely that there were two, on 3 May and 21 May.[2] On the 4th (or, less probably, the 22nd) Milner left a card at Ponsonby's house, on the back of which were recapitulated the four main points of their conversation of the previous days, together with a letter discussing them in full. This letter Milner always referred to as a " hasty note ", and always professed to have written in a bookseller's on his way home the previous day.[3] It is, however, hardly credible that this long and careful composition was a hasty note. He must, at least, have been a tolerant bookseller to allow Milner to use his shop for the purpose of writing an exposition of his views some 600 to 700 words in length. Milner defined his position as follows :

---

[1] " A.B." p. v ; *Dublin Herald*, 8 Sept. 1808 (*ap.* " A.B." p. xxxv) ; *Morning Chronicle*, 19 Nov. 1808 ; Ward, i. 82 ; *Appeal*, p. 60 ; *Letter to Lord Stourton* (*ap.* Keogh, p. 87) ; *Elucidation*, pp. 6, 9 ; *Letters to a Roman Catholic Prelate*, pp. 4 *et seq.* See also *The Jerningham Letters*, i. 309.

[2] Ward's emendation—23 May for 3 May—is unnecessary, and leads him to misdate the second interview as 22 May. Ward, i. 61.

[3] Keogh, p. 90 ; Milner, *Letters to a Roman Catholic Prelate*, pp. 1-3, 24. Milner puts this note as 21 May, but Ponsonby's speech shows it to have been 4 May.

First, the Catholic prelates of Ireland *are willing* to give a *direct negative* power to His Majesty's Government, with respect to the nomination to their titular Bishoprics, in such manner, that when they have among themselves resolved who is the fittest person for the vacant see, they will transmit his name to His Majesty's Ministers, and if the latter should object to that name, they will transmit another and another, until a name is presented to which no objection is made ; and (which is never likely to be the case) should the Pope refuse to give those essentially necessary spiritual powers of which he is the depositary, to the person so presented by the Catholic Bishops, and so approved of by Government, they will continue to present the names till one occurs which is agreeable to both parties, namely the Crown and the Apostolic See.[1]

So that Milner did commit himself in writing to the un-restricted negative, though not to the selective power ; and did undertake for the willingness of the Irish Bishops to concede it. Milner later admitted that the words " direct negative " were liable to be misunderstood ; but, he con-tended, Ponsonby did not misunderstand them. And he urged that though it was true that no limitation of the veto was expressed, yet it was implied that it should be restricted to a reasonable number of times.[2] From a straightforward reading of the note it would be hard to deduce this. However, it is obvious that whether or no Ponsonby was justified in propounding the unlimited negative, he had no ground in Milner's note for the bringing forward of the selective power. He was misled, as his speech shows, by the normal procedure of *Dignus, Dignior, Dignissimus.* At the second interview with Ponsonby on 21 May Milner seems to have outlined his views in the terms which he embodied in his Protest of 26 May.[3] On that day, too, he wrote at Ponsonby's request to the four Irish Catholic Metropolitans and informed them, *inter alia,*

---

[1] *Parl. Deb.* xvii. 218, 25 May 1810. The italics are mine.
[2] Milner, *Letters to a Roman Catholic Prelate,* pp. 24-25.
[3] Ward, i. App. B, p. 235.

that they were in no way bound to the Whigs.[1] And, finally, on 26 May, Milner called on Ponsonby and showed him the Protest ; to which, according to Milner, Ponsonby replied : " I am not surprised at your alarm : I do not pretend that you authorized me to say all that I did say ; but I was at liberty to argue as best suited my cause. For the rest, this Paper is a fair paper, and you have my consent to circulate it."[2] Ponsonby's version was that Milner asked him to sanction the Protest, which limited the veto to the rejection of only a few candidates. Ponsonby refused. He had never intended, he said, to give the Crown a direct nomination, but to withdraw his words at this point would make a bad impression. He authorized Milner to state his (Ponsonby's) views, but not to disclaim the veto.[3] And he expressly admitted that he had no direct authorization of the veto from Milner at all.[4]

So from all this imbroglio the fact emerges that once again Ponsonby had proved himself a bungler. He had exceeded the limits which Milner had laid down as probably acceptable, and had thus alarmed him when it was most important that he should be conciliated. Ponsonby, moreover, by his foolish refusal to correct the reports of his speeches, had allowed the Irish agitators to fasten an indiscretion of Grattan on to him, and use it for their own purposes to wreck the project.

The Whigs indeed took insufficient pains to make sure of their ground. They mistook the rash coöperative zeal of Milner for complete agreement and definite authorization. Milner has been much blamed in this matter, even by so lenient a critic as Fr. Ward. But in reality his only error was excess of zeal. He may probably be believed when he says that in the beginning he came to London

---

[1] Milner, *Appeal*, p. 31.   [2] Husenbeth, *Milner*, p. 153.
[3] *Parl. Deb.* xvii. 218-220.   [4] *Ibid.* 217.

opposed to the idea of a veto.[1] But having heard from Fingall of the supposed leaning of the Irish hierarchy towards it, he rashly took the plunge, without considering whether it was judicious to commit himself very far. He knew, of course, that there was no theological objection to a limited veto ; and he probably considered it to be a practical compromise.

The fact is, the Veto as I had imagined it, in case its conditions were strictly adhered to, would not have given either power or influence to the Crown, but barely the means . . . of excluding real traitors and disturbers of the public peace from a seat amongst our Prelates.[2]

In a word, it never once entered into my imagination (here I confess my egregious error) that you [the Irish hierarchy] or any part of you, would conceive an alteration in the process of recommending candidates for episcopal institutions, to undermine " the only undestroyed monument of your national grandeur ", any more than the different changes which have taken place in this respect since the year 1682 have done.[3]

The " hasty note " was a *faux pas*, as he had probably perceived even by 21 May ; and he was justifiably annoyed when Ponsonby took advantage of it, and ignored his corrective observations of the later interview. It is unlikely that he ever advocated an unrestricted veto : it seems rather that he did not at first realize that his " hasty note " implied so much.

[1] *Letters to a Parish Priest, ap.* " A.B." p. iv : " So far, indeed, from acquiescing in it, I wrote most pressingly during the last spring to two of your venerable Metropolitans, in order to consult with them on the best mode of defeating it ; and it is a fact which I declare upon my conscience, that my chief motive for going up to London about ten weeks ago, was to oppose the measure, had it been brought forward in Parliament, as I feared would be the case ; being deeply conscious that it was my duty to do so, even at the expense of my life ".

[2] *Elucidation*, p. 9.

[3] *Appeal*, p. 28. Rather characteristically, in his next pamphlet, the *Elucidation*, he adopts this claptrap about " monuments of national grandeur " as his own ; see p. 34.

The Whigs, however, considered that they had not been fairly dealt with. They condemned Milner as a traitor, a canting rogue, one in whom it was impossible to place any confidence.[1] They were wholeheartedly on Ponsonby's side in the controversy.[2] For this, no doubt, Milner's subsequent behaviour was largely responsible. Milner, confronted with the choice between appeasing the Whigs or the Irish, wasted no time in selecting the latter alternative, and entered upon his justification with his usual impetuosity.[3] His letter to the *Morning Chronicle* in November 1808 marks his last attempt to defend the restricted veto. After that, he turned against a veto of any sort, though he never asserted it to be theologically objectionable ; [4] and with language of ever-increasing violence supported the Irish Bishops and attacked the Whigs. His accounts of his own conduct were consistent and accurate ; but to the Whigs they were not the less disagreeable, and they were marred by a certain recklessness of assertion which left both friends and enemies astonished. It was inexcusable, in one so familiar with the facts, in one who had indeed been present at the debate,[5] to ascribe Grattan's unhappy remark about the headship of the Church to Ponsonby. It was brazenly audacious to call his *Letters to a Parish Priest* "a mere mooting essay". It was perhaps a little theatrical to speak so often about shedding his last drop of blood in defence

---

[1] *Dropmore Papers*, ix. 241 ; *Parl. Deb.* xvii. 220. ". . . even *our ladies* here have abandoned him, and have no other excuse for his conduct but to allege, which they seriously do, that they know he has been twice out of his mind, and literally confined in a straight waistcoat " (*Dropmore Papers*, ix. 244).

[2] *Ibid.* 237 ; Grey, *Life and Opinions*, p. 207 ; *Court and Cabinets*, iv. 444.

[3] He said his heart revolted at the idea of having offended the Bishops. *Appeal*, p. 53.

[4] *Ibid.* p. 44.

[5] Milner to *Dublin Herald*, *ap.* " A.B." p. xxxiv.

of the Church's liberties.[1] He had an irritating habit also of sending letters to newspapers and protesting that they had been published without his consent, and contrary to his intention. Like many men who are valorous on paper, he was anxious to propitiate the company in which he found himself, and this gave his conduct an appearance of instability and insincerity. Thus at Stowe, in the autumn of 1808, he seems to have wilted under the awful weight of Buckingham's displeasure, and to have made a recantation which is in direct conflict with everything else that is known of his attitude at this time.[2]

It is not surprising in these circumstances that the Whigs distrusted him, and especially as they had two legitimate grounds of complaint, quite apart from Milner's behaviour after the condemnation of the scheme. First : if Milner, as he alleged, was from the first supporting a strictly limited veto, then he was wasting his time. No Government could consent to such a proposal ; for if the negative could be exercised only n times, it was open to a disaffected hierarchy to propose n impossible candidates in order to carry a traitorous $(n+1)$th. This was an argument, certainly, in favour of the Whig contention that Milner had not really been sufficiently explicit.[3] Secondly : there was nothing in Ponsonby's proposition to conflict with the resolutions of 1799. Fingall had just disclosed these resolutions to the Whigs, and it was natural to assume that they were to form the basis for

[1] Milner, *Supplementary Memoirs*, p. 130 ; *Letters to a Roman Catholic Prelate*, pp. 24-25 ; Keogh, p. 87 ; Elrington, *Reflections on the Appointment of Dr. Milner*, pp. 47-48.

[2] *Dropmore Papers*, ix. 367-368.

[3] See *Royal Veto*, pp. 7, 8-13; *Fourth Letter of Laicus*, p. 21 : yet Milner ("A.B." p. xvii) said he contended so strongly with the Whigs as to endanger friendship. Cf. *Appeal*, p. 60. He later alleged that Grenville stated in 1808 that the veto to be effective must be unrestricted. *Letters to a Roman Catholic Prelate*, pp. 36-37.

the new plan.[1] Here is the very centre of the difficulty, the
ultimate reason for failure. Both Milner and the Whigs
allowed themselves to be dragged into a project which
had no backing more official than that afforded by the
unsure support of a section of the Irish hierarchy, who
gave a lukewarm adhesion to the projects of Lord Fingall.
If Milner had not interfered, the veto would have appeared
more clearly for what it was—a gambit of the Aristocratic
party.[2] Milner gave it a hierarchical tinge. It was a fine
stroke of policy in Fingall to secure him. It was extremely
rash of Milner to enter wholeheartedly into the matter
before he was acquainted with authentic Irish sentiment.
At best he had only the ten signatories of 1799 to support
him—less than half the episcopate.[3] How entirely it was
a Fingallian affair may be seen from the emphasis which
Ponsonby laid, when defending his conduct, upon the fact
that he had had Fingall's approval, immediately after the
debate, and at other times subsequently. He assumed
plainly that what was in accordance with Fingall's views
must necessarily satisfy Milner. Too late Milner saw the
danger and wrote his Protest. He knew that he had no
real authority from Ireland beyond what he enjoyed as
general agent of the Irish Bishops.[4] The *Letters to a Parish
Priest* were a desperate attempt to save his face by
extracting from the Irish Bishops *some* concession[5]—the
" restricted negative "—which would, as Milner must

---

[1] Hippisley, *Substance of a Speech* (1811), p. 12.

[2] As " Laicus " brutally put it : " You were literally but a subordinate agent in the business ; and had you not, in defiance of the
opinions, and contrary to the advice of your friends, thrust yourself
forward into the post of danger, you might have passed almost unnoticed, or at the most come off with only that share of reprobation
which your conduct had previously deserved " (*Fourth Letter of Laicus*,
p. 60).

[3] Cf. *Royal Veto*, p. 21, where this point is strongly made.

[4] *Appeal*, pp. 29-31 ; *Elucidation*, p. 8.

[5] *Appeal*, p. 34, where this is almost admitted.

have known, have proved purely nugatory. But Fingall
had never intended the veto to be a useless arrangement. He had had the suggested arrangement of 1799
in mind throughout. Hence, when Ponsonby set out
a scheme which, though it overstepped Milner's limits,
was none the less in consonance with the resolutions
of the Irish Bishops, he felt himself to be justified on
broad grounds ; and he expected and received Fingall's
approbation.[1]

The veto controversy exhibits the Whigs committing
a characteristically Whig *sottise.* Just as they wished to
make Reform the monopoly of the aristocracy, so they
assumed that Emancipation was the monopoly of the
Fingallians. It never occurred to them that Fingall, though
amiable and well-meaning, was unauthorized, and had no
claims to represent Irish opinion. Nor did they realize
that the ten Bishops of 1799 were, from their sympathy
and connection with the English Government, by no
means representative of the hierarchy at large. Least of
all did they envisage the common people of Ireland presuming to entertain opinions on such a topic. To reject
the veto seemed to them an ingratitude to the nation's
leaders, a spurning of the Promised Land because it was
secured against disorder. No one but a Whig would have
supposed that Fingall was competent to speak for Ireland ;
and no one but a Whig would have persisted in Fingallianism after the reception which Ireland had given to the
veto. Yet that is what the Whigs did.

For the half instructed Catholic layman to negotiate with
Protestant statesmen, to regulate the exercise of the Sacrament of
Orders, and the transmission of spiritual jurisdiction, is a policy
as ridiculous as it is invalid. It can lead to nothing but disappointment and vexation on both sides.

The writer of these wise words was Milner himself. He, at

---

[1] Milner himself stressed the 1799 argument. "A.B." pp. vii, xiii.

least, had learned from the events of 1808 : the Whigs,
apparently, had not.

(c) *The Veto Revived*

Ireland's rejection of the veto, proclaimed by the
resolutions of the Irish Roman Catholic Bishops, made a
great stir in political circles. All parties seemed to be
equally indignant. The Tories of the school of Perceval and
Eldon saw in it, of course, the traditional inability of Papists
to keep faith with heretics.

> The rejection of the Veto [wrote Lord Kenyon] on the part of
> the Roman Catholics, evinces the arrogant pretensions and principles
> of that church . . . but even if granted, we cannot reasonably
> suppose that it would afford a shadow of security.[1]

In Ireland itself, Sir Arthur Wellesley had never looked on
the veto as holding out any promise of a settlement, and he
had developed his objections to it in a little treatise which,
though unfinished, shows in its arguments a truly military
clarity and logic.[2] He attributed the rejection of the scheme
to extremists, and argued that they had compromised their
reputations in Ireland by their double-dealing : which
showed that the Chief Secretary was more in touch with
the Portuguese than with the Irish situation.[3] At the other
end of the political scale, the Irish Democrats had quite a
different theory as to what had happened. Keogh, for
instance, stigmatized the conduct of the Whigs as " a
most finished piece of political depravity " ; [4] and it was the
general opinion of the fiercer partisans, then and afterwards,

---

[1] Kenyon, p. 53.
[2] Add. MS. 38079. This is a draft of notes for a pamphlet written
for Croker, and is a masterly analysis of the veto from the Tory point
of view. As it is not included in either series of Wellington's *Despatches*,
it is here given as an appendix.
[3] Cf. Whitbread's pointed remarks, *Parl. Deb.* xii. 366 *et seq.*
[4] Keogh, p. 21.

that the whole scheme had been a device for supporting
the reputation of the Whigs as friends of Ireland, without
committing them to any project which might be inconvenient for them when they came into power again.[1]
The Fingallians, on the other hand, felt they had been
betrayed ; and even the Bishops took refuge in allegations
of the untrustworthiness of the Tory Government.[2] Like the
Whigs, the Fingallians thought that the resolutions of the
Bishops should at least have contained some statement to
the effect that more favourable circumstances (*i.e.* a Whig
Government) might make the veto no longer "inexpedient ".[3]
Acting upon this line, Lord Southwell and other Catholic
gentlemen of Co. Louth wrote to the Primate, O'Reilly,
endeavouring to extract from him a declaration that the
condemnation of the veto related only to existing circumstances. O'Reilly, a weak man, gave them the reply they
wanted ; but the other Bishops held off and refused to
give any collective declaration in this sense.[4] Lastly, the
Whigs of every section were alarmed at the effect of the
conduct of the Catholics upon public opinion. Thomas
Grenville, writing to Lord Grenville on 19 October 1808,
laments—

the incalculable mischief that has been produced by the protest of
the Irish Catholic bishops, and by Milner's letters on that subject
. . . I find a most eager determination to mark the strongest dissent
from this new violence on the part of Keogh and the democrat
Catholics ; and on this subject my own opinions would lead me to be
as warm in language as my friends are, but the public calamity

---

[1] Thus Wyse (i. 183) : " There was never any serious intention
of listening to the arrangement ; it was thrown out merely for purposes
of division, and the result did ample justice to the Machiavellian policy of
the proposer ". And even Ward agrees (i. 59).

[2] See Troy's excuse to Newport, *Dropmore Papers*, ix. 233-234.

[3] *Ibid.* pp. 235-236.

[4] Keogh, pp. 29-30 ; Hippisley, *Speech* (1810), App. IV ; *Parl. Deb.*
xvii. 43 ; Wellington, *Civil Corr.* pp. 497-499 ; *Dropmore Papers*, ix.
226-228 ; *Royal Veto*, p. 47.

produced by this misconduct of these furious demagogues over-
whelms with me all other considerations. If by this intemperance
and dereliction of all loyal and moderate professions of former times,
they make it thus impossible for us to press, and hopeless for us to
obtain from the country or the King, the real grounds of union and
harmony between Great Britain and Ireland, what can we ever look
to again for the tranquillity of that country, and the safety of this ? [1]

The *Edinburgh Review*, indeed, was less gloomy at the
failure to carry the veto, for though it considered it
foolish in the Bishops to refuse it, still it was for acquiescing
in that refusal. The Catholics, it argued cogently enough,
deny that the Pope interferes save in matters of Church
discipline. If you disbelieve them, of what value are your
penal codes, and the oaths that they impose ? [2]

The majority of the party, however, felt that it would
be dangerous to leave the situation as it was. It was well
enough, no doubt, to oppose the Militia Interchange Act,
or to press for the admission of Catholics to the board of
directors of the Bank, or to set Sydney Smith to plead
the cause of Emancipation and tithe-commutation in the
Edinburgh Review ; [3] but this was not sufficient to form a
basis for united action. Catholic Emancipation was one of
the few issues upon which the Whig party was virtually
unanimous ; but the veto had complicated matters, and it
would be necessary for them to define their attitude to it,
before they could have any assurance of Irish support in
the event of their returning to office and beginning a
programme of conciliation. The issue of mere Emancipation
was becoming barren, and the arguments for it had

[1] *Dropmore Papers*, ix. 230-231.

[2] *Edinburgh Review*, April 1809, article v.

[3] The Militia Interchange Act, which was a success, had been sug-
gested anonymously to Windham in 1807 and rejected by him. Add.
MS. 37886, f. 68; *Parl. Deb.* xi. 714; *Edinburgh Review*, xii. 343; Sydney
Smith, *Letters*, p. 38. The article quoted above seems to have been
written by Malthus: Brougham, *Life and Times*, i. 436. Tithe question:
Parl. Deb. xi. 908, xiv. 625 *et seq.* ; *Independent Whig*, 7 Aug. 1808.

become stale;[1] but the veto controversy was only beginning, and it was sharpened, rather than allayed, by the keen sense of the dangerous situation of Ireland that the Whigs entertained.[2]

To Lord Grey the line of policy which his party ought to pursue seemed now clear. He had no great expectations of carrying Emancipation with the veto conceded; but he felt certain that he could not do so without it. The conduct of the Irish Democrats had irritated him profoundly; and he considered that they had destroyed the chances of the Catholics for the next two reigns. He felt himself therefore at liberty to recommend an unalterable adherence to the principles of the veto.

If therefore the negative on the appointment of the Bishops be a thing reasonable in itself; if it be a security which, considering the particular character of the Papal power, . . . may properly be required, either to allay fears, or to obviate prejudices; if it is a point which cannot be stated to affect injuriously the rights of the Catholic Church, and to which we have something equal almost to positive proof that the Catholics feel no conscientious objection; above all, if we are morally certain that without it the question cannot be carried, and have pledged ourselves by recent declarations to an opinion of its expediency and importance; it seems to me that the interests of the Catholics, no less than our own consistency and honour, require that we should make an early declaration that this concession is indispensable to our future support of the cause.[3]

The majority of the party's leaders, however, felt such a step to be at least premature. They were anxious not to inflame the resentment which the great mass of the Irish people felt at the conduct of the Whigs; and however much they might be convinced of the desirability and practicability of the veto, they were inclined to avoid an avowal until it was forced from them by circumstances.

---

[1] But see M'Kenna's fresh and interesting pamphlet.
[2] Sydney Smith, *Letters*, p. 48 ; *Court and Cabinets*, iv. 235.
[3] Grey, *Life and Opinions*, pp. 209-210.

They had no wish to run their heads once more against a
stone wall of their own building, and they were not all of
them willing that " the benefit of Lords Grey, Grenville,
etc. should . . . be lost to the country for that single
question ".[1]

It is hardly surprising, therefore, that they regarded
with misgiving the resurrection of the question by the
decision of the Irish Catholics once again to petition
Parliament. This decision, moreover, had not been reached
without discussions which showed only too clearly the
progress of the Democratic party in the country. When
the subject had been first mooted, at the beginning of
1809, there had been a strong party against petitioning,
holding it better to decline any further dealings with the
English Government. Simultaneously, the *Southern Reporter*
of Cork published slanders against the Bishops, charging
them with being in the pay of Perceval.[2] It was no wonder
if moderate Irishmen considered that Emancipation " now "
presented " insuperable difficulties ".[3] It was not until
23 May that the Catholic meeting in Dublin finally resolved
to petition ; and in other resolutions they showed that
they were chagrined at previous disappointments.[4] And
the old general Committee of the Catholics, which since
the veto fiasco had ceased to function, was now replaced
by a representative Committee of greatly enhanced
efficiency.[5]

The Irish Catholics had decided that the petition
should be presented in the first fortnight of the next
session, since it was too late in May for its presentation
that year ; but before that could happen much had

---

[1] Sydney Smith, *Letters*, p. 40 ; Grey, *Life and Opinions*, p. 211.

[2] *Dropmore Papers*, ix. 275 ; Wellington, *Civil Corr.* p. 535 ; *Morning
Chronicle*, 30 Jan. 1809.

[3] Add. MS. 35648, f. 12, Marsden to Hardwicke, 29 Jan. 1809.

[4] Keogh, p. 71.

[5] Wyse, ii. xxix, i. 143 ; Plowden, iii. 746-747.

occurred to modify the situation, and to define the Whig position. In September 1809 the Tory Ministry went to pieces, and very soon there came an offer to Grey and Grenville from Perceval. That offer was rejected; and, whatever view we may take of its rejection, it is clear that the Catholic question played a considerable part in it, either as a pretext or as a reason. Grey's refusal, so peremptory and uncompromising, had necessarily entailed Grenville's also; and the whole affair had been transacted almost without reference to the general body of the party; so that it was not until Perceval was established in office, and the Whigs committed to Opposition more certainly than ever, that there was an opportunity to develop the principles upon which the Whig leaders supposed themselves to have acted, and upon which they were to act in the future. Their behaviour had, indeed, erred rather on the side of trenchancy than of guile. Among the topics which the Ministerial flutter made it necessary for them to consider was pre-eminently that of Catholic Emancipation and the veto; and on this topic a long and confused correspondence took place, with Tierney as its centre.

Grey, on the whole, was sorry that the Catholic issue had been allowed to emerge so clearly in Grenville's reply to Perceval.[1] He felt, as Tierney did, that it would be much better to damp down the ardours of the Catholics until the Whigs had made up their minds about their future line of procedure.[2] On this point there was general agreement; and Grenville wrote bitterly to Auckland of

---

[1] *Dropmore Papers*, ix. 362, Grey to Grenville, 3 Nov. 1809.

[2] *Tierney MSS.* Tierney to Grey, n.d. [Sept. 1809]: " Is it possible to persuade the Catholics to be moderate ? Lord Ponsonby seems to think it is not, and I wish he was in Ireland to try what he could do with them. If anything could be arranged by which that unfortunate question could be with the consent of the Catholics postponed for even three years it would give the country a chance at least of getting out of its present difficulties."

the lack of consideration for the exigencies of party
politics which the Irish habitually showed. They were, he
declared:

headstrong, directed in great degree by men who wish for the sake
of their importance to keep the grievance open, and I have never
known a moment, except in the single case of their support of the
Union, when they did not contrive to do their friends all the injury
that could be done. I wish the question not to come forward next
year, but I have hardly a doubt that it will be forced on, and if I
were to attempt to stop it, I should only make them believe that I
wanted to come into office by sacrificing their interests, and I should
give a fresh handle for urging it forward. If they were more mixed
in the political discussions of Parliament and government, they
would learn to know men and measures, times and modes, much
better than they now do.[1]

Nevertheless the Whigs needed a quotable policy. Grey
declared that even if all his colleagues were against him,
he would refuse to come in without some measure of
Emancipation—but what measure, and with what securities,
he could not say, though he thought they might well
discuss the point.[2] He developed his ideas in a letter to
Grenville of 3 November, where he declared himself in
favour of " all such regulations as, without danger of
defeating the end we have in view, may tend to give satisfaction, as the cant is, to the King's conscience, to obviate
the public prejudice, and to provide real or even ostensible
securities for the church ". Foremost among these he considered the veto, and adhered to his views of 1808 in
thinking it the best and indeed the indispensable condition
of Emancipation.[3] Tierney, on the other hand, viewed the
matter more calmly :

A full explanation in the sense you affix to it, is highly desirable,
that is, a " thorough understanding of how much might be conceded,

[1] Add. MS. 34457, f. 565.
[2] Tierney MSS. Grey to Tierney, 3 Oct. 1809.
[3] Dropmore Papers, ix. 363, Grey to Grenville, 3 Nov. 1809.

or what securities might be provided in carrying the measure, to satisfy the King's mind, and to obviate the objections which were generally raised to it". The difficulty will be found in the first branch of the alternative, for upon that there will be considerable differences of opinion among our friends. As to the second I do not see the use of talking about it until we know *what securities the Catholics are disposed to give*, for unless *they* are satisfied as well as the King with what is proposed, we shall not advance a step towards the main point, the removal of religious dissentions, and we shall entangle ourselves in new and unnecessary disputes. Remember, that we have had very recent experience how little disposition there is in the Catholics to grant what we conceived most reasonable to ask.[1]

This was common sense ; and Grey would have realized it if he had not been steeped in Fingallianism. Emancipation according to Whig ideas ; Emancipation conditioned to suit Whig politics ; that was always his aim. It is easy to sympathize with his desire for security for the Established Church ; but it is not easy to understand how, after the events of 1808, he could imagine that a veto forced on Ireland by a Whig Government which professed to be performing an act of justice, could give security. " Complete emancipation . . . subject to all reasonable conditions which do not interfere with private conscience, for the security of the Church, and emphatically to the *Veto* "[2]—that was what he required, oblivious, apparently, of the fact that for the mass of the people of Ireland the veto would interfere with private conscience. The Irish may have been ignorant and wrong ; they may probably have been deliberately misled ; but there undoubtedly existed a notion among the common people that the veto was a point of conscience upon which they could not give way. It was much too late to point out that this was a misconception : if Milner, with all the authority of a Vicar Apostolic, could not prevail against prejudice, what

[1] *Tierney MSS.* Tierney to Grey, 4 Nov. 1809.
[2] *Tierney MSS.* Grey to Tierney, 17 Nov. 1809.

hope was there for the monitory allocutions of Lord Grey ?[1] Tierney was more reasonable : he had no desire to commit the party to a policy which would have no adherents among the general public on either side of the St. George's Channel. Grey, however, understood him to suggest that the Whigs should not stickle upon a point of principle which had no chance of being satisfied in the reign of George III, if they should see an opportunity of conferring on the country the benefit of their services ; and Tierney felt it necessary to explain himself further :

Supposing the King to rest upon this ground of a pledge, I think we have a strong case, and one which I think there is a reasonable prospect of defending with ultimate success, and which I therefore am ready to fight for.

Supposing the demand for a pledge abandoned, the question for consideration amongst ourselves is, shall Catholic emancipation be brought forward, guarding the Church and the constitution by such securities as shall be thought reasonable and sufficient. If that be decided in the affirmative and pronounced indispensable as the condition of office, and the King be resolved not to agree to it, then before I committ myself to a course of action and systematic party opposition I must be convinced that by so doing I have a reasonable prospect of carrying the point contended for by obtaining on my side the sense of the country against the prejudices of the crown, and making my way by numbers. A fair estimate of this probability will be best formed by consulting those of our friends who have had opportunities from attentive observation, widely spread connections, and extensive communications with different classes of men, of judging what the public opinion is likely to be. If their report be upon the whole encouraging, whatever may be my individual opinion I shall readily fall into the ranks. But if the result of such consultation should be that whether from principle or prejudice the general sense of the country is in this instance with the King, I must pause before I commit myself in the present state of public affairs both foreign and domestic and in a House of

[1] Milner assured Hippisley at this time that he hoped never to hear of the veto again. *Dropmore Papers*, ix. 356.

Commons composed of such materials as this is, in a system of regular opposition.[1]

Tierney was referring to a contingency which had not occurred, and which was not likely to occur ; still, he was undoubtedly adopting an attitude which differed considerably from Grey's rigid adherence to an arbitrarily determined solution. Here was a point of controversy within the party, which might prove very awkward. The Whigs were rent by dissensions about Reform ; some of their most distinguished members were heretical on the question of the war ; the leadership of the party was indeterminate, or worse ; but on Catholic Emancipation they had hitherto been united. The threatened split never took place, for the necessary conditions which Tierney postulated were never fulfilled ; but the differences of opinion upon the question contributed to the sense of discomfort and disharmony which hampered the Whigs in Parliament.

What was the attitude of the Grenville branch of the party in these circumstances ? Grenville still believed that the veto would be workable if a Whig Government came into office ;[2] but the events of the autumn of 1809 made it necessary for him to define his views more precisely. On the one hand he was again approached by the Irish Catholics to present their petition ; and on the other he became a candidate for the chancellorship of Oxford University, an office which the death of the Duke of Portland had left vacant. Grenville's claims to the chancellorship were based upon his undoubted classical

[1] *Tierney MSS.* Tierney to Grey, 28 Nov. 1809. Cf. *ibid.* Tierney to Grey, 24 Nov. ; *Dropmore Papers*, ix. 362-364 ; and Brougham's attitude : " My only doubt is . . . how far it would be wise or consistent with the former conduct of the party to insist upon the *whole question* being granted, as a *sine qua non* of their giving the country the assistance of their services ". Aspinall, *Brougham*, pp. 17-18 ; Holland, *Further Memoirs of the Whig Party*, p. 45.

[2] Add. MS. 35648, f. 171. Marsden to Hardwicke, repeating a conversation he had had with Grenville.

scholarship, of which he was very proud ; but this qualification was not likely to carry the day if he were suspected
of endangering the security of the Church by his com-
plaisance to the Roman Catholics. And, conversely, his
position with the Catholics would be compromised if it
were supposed that he had betrayed their interests in order
to secure his election. As regarded the Church, his position
was made easier by the fact that he enjoyed the support of
the Archbishop of York and several of the Bishops, who
might be supposed to guarantee his orthodoxy ; and he had,
in addition, the uncommon experience of being canvassed
for by both the Prince and Princess of Wales.[1] All the same,
he found it desirable to explain himself. This he did in a
letter to Dr. Hodson, the Principal of Brasenose, which
was intended for private circulation. In it he declared
that the persistent agitation of the Catholic question was
not his fault ; that he had broken off the negotiations of
September 1809 on the point of the unconstitutional
pledge ; and that the security of the Establishment had
always been his peculiar care.[2] The condition for his
acceptance of office, and his contemplated policy in it,
were left in decent obscurity. It is plain, however, that he,
too, was taking refuge in the veto. As an upholder of it, he
could claim to be at once the friend of the Catholics and
the protector of the Church.[3] Certainly his letter had the
effect he had hoped, for he was elected to the chancellorship in spite of the strong challenge of Lord Eldon, who

[1] Add. MS. 37909, ff. 268-276 ; *Glenbervie Diaries*, ii. 43 (for the
Princess) ; Windsor Arch., George IV, John Cole to the Prince, 17 Nov.
1809 (for the Prince) ; Add. MS. 37909, ff. 250 *seq.* (for the election generally). Nine Bishops voted for Grenville. Sydney Smith, *Letters*, p. 64.

[2] *Dropmore Papers*, ix. 359-362. This letter was approved by the
party ; *ibid.* 387. See the taunts of Keogh, *op. cit.* p. 42.

[3] Compare the letter of the Bishop of St. Asaph to Grenville, *Dropmore Papers*, ix. 344-345 : " . . . I was confident that question could
not well be brought on by your Lordship till the Catholics gave you
the same ground which they revoked since you last recommended their

had the patronage and influence of the Court as well as of the Lord Chancellorship to support him. But Sydney Smith was perhaps not unjustly nervous at this victory, which threw Grenville into dangerous Tory company once again.[1]

It was perhaps significant that Southey accepted an invitation to write a triumphal ode, to be recited at Grenville's first Encaenia.[2] From the point of view of the maintenance of the coalition, it was fortunate that Grey, too, clung to the veto. Still, to the Whigs in general, and to the Catholic party in England, Grenville's election seemed a splendid success. Lord Carlisle wrote to Edward Jerningham: " Our victory over No Popery ! and that rascally cry, by Lord Grenville's election at Oxford, we hold to be most important. It was the most honourable mode of washing away the stain of our being enemies to the Established Church, because we wished to extend substantial relief to our Catholic brethren."[3] Towards the Irish Catholics, however, Grenville's attitude at this time was cool. He resented the resolution whereby they had decided that he should present their petition, as though his consent could be taken for granted.[4] He was, moreover,

petition to a Committee . . .". Though to an anonymous correspondent Grenville wrote : " The Catholic question . . . does not in my opinion justly belong to the merits of this election " (*ibid.* 404). And see Coker, *Some Reflections on the Late Election of a Chancellor of the University of Oxford*, p. 14.   [1] Sydney Smith, *Letters*, p. 65.

[2] Nat. Lib. Wales MS. 4814, f. 43. The poem was written, but arrived too late.

[3] *Edward Jerningham and his Friends*, p. 69 ; Add. MS. 35648, f. 279. Lord Braybrooke to Hardwicke : " I look upon Lord Grenville's triumph as the only thing like hope left to us ; for at least it proves that enlightened bodies of men begin to think for themselves. . . ".

[4] *Dropmore Papers*, ix. 377 ; Add. MS. 37888, f. 209. Grenville to Windham : " One of our first topics of consideration is, what we are to do with the Irish Catholic Petition which they have a little cavalierly resolved that *I shall* present, but which certainly after the disavowal of us all on the subject of the Veto, comes in circumstances perfectly

pressed by his friends to make public the substance of his letter to Hodson, for they felt that if he again presented a Catholic petition, after the veto had been disclaimed in Ireland, without some sort of protest, it would appear as an admission of previous error.[1] Grenville himself was perhaps not averse to the opportunity of drawing up a dignified and well-turned manifesto. At all events he accepted the suggestion, and developed his point of view in his *Letter to Lord Fingall*, which was published early in 1810. The occasion for it was the necessity of explaining his conduct with regard to the impending Irish petition; the cause lay in his desire to signify, in the most emphatic manner, his unyielding resistance to the Democratic party in Ireland, and his determination to persist in his first opinion about the veto.

Grenville began upon the question of the petition. He would, he said, present it, as he felt bound to do so; but he declined to move any motion upon it. Circumstances had changed too much for that. The Government had grown more hostile to concession; and the Democrats in Ireland had succeeded in misleading their Bishops. He deplored the attitude of mind which regarded Emancipation as merely the repeal of "a few partial disqualifications"; on the contrary, "much must be done for mutual conciliation, much for common safety, many contending interests must be reconciled, many jealousies allayed".[2] The

new. The bent of my own mind is to offer to *present* their Petition if they wish it, for I see no sufficient reason to exclude them from laying their complaint before Parliament, however contrary the time and mode of doing so are to my judgment; and to that I believe of almost all their friends in Parliament. But to *decline* making any motion on the subject at least until we are assured that the Petitioners are disposed to receive with duty and submission any arrangement not inconsistent with the known principles of their religious faith, with which Parliament shall think fit to accompany this great measure."

[1] *Dropmore Papers*, ix. 414; *ibid.* 343, for Auckland's view.
[2] *Letter to Lord Fingall*, pp. 9-10.

conduct of the Irish had not made this any easier ; and
Grenville confessed to bitter disappointment at the rejection of the veto—a safeguard allowed by the Pope in
some form or other in almost every European country but
this, and one admitted not to conflict with any point of
doctrine.[1] The effect of this conduct—

must be not only to revive expiring prejudices, but to clog, with
fresh embarrassment, every future discussion of any of the measures
connected with your Petitions. To myself unquestionably the difficulty of originating at this time any fresh discussion respecting
those measures does, in such circumstances, appear almost insuperable. . . . But nothing can . . . in the mean time be more
injurious to your Cause than any attempt, by partial and precipitate
decisions, to prejudge its [the question's] separate branches, or to
limit its unreserved discussion.[2]

In more direct language, Grenville declined to make any
exertion on their behalf in Parliament, until they should
conform to his views as to what safeguards were necessary
and admissible for the protection of the Establishment.
The letter was very like an ultimatum. Grenville believed
that he had found the *via media* between committing
himself to the extreme Irish demands (and thus to certain
opposition) and sacrificing his reputation as the Catholic
champion. The *Letter to Lord Fingall* was in reality the
declaration which Grey had wished to make in 1808, and
which had then been condemned as inexpedient and
gratuitous. The Oxford election and the embarrassment of
a new petition had now made further silence impossible.
Grey, of course, concurred in the *Letter*, and Tierney did
so too, for from his point of view it did not commit them
to impotence, and that was much.[3] Thomas Grenville had
long urged this move on his brother, and the Marquis of
Buckingham was also satisfied.[4] But there were those in

[1] *Ibid.* pp. 11-13.   [2] *Ibid.* pp. 13, 15.
[3] Grey, *Life and Opinions*, pp. 236-237.
[4] *Dropmore Papers*, ix. 433 ; x. 7.

the party who disapproved. The Duke of Bedford, Lord
Holland, Lord Fitzwilliam, Elliot, and Whitbread were
decidedly against placing undue weight on the veto.
They were sorry to see any barrier erected against Emancipation, and they feared that the *Letter* might prove
such a barrier.[1] It seems doubtful, moreover, whether the
Letter to Lord Fingall was quite the ideal compromise
that Grenville imagined it to be. It was to be abandoned
for other experiments in " security " very soon ; and its
efficacy in saving the Whigs' reputations was at least
questionable. Honest men like Horner, and clever men
like Brougham, concurred in thinking that the only hope
for the Whigs, and for the country, lay in their steady and
powerful support of the Catholic question whenever it
was brought forward.[2] And here was Grenville dissociating
himself from it in public for the sake of a device of
doubtful value![3] The difference of opinion ran on lines
very similar to those in the case of Reform: on the one
side there is Grenville, Grey, Lansdowne, and Tierney ;
and on the other the more liberal Whitbread, Holland
House, and the Bedford clique.[4]

Grenville's *Letter* soon drew replies to it. Milner and
Keogh attacked it from different angles ;[5] an anonymous
Answer thrashed out the arguments for and against the
veto once again ;[6] and Trotter roundly asked Grenville

[1] *Court and Cabinets*, iv. 419 ; Holland, *Further Memoirs*, p. 42.

[2] Horner, ii. 24 ; *Life and Times of Brougham*, i. 492 ; Sydney Smith,
Letters, pp. 63, 70. Horner (*op. cit.* ii. 18) thought it significant that
Cobbett had taken up Catholic Emancipation. Milner had been writing
letters to the *Political Register :* Milner, *Letters to a Roman Catholic
Prelate*, p. 26.

[3] Grey was equally against a motion, though he promised support
if it was made. *Life and Opinions*, p. 214.

[4] Whitbread later praised the *Letter*, but adhered to his opinion
that the veto was unessential. *Parl. Deb.* xvii. 182 * *et seq.*, 25 May 1810.

[5] Milner, *Elucidation*, especially pp. 37, 40 ; Keogh, *passim*.

[6] *Answer to Grenville*, pp. iv-viii, 12-16, 21, 32.

whether he proposed to abandon the Catholics altogether, if he could not get his own way.[1] Against these, even the eloquent appeals of Thomas Moore were in vain.[2]

Among the earliest consequences of the publication of the *Letter to Lord Fingall* was a series of discussions with the English Catholics which eventually terminated in an understanding. The English Catholics were docile and eminently respectable, and in ecclesiastical politics they tended to Fingallianism. They had been for some years rather under a cloud, in consequence of the temerities of their leader, Charles Butler, who had been responsible for the invention of " Protestant Catholic Dissenters ", and whose *Red Book* and *Blue Books* had alike been condemned by the Vicars Apostolic.[3] The Catholic laity in England had since then tended to be on cool terms with its clergy, and particularly with Milner, whose zeal might be indubitable, but was occasionally a nuisance. The other Vicars Apostolic certainly found him a difficult and arrogant colleague.[4] The laity tended to be an aristocratic and rather esoteric party, and at this time their social centre was the Marchioness of Buckingham.[5] In 1807 they had founded a club and buried their grievances against their clergy, and in the following years had collaborated with them in attempts to improve their position.[6] The English Catholics were on good terms with the Fingallians in Ireland, and this caused Milner to look upon their activities rather sourly.[7] They had, moreover, at Grenville's

---

[1] Trotter, *A Letter to Lord Grenville*, p. 6.

[2] Moore, *Letter to the Roman Catholics, passim.*

[3] Milner, *Letters to a Roman Catholic Prelate*, p. 9 ; the witness of an enemy, but on this occasion a truthful one.

[4] Ward, i. 24, 66.

[5] Jerningham, i. 309 ; Plowden, iii. 793 n.

[6] Ward, i. 99-100, 101-102 ; *Dropmore Papers*, ix. 194.

[7] Add. MS. 35649, f. 221, gives a sample of the engraved cards on which " The Lords and Gentlemen who were appointed delegates " for the Catholics of Ireland expressed their thanks to their English supporters.

request, refrained from petitioning Parliament in the session of 1809.[1] But they felt that they could not allow the *Letter to Lord Fingall* to go without some further explanation, if such were to be had. Jerningham, their Secretary, was deputed to see Grey and Grenville. The English Catholics were afraid that the Whigs would refuse support to their petition, which was at this time preparing, and into which they were quite resolved not to incorporate any clause involving the veto. Grey and Grenville were firm. They insisted upon some declaration of willingness to accept a reasonable arrangement with regard to the nomination of Vicars Apostolic. Jerningham disliked the word " nomination " ; and after a conference between the Whig magnates on the one side, and the leading English Catholics on the other, Grey with his own hand drew up the following clause to be attached to the petition.[2]

That the English Roman Catholics, in soliciting the attention of Parliament to their petition, are actuated not more by a sense of the hardships and disabilities under which they labour, than by a desire to secure, on the most solid foundation, the peace and harmony of the British Empire ; and to obtain for themselves opportunities of manifesting by the most active exertions their zeal and interest in the common cause in which their country is engaged, for the maintenance of its freedom and independence ; and that they are firmly persuaded, that adequate provision for the maintenance of the civil and religious establishments of this Kingdom may be made consistently with the strictest adherence on their part to the tenets and discipline of the Roman Catholic religion; and that any arrangement on the basis of mutual satisfaction and security, and extending to them the full enjoyment of the civil constitution of their country, will meet with their grateful concurrence.[3]

This moderate and statesmanlike declaration gave all the advantages of adherence to the veto, without the odium

[1] *Dropmore Papers*, ix. 298, 301.
[2] Ward, i. 253, 111-113 ; Butler, *Historical Memoirs*, ii. 197-198.
[3] Ward, i. 113.

attaching to it. It was a gesture of good-will, or as Butler described it, " a mere general expression of good humour ".[1] It shows more common sense on the Whig side than one would have given them credit for, and it was the first step away from the policy of the *Letter to Lord Fingall*, and towards the definitive renunciation of the veto in 1812. But in itself it was unfortunately quite as objectionable to the Catholic extremists, among whom Milner must now be reckoned. All efforts to induce him to sign the petition failed ; though he told the Catholic Lords that they might do so, for all he cared.[2] At a general meeting at the St. Alban's Tavern on 1 February 1810, Grey's declaration was carried, and became the famous " Fifth Resolution ". The meeting was a stormy one, and at a Catholic dinner held afterwards, Milner contrived to entangle himself in two new quarrels, which each in due time produced its litter of violent controversial pamphlets.[3] However, the petition was widely signed in England, and ultimately presented by Grey and Windham.[4] More important, it was backed by the resolution of a synod of Vicars Apostolic and their coadjutors which met on 20 February, and by four votes to two (Milner and Gibson dissenting) approved a limited negative, with the Pope's consent, provided that all securities were taken to prevent its conversion into a direct negative.[5] If this was what the Fifth Resolution implied, it is easy to see why its moderation appeared fallacious to hostile critics, and in particular to Milner, who had touched this thorny topic before, and found it dangerous.[6] After his fashion, Milner now broke out into

[1] Butler, ii. 200.

[2] Milner, *An Explanation with Dr. Poynter*, p. 16 ; Ward, i. 114-122.

[3] Milner, *Letters to a Roman Catholic Prelate*, pp. 51 *et seq.* ; Ward, i. 120-123 ; Hippisley, *Speech* (1810), App. V ; Jerningham, i. 363.

[4] Grey, *Life and Opinions*, p. 238.

[5] Ward, i. 125.

[6] Milner, *Elucidation*, p. 31 : he declared it contained " everything of the Veto except the name ". *Letters to a Roman Catholic Prelate*, p. 28.

outrageous attacks on his fellow Vicars Apostolic, and in
particular on Dr. Poynter. Even more injurious were his
his comments on the English Catholic laity and their
leader Charles Butler, whom he pursued with a venomous
hatred and complete disregard for truth which even Fr.
Ward cannot condone.[1] His controversial methods in these
later quarrels make it difficult to be fair to his conduct
in 1808.

It was in Ireland that both the Grenville manifesto and
the Fifth Resolution produced the sharpest emotion.
Ireland had been ecclesiastically on tenterhooks since a
private scheme by the inevitable Hippisley had leaked
out through a breach of confidence at the end of 1809.[2]
The report of the Fifth Resolution reached the Irish leaders
just when they were preparing a new petition, and it
powerfully affected them. Their representatives in London
were directed to decline any association with the English
Catholics ; and the Irish ecclesiastics as a whole considered the resolution as frivolous and insulting.[3] The
Bishops met in synod on 24 and 26 February, and on each
of these days passed sets of resolutions—six on the first
day, seventeen on the second. Protestations of loyalty,
assertions of their sole right to ecclesiastical authority,
appeals for Emancipation, form the bulk of them ; but in
the resolutions of the 26th there are two new points which
show that the Irish were not insensible to the necessity
for some show of conciliation. They agreed not to acknowledge the validity of any Papal Bulls so long as Pius VII

[1] Ward, i. 150-167 and App. D (for the synod of Durham), p. 26
("And it is hardly an exaggeration to say that his feelings towards
Charles Butler amounted almost to a monomania ") ; Jerningham, too,
was attacked. " Edward is in a dreadful warfare with Bishop Milner,
whom I am quite vexed about, as he is writing violent letters to Lord
Grey and Mr. Grattan " (Jerningham, i. 366).

[2] Keogh, p. 31 ; Court and Cabinets, iv. 423 ; the Jubilee, however,
had provoked demonstrations of loyalty. Add. MS. 35648, f. 209.

[3] Wyse, ii. xxx ; Ward, i. 144 ; Plowden, iii. 788.

was a captive—an undertaking which was worth much,
on the assumption that the Bishops were loyal. And in the
Sixteenth Resolution they expressed their wish to conciliate
in the following terms :

> *Resolved*, That as to arrangements regarding our church, and
> said to be intended for accompanying a proposal for the emancipa-
> tion of Irish Roman Catholics, prudence, and a regard for our duty
> forbid us to pronounce a judgment, whereas the rumoured arrange-
> ments have not been ascertained by us through any channel. How-
> ever we declare, that no spirit of conciliation has ever been wanting
> on our part ; that we seek for nothing beyond the mere integrity
> and safety of the Roman Catholic religion . . . nor may we be
> justly reproached for our solicitude in guarding those sacred things
> for which we are bound to watch, and bear testimony with our
> lives, if required.[1]

The mysterious first sentence refers to a rumoured project
for giving the priests salaries from Government, an honour
which the Bishops had already declined stiffly in one of
their resolutions of 24 February ;[2] and also to the idea of
" Domestic Nomination ", which was at this time much in
the air, and by some was thought to offer a practicable
alternative to the veto. After all, if Papal Bulls were to be
refused while the Pope was in captivity, it seemed *prima
facie* reasonable to the innocent Protestant mind that the
formality of the Pope's coöperation in filling vacant sees
should be done away. It even seemed so to some Catholics,
for a county meeting at Naas passed a resolution in this
sense a little later in the year.[3] Keogh, with admirable
consistency, would have vested nomination in the people,
if there were to be any changes made ; but in this Ireland

---

[1] Given in Milner, *Elucidation*, p. 59.

[2] Given in *Answer to Grenville*, p. 44 : " We neither seek nor desire
any other earthly consideration for our spiritual ministry to our
respective flocks, save what they from a sense of religion and duty
voluntarily afford us ".

[3] Jerningham, i. 366 ; Hippisley, *Speech* (1810), App. V.

was not prepared to follow him.[1] The Whigs, however, were prepared to try Domestic Nomination. In the *Letter to Lord Fingall* they had clung to the veto ; in the Fifth Resolution they had clung to an undefined " security " ; and despite the declaration of the Irish Bishops they clung now to Domestic Nomination. The scheme was formally brought forward when Grattan moved to consider the petitions in June. Grattan spoke at tedious length ; Hippisley had a private plan as usual ; Ponsonby used the opportunity to produce the *pièces justificatives* of his quarrel with Milner, and that was all. A majority of the Irish members present voted for the motion ; but it was, of course, easily defeated. This was fortunate ; for the Irish laity had, on 2 March, followed the example of their clergy and damned the veto, the Fifth Resolution, and all variants of each, in a way which was felt by all parties to be final.[2] The *Edinburgh Review* accepted the verdict, and in a masterly article urged the Whigs to acquiesce in it ; and when Jeffrey took this line it was time for the Whigs to change their tactics.[3]

It was time, indeed, for the Irish problem was changing while they were wrangling. Emancipation, it was increasingly felt, would not be sufficient. Ireland needed better land laws, a better economy, and better education. It was to no purpose that Englishmen pointed out that Ireland had had the better of the financial bargain at the Union, while the number of Irish bankruptcies was increasing by leaps and bounds. Irishmen ignored the fact that 1810 and 1811 were peak years for bankruptcies in England also. The movement for Repeal, which had hitherto been sporadic, began now to be vocal and centralized. In

---

[1] Keogh, p. 75.

[2] *Parl. Deb.* xvii. 17-295 ; Grattan, v. 376 n., 409 ; Hippisley, *Speech* (1810) ; *Morning Chronicle,* 5 June 1810 ; Add. MS. 35648, f. 333, for Fingall's view of Domestic Nomination.

[3] *Edinburgh Review,* xvii. art. i, Nov. 1810.

Dublin it was particularly strong ; and it won a notable victory when Grattan consented to present a Repeal petition on behalf of the freemen and freeholders of that city.[1] Had it not been for the organizing genius of O'Connell, who saw that success could only be won by intensive concentration on one goal, and that the easier one, Ireland might at this time have flung herself whole-heartedly into the Repeal agitation. O'Connell kept her to the more practical issue of Emancipation ; [2] but the Emancipation he desired was complete and full, and not hedged about with Whig reservations. Pamphlets, growing ever bulkier, still flew between the vetoists and their adversaries ; and when the hail of them seemed to be thinning, there came powerful reserves from the pen of *Columbanus* —in private life the librarian at Stowe—who, in his successive epistles *ad Hibernos*, lashed the Bishops, attacked the clergy, fell into heretical opinions, but yet managed to keep his Grenvillian propaganda discreetly in the background.[3] But *Columbanus* bordered on the fantastic, without avoiding the tedious. Meanwhile in Ireland the Catholics were organizing themselves with a deliberate thoroughness which put the amateurish exertions of Fingall quite in the shade ; and when by an unlooked-for mercy the King lost his reason, they were powerful, united, and expectant. And it had become clear that sooner or later the Whigs would have to revise their policy.

(d) *The Catholics and the Regent*

The Catholics had apparently good reason to greet the Regency with satisfaction and hope. For many years

[1] *Morning Chronicle*, 11 Oct. 1810 ; Fitzpatrick, *Cloncurry*, p. 284 Grattan, v. 419 ; Plowden, iii. 892 ; Keogh, pp. 47, 54.

[2] Though O'Connell did support Repeal at this time. Dunlop, p. 32.

[3] *Columbanus*, i. 3, 12, 35, 83, 91, 105-109 ; ii. lx ; iii. 15, 115, 140, give the gist of his arguments. There remains *Columbanus*, iv. for those inclined to pursue them further.

the Prince of Wales had systematically opposed his father's policies. He had been connected with the Whig party sufficiently closely to share their desire for Catholic Emancipation, but not closely enough to share the odium of the veto. Both the Irish and the Whigs now expected from him a more favourable regard and a more open patronage than in the days when he was merely Prince of Wales. His nearest friends, Lords Donoughmore, Hutchinson, and Moira, were all enthusiasts for the Catholic cause. The Prince was, moreover, bound by explicit promises. In 1807 he had commanded Ponsonby and Bedford, when they were of the Government of Ireland, to tell the Roman Catholics that " he would never forsake their interests ".[1] In 1808 the promise had been renewed, in an interview with Holland and Fingall ; [2] and he was said to have given a written promise to Lord Kenmare.[3] Hutchinson described him as having been committed " over and over again ".[4] These might seem solid grounds for confidence ; but they were rendered less so by the peculiarities of the Prince's character. The circumstances of politics contrived at this time to upset him, and the strain on his friendships was considerable. For he was in office, while they remained in Opposition ; and the one state of affairs seemed no less permanent than the other. The Prince developed a Ministerial mentality ; he became a performer, while his friends remained in the ranks of the critics, and, to his annoyance, were too often unwilling to exchange their position for a more active one. The Prince believed that his friends ought to rally round him, even if it meant a union with former political enemies :

---

[1] *Parl. Deb.* xxii. 1011 ; Windsor Arch., George IV, n.d. in 1812 papers, Bedford to the Prince; Windsor Arch., George IV, G. D. Keogh to ?, 11 March 1812, promising secrecy on the point.

[2] Holland, *Memoirs of the Whig Party,* ii. 251.

[3] *Life and Speeches of O'Connell,* i. 174-175.

[4] Francis, *Memoirs,* ii. 371.

his friends had other views.[1] It was, therefore, fallacious to build hopes on the Regent's friendship for Moira and Hutchinson. His promises, moreover, were to be interpreted in the light of his own system of casuistry and self-deception : " I had early discovered ", said Hutchinson bitterly, " a close connection between promise and retractation ".[2] The disappointment of the Whig hopes of office, in February 1811, was the first sign that the Catholics might have mistaken their man. Another blow followed hard upon it, and opened a question which was to agitate Ireland and the Whigs for the better part of a year.

The Catholics in Ireland had latterly been improving their organization. A scheme for local boards having broken down, they fell back upon a system of representation which had already been applied to Dublin in 1809, and which was now extended to the whole country.[3] On 1 January 1811 Edward Hay, the Secretary to the Catholic Committee, sent out notices bidding the Catholic managers in each county return ten delegates to the Catholic Committee.[4] On 12 February Wellesley Pole, the Chief Secretary, after consultation with the Irish Attorney-General, but without the knowledge of the English Government, launched a circular letter to the magistrates prohibiting these elections. He based his action upon the Convention Act of 1793, which prohibited the election of delegates for the pretended purpose of petitioning. The consternation was considerable in England as well as in Ireland ; and it was regarded as sinister, or at least unfortunate, that the Prince should have begun his Regency in such a manner. Before the

[1] *Dropmore Papers*, x. 166 : " The Prince certainly has an idea that his friends ought to come forward whenever he chooses to call upon them, *without regard to who is his minister*. This is a strange fancy, but still it exists, and *very strongly too*."

[2] Francis, *Memoirs*, ii. 371.

[3] Wyse, i. 143-144 ; Pole, *Speech* (1811), pp. 9-11.

[4] Add. MS. 38246, ff. 1-2, 38.

Whigs could exhaust their eloquence upon it, Pole had gone further. On 26 February he sent officers to disperse the Catholic Committee as an unlawful assembly ; but they withdrew upon the declaration of the chairman, Lord Ffrench, that the meeting was merely a private assembly of Catholic gentlemen.[1] A projected conference between the Catholics and the Minister never took place, but the Committee later reassembled without interruption ; and on 8 March O'Connell carried at an aggregate meeting a resolution to address the Regent to remove Pole and the Duke of Richmond (the Lord Lieutenant) from their offices.[2]

In the debates on these events the Whigs, embittered perhaps by their disappointment of office, sharply criticized Pole. His rashness and vanity laid him open to attack. Even so staunch a Tory as Richmond had objected to his coming to Ireland, and lived to regret the damage done to the Government by his unpopularity.[3] The Whigs now enquired why he had waited so long after the publication of Hay's letter, and had then acted so precipitately that there was no time to appeal to the home Government ; they wished to know by what right he ordered magistrates to commit those taking part in such elections ; they abused the Convention Act as an infamous law, mercifully long dormant, but now revived by a tyrannous Government ; and they asked why Pole had not issued a proclamation, if he must issue anything.[4]

Many of these points were unanswerable. Lord Eldon, in public and in private, condemned Pole's letter as

[1] Pole, *Speech* (1811), pp. 46-50.

[2] *Life and Speeches of O'Connell*, i. 97-103 ; Dunlop, *O'Connell*, p. 37.

[3] *Bathurst Papers*, p. 126 : " His temper is rather too warm, and he would try to do jobs for the Queen's County " ; *ibid.* p. 155 : " Pole's unpopularity is against us. His manner is not conciliatory, and even our best friends are often out of humour with him."

[4] *Parl. Deb.* xix. 1-18, 54, 270 ; *Morning Chronicle*, 18 and 23 Feb. 1811 ; *Dropmore Papers*, x. 125 ; Grattan v. 447-448 ; Wyse, i. 175.

slovenly in expression and indefensible in law.[1] The Whigs
were right in insisting that the proper method of procedure was by proclamation, and Pole's lame reply to this
point convinced nobody.[2] He was, however, able to show
that he knew nothing of the projected elections until
early in February, and that if he had waited for advice
from England, they would have taken place before he
could act.[3] The core of the discussion was the meaning of
the Convention Act, and as on this point the lawyers
differed, it was hardly surprising that the laymen judged
on party lines; as they did also on the question of the *bona
fides* of the Catholic Committee.[4] Still, it would be rash to
condemn too hastily the violence of the Castle. It is clear
that the Catholics did not regard the Convention Act as
dormant. In all their meetings they had taken the most
elaborate pains to keep within it. In 1806 they had discussed
the limitations it imposed on them; in 1809 they declared
that the managers of their petition were not to be regarded
as representatives; and in 1810, when the Catholic Committee proceeded to business, it discussed, not the petition,
but " Catholic affairs "—upon which Lord Ffrench warned
them that they were exceeding their powers, and repeated
his warning in similar circumstances on 2 February 1811.[5]
Hay in his letter was careful to point out that the Convention Act " does not interfere with the subject's undoubted right to petition Parliament, nor of course with
the only method by which so large a body as the Catholics
of Ireland could concur in forwarding a Petition . . . ".[6] The

---

[1] Holland, *Further Memoirs*, p. 98; *Life and Speeches of O'Connell*,
i. 117; *Parl. Deb.* xix. 693-700.

[2] " I never heard it contended that a Proclamation was necessary
to enforce statute law of the land." *Speech* (1811), p. 34. See *Morning
Chronicle*, 26 Aug. 1811, for a sound article on proclamations.

[3] *Bathurst Papers*, p. 156; Add. MS. 34458, ff. 203-204.

[4] The division was 43-80. *Parl. Deb.* xix. 55.

[5] Plowden, ii. 321; Pole, *Speech* (1811), p. 7; *Life and Speeches of
Plunket*, i. 301; Dunlop, p. 36.   [6] Add. MS. 38246, ff. 1-2.

Government, however, believed, and subsequent events proved them correct, that the petition was merely the pretext for the setting up of what was virtually a Catholic Parliament. These assemblies of delegates had discussed matters of general policy before, and there could be no doubt that they would do so again. It was all very well for Donoughmore to contend that " the object of the Catholic Committee in assembling the meeting of so many of their brethren, appeared to be no other than to give greater weight and effect to the petitions, which they had to present to both Houses of Parliament " ;[1] but as Perceval pointed out elsewhere, Hay's letter envisaged a more general activity. " It is highly desirable ", Hay had said, " that the Committee should become the depository of the collective wisdom of the Catholic body. That it should be able to ascertain, in order to obey, the wishes, and clearly understand the wants, of all their Catholic fellow subjects." [2] Such a body would not differ greatly from a Catholic Parliament. Lord Grenville admitted that " if so large a meeting were assembled by delegation, contrary to law, and for undefined purposes, it would be dangerous to the public peace ".[3] There is no doubt that the Government were genuinely afraid of the erection, within the letter of the law, of a semi-permanent Irish Catholic Parliament. They had been watching the movement for some time with uneasiness ; the speeches of the delegates seemed to them violent, if not treasonable ; and they were afraid of the great *éclat* of their proceedings throughout Ireland.

The Committee have assumed to themselves all the forms of the House of Commons.—They debate as nearly as possible in the same order as the House of Commons debate.—They have regular orders of the day.—Regular notices of motions, taken down by the Secretary at the Table in writing, without which they reckon it irregular to discuss any question.—They have reporters for their debates, and

---

[1] *Parl. Deb.* xix. 14 *et seq.*   [2] *Ibid.* 40.   [3] *Ibid.* 11.

their Chairman signs all their minutes and proceedings as the Speaker does those of the House of Commons.[1]

The Government position at this time was that they were prepared to tolerate the assembly, as long as it stuck rigidly to the business of petitioning: on 26 February they took Ffrench's word on that point. There was no real inconsistency in their actions. The Whigs, however devoted to Catholic Emancipation they may have been, must have realized that on broad grounds the Castle was justified. Their attack was prompted perhaps by the known irascibility and unpopularity of Pole: for Grey later confessed that he could not see how such an Act as the Convention Act was to be administered leniently.[2] If the Catholic Committee was to be allowed unlimited rope, it would have been simpler to repeal the Union altogether, and few Whigs wanted that.

Neither O'Connell, who now clearly assumed the lead in Irish affairs, nor Pole was minded to let the matter drop. At a Catholic meeting on 9 July O'Connell outlined a new scheme for the election of delegates, and offered to provide a test case in his own person.[3] On Ryder's advice, Pole replied this time with a proclamation.[4] Dr. Sheridan, Kirwan, and others who had taken part in the meeting on 9 July, were arrested and brought to trial; and to the delight of Ireland—and of the Whigs—on 21 November Sheridan was acquitted.[5] The Catholic Committee met on

---

[1] Add. MS. 38246, f. 39; also *Bathurst Papers*, pp. 154, 156 (all these letters from Richmond); Pole, *Speech* (1811), pp. 11, 21.

[2] Add. MS. 34458, f. 210, Grey to Auckland.

[3] *Life and Speeches of O'Connell*, i. 115-118; Dunlop, p. 38.

[4] *Bathurst Papers*, p. 158.

[5] *Life and Speeches of O'Connell*, i. 118; *Dropmore Papers*, ix. 389 (wrongly dated); *Independent Whig*, 30 Nov. 1811; *Bathurst Papers*, p. 159, for Richmond's comment; Nat. Lib. of Wales MS. 2791, for a neutral view (C. Wynn to H. Wynn, 2 Dec. 1811); *Morning Chronicle*, 31 Jan. 1812; Wyse, i. 177; *Reminiscences of Daniel O'Connell*, by a Munster Farmer, pp. 19-20, contain uncorroborated, and perhaps inaccurate, details.

19 October, despite the "peevish and unwarrantable interference of Mr. Pole ",[1] in the Fishamble Street Theatre, whose galleries, we are told, were crowded with ladies.[2] A police raid was luckily too late, but they thought it wiser to disperse for the moment. Another meeting on 23 December, after an attempt at equivocation by Lord Fingall, terminated in his forcible extrusion from the chair by the officers of justice.[3] Undaunted, the Catholics met as *individuals* at D'Arcy's coffee-house, and later as the "Catholic Board"—this meeting being made notable by the presence of Shelley.[4] The issue was now centring round the right to name delegates at all, rather than as to whether the Catholics were confining their activities to petitioning ; but these developments brought little new from the Whig side. There was, however, a disposition to concede that the Government might have a shadow of reason on their side, and that the attack ought properly to be made upon the Convention Act itself rather than upon the administrators of it.[5] The subject came up

[1] *Morning Chronicle*, 5 Aug. 1811.

[2] Add. MS. 37296, f. 3.

[3] Dunlop, p. 40 ; *Life and Speeches of O'Connell*, i. 121-124. The following dialogue took place.—Hare [the magistrate]: "I ask, is it a meeting of the Catholic Committee, composed of the peers, prelates, country gentlemen and other in the city of Dublin ? " Fingall : ". . . We are met for the sole legal and constitutional purpose of petitioning ". Hare : " My Lord, I ask you . . . in what capacity are you met ? " Fingall : " We are met for the purpose of petitioning parliament " (*etc. etc., ad libitum*).

[4] Dunlop, pp. 39-40 ; *Life and Speeches of O'Connell*, i. 124, 128, 136. Shelley continued in Ireland in 1812, still very enthusiastic for Catholic Emancipation, which led him to float propaganda in its favour, in bottles, down the Irish rivers. His *Address to the Irish People*, which appeared in 1812, is a curious document. The Emancipation he advocates there appears as Catholic in the widest sense of the word and is combined with Shelley's characteristic political quietism, and a (perhaps well-merited) injunction to O'Connell not to get drunk. Shelley, *Prose Works*, i. 331.

[5] *E.g.* *Dropmore Papers*, x. 161. Thomas Grenville to Lord Grenville, 4 Aug. 1811 : " I certainly cannot wonder that if the Ministers resist the Catholic question, they should feel it necessary to prevent the

repeatedly in the debates on the general question of
Catholic Emancipation, and its importance was undoubted ;
but as the significance of O'Connell's tactics became more
apparent and their success more obvious, it lost its interest
as a topic for party controversy.[1]

The centre of interest, both for Ireland and the Whigs,
lay not in the debates at Westminster nor in those too-
similar debates at the Fishamble Street Theatre, but in
the ceaseless debate which raged round the unhappy
Regent. The anxiety of the Prince's friends had grown
steadily throughout 1811. From the moment of the King's
insanity they had felt that much depended upon the
good behaviour of the Irish. The Prince, they knew, disliked above all things to be pestered and browbeaten, and
there was but too much reason to fear that the Irish
might offend him in that way. As early as January 1811,
Donoughmore had, with difficulty, averted a projected
address to him (O'Connell had urged it upon the Catholic
Committee) as being likely only to embarrass still further
" an already embarrassed, fettered, insulted man ".[2] They

assembly of an Irish parliament of Catholic delegates ; and when it is
made illegal to elect delegates or to hold a meeting of them, Councillor
Scullie [sic] cannot convince me that after passing that law, it is still
legal to elect delegates and hold a meeting of them. Government, therefore, seem to me to have the law with them on this subject. . . ." See also
Nat. Lib. of Wales MS. 2791, C. Wynn to H. Wynn, 2 Dec. 1811 ; Parl.
Deb. xx. 570, 11 June 1811, where Hutchinson threatens to bring in a
Bill to repeal the Act; the Morning Chronicle, 7 Aug. 1811 ; Grattan, v.
458-459 ; Horner, ii. 102.

[1] Parl. Deb. xxi. 454. Erskine attacked the interpretation which made
delegation the offence ; Wellesley defended the Government (ibid. 408).
On 3 Feb. 1812 Pole made another defence (ibid. 534). Canning
supported him ; and Grattan admitted that the conduct of the Catholics
was " not altogether constitutional in every point " (ibid. 664)—an admission which, as Croker (ibid. 667) pointed out, blew up the Whig case.
The Whigs disliked Croker, and suspected him of being the arch-
propagandist against Emancipation. Morning Chronicle, 17 Jan. 1812.

[2] Windsor Arch., George IV, Donoughmore to Hay, 17 Jan. 1811; Life
and Speeches of O'Connell, i. 63 ; Life and Speeches of Plunket, i. 297-298.

feared, and with good reason, that his decision to retain
Perceval would make matters even more difficult for him ;
and Hutchinson felt obliged to warn the Irish that their
hopes might after all be disappointed.[1] All parties agreed
that it was fortunate that he had not been consulted by
Pole before the launching of the attack on the Catholic
Committee ; but when it was rumoured that he approved
of that measure, Moira, for one, refused to believe it.[2]

Nevertheless the Prince's actions were ominous. When
the Irish Roman Catholics presented a petition to him at
the end of May, they received no answer.[3] They were,
moreover, unwise enough to address him against the
Militia Interchange Act, a measure which had given satisfaction in Ireland, and against which Grattan refused to
present a petition.[4] It was thought advisable for Archbishop Troy to transmit to Moira a dignified protestation
of loyalty (in which Milner concurred), which was to be
passed on to the Regent.[5] The intentions of the Regent,
however, were still obscure ; and the best that the Whigs
could hope for was that, as Buckingham had prophesied,
his object was to gain time, " negotiate with the body of
the Catholics for their claims, and with individuals for
his Ministry ".[6] The ground for their hope was not good,
for it was based on a misunderstanding of the Regent's
position. To him the contest seemed to be one between
reason backed up by religious conviction on the one side,
and his friendships and aversions on the other. The Regent
had no doubt of his antipathy to the Catholics ; and it

[1] Grey, *Life and Opinions*, p. 278; *Life and Speeches of Plunket*, i. 299.

[2] Windsor Arch., George IV, Moira to McMahon, 18 March 1811 ;
Bathurst Papers, p. 155.

[3] Windsor Arch., George IV, Sir F. Goodden to McMahon, 3 June 1811.

[4] Windsor Arch., George IV, Fingall to McMahon, 11 June 1811 ;
Grattan, v. 442; Add. MS. 35649, f. 227 ; *Life and Speeches of O'Connell*,
i. 114.

[5] Windsor Arch., George IV, Troy to Moira, 31 July 1811.

[6] *Dropmore Papers*, x. 193, Buckingham to Grenville, 23 Jan. 1811.

was only the fear of subordinating himself to Perceval, whom he disliked, feared, and tried to bully, that kept him in a state of indecision. ". . . Whether the King lives or dies," wrote Thomas Grenville, " the Irish dilemma at Carlton House continues to be equally out of reach of any obvious solution " ;[1] but the reason for this was the difficulty of choosing between Perceval and Catholic Emancipation : the Whigs, as its champions, were hardly in question.

If the Regent had chosen Emancipation, he would have entrusted his Government first and foremost to his own friends—Moira, Sheridan, Adam, and the two Hutchinsons. But the Regent was now perceptibly inclining towards Perceval. The awkward financial questions raised by the Regency—the Prince's debts, the Queen's Household, etc. —had been satisfactorily settled. The limitations of the Regency Bill would soon be over and forgotten. The influence of the Dukes of Cumberland and York was increasing, and was much strengthened when the Prince was, in the early autumn, laid up with a strained tendon at Oatlands, the Duke of York's house.[2] Moreover, he was falling out of friendship with Moira and Donoughmore as his friendship for Lady Hertford and her relatives increased and his enthusiasm for Catholic Emancipation diminished. There chanced at this time to be a vacancy for an Irish representative peer, and the contest lay between Lord Gosford and Lord Leitrim. Leitrim was the Prince's candidate, and was energetically canvassed for by Donough- more and Hutchinson ; Gosford was Perceval's man, and in the end the Prince's support was transferred to him, with the result that Leitrim was beaten, and the Hutchinson brothers were infuriated.[3] Simultaneously with this blow

[1] *Ibid.* 162.

[2] The Regent had been teaching the Princess Charlotte the Highland Fling, and was " leading his daughter briskly along, when his foot came into violent contact with the leg of a table ".

[3] *Morning Chronicle,* 17 Aug. 1811; Windsor Arch., George IV [1, 2, 5 July 1811], for Donoughmore's efforts ; Grattan, v. 457.

to the Whig hopes came the Prince's sanction of Pole's
proclamation ; but the Whigs still refused to believe that
the Prince had abandoned Catholic Emancipation, and
Grenville, with misplaced ingenuity, found an explanation :

I believe the fact about the Irish business to be [he wrote to
Auckland] that the Prince Regent sanctioned the proclamation on
the ground of having agreed to let the Ministers go on in their own
way, and reserving to himself his own more tolerant principles and
opinions.[1]

A course of action which he condemned as " undignified,
unmanly, and unconstitutional ".

Lord Moira had long watched the Regent's proceedings
with agitation. He was a true friend to the Catholics ; and
many had hoped that the Regent might perhaps send him
to Ireland in place of the Duke of Richmond, who was far
from popular there.[2] But in these days Moira rarely saw
the Prince ; and his letters to McMahon show that he was
equally alarmed as regarded politics, and wounded as
regarded friendship. He was too honest to hide his opinions ;
and he was genuinely anxious for the Prince's welfare, and
the success of his reign. He therefore addressed to him a
letter in the course of which he wrote :

Those anxious feelings for the prosperity and honor of your
Royal Highness which will never cease while I have life, impel me
to solicit earnestly that you will condescend to read the remarks,
on the late steps against the Catholics, contained in the news
papers I presume to send. There is no merit in the stile ; and the
publication is ill-judged if not mischievously intended : but it is
an accurate expression of what is thought by an infinite majority
of the people of Ireland as far as I can gather from my letters : and

---

[1] Add. MS. 34458, f. 262, 18 Aug. 1811 ; see, too, *Morning Chronicle*,
13 Aug. 1811.

[2] *Life of Plunket*, i. 299 ; *Independent Whig*, 30 Nov. 1811, quoting
Dublin Evening Post. Richmond " shocked even the Irish by constant
drunkenness, and was latterly a complete partisan upon the Catholic
question " (Add. MS. 34458, f. 561, G. Eden's view).

the point is much too serious not to claim your Royal Highness' consideration. If the discontent of Ireland be unavoidable, it is to be met firmly like any other calamity which foresight cannot parry. If it be capable of prevention, it can never be for the interest of your Royal Highness to let an evil pregnant with such formidable consequences be gratuitously entailed.

I refer myself, Sir, to your own observation whether I have not, in the confidential intercourse to which you have deigned to admit me, most strictly abstained from any unfavourable remarks upon the measures of your Ministers. I have thought such censure secretly offered to your ear would be not only unconstitutional but unworthy. When I can bring myself to address Your Royal Highness upon a public topic, in deviation from a principle so strongly defined, my judgment may be in error, but my heart must be conscious of an imperious duty.

Without exactly analyzing the policy, for I am sure they would then reject it, Ministers may indistinctly perceive a benefit for themselves in involving your Royal Highness in what they think only a petty contest with the great body of the Irish people. The opposition of sentiment between your Royal Highness and the Ministers respecting the mode in which Ireland should be treated formed the great obstacle to your retaining them, when you should have to act professedly according to your own wish, in your counsels. This obstacle they might imagine they should remove if they could implicate you in differences with the Catholics on any collateral ground. Unfortunately, an incorrect procedure is never sure to stop where those who hazard it may wish. The zeal, or the intemperance, or the designs of associates will always be likely to improve upon the measure and give it a quality it was not intended to possess. The petulant insults in which the dependants of Adminstration indulge themselves towards the Catholics can do no good, and not only may but must do excessive harm. Those sneers do not apply to a few insignificant individuals but to a vast connected body conscious of numerical strength and equally sensible of the advantage which the difficulties of the empire gives to them at this juncture. It is easy for clever men with profligate view to sharpen and direct the indignation of a multitude so wantonly provoked. One must be mentally blind if one is not aware that separatists, neither few in number or of inferior class, are actively at work in propagating their doctrine ; and no expatiation is requisite to show what would be the amount of the inconvenience were the mass of the Catholics to embrace that disposition through disgust or resentment. I do firmly believe that the greatest bar which the separatists have experienced in inculcating notions very seducing for the common people has been the confidence entertained throughout Ireland that under your Government there could not be a continuance of oppression. This opinion is too inestimable to be risked lightly. A rebellion, unconnected with any other circumstances, must be regarded as one of the greatest calamities to the empire : But we know that it could not be unconnected ; we know that Buonaparte would not let slip the moment of our embarrassment ; and, with all our just reliance on ourselves, there is no measuring the degree of wound which his sagacity and enterprise might in such a case inflict. He is watching for this juncture, which I doubt not he has secretly been endeavouring to create.[1]

Whether this letter produced any effect, it is impossible to say. Neither the Hastings Papers nor the Windsor Archives contain any trace of a reply. But Moira was by no means the only observer to realize that Irish hostility to England might be envenomed if the Regent disappointed expectations.[2]

The state of Ireland might certainly give cause for anxiety. Agrarian outrages had been frequent early in the year, and the state of affairs in Tipperary and Waterford was said to be more serious than at any time since 1798.[3] Among the papers of Lord Moira preserved at Windsor is an excellent analysis of the state of the country by one Sterne Tighe, a Protestant, but an anti-Poleite.[4] He em-

[1] Windsor Arch., George IV, 19 Aug. 1811; another letter of Moira to McMahon, in a similar strain, occurs on 1 Dec. 1811.

[2] Nat. Lib. Wales MS. 2791, C. Wynn to H. Wynn, 3 Oct. 1811 ; Add. MS. 35649, f. 339, Denis Scully to Hardwicke, 9 Dec. 1811.

[3] Add. MS. 35649, f. 83, Dugald Campbell to Hardwicke, 22 Jan. 1811. Contrast Miss Godfrey's view : " You think, I dare say, in England, that we are all in an uproar about the proclamation and the Roman Catholic petitions. I really don't believe that there are fifty people in all Ireland that think upon the subject after the meetings are over. . . . " Moore, *Letters*, i. 261.

[4] Windsor Arch., George IV, *sub* 26 Sept.; see also letters to Moira, 11 and 18 Sept.

phasizes above all the fact that the Castle must cease to be a party and must rise to its responsibilities as a Government. The *Morning Chronicle* in a couple of leading articles developed this theme and, like Grattan, bewailed the state of Irish finances.[1] But though the condition of Ireland might be discussed in the newspapers, there was no corresponding general movement towards Catholic Emancipation in England. The agitation was confined to Parliament, and even there it made slow headway. Outside it the only important recruits were Cobbett and Peter Finerty, and they were recruits of doubtful value, though O'Connell was glad enough to get them.[2] The educated classes were still, on the whole, against the Catholics, and the mob still rose to " No Popery ! " One of the shrewdest observers of the political scene, Colonel Willoughby Gordon—no friend to the bigots—gave it as his opinion that :

as an English question, the Catholic petition is decidedly unpopular, and unless the temper of the people is very much changed, there is nothing which would be more likely to create a popular ferment, if handled by designing knaves, (of which there is never a scarcity) than a Catholic concession.[3]

And the view of the Tory backwoodsmen was expressed by Fuller, when, in the debate on Pole's letter, he said :

I have no great faith in Catholic Emancipation. I think that there is a radical and rooted antipathy between England and Ireland. [Order !] Well, then, try Catholic Emancipation, if you think that it will do. I care no more for a Catholic than I care for a Chinese. Give the fellows in their red waistcoats and their blue breeches every thing they want. But it won't do. No, let the great men of the country go home, in place of spending their money here ; let them regulate their tenantry and their estates, and not hear of them only through those secondary persons whom they employ. [Hear, hear !]

[1] *Morning Chronicle*, Feb. 1812 ; Grattan, v. 437.
[2] *Life and Speeches of O'Connell*, i.77 ; *Columbanus ad Hibernos*, i. 26.
[3] Windsor Arch., George IV, Gordon to McMahon, 15 Nov. 1811.

That will do more to conciliate Ireland than all the measure there is so much work made about.[1]

This state of affairs—Irish danger and English apathy—affected the situation in two ways : it turned the Regent more decidedly away from Catholic Emancipation as being " an unpopular question " ; and, conversely, it drove the more thoughtful Tories to the conclusion that even Emancipation might be preferable to civil war. Even in 1811 a newspaper under Dundas influence had shown an inclination in this direction.[2] Inside the Cabinet Wellesley, and outside it Castlereagh and Canning, were known to be favourable in principle to some concession ; and they pushed on the campaign with vigour in the spring of 1812 after Wellesley had resigned. The Whigs were not free from nervousness that Perceval might turn round suddenly and " dish " them.[3] Towards the end of February 1812 the Regent was said to have announced that he had settled the Catholic question on a *laissez-faire* basis—it was no longer to form a " Government question ". Perceval made diplomatic denials, but they turned on verbal points, and, in essence, the report was true.[4] It is most unlikely that the Prince seriously contemplated the speedy success of the movement for Emancipation. His real motive was to obtain the adhesion of Castlereagh as a compensation for the loss of Wellesley, and Castlereagh refused to join the Government unless he were allowed to vote at his discretion on the question.[5] So that the Whigs were now worse off than before, since they were no longer the sole upholders of the

[1] *Parl. Deb*. xix. 49, 22 Feb. 1811 ; cf. *Morning Chronicle*, 29 Aug. 1811.

[2] Windsor Arch., George IV, Moira to McMahon, 1 Oct. 1811.

[3] *Dropmore Papers*, x. 195, 26 Jan. 1812.

[4] *Court of the Regency*, i. 251 ; *Morning Chronicle*, 24 and 26 Feb., 2 March, 11 June 1812 ; Nat. Lib. Wales MS. 2791, C. Wynn to H. Wynn, 24 Feb. 1812 ; *Parl. Deb*. xxi. 1013.

[5] Add. MS. 34458, f. 345 ; *Parl. Deb*. xxi. 635, 1022.

Catholic cause. It was no wonder that they poured scorn
on *laissez-faire*, for they knew the Regent intended it to
mean very little. He had not thought of it until after the
Whigs—as he expected—had refused the offer contained
in his letter to the Duke of York. The Regent had a
marvellous capacity for feeling himself ill-used, and he had
already decided that the Catholics had treated him un-
gratefully and unkindly, because he had not immediately
granted their wishes. He resented their hostility, and was
indignant that they should claim Emancipation as a right
rather than as a boon. He expressed his feelings on this
point, not without bad language and at enormous length,
to the Archbishop of York—a confidant selected no doubt
because the Prince sensed intuitively that his conscience
was going to be involved—and the Archbishop passed the
information on to the Grenvilles.[1]

The Prince's rake's progress to Toryism infuriated
his former friends, and the letter to the Duke of York
gave them a chance to show their feelings. The Duke of
Norfolk warned the Prince against the course he was
taking, and bluntly refused the Garter ;[2] and Lord Moira
redoubled his exertions for the Catholic cause. Only the
Duke of Northumberland followed his master obediently.[3]
Hutchinson, who had already declared his intention of
breaking with " a certain person ", and had moved to
repeal the Union (to the alarm of all good Grenvilles)

---

[1] *Dropmore Papers*, x. 220-222, 227 ; *Court of Regency*, i. 191, 178,
155 ; cf. Add. MS. 34458, f. 234, Hatsell to Auckland : " What does Lord
Grenville say, to the change of language in the Catholics, from *favour*
to a *claim of right* ? This was always to be apprehended from *Them*
and from the *Independents* who are All agog to renew the scenes of
1648. . . ." The Regent might well have concurred. Hatsell at this time
was a very old man.

[2] Jerningham, ii. 17 ; Windsor Arch., George IV, Norfolk to Regent,
17 Feb.

[3] Add. MS. 30118, f. 186, Sir Robt. Wilson to Grey, 13 Dec. ;
Windsor Arch., George IV, Northumberland to McMahon, 18 Feb.
1812, enclosing a letter of the same date to the Regent.

was now reported to have said that the Catholics would
in future ignore the Regent entirely.[1] His brother
Donoughmore was still angrier, and more reckless, for he
had apparently been made the channel for two of the
Regent's promises to the Catholics, and resented having
been put in a false position.[2] His revenge did him no
credit. On 21 April 1812 he presented the Irish petition,
in place of Lord Holland, who kept discreetly in the
background ; and in the course of his speech he made an
attack upon Lady Hertford so gross, and so unwarranted,
that Moira, though voting for the motion, " anguishedly "
defended the Prince from the imputations cast upon him.[3]
Making all allowances for the peculiar family feeling among
the royal brothers, it is still astonishing to find even the
egregious Duke of Sussex voting for such a motion, after

[1] *Parl. Deb.* xxi. 124 ; *Court of Regency,* i. 180, 240.

[2] Holland, *Further Memoirs,* p. 125 ; O'Connell's speech of 18 June
1812 is in *Life and Speeches of O'Connell,* i. 173 *et seq.*

[3] " What phantoms have they [the Government] not conjured up to
warp the judgment, to excite the feelings, and appal the firmness of the
Royal mind ? But though the evil genius should assume a mitred, nay,
more than noble form, the sainted aspect which political bigotry delights
to wear, or the lineaments of that softer sex, which first beguiled man
to his destruction—though to the allurements of Calypso's court, were
joined the magic and the charms of that matured enchantress, should the
spirit of darkness take the human shape, and issuing forth from the inmost
recesses of the gaming-house or brothel, presume to place itself near the
Royal ear ;—what, though the potent spell should not have worked in
vain, and that the boasted recantation of all incumbering prepossessions
and inconvenient prejudices, had already marked the triumph of its
course—though from the Royal side they should have torn the
chosen friend of his youth and faithful counsellor of his maturer years
[Moira ?] . . . though they should have banished from the royal counsels
talents, integrity, honour, and highmindedness like his, and should
have selected for the illustrious person, an associate and an adviser
from Change Alley and from the Stews—though they should have thus
filled up, to its full measure, the disgusting catalogue of their enormities,
we must still cling to the foundering vessel. . . ." (*Parl. Deb.* xxii.
524-525, 656-657) ; Holland, *Further Memoirs,* p. 125. Moira still hoped
for the Prince's reconversion ; cf. Redding, *Regency,* i. 225.

such a speech.[1] In comparison with this, the notorious
" Witchery " resolutions of the Catholic Committee—
resolutions which were foisted upon them by Donoughmore and which complained of the " fatal witchery of an
unworthy secret influence "—were mild indeed.[2] Grey and
Ponsonby were less offensive, but equally explicit, in
declaring that the Regent had broken his promises ; and
their plain speaking undoubtedly wounded him. Whitbread, too, attacked him as the only remaining obstacle
to Emancipation.[3]

Whitbread was too sanguine, as the future was to
show ; but it was true that the cause had recently made
headway. To this result three factors contributed : the
reconciliation of the Irish and the English Catholics ; the
reappearance of the Aristocratic party in Ireland ; and
the consequent moderation of the Whigs upon the question
of the veto. The English Catholics, having thrown the
bombshell of the Fifth Resolution in 1810, had since
then been mildly contemplating the effects of its ex-
plosion. They had taken no overt step ; they had refrained
from annoying the Regent ; and they felt themselves
encouraged by the support, and stimulated by the society,
of the Duke of Sussex.[4] They now re-established concord
with their Irish brethren at a great dinner at the Thatched
House Tavern. " It went off extremely well," wrote Sir
George Jerningham to Lady Bedingfield, " and I trust all
animosity is now done away between the two bodies." [5]

---

[1] *Parl. Deb.* xxii. 530. The *Edinburgh Review* praised him greatly;
see vol. xx. 54-58.

[2] *Life and Speeches of O'Connell*, i. 167, asserts that Dennis Scully com-
piled them; Grattan (v. 484) seems to favour Donoughmore's authorship.

[3] *Parl. Deb.* xxii. 984 *seq.*

[4] Add. MS. 37889, f. 110; Jerningham, ii. 20-22: "I saw the élite . . .
assembled . . . to pay their respects to their eloquent and well-informed
spokesman, the Duke of Sussex ". A mild petition was indeed presented
to the Prince in April 1812 : Ward, i. 179.

[5] Jerningham, ii. 20.

The controversy over the Convention Act brought Lords Fingall and Ffrench once more into the forefront of the battle. The Aristocratic party had largely recovered from the fiasco of 1808. The Keogh period was over ; and O'Connell was not the man to decline their support from democratic prejudice. The Fingallians, however, did not venture to revive the veto. They were too pleased at being allowed to become, if not the leaders, at least the figureheads of the movement once again. In 1811 it was considered, both by Lord Moira and by the Bishop of Limerick, that there was a good chance of retaining the movement in these " respectable " hands.[1] In these circumstances, the Whigs could think of resuming more direct relations with the Irish Catholics ; and they began gradually to loosen their old, tenacious grip upon the veto. Even in 1811 there had been signs that the veto was no longer regarded as so vitally necessary as hitherto ; [2] and by the beginning of 1812 it was apparent that it would, if necessary, be surrendered. " Present us with a *fait accompli*", said the Catholics, " which does not interfere with our religion, and we will accept it. But let us have none of these preliminary public negotiations." [3] When John Joseph Dillon, the author of the articles in the *Morning Chronicle* signed " Hibern-Anglus ", offered to undertake a tour in Ireland on behalf of Grenville and the veto, his offer was politely declined.[4] Grenville in the House of Lords on 31 January 1812 asserted—

that he had never regarded the Veto as a *sine qua non*. He had expressly said in his letter [to Lord Fingall] that it was an arrangement to which he attached no great importance. . . . [5]

---

[1] Windsor Arch., George IV, Bishop of Limerick to ?, 20 June 1811.

[2] Sir John Hippisley stuck to it, however, as late as April 1812 ; *Parl. Deb.* xxii. 762-795.

[3] *Ibid.* xx. 369, 645; *Dropmore Papers*, x. 200-201 ; *Morning Chronicle*, 3 Feb. 1812.

[4] *Dropmore Papers*, x. 172-174, 175.   [5] *Parl. Deb.* xxi. 476.

And Ponsonby a few days afterwards echoed his words :

I lay little stress on the Veto. I look upon all securities of this kind in a very inferior point of view. I think the Catholics, like other men, must be governed by their interests and affections.[1]

Such a *volte-face*, of course, laid the Whigs open to easy retorts, which Eldon and Perceval did not fail to make ; [2] and even Tierney's defence of their position—much the ablest that was made—could not quite reconcile their past with their present professions.[3] The ill-disposed press took a malicious pleasure in reporting that Lord Grenville had become a Catholic, which annoyed him very much.[4] Nevertheless the Whigs persevered ; and in the debate on Canning's motion, Ponsonby set the seal on their recantation by declaring that the best security of all was complete Emancipation.[5]

The Catholic debates throughout the spring of 1812 had—despite dull speeches—shown mounting minorities for Emancipation.[6] Even the tyrant Pole was converted to liberal principles ; [7] and when, after the Ministerial crisis was over, Canning produced his motion for an enquiry into the Catholic claims in the succeeding session, it was carried easily in the Commons, and lost only by one vote in the Lords. The Catholics were jubilant, and confidently expected Emancipation in 1813.[8] Moira, who knew better,

[1] *Ibid.* 661.

[2] *Ibid.* 1031 (Perceval) ; *ibid.* xxii. 694 (Eldon).

[3] *Ibid.* xxi. 1028.

[4] *Morning Chronicle*, 18 March 1812 (quoting another paper) ; *Dropmore Papers*, x. 187.

[5] *Parl. Deb.* xxiii. 705 ; cf. Grenville at *ibid.* xxii. 684.

[6] *The Bath Archives*, i. 365 (dull speeches). Minorities of 135 for Morpeth's motion, 4 Feb. (*Parl. Deb.* xxi. 669) ; 215 for Grattan's, 23 April (*ibid.* xxii. 1040) ; 102 peers for Donoughmore's, 21 April (*ibid.* 703).

[7] In order not to split the family. Add. MS. 37296, f. 398.

[8] Canning's motion, *Parl. Deb.* xxiii. 710 (carried by 235–106). Add. MS. 34458, f. 369 (Grenville), f. 343 (G. Eden) ; Jerningham, ii. 19 ; Canning on his tactics. Add. MS. 37296, ff. 317-319.

preferred to retire to the congenial gloom of an Indian Governorship:[1] and the *Edinburgh Review* added a note of warning to its paean: "The Catholic cause is at this moment endangered by too confident an assurance of easy victory. The controversy is, indeed, triumphantly terminated. The bigots are silenced on every ground of justice or policy."[2] There still remained the alarms of a few extremists,[3] but in Parliament, at any rate, the victory seemed as good as won. The revival in 1813 of the question of "Securities" was an anticlimax as unexpected as it was disastrous.

The Whigs had fallen from power in 1807 as the self-styled champions of Emancipation. They had maintained their championship under the easier circumstances of Opposition, on the whole, with consistency, credit, and sincerity. On innumerable occasions they defended the liberties of the Irish people and the rights of the Catholic Church; and they were vigilant, zealous, and pertinacious in opposing the Government's policy of "vigour" in Ireland. Their divisions might be small, but at least they gave a sign that there were some M.P.'s who were not prepared to allow Irish affairs to be settled in a casual and haphazard manner at the discretion of an unsympathetic Government. In the two years that followed on the episode of the veto, the party admittedly adhered too rigidly to the policy of its adoption, oblivious of the wishes of the Irish people. It must be remembered, however, that the Whigs had to look at the position from the Parliamentary angle. They had first to ask themselves what was possible at Westminster. They believed in the half-loaf. They were prepared

[1] Moore, *Letters*, i. 313.   [2] *Ed. Rev.* xx. 360.
[3] See the agitated letter of Newenham. Add. MS. 38248, ff. 10-11; *Life and Speeches of O'Connell*, i. 170, for Lord Ross's comment on Perceval's assassination; and Coleridge's view in Crabb Robinson, *MS. Diary*, 23 Jan. 1811.

to sacrifice much to carry a conciliatory gesture. Unfortunately it took them too long to realize that for the sake of a conciliatory gesture they were alienating the affections of Ireland. They were knocking their man down in order to demonstrate their friendliness by assisting him to rise. They were not at all in touch with young Irish opinion. A few of them knew Denis Scully, and all of them knew Lord Donoughmore; but they did not know O'Connell, and it was no compensation for that omission that they were hand in glove with Lord Fingall. The result was that Irish affairs began to move without them, and the Irish Catholics began to organize on lines which would eventually make them independent of their Parliamentary patrons. In the light of after-events, it is obvious that the Whigs would have done more justice to their good intentions by adopting a more extreme and less compromising attitude from the start. The veto rankled in Ireland at least as much as in England, and it obscured the gratitude which was certainly due to the Whig leaders. For they could expect little but evil from England as the result of their efforts. There can be no doubt that their support of Emancipation reacted most unfavourably on their position in this country. It was not then, and it never became, a vote-catching question. It played an important part in every negotiation for allies that the Whigs undertook, and, as often as not, it proved an obstacle to union. It came up as a vital issue on the four occasions when there was a possibility of their accepting office; and on those occasions it certainly contributed to keep them out. When their warnings were not heeded, when Ireland became a source of danger, they were unfortunate in that they were compelled to share the credit for pressing on the question with many of their rivals. The Whigs fall into the background, where Catholic affairs are concerned, in the years 1811 and 1812. The Regent, O'Connell, and Wellesley Pole replace Ponsonby, Keogh, and Fingall in the centre of the stage ; and later it is Canning, not Grattan, who carries the last triumphant motion. The Catholic question, in fact, had ceased to be the preserve of the Whigs. It had become, like the slave trade, a non-party issue ; and the date for this change (1812) marks, therefore, the end of the short but distinctive period in which it had been their proud monopoly. The characteristic Whig blend of idealism with factiousness was no longer the driving spirit behind the agitation.

CHAPTER II

THE WHIGS AND THE WAR

WHILE the Talents were engaged in endeavouring to hoodwink George III over the Catholic Bill, Napoleon and Alexander were on their way to Friedland and Tilsit. For England the situation appeared gloomy. The Tsar was the last Continental ruler of importance to keep up the fight against French domination. In Sicily, the Queen of Naples maintained an independence which was likely to last no longer than the occupation of the island by British troops and the patrolling of the Straits by British ships; and in Sweden Gustavus IV was known to be not unwilling to indulge his monomania against Napoleon at the expense of the British taxpayer : but of serviceable allies, actual or potential, we had none. Europe was lost to us ; and it needed the cruel spur of the Continental System to prick it into activity.

On the sea our prospects were brighter. The campaign of Trafalgar had put an end to the danger of invasion, and in a year or so the action in Basque Roads was to prove that the French Navy had little chance against British experience and seamanship. The result of this superiority was a clean sweep of the French possessions overseas, and a series of successful attacks on the colonies of their allies, the Spaniards and Dutch. These acquisitions, it was hoped, would be sufficient, indeed more than sufficient, to balance the loss of Hanover, when the time came for a pacification and an exchange of conquests. The position gave every sign of becoming a stalemate. Napoleon was master of the Continent ; Great Britain of the ocean and the colonies. Both

sides realized this fact almost simultaneously. Napoleon
was driven to undertake the Continental System, a task
beyond the strength of any power ; and British Ministers
were forced to recur to the efforts of the early days of
the war, and adventure a large force upon the Continent
of Europe, instead of concentrating their attention upon
the " filching of sugar islands ".

The Talents, however, had given no sign in their
short Administration of being alive to the necessity of
an altered policy. Under the influence of Grenville and
Windham they had persisted in the tactics of Pitt. The
strength of the country was dispersed in expeditions
usually ill-conceived, often ill-executed, and sometimes
absurd. Thus Admiral Duckworth had been sent to coerce
the Porte, with a view to aiding our ally Russia. He had
sailed with his fleet up and down the Sea of Marmora, had
found difficulty in taking efficacious action, and had
returned empty-handed, with some danger and a little
damage to his ships from the shore batteries of the
Dardanelles.[1] Another force had been dispatched to
invade Egypt, more with a desire to forestall Napoleon,
who was suspected of renewed designs upon that country,
than with any clear idea of the benefits to be obtained
from such an expedition. After meeting with several
severe defeats, this army was ultimately withdrawn by
Castlereagh, having in six months' campaigning added
little to the glory of the British name.[2] For the attack on
Buenos Ayres the Talents were not directly responsible ;
but some of them, and in particular Windham, must bear
some share of the blame for the ultimate failure.[3] They
had indeed one great victory to their credit—that of
Maida ; but neither it nor the preservation of Sicily can

[1] Fortescue, *History of the British Army*, vi. 6.
[2] *Ibid.* 13-17.
[3] *Ibid.* v. 432-437. There is a MS. narrative of this expedition, which
Fortescue does not seem to have used, in Add. MS. 37887 at ff. 43 *et seq.*

be counted to them for merit, since each was due to the initiative of the general on the spot. The military exploits of the Talents were, therefore, far from glorious. They committed all the blunders for which they had censured Pitt, and they failed to provide the inspiring leadership which had alone made those blunders tolerable.[1] And if their expeditions came to grief, so also did their foreign policy. By their refusal to renew the subsidy to Russia after Austria had made peace they gave the Tsar an excuse, if they did not provoke him, to listen to the overtures of France. Crabb Robinson, reporting on foreign affairs for *The Times*, found the Whigs everywhere reproached and derided.[2] Sir Robert Wilson was forced to endure the tirades of Woronzow against the " Foxistes ", and hear him praise the superior firmness and intelligence of their successors.[3] The Whigs may be acquitted of an intention to desert our ally ; but it is not easy to exculpate them from an undue casualness in their treatment of him.[4] Their efforts for peace, though more meritorious, had been even less successful. They had imported into the sphere of foreign policy that spirit of idealism which had carried through the abolition of the slave trade, and they had found that they were dealing with an uncompromising realist. The death of Fox, while the negotiations were still pending, saved him from the shattering of an illusion fostered in the happy irresponsibility of Opposition, and chivalrously persisted in under the realities of office. Such an experience should have made the Whigs better able to understand the difficulties of their successors.[5]

[1] The *Morning Chronicle* naturally blamed the generals : 13 June 1807.

[2] Crabb Robinson, *Diary*, i. 124.

[3] Add. MS. 30105, ff. 97-98.

[4] The *Morning Chronicle* of 26 May and 10 Dec. 1807 did its best with intractable material ; and as late as 1813 the *Edinburgh Review* grew warm upon the subject (xxi. art. x).

[5] Coquelle, *Napoleon and England*, ch. xix, gives the best account of the Whig attitude during these negotiations.

The blunders of the Talents are important, because they gave the Tories a fatally easy opportunity to reply to criticism with a *tu quoque*, and because they had their effect upon the public mind. The country had too little confidence in the Whigs to wish to turn out the Tories ; and for this state of affairs the badness of their record when in office was largely responsible. Not entirely, however : for it could not escape observation that the Whigs were deeply divided upon the conduct of the war, and even upon the necessity for its continuance.

There was a school of opinion in the country that continued to regard the war as a struggle forced by us upon a peace-loving French Emperor. Its views found expression in such papers as the *Independent Whig* : its most distinguished member was probably Hazlitt. To the end of his life Hazlitt remained quite unbalanced where Napoleon was in question ; but many who did not share his fanatical adoration of the Emperor concurred in his opinion about the war :

> We chose to rest a dispute, which was to involve everything near and dear to us, on a diplomatic ambiguity ; on a technical question as to the manner how and to whom we were to give up a barren rock which was of no use to us, and to which we had resigned all pretensions. . . . It was not the danger of invasion which produced the taking up of arms, but the determination to take up arms which produced the fear of invasion.[1]

The Whigs, as a whole, had long since got over their Napoleonic phase ; but an appreciable section of them held that it was futile to continue the war, and that peace might be had for the asking. Most important of these was Whitbread. His speech in the House of Commons on 5 January 1807 marks the beginning of that series of differences with the bulk of his party which was to lead to such disastrous dissensions in the future. He contended that

[1] Hazlitt, *Works*, i. 96.

our negotiators had treated as an ultimatum terms which
France had proposed expressly with a view to their being
withdrawn later.[1] He accused them of showing a lack of
imagination and flexibility; and he lamented their insistence on the satisfaction of *all* of Russia's demands. It
seemed to him that the negotiations had been conducted
throughout with undue caution.

> Sir [he said], I am upon principle, as well as from feeling, in all
> transactions of life . . . an enemy to perpetual and endless suspicion.
> It is not the character of wisdom, and it impedes the progress of
> human affairs. . . . Good God ! if peace be not the issue of the
> contest, whither are we hurrying ? Contemplate, Sir, if you can
> with composure, these two mighty Empires exerting their utmost
> efforts, each for the destruction of the other ; and think upon it, if
> you can without horror, that before the contest be ended, one or
> other must be destroyed.[2]

And he moved an amendment to the Address in the very
words in which Howick had moved the amendment upon
the rupture of the peace of Amiens—an unnecessarily
malicious touch.[3]

This debate marked out the two divergent points of
view, between which most Whigs hovered for the next
few years. On the one hand were Whitbread and his friends,
zealous above all things for peace, and impartial to the
point of being unpatriotic ; and on the other the much larger
body which followed Grey and Grenville, who professed
their desire for an honourable peace, but acknowledged
that it was at the moment difficult if not impossible to
obtain, and confined their criticism, therefore, to the
methods adopted in prosecuting the war. The questions
outstanding between the two countries were too vexed
for easy arrangement ; and the problems of Hanover
and Sicily were perhaps in 1806 hardly susceptible of

---

[1] *Substance of a Speech . . . on 5 Jan. 1807*, pp. 22, 23.

[2] *Ibid.* pp. 63, 66.

[3] *Ibid.* p. 68 ; *Life and Times of Brougham,* i. 390-392.

satisfactory solution.[1] Nevertheless Whitbread by no means stood alone. In April 1807 an article in the *Edinburgh Review* on " The Dangers of the Country " took much the same line. The reviewer emphasized the fact that " peace at any price " was no part of his programme : peace must be honourable if not glorious. But he denied that a glorious peace was obtainable. The war had been undertaken to put a stop to French aggressions ; yet every campaign had resulted in fresh conquests for France at the expense of our allies. The possible objects for which we were contending were : first, the restoration of the Bourbons ; secondly, the compensation of our allies ; thirdly, the retention of our conquests ; and fourthly, security. Of these, the third was unworthy of us and the first two were unattainable. And he urged that security was more surely obtainable by a wise peace than by a protraction of the war.

The game, we fear, is decidedly lost, as to the Continent of Europe ; and for our allies to persist in it, will only be to push their bad fortune. . . . We have more foreign settlements already than we have any good use for ; and it would be the height of imprudence to think of keeping all that are now in our hands even if their original owners were quite willing to relinquish them.[2]

Even the *Morning Chronicle*, which had been warlike as long as the Talents were in, grew downcast now that they were out, and began to reflect that since it was hopeless to reduce France by maritime action, we might gain all that we were then gaining from the war by a cessation of hostilities.[3]

At this juncture too, William Roscoe, a well-known Liverpool Whig, published a pamphlet which attracted widespread attention, entitled *Considerations on the Causes*,

[1] Grenville declared, to Cobbett's great disgust, that " Hanover should be as dear to us as Hampshire ". *Political Register*, xiii. 69.

[2] *Edinburgh Review*, x. 19, 20. This article gave great offence to the Tories of Edinburgh : Scott, *Letters*, i. 400.

[3] *Morning Chronicle*, 16 March 1807, 15 Aug. 1807.

Objects and Consequences of the present war, and on the Expediency, or the Danger, of Peace with France. In Roscoe's opinion we had ceased to fight for our allies : we fought merely for our existence. But this was our own fault. We entered the war again, on the breakdown of the negotiations of 1806, not to preserve the established order, nor to restore the Bourbons, nor for the sake of an indemnity— but solely to fulfil our pledges to Russia, who, through our stupidity, had since deserted us. Now that Russia was our enemy, we were entitled to neglect her interests ; so that there remained no subject of difference between France and England to account for a continuance of hostilities.[1]

In the summer of 1807, therefore, there was a considerable movement in favour of peace. In the manufacturing districts it was particularly strong, and petitions for peace were actually presented from Bolton, Oldham, and Manchester.[2] In the West Riding of Yorkshire, too, there was a similar agitation. But here the other half of Whig opinion came into play. Lord Milton, the Whig member for the county, persuaded his constituents to refrain from petitioning, on the ground that to petition for peace would be an encouragement to the enemy to continue the war.[3] Grey and Grenville emphatically approved his action and supported his arguments.[4] They endeavoured, without success, to convince Whitbread of their validity, or at least to induce him to be quiet ; and Grey wrote to him expressing a hope—

that nothing will be hazarded either in language or action, without the most serious consideration of the consequences it may produce.

---

[1] *Considerations* (etc.) pp. 10, 59, 60. Whitbread cordially approved Roscoe's pamphlet ; and when, in the next year, he published a sequel to it, Whitbread revised and emended it before publication. *Life of Roscoe,* i. 426, 435.

[2] *Parl. Deb.* x. 692, 708, 1182.

[3] *Morning Chronicle,* 5 Nov., 17 Nov. 1807 ; *Parl. Deb.* x. 47.

[4] *Dropmore Papers,* ix. 157 ; *Life and Opinions of Grey,* pp. 178-179

Above all, I hope that nothing will be done to encourage a clamour for peace, against which I must set my face decidedly and strenuously.[1]

But Whitbread was not to be repressed. A party dinner was held at Lord Grenville's house just before the beginning of the session of 1808 ; and Whitbread chose this occasion, when harmony was above all desirable, to begin upon the subject of peace—

in so hot, and I must say, so wrong-headed a manner, that I am afraid the impression must have been very unfavourable. . . . Grenville seemed quite dumbfoundered, and hardly spoke a word. . . .[2]

Here, then, was a fruitful source of discord.[3] Whitbread had not been in the Cabinet in 1806 ; he had not realized that in their negotiations the Whigs had been set an impossible task. Grey and Grenville were certainly prepared to collaborate in attacks on the Tories, for, after all, they must not allow the Ministers to become complacent ; but they could not follow Whitbread into a general attack upon the war.

On the question of peace [wrote Grey] I think the case so clear that I hope there will be no difference when we consider the subject calmly. I think nothing could be more damning to our reputations than any attempt to take advantage of the cry which has arisen in Yorkshire.[4]

To Grey, Whitbread's actions must have seemed the tactics of an angular and disappointed colleague.

The question of peace came up, despite the efforts of the leaders, at the beginning of the session of 1808. Much had happened since the last meeting of Parliament. The

---

[1] *Life and Opinions of Grey*, pp. 178-179.
[2] *Ibid.* pp. 179-180.
[3] As was indeed generally realized. Nat. Lib. Wales MS. 4812, f. 199, for Southey's view.
[4] *Tierney MSS.* Grey to Tierney, 20 Dec. 1807 ; Grenville's similar views in Add. MS. 34457, f. 394 (to Auckland, 29 Dec. 1807).

Ministers had been distracted by the evil legacy of the Talents ; and in quick succession had come the news of the mutiny at Vellore, the failure at Buenos Ayres, and the final disaster in Egypt. The Treaty of Tilsit had been signed, and the Continental System seriously inaugurated. In this emergency the reply of the Government had been vigorous to the point of brutality. Acting on confidential information as to the secret clauses of the Treaty of Tilsit, they had dispatched an armament which attacked Copenhagen by sea and land, and exacted the cession of the Danish fleet. One other success they had had, or rather they had shared it with Lord Strangford : they had managed to convey the royal family of Portugal to Brazil, and thus had baulked the attempt of Napoleon to treat the Braganzas as he afterwards treated the Spanish Bourbons. They had in the meantime been carrying on an unpromising negotiation for peace through the mediation of Austria and Russia ; and it was their failure to bring it to an issue that provoked Whitbread to attack them, although he had not seen the papers upon which his motion was to be founded at the time he gave notice of it.[1]

On 29 February 1808 he brought forward three motions. The first condemned the insistence upon an impartial mediator ; the second censured the general conduct of Ministers in the negotiation ; and the third asserted " That there is nothing in the present state of the war, which ought to preclude His Majesty from embracing any fair opportunity of acceding to, or commencing, a negotiation with the enemy on a footing of equality for the termination of hostilities, on terms of equity and honour ".[2] In his long speech he recapitulated most of the familiar arguments for peace ; but, in addition, he protested against the personal hatred with which the

[1] Grey, *Life and Opinions*, p. 180 ; Coquelle, pp. 158-176, justifies Canning.

[2] *Parl. Deb.* x. 856.

Tories pursued Napoleon, and pointed out that in the matter of political morality it ill became the English to cast a stone. And he concluded with this characteristic passage :

> Having mentioned the name of Mr. Fox, I willingly acknowledge myself his true and genuine disciple. I am only feebly urging the sentiments which he would have forcibly uttered, if he had not been unhappily taken from us. I trust that I am treading in his footsteps ; would to God that his countenance were now upon me ! would to God, this humble effort over, I could feel myself as I have often done, secure under the impenetrable aegis of his eloquence ! [1]

The eloquence, however, was on this occasion on the other side. Whitbread did indeed get as many as 58 votes for his third motion, and 70 for his first. But the Whigs were divided, almost leaderless in the Commons, and particularly irritated just then by Ponsonby's mismanagement ; so that it would be incorrect to see in the 58 the partisans of a wholehearted peace policy.[2] Among them were such men as Horner, Abercromby, Piggott, and Sheridan, who were by no means of Whitbread's group.[3]

Whitbread's motion, however, was merely the prelude to the real business of the session, which was to pass judgment on the expedition to Copenhagen. This offered an opportunity for reasonable criticism ; the moralists, no less than the politicians, were divided.[4] The Whigs made good use of it. They were nearly unanimous in reprobating the expedition, not only on the score of its impolicy

---

[1] *Parl. Deb.* x. 801-853. The *Morning Chronicle*, 13 Jan. 1808, admitted that the Government was right to reject the Austrian mediation.

[2] Grey, *Life and Opinions*, pp. 181-182. See below, p. 327.

[3] *Parl. Deb.* x. 870.

[4] Lord Teignmouth, Coleridge, Wilberforce, for it ; Southey and many of the " Saints " against. *Memoir of Lord Teignmouth*, ii. 137 ; Coleridge, *Works*, ii. 275 ; Wilberforce, *Life*, iii. 345 ; Nat. Lib. Wales MS. 4812, f. 202.

but as an immoral act.[1] In the first six months of 1808
Whig speeches were liberally sprinkled with sarcasms on
the "new morality"; and Lord Erskine said "that if
Hell did not exist before, Providence would create it
now, to punish ministers for that d——able measure".[2]
Only Thomas Grenville supported Canning's action, which,
in his opinion, had been taken upon "a principle which I
know not how we are to attack without making ourselves vulnerable upon our former orders respecting
Lisbon ".[3] It was feared for a moment that these heresies
might affect Lord Grenville, but that misfortune was
happily averted.[4] Criticism began on the first day of the
session, for the Lords Commissioners' Speech contained a
reference to the expedition, and the Opposition, not
unnaturally, declined to approve it before having had an
opportunity of making themselves acquainted with the
relevant papers, which the Government had not as yet
produced. Some of the Whig peers, headed by the Duke of
Gloucester, entered a Protest upon the Journals of the
House upon this account.[5] In the Commons the Whigs took
the same attitude; but they found it very difficult to make
Canning produce the papers they desired. When at last he
did so, towards the end of February, they were so garbled
by excision, that Garlike (lately Envoy Extraordinary

[1] *Morning Chronicle*, 17 Nov., 7 Oct. 1807 ; *Tierney MSS.* Tierney
to Gen. Maitland, Sept. 1807 : " If any evidence entitled to credit exists
that there was an understanding between the Danes and the French
by which the latter were to have the assistance of the Danish fleet
Ministers have acted boldly but justifiably. If no such evidence is to
be found . . . our conduct has been no better than piracy."

[2] Leveson-Gower, *Correspondence*, p. 315.

[3] *Dropmore Papers*, ix. 144 ; also *ibid.* 148. The Talents had projected
a similar enterprise against the Portuguese fleet, when it had seemed
likely to fall into French hands ; and Howick had almost threatened war
if the neutrality of Denmark were not more benevolent.

[4] *Tierney MSS.* Tierney to Howick, 26 Nov. 1807 ; Add. MS. 34457,
ff. 327, 367.

[5] *Parl. Deb.* x. 14, 16, 58, 69, etc. ; *Protests of the Lords*, ii. 384.

and Minister Plenipotentiary to Denmark), who felt his reputation to be concerned, began an angry correspondence with him, protesting against the misrepresentation to which these omissions gave rise. It does not appear that he was given any satisfaction.[1] Canning indeed behaved with quite unnecessary tortuousness, and gave every ground for the suspicion entertained by some of the Whigs that the reasons publicly assigned for the attack would not bear inspection. They did not believe the story of the secret articles ; and though the Grenvilles, at any rate, realized that Canning could not produce evidence of their authenticity without endangering the source of his information, they still pressed for it.[2] They believed, or affected to believe, that the Danes could and would have made effective resistance to Napoleon. Earl St. Vincent was brought forward to testify that the island of Sjaelland (Zealand) was easily defensible against an army in Jutland.[3] The value of the vessels captured was minimized, the sufferings of Copenhagen were magnified for party purposes. It was represented that by setting the whole Danish nation irrevocably against us, we had defeated our own object, and lessened our security rather than increased it.[4] Ponsonby satirically enquired why we had so rashly abandoned Sjaelland : " Why so shabby in our iniquities ? When we imitated the atrocities of the ruler of France, why not imitate the grandeur and magnitude of his designs ? " ; and a correspondent of the *Morning Chronicle* ironically suggested that the island should be given as a kingdom to Sir Home Popham.[5] As Grey put it :

[1] *Dropmore Papers*, ix. 183.

[2] Add. MS. 35647, ff. 122, 126. G. Jackson, though friendly to Canning, thought his attitude a mistake. *Jackson Diaries*, ii. 236.

[3] *Parl. Deb.* x. 375 ; Brenton, *St. Vincent*, ii. 270, thinks he was in error.

[4] *Tierney MSS*. Howick to Tierney, 8 Nov. 1807.

[5] *Parl. Deb.* x. 265 ; *Morning Chronicle*, 16 Oct. 1807. Pasley, *Military Policy of the British Empire*, p. 222, agrees.

If I were put to choose whether I would have Denmark, deprived of her navy, an inveterate enemy as she now must be, and still possessing great means of annoyance, or preserving a doubtful neutrality, or at the worst an unwilling instrument of the hostility of France, I should have no hesitation in preferring the latter ; and this without taking into account the loss of national character, and the enmity of every other power in Europe, which I fear must be the result of this act of violence and injustice. For this, eighteen sail of the line and fifteen frigates, will be but a poor compensation. . . .[1]

The Whigs had an arguable case ; but they do not seem to have made the best of it. On Ponsonby's motion of 3 February they could only divide 108 against 253 ; on Whitbread's five days later only 75; on Sharp's on 21 March only 64. They opposed, also, the vote of thanks to the commanders ; but for this their division sank to 19.[2] The attack on the Copenhagen expedition was a failure.

Equally unsuccessful was their attempt to deride the Portuguese emigration to the Brazils. They had long persisted in believing this to be impossible ; when it was accomplished, they pretended that it was of no significance. They described the benefits to our trade which might fairly be expected to ensue, as chimerical ; or alternatively, as attributable neither to Lord Strangford nor to the Government, but simply to undeserved good fortune.[3] They were captious, too, about the Government's Swedish policy ; and Perceval's rebuke of their attitude

[1] Add. MS. 37847, ff. 261-262.

[2] *Parl. Deb.* x. 182, 310, 396-397, 1235. The Tories were dissatisfied with these divisions. Bulwer, *Palmerston*, i. 81.

[3] *Parl. Deb.* x. 58 etc. ; *Morning Chronicle*, 26 Sept., 23 Dec. 1807, 5 Jan., 18 Jan. 1808 ; *Edinburgh Review*, xii. art. xiv ; *Dropmore Papers*, ix. 143 ; Manchester, *British Pre-eminence in Brazil*, for an admirable account of Strangford's achievement and its consequences ; Wellington, *Despatches*, vi. 329 : " Great Britain has ruined Portugal by her free trade with the Brazils. . . . Portugal would be now in a very different situation as an ally, if our trade with the Brazils were still carried on through Lisbon."

was both well-merited and effective.[1] It was felt, indeed,
by some of their own party that the Whigs were too
undiscriminating in their attacks on the Government.
Lyttelton, for instance, had refused to vote against
Copenhagen ; and Sir Thomas Turton, in reference to a
speech of Whitbread's, " deprecated severely this perpetual
recurrence to subjects undertaken for the purpose of party
spirit and personal enmity ".[2] There was too much party
bitterness and too little constructive criticism in their
attacks. Recrimination was the order of the day ; and the
Tories were equally to blame for this state of affairs. They
fell too easily into the habit of deflecting criticism by a
reference to the failures of their predecessors. " The
character of Parliament is changed ", wrote an anonymous
pamphleteer ; " Business drags heavily . . . [nothing but]
personalities, . . . accusations, retorts, and breaches of
order ".[3] The " testiness " of Opposition, of which he complained, made it difficult for Ministers to get through their
business : " According to the present style of parliamentary
proceedings, the executive ministers are so completely
occupied with answering the accusations brought against
them for their conduct in the preceding year, that they
have no time to attend to any plan for the ensuing one :
it results from this that the British government is constantly
six months behindhand with the events of the day . . . ".[4]
This is an obvious exaggeration, but it does contain a
grain of truth. It would be unfair, however, to blame the
Whigs for this state of affairs. The evil lay rather in the
system which crammed the activities of Parliament into
the first six months of the year—the time when campaigns

[1] *Parl. Deb.* x. 1165.   [2] *Ibid.* 302, 1360.
[3] *Public Spirit*, p. 69. Cf. *Short Remarks on the State of Parties at the
close of the year 1809*, p. 13 : " certainly the number of persons who at
the present time talk of objecting to certain parts of the late ministers'
conduct, and of assisting any steps which may be taken to throw censure on them in particular instances, is by no means trifling . . . ".
[4] Leckie, *Survey of Foreign Affairs*, pt. ii. 36.

were preparing—and allowed the summer and autumn to pass without a meeting of the Houses. They had, therefore, to examine and thrash out the achievements of the past six months before they could proceed to prepare for the new campaign. If this examination was to be omitted, the Opposition could hardly claim to be doing its duty by the nation.

None the less it is clear that the Whigs were at this time barren of constructive ideas about the conduct of the war. Quite apart from men like Whitbread and Roscoe, who held that, as we had nothing to fight for, it was futile to determine more effective ways of fighting; the Whigs, as a body, could suggest no means of retrieving the war from the backwater into which it had drifted. They recognized that small diversions were of no value, but they refused to proceed to the conclusion that the only method remaining to us was intervention on the grand scale on the Continent of Europe. On the contrary, they disliked the idea of continental commitments.[1] The Tory Ministers were at least feeling their way towards this solution of the problem; and perhaps they might have risked a serious effort in the Baltic or on the North German coast if the sudden outbreak in Spain had not opened up the ideal opportunity for intervention. Two questions at once arose. Would the Government throw itself unhesitatingly into the struggle and trust the armies and fortunes of the nation to the uncertainties of a popular outbreak ? And were the Whigs to countenance this venture as against any other continental enterprise ?

In June 1808 the delegates of the Asturias arrived in London to ask for help ; and a fortnight later Sheridan brought the matter up in Parliament. He is said to have been drunk when he made his speech,[2] but it was not

---

[1] Add. MS. 34457, f. 324 (Grenville's view) ; *Morning Chronicle*, 20 July 1807 ; *Independent Whig*, 21 Aug. 1808.

[2] Coupland, *Wilberforce*, p. 356.

unworthy of the man and the occasion. He disclaimed any desire to dictate a policy to the Government, and professed himself anxious only to bring the question prominently before the House. But he insisted earnestly on the necessity for vigorous and determined action :

> In my opinion, we must not deal in driblets ; we must do much or nothing. . . . Instead of striking at the core of the evil, the administrations of this country have hitherto contented themselves with nibbling at the rind . . . they have gone about filching sugar-islands and neglecting all that was dignified and all that was consonant to the truly understood interests of this country. I wish, therefore, Sir, to let Spain know, that the conduct which we have pursued will not be persevered in, but that we are resolved fairly and fully to stand up for the salvation of Europe.[1]

Sheridan's speech was cordially received by the Government ; by the Whigs with less satisfaction. They felt that Sheridan was precipitate, and that he took too much upon himself in presuming to speak for his party. Ponsonby and Whitbread were cautious, but, on the whole, disapproving, affecting to consider the time inopportune ; and Grey in his correspondence subsequently spoke severely of Sheridan.[2] Windham, however, supported him ;[3] and very soon the mass of the party was caught up in the extraordinary wave of enthusiasm which passed over the nation. For a moment the Whigs were in full agreement with their adversaries as to the policy to be adopted : they differed from them only in being relieved from the necessity of considering its practicability. The spectacle of a nation rightly struggling to be free appealed irresistibly to a party which had applauded the France of 1792. " Spain ! Spain ! " cried Horner, " I am in a fever till I hear more about Dupont and the passes of the Sierra Morena."[4] Holland, and Grey, and Brougham re-echoed Horner's cry ; and men so diverse as

---

[1] *Parl. Deb.* xi. 888.   [2] Grey, *Life* and *Opinions*, p. 219.
[3] *Parl. Deb.* xi. 893-895.
[4] Horner, *Memoirs*, i. 427 ; see also *ibid.* ii. 157.

Moira and Cartwright concurred.[1] The *Morning Chronicle*
was not a whit behind the popular assemblies in enthusiasm:[2]

At this moment, the English people would cordially acquiesce
in any effort, however expensive, that could assist the cause of
that brave and noble nation, so truly and intimately do they sympathize in the struggle of a people for liberty.[3]

And in July the columns of the paper began again to be
filled with satirical poems about "Boney" and "Nap",
of a type that had been long absent from them.[4] Even the
more phlegmatic Grenvilles warmed at length to a grudging
approval, though their hopes were never very high, and
though they were inclined to attribute Napoleon's ill-
success to the difficulty of the country—a factor which
they conveniently forgot when later they passed judgment
on English defeats.[5]

The Whigs were now above all anxious that a proper
force should be sent to the Peninsula under a competent
general—no "whiskered martinet" or Royal Duke, but a
man such as Sir Hew Dalrymple, "who has gained the
confidence of the Spanish people".[6] The force must be a
real army : for no mere expedition would now suffice. The

[1] Brougham, *Life and Times*, i. 413, where Grey says : " To assist
the Spaniards is morally and politically one of the highest duties a
nation ever had to perform ". *Correspondence of Sir John Sinclair*, ii.
App. II, 8 (for Moira) ; Holland, *Further Memoirs*, p. 13 ; Cartwright,
Life, i. 368-369 ; Roscoe, *Life*, i. 443.

[2] Add. MS. 27838, ff. 325-326, f. 332, give resolutions of Westminster
and Middlesex meetings. See *Morning Chronicle*, 2 July 1808.

[3] *Ibid.* 15 June 1808.

[4] *Ibid.* 25 July 1808.

[5] Add. MS. 34457, f. 435 ; Holland, *Further Memoirs*, p. 14. Brougham
thought the Grenvilles too gloomy : *Brougham and his early Friends*,
ii. 314.

[6] Windsor Arch., George IV, Moira to McMahon, 9 Sept. 1808,
where the rumour of the Duke of York's going out is lamented on
account of the Duke's anti-Catholic bias. *Morning Chronicle*, 18 July

Morning Chronicle repudiated as "mercantile" and ungenerous the suggestion that the Spaniards should hand
over a fortress (*e.g.* Cadiz) in pledge to us ;[1] though later
their refusal to do so was made the basis of a charge of
ingratitude. The *Morning Chronicle,* indeed, entertained
the most extravagant hopes. Our 30,000 men in Portugal,
after subduing that country, should be moved, not to
Spain, which had no need of them, but to Italy, where
they were to assist Austria and simultaneously effect
Italian unity.[2]

The news of the Convention of Cintra shocked the
enthusiasts into a closer connection with reality. Curiously
enough, there was no rioting ;[3] but popular opinion was
profoundly moved. Its expression varied from the heavy
splendour of Wordsworth's *Tract* to the rather cheap
remark of Erskine that henceforward humiliation should
be spelled Hewmiliation. Immediate criticism fastened
rather unfairly on the defects of the Convention and
ignored its undoubted advantages, perhaps owing to Sir
Hew's carelessness in delaying the sending of dispatches
to England, so that the first news came from the Portuguese, who naturally made the worst of the case.[4] But the
Morning Chronicle, though stunned at first,[5] rallied to
make some very pertinent remarks about the conduct of
the expedition :

If Sir Arthur Wellesley was a proper person to conduct the
expedition, why was he superseded ? If Sir Harry Burrard was an

1808, for the suggestion of Dalrymple ; Add. MS. 34457, f. 413, Grenville to Auckland : "Lord Chatham (what a choice ! if they knew him
as well as I do !) and his army are destined for Lisbon ".

[1] *Morning Chronicle,* 16 June 1808 ; *Jackson Diaries,* ii. 251.

[2] *Morning Chronicle,* 11 Aug., 9 Sept. 1808.

[3] It was suggested that the fire at Covent Garden distracted the
mob's attention. *Lyttelton Correspondence,* p. 29.

[4] Oman, *Peninsular War,* i. 278.

[5] " One is constantly tempted to believe that it is a dream . . ."
(*Morning Chronicle,* 19 Sept. 1808).

improper person, why was he sent out ? And if Sir Hew Dalrymple was the fittest of the three, why was he not appointed from the beginning ? [1]

It was unfair, however, to attack Sir Arthur's reputation and cast doubts on the merits of his victory at Assaye ; and the Wellesleys seriously contemplated bringing an action for libel in respect of this article.[2]

The fiasco of the Convention was soon to be followed by the unhappy campaign of Moore, whose progress was followed with anxiety as the year drew to its close. In these depressing circumstances there appeared among the Whigs a new division more serious than that upon the question of peace. Should they continue to support the Peninsular venture or no ? To some of them, and above all to Lord Holland, it seemed that to fight for Spain was to fight for light against darkness, liberty against tyranny, Whig principles against despotism. To them it seemed that the Spanish struggle concentrated the issues of the war in such a form that no moral man, and, therefore, no Whig, could refuse his support. If ever events justified a war, they did so here. Dissensions, treacheries, incompetence on the side of the Spaniards, were regrettable (if authenticated) but they were emphatically to be endured. On the other side there was an increasing body of Whig opinion which regarded the Peninsular war as erroneous in principle, and hopeless in fact. From the very beginning, there had been a few Whigs who had stood out against the enthusiasm of the moment, and deprecated inter-ference in the Peninsula. Whitbread, in his *Letter to Lord Holland* of June 1808, while professing to yield to no one in his enthusiasm for the Spanish nation, had opposed the sending of an expedition. True to his pacificism, he proposed to get the French out of Spain by negotiations in

---

[1] *Ibid.* 28 Nov. 1808.
[2] *Ibid.* 14 Oct. 1808 ; Add. MS. 37309, ff. 259 *et seq.*

which England was to make sacrifices sufficient to salve
the Emperor's wounded prestige.[1] And these fantasies
were sympathetically reviewed in the *Edinburgh Review*,
which regarded the breaking-off of the negotiations of
1806 as an occasion

> when the Whigs themselves manifestly deserted their ancient
> tenets, and, betrayed by false hopes of Continental victories, or
> debauched by the enjoyment of power, adopted the language and
> view of their ancient adversaries.[2]

The *Review* despaired of the Continent, and deprecated the
renewal of coalitions or the declaration of war on France
by other powers. There was no hint of appreciation of the
fact that even an unsuccessful war might be a successful
diversion. The *Independent Whig* was even more hostile.
It doubted whether Spain was worth defending ; it hinted
that our only object was further colonial prizes ; and it
tartly remarked that we had much better remember the
starving workers of our own country, and the unfortunates
languishing in our own gaols, than go crusading for an
abject people in a cause of doubtful justice.[3] Such views
were far from popular in the summer of 1808 ; [4] but they
gained strength as affairs in the Peninsula went from bad
to worse, and by the end of the year they were held in
one form or another by a considerable section of the
Whig party. Grenville and Whitbread agreed in this, if in
nothing else, that they deplored the line taken by Lord
Holland and his friends. In some cases the opposition to
the Spanish venture arose from a dislike of interference

---

[1] I have been unable to find this pamphlet. A review appears in
Edinburgh Review, xii. 433 *et seq.*

[2] *Ibid.* 435.

[3] *Independent Whig*, 10 July, 4 Sept. 1808.

[4] *E.g.* Cobbett's attacks : *Political Register*, xiii. 961-965 ; xiv. 386.
Cartwright wrote to Whitbread protesting against his lack of enthusiasm
for a cause so closely connected with Reform. *Ibid.* 110-115.

on the Continent; in some, from a reluctance to approve a
Ministerial policy; in some, from a desire for peace; in
many, from an honest conviction of the hopelessness of
further efforts. For whatever reason adopted, this view of
affairs drove the Whigs who held it into lamentable errors
and indiscretions. It added greatly to their unpopularity;
it compromised them as supporters of democracy; it
accorded ill with their past professions; and, as it turned
out, it put them constantly in the position of seeing their
prophecies confounded by facts.

There was thus a sharp conflict of opinion in the Whig
camp; and it grew ever sharper as it became obvious that
the Spanish war would not be a swift and easy victory.
Brougham, in his famous " Don Cevallos " article in the
Edinburgh Review, warned his readers of the probable
ardours of the contest. But the *Edinburgh Review* in a
single quarter had entirely changed its note. It was no
longer pacifist. It urged vigorous action in the Peninsula,
larger armies, closer coöperation; and though it made
the mistake of considering Portugal irrelevant to the issue
in Spain, it definitely abandoned its former attitude of
insularity. It accepted a Continental System of some sort,
and recommended generous efforts in the common cause.[1]
Brougham's spirit thus rose with adversity; that of the
Grenvilles sank ever lower; that of Auckland lowest of all.
The game was played out, they felt;[2] the "silly notion
that Don Somebody with the peasants of Galicia was to

---

[1] *Edinburgh Review*, xiii. 219-231 ; Aspinall, *Lord Brougham and the
Whig Party*, pp. 19-20, for Brougham's authorship ; Scott, *Letters*, ii.
106, for the effect of the article in Edinburgh.

[2] " Why, dear Lady Holland, do you not come home ? It has been
all over this month. . . . Are you fond of funerals ? Do you love to
follow a nation to its grave ? " Sydney Smith, *Letters*, p. 47, Dec.
1808 ; Cockburn, *Jeffrey*, pp. 193-194; Windsor Arch., George IV, Moira
to McMahon, 2 Nov. 1808 (but see his conflicting opinion in Add. MS.
37888, ff. 102-103). There were times when Brougham was gloomy too.
Life and Times, i. 421-425.

overturn Bonaparte and beat the whole French army commanding all the resources of Europe " was discredited ;[1]
and the Government persisted only in order " to nurse in
the public mind the inconsiderate and womanish enthusiasm to which they have abandoned themselves ". [2]
And Buckingham with sonorous pessimism considered
that " the prospects are closing fast around us ; and the
moments for managements are gone by ".[3]

Ponsonby and Grey continued to the end of the year
to take a more hopeful view, and it was plain that a
considerable section of the party still agreed with them, for
Grey feared that a debate on Spain would cause many
Whigs to rally to the Government.[4] The news of Coruña,
indeed, did something to shake Grey's optimism, but
nevertheless it seemed likely that when Parliament met
in January 1809 the Whig Opposition would not be very
formidable. The Grenvilles, who were more emphatic than
anybody else in the condemnation of the Government's
policy, were too patriotic, and too anxious at the danger
of the country, to desire a factious Opposition.

> The only question [wrote Lord Grenville in December], can be
> what we owe to our own characters in such a moment, and what we
> owe to the country in point of duty, however hopeless. But I feel
> a strong reluctance to these wordy wars, at a moment when the
> country itself has not, perhaps, two years more of existence. . . .
> I am sick of politics, and entertain a most melancholy picture of
> what is to come.[5]

The bulk of the party was solid for the prosecution of the
war in some form—there was little or no support for

---

[1] Add. MS. 34457, f. 491, Grenville to Auckland (about Dec.–Jan.).
Cf. Add. MS. 35648, f. 3, Grenville to Hardwicke, 2 Jan. 1809.

[2] *Dropmore Papers*, ix. 255.

[3] *Ibid.* 282.

[4] *Ibid.* 270 ; Add. MS. 34457, f. 498 (Grey) ; *Dropmore Papers*, ix.
256 (Ponsonby) ; Add. MS. 37906, f. 329 (Windham).

[5] *Court and Cabinets*, iv. 288.

Whitbread in Parliament—but they found themselves quite unable to agree as to what that form should be ; and in consequence, they moved no amendment to the Address. St. Vincent, like Grenville, condemned the theory of continental expeditions ; Ponsonby and Moira, on the other hand, concentrated their attacks on the way in which the expeditions had been carried out.[1] The condition of the party was indeed chaotic : everywhere was indiscipline, disorder, cross-purposes. Grenville advocated a reliance on guerrilla warfare, holding that no regular army which we could produce could face Napoleon's 500,000 ; Ponsonby was for pursuing Elizabeth's methods of succouring the Dutch ; Cochrane desired an amphibious warfare based on Minorca—which would have given his peculiar genius great scope.[2] Both Moira and Ponsonby urged that the proper course would have been to hold the passes of the Pyrenees ; though they simultaneously insisted that Ministers should have taken more time for consideration before venturing an army in Spain at all.[3] The actual delay in sending an army to the Peninsula had not been great ; yet even so, Wellesley found that a landing in the north of Spain had become impracticable owing to the broken state of the insurrection in those parts.[4] How, therefore, we were to have held the Pyrenees—a project at best chimerical—was by no means obvious.

The Whigs were not much happier when they descended from general considerations of strategy to the details of Wellesley's campaign. The public was weary of Cintra, and had half forgotten it ;[5] and the Whigs were not able

[1] *Parl. Deb.* xii. 6, 12, 25, 46.

[2] *Ibid.* 13, 50; *Morning Chronicle*, 21 Jan., 23 Feb. 1809, supporting Cochrane's plan.

[3] *Parl. Deb.* xii. 25, 46 *et seq.* There was a strong feeling that we should have landed at Santander. *Morning Chronicle*, 21 Jan. 1809 ; Add. MS. 37888, ff. 44-45 (Windham). Andalusia and Catalonia were also suggested. Add. MS. 37888, ff. 102, 104.

[4] Oman, i. 227, 228.   [5] *Jackson Diaries*, ii. 345, Jan. 1809.

to fan the embers of its indignation. When the vote of
thanks to Wellesley for the victory of Vimeiro was before
the House, Whitbread made a preposterous demand for the
inclusion of Sir Harry Burrard, who had not come ashore
until the battle was over ; but he found no support for
this amendment, and was ultimately induced to withdraw
it.[1] In the debate on the Convention itself, the Whigs had
decidedly the worse of the argument. Petty, who opened it,
was moderate and reasonable, but he did not succeed in
proving his case. He contended that the Government had
sent an army to Portugal, when they should have sent it
to Spain ; and that it was through the inefficiency of
Ministers that the generals were obliged to conclude the
Convention, since the cavalry and equipment necessary
for a successful pursuit of Junot were lacking. He was
rightly severe upon the preposterous changes in the
command ; but in his comments on the military operations
he was betrayed by ignorance into many blunders.[2] Sir
Arthur Wellesley himself, in a most able speech, completely
refuted his arguments. He showed conclusively that the
question of the ability of the army to move forward after
Vimeiro was never at any time raised as a ground for the
conclusion of the Convention. He made it clear that he
considered that the Government had done their best; and
that the Convention was really the result of Burrard's
refusal to pursue the enemy after Vimeiro, and of Dalrymple's inactivity on the following days. As to the point
of the expediency of conducting a campaign in Asturias
rather than in Portugal, he pointed out that when he
arrived in Galicia in search of information, he found that
although the army of the Asturias had just sustained the
disastrous defeat of Rio Seco, even so the Galicians urged
him to direct his attack on Portugal.[3] Junot's army was

---

[1] *Parl. Deb.* xii. 153.   [2] *Ibid.* 897-917.

[3] *Ibid.* 928-936. Wellesley's comments at the time of Vimeiro bear
out his defence of the Ministry, though he complained of lack of

isolated and comparatively small ; Lisbon was disaffected ; Oporto had already set up a Junta.[1] The Spaniards felt that a British force advancing from Portugal would embarrass the French and form a valuable connecting link between the still uncoördinated Spanish armies of the north and south. Subsequent events proved this reasoning to have been correct in every particular ; but in any case it would have been reasonable when attempting to assist an ally not to ignore his views as to how that assistance could most usefully be rendered. Wellesley's arguments, however, fell on deaf ears. The remaining speeches from the Opposition benches produced no new point, and ignored his refutation of the old ones. An unusually large minority of 153 voted for the motion, but the Government had no difficulty in defeating it by a margin of 50.[2]

The attack of the Whigs upon the Swedish fiasco had more justice, if less success ; for the chief difficulty of Sir John Moore had lain not so much in the mad notions of Gustavus IV as in the weak and impracticable instructions with which he had been sent out. The shabby treatment meted out to Moore by the Ministry made him, in spite of himself, a party man. Though admittedly the most distinguished officer in the army, he had been slighted, passed over, and insulted, probably because he had allowed his contempt for Canning's policy to emerge too clearly.[3] It was in a confused effort to advance Wellesley and jockey Moore that four successive commanders were

cavalry, poor quality of horses, and imperfect Commissariat arrangements. Wellington, *Despatches*, iv. 59, 69, 81, 100-101, 112 ; Fortescue, *History of the British Army*, vi. 215-235.

[1] Oman, i. 206-219.

[2] *Parl. Deb.* xii. 974 ; *Morning Chronicle*, 24 Feb. 1809, analyses the minority, which included 33 county members (including the Irish county members).

[3] Fortescue, *History of the British Army*, vi. ch. xvii ; *Life of Moore*, ii. 104-106, gives his interview with Castlereagh, where he complained of the " unhandsome treatment " to which he had been subjected.

sent to Portugal in 1808 ; [1] and when at last Moore was
sent to command in chief, he was sent, or so it seemed to
his friends, on a mad and impracticable enterprise which
was certain to end in disaster.

> Sir John Moore [wrote Lord Holland] was in habits and opinions
> more connected with the Whigs than with their opponents. He was
> sincerely lamented by that party ; and in vindicating his memory,
> sometimes from reasonable criticism, at others from malevolent
> aspersions, many members of it were hurried into disparaging a
> cause in which they thought he had been sacrificed by Ministers.[2]

It was under the influence of such feelings that
Ponsonby raised the question of Moore's campaign in
the Commons on 24 February. His speech was full of con-
tradictory exhortations, and charges which neutralized
each other. The Government was attacked in the same
breath for its lack of caution and for its lack of promptitude.
" No British force found its way into Spain until all the
Spanish armies had been overthrown, and Madrid had
again capitulated to Bonaparte " : but, apart from the
inaccuracy of the statement, the delay was chargeable
not on the Government, but upon the disturbed state of
Portugal, which kept Dalrymple fully occupied at Lisbon
settling the details of the Regency and carrying out the
terms of the Convention. It is true that he made little
effort to prepare for a march into Spain, in the way of
collecting baggage animals, and ascertaining by personal
investigation the state of the roads to the eastward ; but
that was the fault, not of the Ministry, but of a harassed
and unenterprising officer.[3] Ponsonby again raised the
question of the defence of the Pyrenees, and went so far
as to say that

---

[1] Wellington, *Despatches*, iv. 142-143, gives Wellington's comforting
letter to Moore urging him to ignore slights.

[2] Holland, *Further Memoirs*, p. 25.

[3] Oman, i. 279-290, and see Add. MS. 35647, f. 343, for letter from
Spain complaining of this delay.

if a British army landed at St. Andero [*i.e.* Santander] could be of
no avail for that object, if the French could not, by any effort on
our part, have been shut out from Spain . . . whether that was
not a good reason why a British army should not have been sent
into Spain at all ?

Ponsonby, then, was willing to fight to keep the French
out of Spain, but unwilling to fight to expel them. He
would, in fact, refuse to fight except in what he considered
the most favourable defensive position. If that position
could be turned, or if it proved to have been a figment of
his imagination, the Spaniards might shift for themselves.
He completely failed to realize the essentials of the situation
in Spain. Instead of reprobating Moore's delay at Salamanca,
he demanded to know why he had not retreated from that
place instead of advancing to Sahagun.[1] The best that can
be said for him is that he refrained from the disgraceful
nonsense in which Erskine indulged, in the corresponding
debate in the Lords. Erskine observed that

if His Majesty's ministers' plans had been overpowered by any
unforeseen circumstances, he would have come forward as their
advocate ; but they acted without system, and ran headfore-
most into everything that was wrong ; by which means everything they undertook was defeated, and at the end they would be
lost themselves ; that loss would be but trifling, compared with the
lives of the 35,000 men they had endangered. He was of opinion
that it would have been better for the service of the country, had
the men who lost their lives in the late campaign, been shot in St.
James' Park. The men who were sent to Spain, were sent there to be
massacred, without any prospect of their being able to do any good.[2]

Other Whigs, such as Grey and Whitbread, endeavoured to
fix the blame for what they considered to be a disaster
upon Frere, or upon his ill-chosen agent Charmilly ;[3] but

---

[1] *Parl. Deb.* xii. 1057-1119, for this debate.

[2] *Ibid.* xiv. 169-170.

[3] *Ibid.* 122 *et seq.*, 482. The *Tierney MSS.* contain a curious correspondence (June 1809) between leading Whigs about Charmilly, who
resented their remarks, and tried to call them out. Charmilly had been

none of them showed the slightest appreciation of the fact
that Moore's diversion had in fact saved Spain. Like
Moore himself, they were blind to the futility of marching
to help our ally, and then retreating without having so
much as seen the enemy, upon the mere rumour that the
French army might turn in our direction. They did not
reckon with the damaging effect of such a course upon
our prestige. They neglected the fact that, as Wellington
on another occasion pointed out, a British army on the
Continent acted as a magnet to Napoleon.[1] All they saw
was that we had failed to retreat when retreat might still
have been safe and dignified ; that, on the contrary, we had
waited until the last possible moment to effect an escape
which had been very costly in men and money, and which
had terminated in the death of our most distinguished
commander, and a chancy battle with our backs to our
belated transports. Instead of seeing in our transports, as
Wellington later did, a secure base for all our efforts, they
saw in them a confession of failure. And, estimating the
campaign as a failure, they were led to blame, not their
favourite Moore, who had very nearly made it so, but
Frere, or Castlereagh, or Charmilly. Nor did they realize
that the much-canvassed horrors of the retreat from
Sahagun had been caused in no small degree by Moore
himself, who, in his relentless haste to reach the coast,
neglected to delay the French by rear-guard actions at
several very easily tenable positions, where there would
have been no great danger of bringing on a general action.[2]

Moore's advance might perhaps (though surely fallaciously) be adjudged a concession to political necessity at

usurer-in-chief to the *émigrés* ; and Jackson considered him " a very
dangerous *chap* ". *Jackson Diaries*, ii. 344. Frere, *Works*, i. 99, gives
his point of view.

[1] Wellington, *Despatches*, iv. 129. Moore did not realize this either.
Moore, *Narrative*, App. DD, Moore to Castlereagh, 16 Dec.

[2] Oman, i. 568, 571 ; a correspondent of Windham's in Coruña made
the same criticism. Add. MS. 37888, f. 75.

the expense of military orthodoxy. If the Whigs considered
it in that light, their criticisms become more comprehensible ; and in so far as attention to the political side of the
campaign was the result of pressure from Frere, and from
the Government, they were right in seeking to attach
responsibility to them ; though the determining cause of
Moore's advance was a French dispatch fortuitously inter-
cepted, and not Frere's agent Charmilly. But it is strange
that they should have failed to realize its value as a
diversion. Moore's *Narrative,* which appeared soon after his
death and which was read with indignant interest by
every good Whig, contains the most explicit recognition
by Moore himself that his diversion had achieved its
object :

> The diversion made by our march upon Sahagun, though at a
> great risk to ourselves, has been complete . . . the march of the
> French on Badajoz was stopped when its advanced guard had
> reached Talavera de la Reina ; and everything disposable is now
> turned in this direction.[1]

The *Morning Chronicle* is an exception in its appreciation
of the true facts of the case.[2] Even observers in Spain were
at fault ; the Hollands were furious when Moore retreated,
and Lady Holland, on hearing the news from Coruña,
made the venomous remark that " it required such an end
to redeem his reputation ".[3] No doubt the feeling that the
expedition had been a failure was increased by the currency
which Moore's *Narrative* gave to reports of the apathy and
selfishness of the Spaniards,[4] and also by the unusual sight

---

[1] Moore, *Narrative,* App. EE, p. 301 : to Castlereagh, 28 Dec.; pp.
144-162 give the crisis of the campaign. *Life of Sir John Moore,*
ii. 166-179 ; Oman, i. 540, 542, and Fortescue, vi. 315-321, 395, are
in substantial agreement. We know that Creevey read this *Narrative.*
Creevey, *Life and Times,* p. 43.

[2] *Morning Chronicle,* 12 Jan. 1809.

[3] *The Spanish Journals of Lady Holland,* pp. 233, 280.

[4] Moore, *Narrative, passim* ; Wilkins, *Baird,* pp. 221, 226-227, 241 ;
Add. MS. 35647, f. 334 (letter from Spain to Hardwicke).

of soldiers disembarking in England within a day or two
of a great battle, with all the miseries of the retreat visible
in their ragged, wounded, and emaciated condition.[1]
These things gave ground to the Whigs for attacks on the
Ministers. But it required no ordinary obstinacy to maintain,
as Grey did nine months later, that Moore's campaign had
been of no importance.

It did indeed create a diversion, which drew off Bonaparte with
his main force for three weeks or a month. But being then free from
all uneasiness with respect to any British army, which for the
purposes of the campaign was annihilated, he had *champs libre*
[*sic*] for his further operations against the Spaniards ; and he would
have made short work if he had not been called off by Austria. This,
in truth, was the real diversion.[2]

The Austrian war of 1809 put a new complexion upon
the problem of our military strategy. To those who regarded continental intervention as not bad in itself, but
yet were disinclined to risk another army in Spain, it offered
a possible alternative policy. A diversion in North Germany
was considered by many to be a hopeful venture, in view
of the unrest known to prevail there. Ministers, however,
were not disposed to give up the game in Spain so
soon, and they were rightly dubious as to the prospects
in Germany. They determined, therefore, on a project
long known to previous Ministries, and certainly feared
by Napoleon : the sending of an expedition to the Scheldt
to capture the island of Walcheren, the town of Flushing,
and the fleet of Admiral Missiessy, which was at that time
lying shut up in the river. A large expedition under the
joint command of Lord Chatham and Sir Richard Strachan
failed completely to carry out a project which had always
been dubious, and which unfavourable circumstances had

---

[1] Oman, i. 596-597.
[2] Brougham, *Life and Times*, i. 477, Grey to Brougham, 22 Nov.
1809. The Hollands had now veered to a more charitable opinion of
Moore : *ibid.* 482.

conspired to make impossible. The diversion to assist Austria had failed. Ministers, however, had better fortune in Spain. Wellesley, reappointed to the command, brilliantly justified himself. Taking Oporto in splendid style, he chased Soult pell-mell out of Portugal ; but an advance into Spain which was perhaps a little rash ended in the hard-won victory of Talavera, where he was compelled to leave his wounded to fall into the hands of the enemy.

The Whigs, as was to be expected, were not unanimous in their opinion of the plans for this summer's campaigning. Grey, for instance, would have preferred to concentrate all our energies on the Peninsula rather than dissipate British forces by a diversion really excentric to our strategy.[1] Moira, on the other hand, would have preferred a North German expedition.

Instead of that, you dispatch Sir A. Wellesley to Portugal to drive out of that country a French force which was ordered into it for no other purpose than to induce you thither. You give in to that obvious trap altho' there is not a Common Councilman in London, so much of a Cockney as to judge otherwise, than that the possession of Portugal would be a weight instead of an advantage.[2]

There was undoubtedly a feeling that after the two previous failures it might be unwise to adventure another army into Spain. George III was certainly of that opinion, and he consented to the appointment of so junior an officer as Wellesley only because it was unlikely that any very large force would be entrusted to one so young.[3] Wellesley, indeed, like Moore, became a party question. His connection with the Government had been too close and too recent for it to be otherwise ; and it is, therefore, not surprising that he should have been attacked with less charity

[1] *Tierney MS.* Grey to Tierney, 24 July 1809.
[2] Windsor Arch., George IV, Moira to McMahon, 23 July 1809.
[3] Add. MS. 38243, ff. 168-170, George III to Castlereagh (copy), 3 Oct. 1809.

than had been extended to Moore. The Wellesleys were good friends to the Grenvilles, with whom they kept up a cordial correspondence, and whose influence sometimes averted Parliamentary attacks upon them ;[1] and Sir Arthur was always a favourite of Windham.[2] But when the officers serving under him presented Sir Arthur with a piece of plate, the *Morning Chronicle* was indignant at so tangible an expression of party prejudice.[3] Lord Wellesley too, when he succeeded Frere in Spain, had to contend with a good deal of misrepresentation in the press at home, where he was described as " going through the mummery of dancing upon the French flag " and represented as being ambitious for Spanish titles.[4] If the *Morning Chronicle* did occasionally, in 1809, profess confidence in Sir Arthur as a general, it was only in order to contrast his ability with the ineptitude of the Ministry.[5] The Whigs, therefore, looked sourly on the Spanish campaign of 1809. After blaming Wellesley's long delay in Portugal, they did not scruple to censure him for advancing into Spain :[6]

The testimony of every officer in Lord Wellington's army, who has communicated with his friends, is against the line of conduct which he pursued. He thought only of rapidity, and not of subsistence. He hurried on, outstript his commissariat, forced himself into a predicament from which he could not escape without fighting, and in which he could reap nothing but honour by the sacrifice of one-fourth of his followers.[7]

But many officers were indignant at the despondent tone

[1] *E.g.* on 1 Feb. 1810. Creevey, p. 127 ; *Court and Cabinets*, iv. 421.
[2] Add. MS. 37906, f. 345.
[3] *Morning Chronicle*, 26 March 1809.
[4] Knighton, *Memoirs*, i. 94, 126. Knighton accompanied Lord Wellesley as his physician—his first step to a distinguished career.
[5] *Morning Chronicle*, 26 May 1809.
[6] *Ibid.* 4 Sept. 1809 ; see Wellington, *Despatches*, iv. 443, and especially v. 338-339, for an elaborate defence of his delay.
[7] *Morning Chronicle*, 10 Oct. 1809.

of the English press.[1] Yet Talavera was considered to have
been a mistake even by the Grenvilles. Auckland excelled
himself when, lamenting that the battle should have been
fought, he added :

At the same time, I do not mean to object to the general expediency of annoying the enemy, and of enuring, in times so
perilous, our armies to the energies and usages of warfare.[2]

No doubt the news of the behaviour of Cuesta upon the
occasion greatly contributed to this feeling of depression.
The Whigs were fully informed of the circumstances of the
case through their correspondents in Spain, and news of
Wellington's indignation must have reached them too.[3]
The result was to raise the indignation against the Spaniards,
into which the Whigs who disagreed with Holland had
always been prone to fall, to boiling point. Despite
occasional reports in a contrary sense,[4] the friends of the
Whigs in Spain painted upon the whole a gloomy picture
of Spanish apathy and incompetence. Mistrust of the
Spaniards had always been one of the arguments against
the point of view of Lord Holland. It had led the Whigs to
oppose the making of a treaty with the insurgents.[5] This
attitude had a good deal of justification. There can be no
doubt that the Hollands, for instance, were too sanguine,
and too blind to the weaknesses of the Junta. "I believe he
[Lord Holland] would give the lives of ten English to save
one Spaniard ", observed Sir John Cradock ;[6] and Lord
Paget was hardly exaggerating when he wrote to him :

[1] *E.g. Jackson Diaries*, ii. 492, complaining of *The Times*.
[2] Add. MS. 35648, ff. 125-126, Auckland to Hardwicke, 15 Aug. 1809.
[3] *Court and Cabinets*, iv. 359, 362 (Berkeley and Fremantle) ;
Morning Chronicle, 12 Aug. 1809 ; Wellington, *Despatches*, iv. 497.
[4] Nat. Lib. Wales MS. 4814, f. 41, Henry Wynn to C. Wynn, 9 May
1809 ; Ward, *Letters to " Ivy "*, p. 81.
[5] *Morning Chronicle*, 14 March, 1 April 1809.
[6] *Spanish Journals of Lady Holland*, p. 250 note.

You talk to a parcel of people snug upon the coast, and who, knowing your enthusiasm for the Spanish cause, flatter *your misconceptions* of the state of the country, and from the language of such people you form your judgment of the dispositions of the Spanish nation. *'Tis one not worth saving.* Such ignorance, such deceit, such apathy, such pusillanimity, such cruelty, was never both united. There is not one army that has fought at all. There is not one general who has exerted himself, there is not one province that has made any sacrifice whatever. There is but one town in all Spain that has shown an atom of energy. We are treated like enemies. The houses are shut against us. The resources of the country are withheld from us ; we are roving about the country in search of Quixotic adventures to save our own honor, whilst there is not one Spaniard who does not skulk and shrink within himself at the very name of Frenchman.[1]

It seemed incredible to Grey that, after the experience of Talavera, Holland could still maintain faith in Spain ; [2] and though when Holland came home in the autumn of 1809 he seemed less optimistic, he still irritated the Whigs by using " the same arguments as Ministers ".[3] Holland indeed might argue, as a detached military expert like Pasley argued, that the inefficiency in Spain lay in the Junta and the generals ; that the heart of the common people was sound ; that a more unified organization, in particular a closer connexion with the English general, would largely remedy these evils ; and that at the very worst, the activities of the guerrillas made Spain still incomparably the best field for a Continental expedition.[4] There was a good deal of policy in the Whig views ; a good deal of party tactics ; for they could be oblivious of the shortcomings of Cuesta when it was necessary to decry Wellington.

[1] *Spanish Journals of Lady Holland*, p. 376.
[2] *Life and Times of Brougham*, i. 439 ; *Tierney MSS.* Grey to Tierney, 25 Aug. 1809.
[3] *Tierney MSS.* Grey to Tierney, 21 June 1809.
[4] Pasley, *Military Policy of the British Empire*, p. 196 *et seq.*

After Wellington's retirement into Portugal they affected to consider the enterprise as desperate. It was difficult to conceive what rational object Ministers could have in sending out reinforcements to the Peninsula, for now that Austria had concluded peace, there was no hope that we should be able to maintain a footing there any longer.[1] The *Independent Whig* went further—so far, that Ministers took the Attorney-General's opinion ; but though this proved favourable, it discouraged prosecution. The *Independent Whig* had said :

Viewing the crusades in which the policy of our government are [*sic*] now engaged, but as the frantic and visionary pursuits of treachery and folly, every success which may accompany the valour of our armies we can consider but as HUMAN BUTCHERY, perpetrated for the PERSONAL SPLEEN AND VINDICTIVE RAPACITY of the British Ministry ! [2]

These were not the opinions of the nation, nor were they those of Wellington, who was decidedly of the opinion that Portugal could, and ought to, be defended.[3] Already some officers on his staff had discerned the strength of the Torres Vedras position ; [4] and provided the army could get money and provisions, there seemed no reason to be depressed about the future. It was just here, however, that we came nearest to failure. The correspondence of Wellington is filled with complaints and supplications. He is always short of money, always in debt, very often short of food.[5] The Commissariat, a department to

---

[1] *Morning Chronicle*, 2 Sept., 28 Oct. 1809.

[2] *Independent Whig*, 20 Aug. 1809.

[3] Wellington, *Despatches*, v. 269-270, 310.

[4] *Burghersh Correspondence*, p. 22. Burghersh was *aide* to Wellington.

[5] Wellington, *Despatches*, iv. 279, 280-281, 344, 346, 385, 399, 427, 520 ; v. 386. "It will be better for Government . . . to relinquish their operations . . . if the country cannot afford to carry them on " (*ibid.* iv. 445). "It is not my fault if the British Government have undertaken . . . a larger concern than they can find means to provide for " (*ibid.* 493).

which he always gave particular attention, was but newly
organized, and inefficient : and the transport system was
thoroughly unsatisfactory.[1] The war was costing at this
time not far short of £250,000 per month ; and as yet the
Government had found no Herries and Rothschild to solve
the problem of furnishing so large a sum.[2] If the Whigs had
concentrated their criticisms on these matters ; if they
had kept off tactics and strategy, they would have had an
arguable case against Ministers, and really performed a
useful service. But it was rare for them to make much of
these points : they referred to them, if at all, rather as
supplementary items in the attack on the Government.[3]
And even had they taken this line, they would probably
have overstated their case. Wellington himself generously
recognized the difficulties under which the Government
laboured, and the efforts they were making to assist him :

> . . . acting as I do confidentially with Ministers, and acquainted
> as I am with their means, the employment for them, and the difficulties
> of all descriptions which in these days they have to contend with,
> I should not act fairly by them if I were to speculate in my dispatches
> upon advantages which would result if certain measures were
> adopted, which measures I know it to be out of their power to adopt.[4]

And, even with those scanty means, " the fact is, that the
British army has saved Spain and Portugal during this
year ".[5] Wellington was thankful that he had his friends
Liverpool and Bathurst to support him in the Cabinet,
now that Castlereagh was gone ; and he congratulated

---

[1] *Despatches*, v. 13, 15, 32 ; iv. 285 : " The agent of transports is
the worst hand I have seen of that description ". *Operations in Spain*,
pp. 82-84, emphasizes this, too, and relates how an incompetent and
drunken transport commander mistook England for Guernsey.

[2] *Despatches*, v. 173-175 ; Cunningham, *British Credit in the Napoleonic War*, pp. 9, 70 ; Corti, *Huset Rothschild*, i. 113. In 1810 it cost
£421,500 per month. *Despatches*, vi. 168.

[3] *Morning Chronicle*, 2 March 1809, has a good article on these points.

[4] *Despatches*, v. 326, to Villiers, 6 Dec. 1809.

[5] *Ibid.* 349.

them on having survived the crisis of September 1809.
Perceval's was a weak Government, and its desperate
anxiety to avoid disaster and win cheap successes was a
reflection of its weakness, and was galling to Wellington;
but there can be no doubt that he preferred it to the
negative policy of Grey and Grenville.[1]

That same Cabinet crisis of September had disastrously
delayed the evacuation of Walcheren. There had been a
disposition in some Whigs to look not unfavourably on
the expedition, as being at least a characteristically British
object, and as promising, at any rate temporarily, a cheap
and easy success.[2] When it failed, it was, of course, heavily
damned in the Whig papers; though Lord Moira perversely
held that, failure for failure, Lord Chatham came out
better than Lord Wellington.[3]

Parliament met on 23 January 1810, and immediately
the Opposition began upon Spain and Walcheren. In the
course of the session there were no less than seven debates
on the affairs of the Peninsula, and every conceivable
criticism was brought forward. Broadly, the attacks fell
into two main groups. On the one hand were those which
criticized the conduct of the campaign and the activities
of the Wellesleys; and on the other, those which exculpated
the commander and blamed the policy of the Government.
The attacks on the Wellesleys passed the bounds of decency.
When the vote of thanks to Wellington came up in the
Lords, Suffolk denied that Talavera was a victory;[4] Grey
went even further and affirmed that it was a disaster. After
impugning Wellington's veracity by expressing a preference
for Spanish accounts of the battle, he went on to criticize

[1] Add. MS. 38244, ff. 98-110, Liverpool to Wellington, Dec. 1809;
Despatches, v. 276; vi. 181.
[2] *Morning Chronicle*, 19 July 1809; Brougham, *Life and Times*, i.
444.
[3] Windsor Arch., George IV, Moira to McMahon, 8 Sept. 1809.
[4] *Parl. Deb.* xv. 136.

the general's dispositions with an incautious effrontery which is astonishing.[1] In the debate in the Commons on the same subject, despite the efforts of Ponsonby, the more reckless Whigs got entirely out of hand. Milton's observation that Wellington had merely extricated himself from a scrape into which he should never have got, had some truth in it; but his suggestion that he fought the battle to gain a peerage was disgraceful.[2] Tarleton censured Wellington's dispatches as "vainglorious, partial and incorrect";[3] and Whitbread confessed that he preferred Cuesta's.[4] On this occasion, however, there was no division.

All our indignation against Wellington ended in smoke. Opposition to his thanks was so unpopular, that some of the stoutest of our crew slunk away, or rather, they were dispersed by the indefatigable intrigues of the Wellesleys and the tricks of Tierney. . . .[5]

But on the question of the grant of a pension they did better, and managed to divide 106 in the Commons.[6] Even then the rancour of the extremists was not satisfied, and Creevey and Waithman drew up a petition against Wellington's annuity which Waithman managed to carry in the Common Council, and which was actually received by the House of Commons, to Creevey's great satisfaction.[7] The only temperate and sensible remark uttered upon this question came from Lord Grosvenor, who pointed out that the thanks of the Houses were becoming cheapened by being granted for actions of less than the first importance.[8]

---

[1] *Parl. Deb.* xv. 140.

[2] *Ibid.* 280. Cochrane's attack on the pensions of the Wellesleys was among the most effective. On the basis of pensions for injured seamen he assessed Wellington's pension as = 426 pairs of lieutenants' legs : and Arden's as = 1022 captains' arms. Fortescue, *Dundonald*, p. 90.

[3] *Parl. Deb.* xv. 287.

[4] *Ibid.* 297. But he had done his best to stop the amendment being made. *Court and Cabinets*, iv. 421.

[5] Creevey, p. 167.

[6] *Parl. Deb.* xv. 467.

[7] Creevey, pp. 130-131.

[8] *Parl. Deb.* xv. 137.

The other half of the Whigs declined to blow upon Talavera. Windham compared it to Crécy ; and Grenville paid his more sober tribute.[1] It was the system of continental expeditions, not the actions of our commanders, that aroused his reprobation. And if we must act in Spain, he urged again that the true policy would have been to hold the line of the Pyrenees ; though it is not clear how he reconciled this theory with his remark a little earlier, that it had become useless in modern warfare to defend mountain barriers.[2] On the major question, that of hostility to expeditions, Lansdowne fully agreed with him.[3] So, too, did Whitbread, but with a peculiar emphasis of his own. To him, expeditions were " gladiatorial exhibitions " which unduly delayed the conclusion of peace.[4] There were not found many to concur with him in this view ; but there were very many who condemned the Peninsular war on the ground that Portugal was indefensible against an army securely based on Spain. Tarleton was insistent upon this point, and so was Moira ;[5] while to Newport the enterprise was " hopeless ", to Curwen " absurd ", to Bankes " romantic ".[6] There can be no doubt as to whence the Whigs derived this conviction.

The great disadvantage under which I labour [wrote Wellington in April] is that Sir John Moore, who was here before me, gave an opinion that this country could not be defended by the army under his command. . . . I have as much respect as any man can have for the opinion and judgment of Sir John Moore ; and I should mistrust my own, if opposed to his . . . But he positively knew nothing of Portugal.[7]

It was the old story of party generals. The Whigs believed

---

[1] Tarleton, *Substance of a Speech*, 1810, pp. 15-16.
[2] *Parl. Deb.* xv. 514.   [3] *Ibid.* 532.   [4] *Ibid.* 84 *et seq.*
[5] Tarleton, *Substance of a Speech*, pp. 12-15; *Parl. Deb.* xv. 530.
[6] *Ibid.* xvi. 9 ***, 11 ***, 9 ****.
[7] Wellington, *Despatches*, vi. 5. Moore's opinion in Wilkins, *Baird*, p. 245.

Moore because he was a Whig, and because Wellington was a Tory. They had, of course, some justification. They could not foresee Torres Vedras. They could not know that, when Wellington talked of defending Portugal, he meant, in reality, defending Lisbon. If they meant that the frontier of Portugal was indefensible, they spoke no more than the truth. Wellington himself had written :

There are so many entrances into Portugal, the whole country being frontier, that it would be very difficult to prevent the enemy from penetrating ; and it is probable that we should be obliged to confine ourselves to the preservation of that which is most important, the capital.[1]

Nevertheless it was not until the very end of the session that the Whigs produced a criticism of the campaign in Spain that was worthy of serious consideration. It came, characteristically, from the moderate and sensible Lansdowne, and it combined both branches of the Whig attack. Lansdowne made three strong points : the rashness of the advance into Spain ; the shortage of food supplies ; and the folly of trusting Cuesta.[2] With regard to the first point, he was substantially in the right. As to the Commissariat, the Talavera campaign presented extraordinary conditions which took the French, no less than Wellington, by surprise ; and at the end of it each army was equally near starvation.[3] As to the trusting of Cuesta, the charge was an anachronism. Most of the accusations against that general took their rise from his conduct while co-operating with Wellington on this very campaign. There was nothing more damnatory against him before that junction took place than a strong suspicion of incapacity, and the reputation of being hostile to the Cortes—which latter was,

[1] *Despatches*, v. 89.   [2] *Parl. Deb.* xvii. 471 *et seq.*
[3] Fortescue, *History of the British Army*, vii. 288 : " the campaign of Talavera came to an end simply and solely from want of food ". See *Despatches*, vi. 127, on the novelty of the Commissariat service in the British army.

perhaps, not altogether a bad recommendation. Moreover, he was the only Spanish general with whom Wellington could possibly be expected to coöperate ; and if we were to refuse coöperation altogether, it would be better to leave the country at once and turn our attention once more to " filching sugar islands ".

The debates on the Talavera campaign were much resented in the Peninsula.[1] Wellington was hurt by the suggestion that he was willing to sacrifice his men for the sake of his personal glory—a suggestion so grotesquely inaccurate that only a very mean man, or a very stupid one, would have made it.

> The state of opinion in England is very unfavourable to the Peninsula. The ministers are as much alarmed as the public, or as the Opposition pretend to be ; and they appear to be of opinion that I am inclined to fight a desperate battle which is to answer no purpose.[2]
>
> Depend upon it, whatever people may tell you, I am not so desirous as they imagine of fighting desperate battles ; if I was, I might fight one any day I please.[3]

These persistent and ungenerous attacks on the commander were particularly unfortunate in that they not merely irritated Wellington (that he could bear well enough), but frightened the Government. A disaster in Spain, on top of Walcheren, might be the end of them ; and, consequently, they tried to limit Wellington's activities (the financial situation had already limited his resources) to something " safe and cheap ".

> The government are terribly afraid that I shall get them, and myself, into a scrape. But what can be expected from men who are beaten in the House of Commons three times a week ? A great deal might be done now, if there existed in England less party and more public sentiment, and if there was any government.[4]

---

[1] *Burghersh Correspondence*, p. 41. At home also : see " Britannicus ", *Letter to Whitbread*, pp. 6-10, comparing him to Hanno attacking Hannibal   [2] *Despatches*, vi. 48.   [3] *Ibid.* 8.   [4] *Ibid.* 21.

If Wellington had been a less courageous, or a less generous, commander, he could, without difficulty, have transferred the odium from his own shoulders to those of the Government ; but he preferred to bear the burden of criticism rather than to witness the fall of the only Administration that could afford reasonable security for the successful prosecution of the war by the only method which seemed likely to have any effect upon our adversary.[1]

The effect of the Walcheren expedition had been fatal only to ourselves ; and it was with the Walcheren expedition that the Opposition mainly concerned itself during this session. It afforded them an opportunity for attack which could hardly have been bettered. It marked the climax of their efforts to overthrow the weak Government of Perceval. On 26 January they had scored their first success, when, with the assistance of Lord Castlereagh, they carried a motion for a Committee of Enquiry into the expedition.[2] On 23 February Whitbread followed this up by moving that Lord Chatham's narrative should be produced. It had just been established that Chatham had handed in a memorandum to the King, without the knowledge of his colleagues, and had subsequently had it returned to him in order that he might incorporate into it his more mature thoughts upon certain points. Whether this was unconstitutional (as the Whigs contended) or no, it was in every point of view highly undesirable, and Whitbread was right to press for the production of the document in the House. He was rewarded for his pertinacity with a majority of seven (178–171).[3] On 2 March, pursuing the subject

---

[1] *Despatches*, v. 413 : " . . . I will neither endeavour to shift from my own shoulders on those of the Ministers the responsibility for the (possible) failure . . . nor will I give to the Ministers, who are not strong . . . an excuse for withdrawing the army from a position which . . . the honour and interest of the country require they should maintain as long as possible ".

[2] *Parl. Deb.* xv. 161–210 ; Creevey, p. 124.

[3] *Parl. Deb.* xv. 587. A weak Ministerial division, rather than a strong Opposition.

further, he moved two resolutions, one declaratory of the facts, the other censuring Chatham's conduct in that he " did unconstitutionally abuse the privilege of access to his sovereign ".[1] He had no difficulty in carrying his first resolution ; but he waived the second in favour of an amendment of Canning's, which declared Chatham's conduct reprehensible, and deserving of censure. This, too, was carried without a division.[2] It was, therefore, with a lively expectation of victory that the Whigs prepared for Lord Porchester's resolutions, which were shortly to be debated in the Commons. The occasion was recognized as crucial for the Government. If they should be beaten, resignation was considered certain. Whitbread, curiously enough, was insistent that the resolutions should not be " pared down to try to catch votes " ; an unnecessary austerity which irritated some of his colleagues.[3]

On 26 March Lord Porchester moved his resolutions in a lengthy speech. There were two sets of them—fifteen in all ; but they were all of a declaratory nature except the last, which censured the Government, and the eighth, which asserted that " The expedition to the Scheldt was undertaken under circumstances which afforded no rational hope of adequate success ".[4] Porchester's speech was a complete *exposé* of the rashness and ignorance which had caused the disaster. He rightly laid the blame for the failure upon the Government, who had set their servants an impossible task. He showed that it was the initial tardiness of Ministers rather than the sluggishness of Lord Chatham that had spoilt our best chance ; he quoted the very unfavourable opinions of the five military experts consulted by the Cabinet and he demonstrated that there had been no precisely determined general plan of campaign.

[1] *Ibid.* xvi. 7*.
[2] *Ibid.* 12*. *Commons Journals*, lxv. 147.
[3] *Dropmore Papers*, x. 20 ; Creevey, p. 118.
[4] *Parl. Deb.* xvi. 79.

He also animadverted with just severity upon the disgraceful lack of medical precautions, and upon the fatal delay in effecting the evacuation of the island. Ministers could make no adequate reply. They could indeed plead that considerable damage had been done to the enemy, and they could urge that the very late diversion to Walcheren had Austria's full approval. But on the main question of culpability the Whigs had an impregnable case. Not Sir Richard Strachan, nor even the nervous and unconstitutional Lord Chatham, was to blame, but the men who had devised and dispatched the expedition, and they alone.[1] But, unluckily for the Whigs, the chief of these—Lord Castlereagh—was already out of office, and had been so for nearly six months. The accident of the long summer vacation told once again for the Tories. Perceval did not have to meet a Cabinet crisis while Parliament was sitting ; and by the time the session began, he was seated rather more securely in the saddle. Moreover, as in the case of Cintra, popular indignation was no longer at fever-heat. And, somehow or other, the Whigs bungled their case. When the crucial divisions were taken on 30 March, the Whigs were beaten by majorities ranging from 51 to 23 (275–227 ; 272–232 ; 275–224 ; 255–232).[2] The disappointment was overwhelming. To many it seemed to mark the nadir of the Whigs as a political party.[3] They had had almost every factor in their favour—a good case, strong allies in Parliament, even stronger popular support outside it—yet even so they could not win a single division. The fact is eloquent of the distrust which the Whigs had brought upon themselves among the unattached members of Parliament ; and to this distrust, their attitude to the Peninsular war and their undisciplined state in the House of Commons, had largely contributed. The behaviour of a

---

[1] Fortescue, *History of the British Army*, vii. 93-96, endorses, for once, the Whig view.

[2] *Parl. Deb.* xvi. 421-422.   [3] Ward, *Letters to " Ivy "*, p. 98.

conscientious man like. Wilberforce is a good criterion.
Wilberforce voted steadily against the Government on the
Walcheren enquiry, until on 30 March, in the final division,
he turned round and voted for them.[1] The figures, too, are
eloquent. For censuring the retention of Walcheren, the
Whigs had 224 against 275 ; opposing a motion approving
the retention of Walcheren, they had 232 against 253.
There were, therefore, a good many members who were
unwilling to approve the expedition, but were still more
unwilling to censure it. For this reluctance, as for Wilberforce's behaviour, there can be only one explanation :
the majority of independent members preferred to take the
chance that Walcheren would be a salutary lesson to
the Government, than to risk putting the country into the
hands of a party that had neither policy, nor prospect of
uniting upon one, nor ability to carry it out.[2]

Nevertheless the Walcheren division was considered
disgraceful to the House of Commons. Before the question
had been decided, the *Edinburgh Review* had written that
in the event of a Government majority, " we will venture
to predict, not that the Government is acquitted, but that
the Parliament stands condemned".[3] The extreme Reformers
were almost gratified at a result which gave such force to
their arguments. Even a moderate like Lord Holland
could write :

It was the strongest practical argument ever furnished for a
reform of Parliament ; for the House of Commons on that disgraceful occasion spoke neither the sense of the people whom it
represented, nor even of the individuals who composed its body.[4]

And the editorial detachment of the *Annual Register* was
abandoned, to describe it as an " insult to the people ".

[1] Wilberforce, *Life*, iii. 442.
[2] Ranby, *An Inquiry into the supposed increase of the influence of
the Crown*, p. 54, makes this point well.
[3] *Ap. Political Register*, xvii. 518.
[4] Holland, *Further Memoirs*, p. 47.

The Whigs invented all sorts of explanations of their failure. Some considered that Ponsonby's inadequate leadership and his attempts to push Brougham into the background were really responsible ;[1] others, that the Whigs had not succeeded in proving their case.[2] The *Morning Chronicle* accused the Ministers of using Burdett's case to hinder the enquiry, and rather glumly suggested petitions to Parliament in protest at its result.[3] But the true reason was hit by Ward when he wrote, " The truth is that the country is outrageously against them, and that it prefers anything to the Grenvilles ".[4] And two years later a now regenerate Milton admitted that it was so.[5]

The session was wound up by Grey's resolutions of 13 June. Their object was

to recapitulate the dangers of the country ; to expose the rashness of our policy . . . and to record the public principles of himself and his friends, by marking on one hand, the difference between the system he recommended and that pursued by the Government, and on the other, a line of separation between himself and those reformers who were for circumscribing the powers of Parliament as well as altering fundamentally the basis of the representation.[6]

It was, in fact, an attack on all those leading principles which had constituted the basis of Pitt's Government.[7] But the tone with respect to the war was remarkably firm. All present prospect of peace was acknowledged illusory. Continental interests were repudiated, continental expeditions condemned ; the country was urged to rally to exclusively British interests, foremost among which was the defence of our shores from invasion.[8] Grey's attitude

---

[1] Holland, *Further Memoirs*, p. 46 ; Ward, *Letters to " Ivy "*, p. 98.
[2] *Court and Cabinets*, iv. 430.
[3] *Morning Chronicle*, 28 March, 5 April 1810.
[4] Ward, *Letters to " Ivy "*, p. 99.
[5] *Parl. Deb.* xxiii. 150, 8 May 1812.
[6] Holland, *Further Memoirs*, p. 54.
[7] *The Wellesley Papers*, ii. 16.   [8] *Parl. Deb.* xvii. 535 *seq.*

is noteworthy, for outside Parliament the agitation for
peace, which had died down in 1809, was reviving a little,
and Roscoe, Jeffrey, and Leigh Hunt all supported it.[1]
But Grey was beginning to move gradually towards a
recantation, though it did not actually come until 1811.
This session of 1810 was the last in which the Whigs undertook frontal attacks upon the military policy of the Government. Afterwards there were criticisms in abundance, but
hardly a single division; and the criticisms were usually
confined to matters of detail. If the Grenvilles clung
tenaciously to the idea that operations in the Peninsula
were based upon a fallacy, they refrained from challenging
the Government upon it; and for the most part confined
their lamentations to their private correspondence. It is
to this, then, rather than to the debates in Parliament,
that we must turn for the essence of Whig opinion in the
following two years. The party, of course, remained as
divided as ever upon this as upon nearly every subject.
Horner and Holland were still zealous for larger armies and
greater efforts; the *Morning Chronicle* still hankered after
sugar islands; and the peace party was still in existence.[2]
Yet there was a certain fluidity as between the three
groups; a tendency for Grey and the *Morning Chronicle*,
in spite of grievous relapses, to approximate to the
position of Holland, to criticize the Government, not the
general, and to reprobate lack of success, rather than
misguided aims.

Wellington's campaign of 1810 was very disappointing
to those at home who saw only the results, without taking

[1] *Examiner*, 7 Oct. 1810; Roscoe, i. 482; Roscoe, *Brief Observations*,
p. 14; Cockburn, *Jeffrey*, pp. 189-192. Scott wrote to Southey: "What
do you think of Roscoe's mean-spirited pamphlet ... ? I always thought
that man over-rated, but he seems to have grown actually silly" (Scott,
Letters, ii. 474).

[2] Horner, ii. 68-75, to Jeffrey, 18 Jan. 1811; Cockburn, *Jeffrey*, p.
187; *Morning Chronicle*, 14 Feb. 1811 (on the capture of the Isle-de-
France).

into account the means with which they were achieved.
If the Whigs had been indignant at Talavera, they were
depressed by Wellington's retreat, and by the loss of
Ciudad Rodrigo. The year marked, perhaps, the lowest
point in our fortunes in the Peninsula. There was serious
talk of withdrawal early in the summer, and it had already
been suggested that Wellington should replace Minto in
India. In May there was a great quarrel between Perceval
and Wellesley, because Wellington was not getting the
financial support that his brother considered essential ;
and Wellington himself wrote sharply to Liverpool on this
point.[1] But by November all these difficulties had been
surmounted and, although the financial crisis was approaching its peak, Liverpool was able to give the fullest
assurance of the Government's support.[2] The gradual
revelation of the strategy of Torres Vedras may have
contributed to increase the confidence of the home Government ; but to the Whigs it appeared a very doubtful
expedient. There now appears for the first time, behind the
Whig criticisms of the war, a new military expert. They
had listened to Moira, and they had consulted Dumouriez ;
but they now obtained an opinion from someone who
had actually been in the Peninsula and professed expert
knowledge of the conditions there—Sir Robert Wilson.
The long series of letters which he wrote to Lord Grey
begins to be of importance in the autumn of 1810. In these
letters he deploys his military knowledge in a generous
manner for the benefit of the layman, eschewing false
modesty, imagination, and charity. For Grey he drew maps
of Portugal, better, as he observed, than any maps he
would be likely to buy ; and with these as a basis he systematically criticized Wellington's operations, at an interval
of about a fortnight after they had taken place. It took

---

[1] Add. MS. 38245, f. 131 ; *Despatches*, v. 523 ; Wellington, *Supplementary Despatches*, vii. 262.

[2] Add. MS. 38245, ff. 284-286.

him a curiously long time to realize what Wellington's intentions were; and when he did so he had but little confidence in the Torres Vedras position.[1] Other military men agreed with him—Dumouriez and Moira in particular.[2] The *Morning Chronicle* praised Wellington's retreat, and even congratulated him on the victory of Busaco; but its hopes were still far from high, and it closed the year predicting disaster.[3]

The retreat of Masséna in the spring of 1811 confounded the critics, who then turned their attention to complaints of Wellington's neglect to pursue the French, and harry them out of Portugal.[4] But the carpings of the Whigs were growing unpopular with the nation. The *Morning Chronicle* ruefully admitted it.[5] An independent gentleman of Lower Berkeley Street, Manchester Square, commented on this fact to Sir Charles Hastings:

I hear little or nothing of a change of Ministers, and I think the present people are much stronger in public opinion than they ever were, and that their dismissal will be now far from popular. This is my reluctant opinion. Every prediction on the part of the Opposition with respect to the issue of the campaign—that we should lose our whole army, be obliged to embark in six weeks, etc., etc.,—said much too heedlessly and too frequently, has been successively refuted by the event, and given people a poor opinion of their sagacity, while the others triumph over them and with some reason.[6]

Coleridge in the *Courier* baited them unmercifully, charged

---

[1] Add. MS. 30118, ff. 10, 23, 38-39, 40-41, 50, 58, and especially ff. 62-63, 73.

[2] *Hastings Papers*, iii. 284; *Dropmore Papers*, x. 64; also J. Willoughby Gordon's opinion, Add. MS. 38738, f. 62. Other Whig opinions in Add. MS. 34458, f. 124 (Grenville); Nat. Lib. Wales MS. 4814, f. 51 (Wynn).

[3] *Morning Chronicle*, 16, 20, 26 Oct., 13 Nov., 13, 29 Dec.; see, too, Moira in *Hastings Papers*, iii. 286, approving Busaco.

[4] Windsor Arch., George IV, Moira and Northumberland to McMahon, 8 and 9 April.

[5] *Morning Chronicle*, 7 March 1811.   [6] *Hastings Papers*, iii. 288.

them with rejoicing at our disasters in Spain, and remarked
that it was observable " that the *Morning Chronicle* seems
never to conceive the possibility of any accidents occurring
to Buonaparte, as thinking him, perhaps, especially
entitled to the favour and protection of Providence ".[1]
The *Morning Chronicle* was ruffled by these and similar
attacks, and replied, in the style of the *Eatanswill Independent* :

> . . . we hear the breath of corruption blowing the stigma of dis-
> affection through the halfpenny trumpet of a hacknied scribe,
> and endeavouring to brand the most truly independent men . . .
> with the vilest imputations of joy at the success, and sorrow at
> the discomfiture of sanguinary despotism. This subject would be
> pursued, were it possible to conceive that one rational man in the
> community could be influenced by such noxious, and at the same
> time such impotent ribaldry, which unites the coarseness of a fish-
> woman to the spite of a eunuch.[2]

The *Morning Chronicle* might indeed feel itself aggrieved,
for it had honestly rejoiced at Wellington's success against
Masséna.[3] The popular enthusiasm for the war was being
communicated to the more refined Whig minds by the
cold ratiocination of Captain Pasley, whose great work
on the *Military Policy of the British Empire* had just run
into a second edition, and was having an immense effect on
thinking men. " A fearful work ", Crabb Robinson called
it ; [4] and its demonstration of the necessity of concentrating
our efforts on some single aim, and that the aim to which
our resources were most suited, did much to swing the
waverers, and those intellectuals who always mistrust
popular policies, to a support of the war in the Peninsula.

Perhaps it was Pasley's work that converted Grey in

[1] Coleridge, *Essays*, pp. 842, 886-887.
[2] *Morning Chronicle*, 22 April 1811.
[3] *Ibid*. 16 April 1811. The Grenvilles lamented, indeed, the warlike
tone of the paper. *Dropmore Papers*, x. 129.
[4] Crabb Robinson, *MS. Diary*, i. 25.

the spring of 1811 ; for he certainly seems to have thrown off the influence of Wilson for a short time. By whomever prompted, on 26 April, the occasion of the vote of thanks to Wellington for the delivery of Portugal, he made what was in effect a public recantation. He admitted that he had been mistaken in his doubts as to the policy of a campaign in Portugal, he paid generous tribute to Wellington's abilities, and he added that he believed that Portugal was now secure. He confessed " that if we continued to be left as principals in the war of the Peninsula, he much doubted, still, the chances of our being ultimately successful " ; but upon the whole, the speech represented a complete *volte-face*, and was honestly recognized by Grey to be so.[1] And Auckland, of all men, declared his agreement with it.[2] Grenville was still obstinate, and would have preferred to devote the money that was to be sent to Portugal to balancing the Irish Budget ; he had, however, little support, and when a Bill to provide relief for the inhabitants of Portugal was introduced, it met with almost unanimous Whig approval.[3]

Yet the criticism and carping continued ; less violently, perhaps, than of old, but still in a considerable stream. Both Sir Robert Wilson and Willoughby Gordon spread rumours of a probable evacuation of Portugal, at a time when the private correspondents of the Whigs were taking an exceptionally favourable view of our prospects.[4] And Wilson blamed Wellington for estimating the French force in Spain too low ; though the Whigs had always accused him of estimating it too high in order to add to his own glory.[5] Wilson was sometimes ridiculously perverse. Thus he wrote to Grey on 29 August :

---

[1] *Parl. Deb.* xix. 766-768.   [2] Add. MS. 34458, f. 225.
[3] *Parl. Deb.* xix. 450 *et seq.*, 747, 757.
[4] Add. MS. 30118, f. 108 (Wilson) ; Add. MS. 38738, ff. 83-85 (Gordon) ; *Court of the Regency*, i. 92, 112-113 (Admiral Berkeley and Sydenham).   [5] Add. MS. 30118, f. 118.

The possession of Lisbon is a great disadvantage to the general cause under all the circumstances of its maintenance. If the enemy acquired it by voluntary cession, and if we threw 10,000 men into Peniche, it would require near 30,000 men to preserve it, and this diminution of force would enable us to contend successfully with the residue, whilst Lisbon would be of no real value to the enemy. I consider that position as a kind of trap for the profitless employment of whatever troops are sheltered there.[1]

Such a letter implies that the writer had not grasped that Lisbon meant far more to us than to the French, and that we could hold it far more easily than they could. For a power that controlled the sea, it was an ideally easy place to defend, as Torres Vedras proved. To the French, admittedly, it would be something of a burden, being so far away from the centre of French power, and so liable to have its communications with Spain interfered with. But to deny its value to us was foolish. Apart from its admirable value as the starting-point of all roads to Spain ; apart, too, from its value as a naval base—which would have made it a nuisance in French hands—it was essential to preserve Lisbon, if we were to retain the assistance of Portugal. The old commander of the Lusitanian Legion should have been better able to estimate the effect on our Portuguese allies of such a surrender of their interests. Sir Robert's fantasies would hardly be worth discussion, if it were not that he was constantly pouring such stuff into Grey's ear, and that Grey trusted his judgment above Wellington's. He was, in fact, a new Moore. He elaborately worked out campaigns whereby Marmont was to drive Wellington back to Lisbon, and take Oporto ; but he always assumed that Wellington would be utterly passive, and that no Frenchman ever made a mistake.[2] The *Morning Chronicle* was on safer ground in criticizing the operations of the summer and autumn, which certainly failed to pro-

---

[1] Add. MS. 30118, ff. 125-126.
[2] Add. MS. 30118, f. 155.

duce the results for which Wellington had hoped. " The
laurels of Britain have undoubtedly received some additional wreaths, yet the main pillar of all true military glory
has been wanting, namely, utility." As regards Albuera,
this remark is just ; and even as regards Fuentes de Oñoro
it is intelligible, for Fuentes is still a matter for controversy, and was certainly not one of the more classic of
Wellington's victories.[1] Yet to say that " it is even to be
lamented that Lord Wellington was induced to quit his
lines at Torres Vedras ", was to spoil an arguable case
through exaggeration. Wellington's campaign of 1811 can
only be fairly criticized in the light of his campaigns of
1812 and 1813 ; it was a preliminary essay which failed for
lack of means. Even so, it is difficult to see how the
Morning Chronicle could have justified an expensive
passivity in the neighbourhood of Lisbon ; and it is certain
that if Wellington had adopted such a policy he would
have been bitterly assailed in the Whig press.[2]

The lightning-stroke at Ciudad Rodrigo, in January
1812—" conceived and executed in a manner truly
Wellingtonian "[3]—took the Whig critics by surprise.
Wilson—whose description of the place as " an almost
untenable town . . . that ought to have been carried by
assault on the second night or day " was accepted by
the *Morning Chronicle*[4]—was reduced to minimizing the
achievement by comparing it with Suchet's capture of
Valencia ; and most of the Whigs took this line. To Wilson it
was a mere " trophy " which Wellington should have taken
sooner.[5] The *Morning Chronicle* gravely suggested that the
French had allowed us to take it, in order that we should

---

[1] Fortescue, *History of the British Army*, viii. 174, considers that it
was fought to cheer up the English public ; and Oman, *Peninsular War*,
iv. 343-348, though he justifies it, quotes many hostile verdicts.

[2] *Morning Chronicle*, 17 Sept. 1811.

[3] *Barnard Letters*, p. 203.

[4] *Morning Chronicle*, 14 Feb. 1812.   [5] Add. MS. 30119, ff. 6-8.

waste our forces garrisoning it ;[1] and Auckland decided that the affair of Ciudad Rodrigo, in the opposite scale to Valentia and Blake's army, bears at best the proportion of an ounce to a pound, and a few weeks will prove it too plainly. In the meantime those who wish to deceive themselves and others will be in a fool's paradise.[2]

It was Auckland, however, who was living in a fool's paradise. The taking of Badajoz drove home the lesson of Ciudad Rodrigo—that the Portuguese, and not the Andalusian front, was to decide the fate of King Joseph. The *Morning Chronicle* had not anticipated an attack on Badajoz.[3] Wilson was confounded by it, and for the first time began to ask himself whether he had not been wrong about Wellington.[4] Reports from Spain spoke in terms of confidence of the issue ;[5] and when at last the place fell, the *Morning Chronicle* had no word of criticism to utter.[6] Grey, however, was pessimistic : he considered that all this expense of blood and treasure was fruitless.[7] And Auckland assured him, on the strength of private communications from Portugal, that Wellington had neither men, nor money, nor provisions, and that, in short " that game is up ".[8] One consolation the Whigs had at this time : they saw that the Government was undertaking more seriously that scheme of diversions on the Asturian and Catalonian coast which they had always pressed upon it.[9]

---

[1] *Morning Chronicle*, 14, 15 Feb. 1812.

[2] *Dropmore Papers*, x. 205 ; see too *Examiner*, 9 Feb. 1812 ; Nat. Lib. of Wales MS. 2791, C. Wynn to H. Wynn, 10 Feb. 1812.

[3] *Morning Chronicle*, 27 Jan., 16 March 1812.

[4] Add. MS. 30119, ff. 23-26.

[5] *Milne Home Papers*, p. 154 ; *Dropmore Papers*, x. 232.

[6] *Morning Chronicle*, 25 April 1812.

[7] *Dropmore Papers*, x. 244 ; compare Auckland : " The war in the Peninsula continues in all the activity of a corroding cancer, the mischief of which will never be acknowledged till too late to be remedied " (*ibid.* 285).   [8] *Ibid.* 249.

[9] *Morning Chronicle*, 12 July 1812 ; Horner, ii. 114 ; Oman, v. 336-340, 548 *et seq.*

Wellington was now in Spain, playing his exciting game with Marmont, and was soon to overthrow him at Salamanca. In these circumstances, when a victory might be expected, the *Morning Chronicle* refrained from cavil at the allusion to the affairs of the Peninsula in the Regent's speech at the close of the session.[1] And when at last the news of Salamanca arrived, it gave way to a generous outburst of enthusiasm, unspoilt by reservations, and urged that Wellington be made a field-marshal in order to give him undisputed precedence in Spain.[2] Grey, too, was pleased;[3] and Thomas Grenville showed unusual grasp of the position when he remarked that Wellington's danger lay in a junction of Soult and the remnants of Marmont's army.[4] The mysterious informant who passed political gossip on to the Marquis of Buckingham still retailed preposterous untruths about Wellington's situation, and the lack of support for his efforts by the home Government;[5] but criticism of Wellington himself almost ceased. Only Lord Moira made ungenerous attempts to belittle Salamanca :

Persuaded as I am that the armies opposed to Lord Wellington were always very short in numerical force of that which he

[1] *Morning Chronicle*, 30 July 1812.

[2] *Ibid.* 17, 18 Aug. 1812.

[3] *Dropmore Papers*, 292.

[4] *Ibid.* 290. Auckland's comment is typical: " Marmont's unaccountable folly has given a fortunate brilliancy to Lord Wellington's campaign, which was leading to a lame and impotent conclusion " (*ibid.* 293) : true, but unkind !

[5] *Court of Regency*, i. 385 : " Lord Wellington does not hesitate charging this unpromising aspect of things, not only upon the ill-judged economy of Ministers, who have crippled him, but also upon the failure of the expedition to Catalonia, which your Lordship will hear with indignation and surprise, has actually been stopped by orders from the present wretched Ministers. It is true, they have, since things have taken the present turn, ordered it to go on again,—but the moment—even the season—for efficient co-operation has been wantonly thrown away; . . ." All this is quite untrue. See Oman, v. 558 *seq.*, for the Valencian diversion.

commanded . . . I cannot find brilliancy in his defensive campaigns, nor can I comprehend the policy of such protracted expenses.[1]

And he went on to speak of " our great superiority of strength " at Salamanca. All this was pure delusion. It was extremely rare for Wellington to find himself in marked superiority to his adversary; and at Salamanca the numbers were 49,000 allies (of whom 30,000 were British) and 40,000 French, while the French had a very great superiority in guns.[2] Moira was sound, however, in criticizing Wellington's advance on Madrid, which threw away his best chance of annihilating the French armies in detail ; but this may have been a purely fortuitous judgment, since his next comment went wildly astray. He observed that there was a danger of Suchet pushing round by the upper Ebro into northern Portugal, and taking Wellington in the rear. But this was to neglect the fact that the only hope for the French was an immediate concentration of every available force to crush Wellington ; and to forget that Biscay and Asturias were at this time particularly dangerous for the French ; while Suchet on his part was naturally reluctant to leave the east coast, where he had at least won a modicum of success, and where Wellington's carefully planned (if indifferently executed) diversion kept him in a state of anxiety. Moreover, Wellington's mistake in moving on Burgos did at least block the way for any enterprise of that nature.[3]

The Burgos episode provides an interesting example of the reorientation of Whig criticism. The general underlying principle of it was now that Wellington must probably be right : therefore if there was any failure, the Government was to blame. Not a single Whig voice was raised in criticism of Wellington's conduct of this affair, though it merited far more censure than Talavera or Fuentes de Oñoro ; but, on

---

[1] *Hastings Papers*, iii. 298.   [2] Oman, v. 429, 432.
[3] *Hastings Papers*, iii. 298-299.

the other hand, the Government was most unfairly blamed
in a case where it had done all that could be expected of it.[1]
Yet there was in 1812, as in 1811, no general Whig attack
on the Government's military policy; and the more
moderate and sensible Whigs, such as Tierney, expressly
discouraged any such demonstration.[2] Even the retreat
to Portugal at the close of the campaign failed to provoke
them, though in their private correspondence they returned
to a mood of despair. It was perhaps inevitable that they
should do so; for the opportunity in 1812, when Napoleon
was involving himself with Russia, seemed to have been
unique; and to the observer in England Wellington's
retreat must have appeared like a repetition of 1810 and
1811. The Whigs could not be expected to put the blame
for the hardships of the march upon the proper shoulders—
those of their particular friend and confidential informant,
J. Willoughby Gordon, who had been sent out as quarter-
master by his patron the Duke of York.[3] Nor could they
realize that the situation was essentially different from
that of the two preceding autumns, in that it was now
Wellington, and not the French, who dominated the
situation, and assumed the initiative.[4] Grey, who by
this time entertained more sensible notions of the situation
in Spain than the majority of his colleagues (Sir Robert

[1] *Morning Chronicle*, 7 Nov. 1812; *Dropmore Papers*, x. 317;
Brougham, *Life and Times*, ii. 67. " Mr. Geden " (*i.e.* George Eden)
may be an exception : he writes, " The blundering at Burgos has been
great ", but omits to say *whose* blundering. Add. MS. 34458, f. 422.

[2] *Dropmore Papers*, x. 317 ; Olphin, *George Tierney*, p. 123.

[3] Fortescue, *op. cit.* viii. 616-625 ; Oman, vi. 135-138. Grey wrote :
" I have the most accurate and certain accounts of the retreat
[Gordon's ?]. If the truth should ever be known I have no doubt it
would be found to have been full as calamitous as that of poor Moore.
Our positive loss as great, the indiscipline and plunder at least equal."
Add. MS. 34458, ff. 431-432. Moira blamed the retreat and considered
that Wellington should have risked another battle ! *Hastings Papers*,
iii. 300. The *Morning Chronicle* (2 Dec.) was more appreciative.

[4] See *Morning Chronicle*, 24 Nov. ; Add. MS. 34458, ff. 431-432.

Wilson had gone to Russia, and confined his efforts henceforward to contradicting the reports of Lord Cathcart), realized clearly that our success in Spain was dependent on factors not entirely under our control : on the necessity for Napoleon's concentration on other problems, and on the disunion and jealousies of the marshals ; [1] though he erred in supposing that these factors completely explained Wellington's success, and that without them his position was not such as to hold out any hopes for the future. But he did grasp the fact that the operations in the Peninsula were important, and would vitally affect the issue of the struggle. Grenville, on the other hand, though enthusiastic for war, lagged behind Grey in this particular. The difference between them on this question became more marked during 1813. The Russian campaign had confounded the habitual pessimists in the Whig camp ; [2] and with Wellington's fiery sickle sweeping round from the Douro to the Ebro, the *Morning Chronicle* had become whole-heartedly a supporter of the war in the Peninsula.[3] Yet Grenville and his brother remained stubbornly convinced that campaigns in Spain dissipated the resources of the nation to no purpose. Their theory of our successes there in 1813 was that Providence had intervened, by a change in circumstances which nobody could have expected, to confound prophecies of disaster which had been soundly based at the time they were made.

I am no detractor from Lord Wellington, whose talents I am glad to see rewarded by placing him really at the head of our army ; but it is quite ridiculous to state him as driving the French out of Spain, when, in truth, they are making no efforts in it, but have withdrawn from thence all the *élite* of their army. . . .[4]

An invasion of France they regarded as " desperate folly ".[5]

---

[1] *Dropmore Papers*, x. 300, 294.

[2] *E.g.* Auckland, *Dropmore Papers*, x. 320 ; *Morning Chronicle*, 13 Oct. 1812.   [3] Add. MS. 34458, ff. 546 *et seq.*

[4] *Dropmore Papers*, x. 348, T. Grenville to Lord Grenville, July 1813.

[5] *Ibid.* 349, same to same.

Even the termination of the armistice of Pläswitz and the adoption of a definite attitude by Austria failed to persuade them that it might be worth while to continue efforts in Spain. Lord Grenville wrote to Auckland on 31 August :

The Austrian declaration of war opens a new scene of hopes and fears, and has even a little revived my speculations of possible deliverance from the overwhelming tide of evil which has set in upon us for the last twenty years.

But then, alas, I think what the Courts of Vienna and Berlin and Petersburg are, and my doubts and apprehensions return. Were we not now engaged in that rash and foolish enterprize of Spain, more manifestly absurd to my apprehension now in its greatest height of unlooked-for success, than even at any former period, had we now our army disposeable, and our reserves unwasted, how much might not this country have contributed to turn the scale of this last, decisive, and most awful conflict ! Instead of this we are lavishing blood and money in a quarter where the most complete victory can contribute nothing to the final issue of the cause.

But to whisper, or even to entertain such sentiments is little less than treason against the superior wisdom and combined judgment of the *Morning Post* and *Morning Chronicle* ! [1]

Grey felt it necessary to put in a *caveat* against these opinions of his partner :

I cannot agree with you in thinking that the money spent in Spain has been ineffectual in producing the better hope which now exists ; or that Buonaparte's power, which even in his present circumstances makes you fear more than you hope, would not be much more formidable to the allies if he had to oppose to them not only the armies which he is at present obliged to maintain on the frontier of Spain, but all the military resources which the subjugation of the Peninsula must have placed at his command. I still think that our opinions at the beginning and in the progress of the Spanish contest were well warranted by such data as we then had to reason upon ; and in saying this I shall perhaps be thought sufficiently pertinacious. But I cannot say that as things have turned out,

[1] Add. MS. 34458, f. 546.

contrary, certainly, to my expectations, the event of the Spanish war has not been both honourable and advantageous to this country. I am really most anxious that you should consider well what you say upon this subject, as I fear it may give Liverpool and Company an advantage over you. Why refer much to former opinions ? [1]

Fortunately for Whig harmony, Grenville, too, had his grievance. Grey towards the end of 1813 relapsed into something of the pacific tone of 1810, and Holland, now that Spain was as good as won, agreed with him.[2] But Grenville was grown Pittish again, as our fortunes rose, and as there seemed to be a real chance of shaking off the Napoleonic yoke. The young Grenvilles were enlisting, and some of them even went to the much-maligned army of Spain, so that " Uncle Tom " began to feel proud of his family's exertions in the great cause.[3] Grenville then could bargain with Grey, and after some correspondence they reached a characteristic agreement upon a principle of mutual discretion and forbearance.[4]

At this point must be terminated the account of the Whig reactions to the war. Controversy turned in 1814 more upon terms of peace than upon the method of carrying on the struggle. It is to be regretted that no study of the Whig attitude to the settlement of Europe at the close of the Napoleonic wars has so far appeared, for they showed more good sense in their criticism than might have been expected. From the point of view of the effect of their opinions upon their reputation with the public, it would have been possible to terminate this chapter at Salamanca ; for after the crisis of May–June 1812 the

[1] *Dropmore Papers*, x. 354.

[2] *Ibid.* 351, 355, 356. Cf. Nat. Lib. of Wales MS. 4814, f. 74, for Wynn's condemnation of pacifism.

[3] *Dropmore Papers*, x. 360. Temple and Sir Watkin Wynn volunteered for service in their capacities as colonels of Militia.

[4] *Ibid.* 360-363, 364-365.

chances of the Whigs' coming in were so small that their
views upon the war made little difference to their prospects
one way or the other ; but their criticisms had so largely
concerned themselves with the conduct of the war in the
Peninsula, that it seemed reasonable to carry forward the
narrative to the close of 1813, when the struggle there was
as good as over.

The general effect produced by a study of the Whig
criticisms of the war is not flattering to the intelligence
and judgment of the Whigs as a party. They proved to be
wrong on almost every point of policy, and upon many
points of fact. They prophesied too darkly, and too often ;
and apparently no confounding of their predictions could
convince them of their errors. As Perceval said (misquoting
Pope) :

> Destroy the web of prophecy in vain,
> The creature's at his dirty work again.[1]

They " thought too little of the grandeur of the struggle,
and the obvious certainty that England or Napoleon
must fall to rise no more ".[2] Ward, who was for long quite
Grenvillian in his attitude to the war, early realized that
it was rash to pontificate at a distance.

> Of a few broad features we may perhaps be able to judge, but
> with regard to details and points disputed, even among professional
> men, we neither have, nor deserve to have, the smallest authority.[3]

How much better it would have been for the reputations
of the Whigs, if they had borne this maxim in mind ! Sir
Robert Wilson, Moira, Dumouriez, and such officers as
Wellington allowed leave of absence because their absence
was more helpful than their presence, were no sure foundation for attacks upon a general who had enough to distract
him without having the perpetual irritation of apparently

---

[1] *Parl. Deb.* xxi. 57.
[2] Lord John Russell, *Selected Speeches*, i. 5-6.
[3] Ward, *Letters to " Ivy "*, p. 63, 1 Feb. 1809.

malicious, and certainly ignorant, criticism in England.
The men who could have given a correct impression at
home—the men whom Wellington trusted—never had the
opportunity of doing so, for he could not spare them from
the Peninsula unless it was to recover their health. Consequently the Whigs got into the habit of accepting as
correct the report of any disappointed, depressed, or discontented officer who chose to argue from the purely
casual conditions under his own observation to the state
of the army as a whole, or who from pure ignorance misin-
terpreted the intention of the commander-in-chief because
his rank was not sufficiently senior for him to know more
of it than the orders which immediately concerned him.
When Sir Samford Whittingham first went out to the
Peninsula, a friend gave him one invaluable piece of
advice in this matter : " Never send information home as
certain to be depended upon but on the clearest evidence ".[1]
Whittingham was an exemplary officer, and he took the
advice, but all his colleagues were not so scrupulous.
Again and again Wellington complained on this ground :

   . . . as soon as an accident happens, every man who can write,
and who has a friend who can read, sits down to write his account
of what he does not know, and his comments on what he does not
understand. . . .[2]

The *Morning Chronicle* received letters commenting on
affairs in Portugal from officers who avowed that they did
not know what Wellington's plans were, because he was
" as close as an oyster ", and it did not scruple to print
a letter of a private soldier which the editor had *selected*
as giving a true—and extremely gloomy—account of the
state of affairs at Torres Vedras.[3] Wellington had to prevent
his officers writing " a whining report " upon Albuera,

---

[1] *Memoirs of Sir Samford Whittingham*, p. 32.
[2] Wellington, *Despatches*, vi. 276.
[3] *Morning Chronicle*, 3 Aug. 1810, 1 Jan. 1811.

" which would have driven the people in England mad ".[1]
The spirit of party, as Wellington complained, was as
prevalent in the army as elsewhere ; [2] and he resented the
mischief that was done, not only to him personally but to
the character of the army, by the inspired reports in the
English newspapers.[3] Wellington was unusually anxious
about the press, because it formed the best source of
information about his actions that was available in France ;
for the activities of the guerrillas made it extraordinarily
difficult to get news from Spain to France direct. He even
remonstrated with Liverpool for allowing his dispatches to
appear in the *Gazette*, and thus, perhaps, disclose his plans
to the enemy.[4] There is, however, no doubt that he had
very serious ground for anger at the treatment he received,
and affairs reached a climax with the case of J. Willoughby
Gordon. Gordon had for some time been secretary to the
commander-in-chief at the Horse Guards. He was a friend
of McMahon, and wrote a good many letters to him which
are preserved at Windsor. He was on good terms with
some of the Tory Ministry, but his real friends were Whigs,
and to them he wrote habitually, particularly to Grey and
his circle, detailing such gossip as he could pick up from his
Ministerial acquaintances. He was not, however, " —— "
of the Grenville correspondence, for the Anonymous continued to make his reports while Gordon was in Spain. But
he was a shrewd observer of politics, and his letters, written
in a neat, instantly recognizable, military hand, are always
of interest. He was, at the same time, an ambitious man,
and his correspondence is liberally sprinkled with references
to the possibility of his own advancement. A sardonic fate
sent him a most unsuitable promotion, when, on the advice

[1] Fortescue, *History of the British Army*, viii. 210.
[2] Wellington, *Supplementary Despatches*, vi. 588.
[3] *Despatches*, vi. 582.
[4] *Supplementary Despatches*, vii. 120 ; Add. MS. 38246, ff. 125-128 ;
Despatches, v. 299.

of the Duke of York, he was made quartermaster-general to Wellington, in succession to the efficient Murray. Gordon was an incompetent Q.M.G., and it was his errors that made the retreat into Portugal, in the autumn of 1812, so nearly disastrous. Unhappily the passion for gossip remained with him in his new situation. He applied the methods of the Horse Guards to the staff in the Peninsula, and began to send his little scraps of information home for the benefit of his Whig friends. Growing bolder, he transmitted to the *Morning Chronicle* confidential information of importance, which thus found its way to French eyes. Wellington at this point discovered his practices, and had him recalled as soon as the Horse Guards could manage it.[1]

Such were the sources of information inside Wellington's army from which the criticisms of the Whigs were fed. Believing in reports of this nature, they were led to believe in other sources less and less deserving of credit ; for if they were to· believe Wellington's officers, they could not believe Wellington himself, so that they were driven to accept the Spanish or French account of a battle in preference to the English. Thus, as to a comparatively trivial matter, Wellington complains in 1811 :

I see in the newspapers that Tarleton and the others have accused me of feeding the inhabitants of Lisbon. They have, as usual, taken this from the *Moniteur*. It is positively false.[2]

But the Whigs would take the word of the *Moniteur* even on more considerable matters. Auckland believed Masséna's account of the Torres Vedras campaign, because he had " no apparent motive for exaggerating the advantages and security of the situation " ;[3] whereas Wellington wrote in a " fallacious style " or was even guilty of outrageous falsehood.[4] Against such impenetrable obliquity only time could avail.

[1] Oman, vi. 224-226.
[2] Wellington, *Supplementary Despatches*, vii. 95.
[3] *Dropmore Papers*, x. 77.   [4] *Ibid.* 57.

No doubt the Ministers' system of favouring their own papers, by giving them the news first, inevitably led to a reaction of incredulity, and the difficulty and delay attending the transmission of information made it easy to leap to the wrong conclusion ; [1] yet the Whigs had other, private sources of information which contributed regularly to their knowledge. A steady stream of Whigs visited the Peninsula as private tourists while the conflict was in progress, and by no means all were of the Holland persuasion. Particularly valuable for the accuracy and frequency of their reports were Admirals Berkeley and Fremantle, both relatives of the Grenville family. Berkeley began reporting in February 1809, and his letters supply a useful corrective to the idea that all Whig correspondents were gloomy. On the contrary, he appears usually to have been of an optimistic turn of mind, and certainly had considerable confidence in Wellington. Fremantle, too, was by no means the carping critic that might have been expected. If the Grenvilles despaired about Spain, it was not the fault of their relatives there. Another Grenville connection in Spain was Henry Wynn, younger brother to Charles and Watkin, and a nephew of the Grenville brothers. He went out in the autumn of 1808 as a private individual, after a fruitless attempt to induce Canning to give him some quasi-official position without many duties.[2] He stayed mainly in Andalusia, and his letters are not very informative. With him went still another Grenville nephew, Lord Ebrington.[3] Other Whigs in the Peninsula, of the Holland faction, were Tom Sheridan and his wife ; Lord William Russell and Lord John Russell, sons of the Duke of Bedford ; and William

[1] *E.g.* the *Morning Chronicle* makes bad mistakes about Wellington's taking of Oporto, 25 May 1809.

[2] Leveson-Gower, *Correspondence*, p. 339 ; *Bathurst Papers*, pp. 75, 77 ; Nat. Lib. of Wales MS. 2790 ; Leighton, *Correspondence of Lady Williams Wynn*, pp. 128-136.

[3] *Spanish Journals of Lady Holland*, p. 241.

Ponsonby, the youngest son of Lord Bessborough.[1] Above all, of course, Lady Holland and her Lord, and J. W. Ward. Wellington himself, too, found time to write to Temple and Buckingham, and occasionally, to one or other of the Grenvilles. It is a matter of astonishment that, with this great body of information pouring into Stowe and Dropmore, the Grenvilles should have remained so obstinately blind on the subject of Spain. Grey was not so well served; hence, perhaps, his reliance upon Sir Robert Wilson, J. Willoughby Gordon, and the other military experts.

It is not easy, in a case of this sort, to judge fairly of the Whig point of view. The argument *ex post facto* is too strong. It is too tempting to charge the Whigs with faction when all their offence was lack of foresight. Yet contemporaries were severe upon them. They had to suffer from unscrupulous attacks upon their patriotism. A pamphlet entitled *The French Spy*, which was typical of a class of ephemeral scurrilities, purported to be the account of the intrigues of an agent of Napoleon, who was treating with the Opposition for " peace ", and it enforced the taunt by a reference to previous instances where the Whigs had betrayed their country—as in the American war, and at the time of the Oczakow incident.[2] And enemies of the extremer Whigs did not hesitate to assert that they regarded a possible conquest of the country with composure, since it would affect only the stock-holders, and leave the bulk of the population untouched.[3] These were the views of base and insignificant pamphleteers, but they were held in a milder form by a majority of the population, whose simple patriotism could not tolerate the gloom with which Whigs received the news of Talavera or Torres Vedras. Thus Wordsworth wrote :

[1] *Supplementary Despatches*, vi. 343 ; Frere, *Works*, i. 140 ; *Morning Chronicle*, 7 Feb. 1812.

[2] *The French Spy*, pp. 4 *et seq.*   [3] *Patriots and Whigs*, pp. 32-33.

If Lord Grenville and Mr. Ponsonby think that the privilege allowed to opposition-manœuvring justifies them in speaking as they do, they are sadly mistaken, and do not discern what is becoming the times.[1]

This was hard on the Whigs, who were anxious that the country should follow the best possible policy, and who could not help it if their party prejudice led them necessarily to consider any Tory policy as *ipso facto* a bad one. Even before Coleridge's rancorous genius had begun to gall them in the columns of the *Courier*, they had felt and resented their unpopularity.

Is it then wrong [wrote the *Morning Chronicle*] in the representatives of the people to be occupied with the affairs of the nation in a time of danger ? or do such writers wish the Parliament to be like that of the old Government of France, a place to register, but not to discuss, the edicts of the Court ? . . . What is *public* business, if such inquiry be not ?
If we indignantly reproach a Minister with being the cause of a disgraceful and disastrous convention . . . we are accused of triumphing in the misfortunes of the country. . . . Or, if we warn the government against withholding from 4,000,000 of His Majesty's subjects their just rights, then, by some vile, cowardly, crawling sycophant of Mr. Perceval, we are accused of pointing out to the enemy the most vulnerable part of the Empire !?

The Whigs claimed, with justice, that it was the duty of an Opposition to criticize, and the more emphatically so since the matter was no minor business of Administration, but the very existence of the country. No one who reads the correspondence of the Grenvilles can fail to be struck with the noble tone of patriotism which informs even their gloomiest outpourings. Yet their inability to rise above purely destructive criticism condemned them in the eyes of the nation. Their attacks on the Government were too constant, too petty, and too unproductive of useful

---

[1] Wordsworth, *Prose Works*, i. 207.
[2] *Morning Chronicle*, 3 March, 20 Dec. 1808.

ideas, to convince the country of their sincerity or utility.
As Scott put it :

> Who ever thought he did a service to a person engaged in an
> arduous conflict, by proving to him, or attempting to prove to him
> that he must necessarily be beaten ? [1]

The Whigs had nothing to substitute for the policy of
Castlereagh and the Wellesleys. Even at the crisis of their
hopes, in May 1812, they could bring forward no definite
foreign policy, nor could they frankly accept the policy of
war in the Peninsula. Undoubtedly this had its influence
on the Regent, who, where the war was concerned, was
decidedly under Wellesley influence. If they eschewed a
Continental policy, what could they offer in exchange ?
More sugar islands, whose " filching " some, at least, of
their number condemned ? Their own internal divisions
precluded the adoption of a clear line of policy, and their
jealousy of the Tories restrained them from proceeding to
the only possible exit from the strategic impasse. To the
very end Whitbread and the *Independent Whig* clamoured
for peace, preaching kindness to Napoleon to the last
possible moment and necessitating elaborate dissociation
by Grey when he too turned peaceful in 1814. A few
eccentrics like Hutchinson and Hazlitt publicly avowed
their admiration for Napoleon as late as 1812. Could
public opinion, could foreign nations, make the necessary
distinctions between these extremists and the orthodox
stem of Whiggism ? Would they not turn for safety to the
Tories, who might be corrupt but were certainly warlike,
and reasonably efficient ? G. F. Leckie, who was no admirer
of the Wellesley system of foreign policy, pointed out that
it was no wonder that the Spaniards were something shy
of us, when at any moment a Ministry pledged to desert
them might come into office.[2] And even granting that the

---

[1] Scott, *Letters*, i. 400.

[2] Leckie, " Essay on the Practice of the British Government ", in *The Pamphleteer*, xi. p. 99.

Whigs in office would have been forced by the exigencies of the case to continue the foreign policy and military commitments of their predecessors, was there any reason to suppose that they would carry them out as satisfactorily ?

Will those who neglected their allies and left them in the lurch in Poland, who planned the childish expedition to Constantinople, and formed the idea of conquering Egypt with a handful of men, do any better ? [1]

Their criticisms of Castlereagh's reorganization of recruiting showed that they had no grasp of military organization ; their criticisms of the military operations proved that they were incompetent amateurs in tactics ; their criticisms of the Peninsular project demonstrated that they had not thought out a satisfactory solution of the pressing problems of the higher strategy. Perfect sincerity and good intentions could not countervail against such disabilities, and it is obvious that on too many occasions they allowed themselves to be hurried by faction, pique, and petty jealousy into a mean-spirited carping which it is not easy to forgive. A Whig Ministry would have meant disaster in the Peninsula, for it would have taken them too long to realize and admit that their predecessors had been in the right ; and in the meantime the struggle would have been over. And with the Peninsula lost, we should have been driven back on expeditions to Egypt, or Constantinople, or lines of posts across the Andes, or some such nonsense, until the resurrection of Europe at last allowed us to venture a tardy and inadequate assistance to the victorious armies of Austria and Russia.

[1] Windsor Arch., George IV, Northumberland to McMahon, 29 March 1810.

CHAPTER III

THE WHIGS AND REFORM

(a) *Introduction*

THE struggle for Parliamentary Reform lasted for rather more than half a century. In the course of those years the fortunes of the cause underwent many vicissitudes; but the prospects had rarely seemed so hopeless as in the spring of 1807. That this should have been so is perhaps a little surprising. A Whig Government had just been in office, for the first time for more than twenty years—a Government which included men who had played a great part in the earlier efforts. But for Parliamentary Reform it had done nothing at all. During its tenure of office the question had not been so much as raised in Parliament. It was, indeed, some years since any tangible proposal for the alteration of the franchise had been put before either House. Yet twenty years before, it had seemed not improbable that the movement would be successful in the immediate future. Between 1780 and 1785 hardly a session had passed without a debate on the subject. From the extreme radical scheme of the Duke of Richmond to the last conciliatory attempt of Pitt, every shade of Reform had been mooted.[1] And though the outbreak of the French Revolution had prejudiced Pitt against attempting any immediate solution of the problem, the Minister's defection was the opportunity of an Opposition which had lately been at considerable hazard of seeing itself permanently

[1] For a useful summary of the various Reform schemes see Meadley, *A Sketch of the Various Proposals for Constitutional Reform in the Representation of the People, ap.* Bentham, *Works*, vol. iii.

un-Whigged. When Pitt fell silent the Whigs stole his tune.

They found their chief executant not in Fox, whose love of humanity was too generalized to be easily confined within the limits of the practical, but in Charles Grey, who was young, and fervent beyond discretion. It was Grey who had agitated the question in 1792, 1793, and 1797, supported with something less than his own enthusiasm by his chiefs.[1] It was Grey who had presented the great petition of 1793, whose bitter calculation of electoral influences was a permanent quarry for Reformers in search of damning statistics. It was Grey who had rallied the 93 votes for the astonishingly radical proposals of 1797. Still, whether Grey or Fox, Reform was actively the policy of the Foxites, and dormantly that of the Pittites. Yet after 1797 there was little or nothing. In 1800, indeed, Grey and Tierney had collected 34 votes for an insignificant palliative measure of redistribution, for which the Union was thought to be a suitable occasion;[2] but a division of 34 was pitiable: fifteen years before Pitt had counted 174. After 1800, the years are wholly blank. The Whigs lost hope; they lost conviction. The leaders defaulted. Fox in office took over his predecessor's opinions; as an administrator he felt for the first time the dead-weight of the argument of inexpediency.[3] Place, on the threshold of his career as a Westminster politician, had the *gaucherie* to press him on the subject; but Fox found it convenient to fob him off with a vague promise.[4] Age and the Prince of Wales were already dimming the chivalrous ardour of Sheridan and the passionate eloquence of Erskine. Even Tierney was no longer the Tierney who had been the people's idol, the

---

[1] Meadley, *ap.* Bentham, iii. 555; Veitch, *Genesis of Parliamentary Reform*, p. 118.

[2] Meadley, *loc. cit.*

[3] Green, *Portraits of Pitt and Fox*, p. 36.

[4] Wallas, *Life of Francis Place*, pp. 40-41.

Burdett of Southwark.[1] Tierney, in fact, not content with offending his colleagues by attending the House during the great Secession of 1798, had gone so far as to accept office under Addington as Treasurer of the Navy. Gale Jones, who had helped to secure his return for Southwark, in bitter anger at his apostasy treated him with terrible severity in his *Five Letters to G. Tierney*; and Tierney, who had at one time seemed likely to dispute the succession to Fox with Grey, was greatly shaken in the estimation of the public.[2] Most curious of all was the case of Grey, over whom there came a premature caution and lethargy, and who lost altogether the fire of his earlier years.

It was no wonder, then, that the Talents should have disappointed their followers ; no wonder that free-lances, in and out of Parliament, should have cast gibes.[3] The handicaps under which the Whig Government had laboured had certainly been heavy : that, at least, must be admitted. They had, indeed, had an enormous majority ; but of those patchwork hosts how many were Whigs ? How many would have followed ? " Had they begun their Administration with great and extensive Reforms we ask how many days they would have remained in office . . . ? "[4] Nor was the constitution to be refashioned in a hurry : " natura humanae infirmitatis, tardiora remedia quam mala ", as the *Morning Chronicle* characteristically remarked.[5]

After their resignation, when their opponents taunted

---

[1] Barnes, *Parliamentary Portraits*, p. 59 ; *An Account of the Proceedings of the Electors of . . . Southwark* (12 April, 1809), p. 11.

[2] G. Jones, *op. cit., passim.* See also S. F. Waddington, *Three Letters to Tierney.* Waddington was a man with a grievance : see Cobbett, *Rural Rides* (ed. Cole), pp. 221, 1042. In 1812 he wrote to the Regent urging peace and Catholic Emancipation. Windsor Arch., George IV, 24 Feb. 1812.

[3] *E.g. Parl. Deb.* ix. 208 ; *Political Register*, xi. 492, 587, 1129-1130, etc.

[4] *Morning Chronicle*, 8 June 1807.   [5] *Ibid.* 20 March 1807.

them with failure to embody their principles in action,
there was a disposition in some quarters to blame their
allies, the Grenvilles. How far was this excuse valid ? It
would certainly have been difficult to carry any significant
measure of Reform in a Cabinet of which Lord Grenville
was a member. Lord Grenville was of undoubted ability :
an excellent classical scholar, a patron of letters and a
statesman of long experience. But his activities in politics,
and his accomplishments in letters, had not succeeded in
broadening a mentality originally narrow or softening a
disposition always arrogant and formal. Yet, despite the
creaking gravity of his official correspondence, his private
letters show him to have been a man of warm affections
within the limits of his circle. To his brothers, the Marquis
of Buckingham and Thomas Grenville, he wrote almost
daily ; and to Auckland he could talk of his gardens as
though for the moment forgetful of being a Grenville. The
barony of Grenville, it is true, was a recent creation ; but
his ancient and honourable family had hung for years on
the fringe of the peerage, and for the last half-century had
been slowly collecting that vast agglomeration of lands
which was one day to enable them successfully to press their
claims to a dukedom. Grenville was, in fact, a Whig : of
all the " Venetian Oligarchy ", he was the most Venetian
and the most oligarchical. The sinecures of himself and
his brothers baffle computation : as Joint Teller of the
Exchequer Buckingham alone drew a considerable sum.[1]
If jealousy of the Crown, great territorial possessions, and
an unquestioning assumption of the divine right of the
family to rule the country and be supported by it—if
these be the hallmarks of Whiggism, then the Grenvilles
needed no assaying. But their Whiggism was the creed of
an elder generation—of that Duke of Bedford round whom

[1] McCallum, *Livre Rouge*, p. 94, estimates the family's income from
public sources as £30,000. Leigh Hunt (*Examiner*, 10 May 1812) gave
the figure for 1806 as £55,000.

the Bloomsbury Gang had gathered, rather than of the Duke of 1807, who professed liberal principles and visited Whitbread at Southill. It was pre-Rockingham Whiggism, and the Foxites did not like it. To the Grenvillites, therefore, it was impossible that any reform in the franchise or any attack upon sinecures could be acceptable or even tolerable. So that it is not very surprising that when, on the eve of the election of 1807, Horner and Bennet were commissioned to review for an ungrateful country the benefits received at the hands of the Talents, no mention of Parliamentary Reform was allowed to creep into their brief pamphlet.[1]

But it would be a mistake to infer that only the necessary evil of the Grenville alliance had restrained the Foxites from Reform. It was not only Parliamentary Whiggism that had turned its back at once on its past and on its future. The reservoirs of popular enthusiasm had run dry; the clubs of Reformers had shut their doors. Since the passing of Pitt's severe law of 1794, the popular societies had struggled against adversity with ever-decreasing success. The expenses of trials, the fear of arrest, and the reluctance of the average man to run counter to the law, had all combined to sap their strength. By 1800 they were moribund. This was very serious for the Reforming movement. A minority depends vitally upon good organization to make its full effect; and in the early 'nineties the Societies had very greatly assisted the spread of the agitation. It had been the Friends of the People, not the official Whigs, who had pushed Grey on to the efforts of 1792 and 1793. In an age of a ludicrous

---

[1] *A Short Account of a late Short Administration.* See Horner, *Memoirs*, i. 401, 490-494. Howick's election appeal (Add. MS. 27838, f. 107) does indeed refer to Reversions, the Scottish Judicature Bill, and the effort to check financial abuses; but there is no mention of Parliamentary Reform; Sydney Smith (*Letters*, p. 81) also makes no attempt to include Reform among the achievements of the Talents.

franchise they had provided a channel for the voicing of
new opinions, for their representation and organization,
and for the linking up of like-minded men across the width
of the countryside. These great services were now suspended; and not only because a brutal Government struck
out in blind panic at what it did not understand, but
because the public interest in these societies was diminishing. After 1800 they died out completely.[1] First the
enthusiasm for the peace, then the fear of invasion, wholly
occupied the public mind. The intellectual excitements of
ten years ago were not flat or stale; they were dangerous
drugs which no patriotic Briton cared to use. Public
opinion ceased to excite itself over the Rights of Man and
the principles of the French Revolution, for the excellent
reason that the Revolution was over. Its spiritual urge was
dead, and the intellectual fabrics which had been the
intelligible expression of that urge were crumbling into
ruin. No new editions of Paine were called for; and Godwin
was drifting through the shoals of sordid financial embarrassments to the haven of venerable obscurity where later
Hazlitt found him.[2] It was the epoch when the enthusiasts
were confounded and turned backward: it was the epoch
when the poets took to prose. Southey had already deserted
the Whigs, though he still execrated the Pittites; and
Coleridge agreed with him in tending ever deeper into the
sheltering vale of conservatism.[3] Already Wordsworth had
appeared as the great patriotic poet of the war; and
though he was to produce, in the *Tract on the Convention
of Cintra*, a noble epitome of all that was most solid and
valuable in the political theory of his early maturity, he
was to show in it also that he was approaching his psycho-
logical crisis, and to presage the dilemma which at last

[1] Veitch, pp. 333-338.
[2] Hazlitt, *Spirit of the Age*. Paine's *Age of Reason* was indeed reprinted about this time; but not his *Rights of Man*.
[3] Crabb Robinson, *Correspondence*, i. 52.

forced him, for liberty's and nationality's sake, to the empty husks of the Ultras.[1]

The apathy of the general public was in fact very great. The symptoms which Lord Cockburn noticed in Scotland may be taken equally well to apply to contemporary England. " If any of the measures ", he says, " which twenty years afterwards agitated every political nerve in the kingdom had been propounded, however attractively, they would have fallen to the ground cold." [2] The press reflected this state of affairs. The *Morning Chronicle*, the leading Whig daily paper, was entirely at one with the Talents in their refusal to be drawn into any rash attempt.[3] The *Edinburgh Review*, which reflected the opinions of the younger and more intellectual section of the party, was at least as decided. The Reviewers were convinced that Parliament as then constituted did in fact possess all the reasonable requisites of such a body, for it represented all types and interests and performed its functions to the general satisfaction. Placemen and sinecures were not a serious menace, and family influence was far from undesirable.[4] A whole article was not considered too much for the expression of the *Edinburgh's* horror and abjuration of Cobbett and his " pernicious and reprehensible " doctrines.[5]

In Cobbett, indeed, the Reformers had found one splendid champion. With that forceful contrariness which had once led him to exhibit pictures of King George in the United States, he had swung round from the violent anti-Burdett invective of 1802 to the no less violent pro-Burdett declamation of 1807, and now made head against

[1] Wordsworth, *Prose Works*, ed. Grosart, i. 141-145, 207 ; *Letters*, i. 219, 425.

[2] Cockburn, *Memorials*, p. 263.

[3] See above, p. 174.

[4] *Edinburgh Review*, x. 407, 409, 418.

[5] *Ibid.* 386 *et seq.*

the popular current.[1] For the pacific policy of the Whigs
he had as great a contempt as for the obscurantism of the
Tories. Attached to no party, guided only by his own
tortuous common sense, he was often a voice crying in
the wilderness; but his following was large and his influence
important. The zestful pugnacity of his journalism, though
it was often employed for personal, and occasionally for
scurrilous ends, was always at the disposal of the more
radical projects for retrenchment. To him Grenville was a
parasite, Grey a deserter. In 1806 he had by no means
adopted the point of view of the extreme Reformers.
Corruption, not the iniquities of the franchise, was the
regular mark for his arrows. He had transferred his
allegiance by a natural declension from Pitt to the New
Opposition, and from the New Opposition to the Talents.[2]
But the slackness of the Talents disgusted him; and in
February 1806 he broke with his old friend and patron
Windham, and allied himself with the Burdettites.[3] It
was not long before they converted him to Parliamentary
Reform, and by 1807 the Whigs were compelled to endure
the taunts and gibes which he poured out every week in
the pages of his *Political Register*. In the years that followed
he was by far the most important educative influence
with the masses, on the side of Reform.

Up to a point he was aided and supplemented by
another Sunday paper—the *Independent Whig*, edited by
Henry White. Relatively few copies of this paper are
obtainable; but we know that it was founded in 1805,[4]
and that its career was not untroubled by prosecutions for
libel.[5] From the examples available it is clear that its

---

[1] See in *Edinburgh Review*, x. 388, quotations from *Political
Register*, ii. 51.

[2] Carlyle, *Cobbett*, pp. 103, 108.

[3] *Life and Letters of Cobbett*, i. 322.

[4] See *Independent Whig*, 1 Jan. 1809.

[5] *Ibid.* 10 July 1808, 1 Nov. 1811.

editors were both able and enlightened : they were keen
Reformers, very interested in social questions, and far
from tender of the feelings of the Whig leaders. It is clear
then that, bad as the situation was, there were yet Reformers
enough in London and the Home Counties to support two
Sunday newspapers of a Reforming complexion.

There were, in fact, a few democratic pilots who had
weathered the storm of patriotic reaction. Conspicuous
among them was Major Cartwright, who for years had been
the self-constituted pamphleteer and general fugleman of
the movement. Cartwright's optimism was perhaps the
facile optimism of a foolish man ; for Cartwright was
certainly not a very wise one. His intellectual equipment
was not equal to the gravity of his cause or the exhaustless-
ness of his energy. He was the victim of an *idée fixe*, and
was lamentably ignorant of the history of the constitution
for whose primitive purity he was always clamouring.
Still, the Major had spirit and pluck, and he refused to be
cast down by the apathy which he saw all around him.[1]

All could not share Cartwright's optimism. John Gale
Jones in particular bitterly lamented the failure of the
Talents to realize the hopes of the Reformers, and blamed
Fox because he did not " fulfil the anxious expectations
of the country, and retrieve his reputation ".[2] He was
unsparing in his denunciation of the system the Whigs
were pursuing :

. . . the present extraordinary crisis: the attempts evidently making
by a powerful and corrupt junto to destroy the elective franchise,
and poison the very fountain of our liberties : the general anxiety
that justly prevails at the alarming study of a *Paper aristocracy*,
that appears to aim at absolute power and rise paramount alike
over the King, the nobility and the people :[3] render it an imperious

[1] *Life and Correspondence of Major Cartwright*, i. 240, 300, 352.
[2] *Five Letters to G. Tierney*, p. 20.
[3] Compare Palmerston's judgment : " They had called a new Parliament, in the elections for which the influence, direct and indirect, of

duty in every man . . . to hasten forward, avow his undisguised sentiments, and prevent, if possible, his country from becoming a prey either to domestic slavery or foreign subjection.[1]

Other tenacious Reformers gathered round the hospitable table of Colonel Bosville in Welbeck Street, and these included Major James, Thelwall, and Sir Charles Wolseley.[2] These gatherings of the faithful might begin to believe, in the spring of 1807, that they had seen the worst of their times. Even amid the vituperation of Waddington's *Three Letters to Tierney*, we find an unexpected appeal to the petition of 1793 ; and in 1805 the Duke of Bedford, in correspondence with Cartwright, had declared the necessity for a radical amendment of the system of government.[3] In 1806 two great partisans turned their attentions to Westminster politics—Cobbett in his *Political Register*, and Francis Place in private conversation with other prosperous traders like himself.[4] Since the decay of the clubs, Place had quite retired from political activity, but five years' quiescence had not dulled his abilities or modified his views. Place had no opinion of Fox, and little of any of the other official Whigs. He had hammered out for himself his political, no less than his religious convictions, and he was a wholehearted Reformer. He brought to the cause a dogged ingenuity and a sound business head, and under his guidance the turbid waters of Westminster politics had

the Government had been exerted to an extent and with a success beyond example . . . the multitude . . . began at last to give them credit for the abilities of which they claimed such exclusive possession; and keeping the King as a sort of State prisoner, by allowing none but themselves to approach him, they began almost to consider themselves as a fourth branch of the government of the country " (Bulwer, *Palmerston*, i. 62).

[1] *Five Letters to G. Tierney*, pp. iii, iv.

[2] Redding, i. 237-250 ; Add. MS. 27838, f. 10. See *Life of Sir Robert Wilson*, i. 56-58, for a good description of Bosville's dinners.

[3] Cartwright, *The Comparison*, p. 61.

[4] Add. MS. 35143, f. 131, for Place's account of how he turned politician.

been set to turn the wheels of progress. In October 1806 there was a general election. A new ally, and a valuable one, had been secured in the person of Sir Francis Burdett himself; and between them they all but carried the election of Burdett's creature, James Paull, whose ambition it was to play Francis to Wellesley's Hastings, and who was already in the confidence of the extremer Whigs. When the Talents fell, the electors of Westminster were encouraged to fresh efforts, which this time were crowned with success. Burdett and Paull were put up; and despite a miserable quarrel between them, and extreme shortage of funds, the Westminster Committee obstinately continued the contest. All their efforts were now concentrated upon securing Burdett's election; Horne Tooke lent his powerful support; [1] and at the close of the poll Burdett was triumphantly returned with a handsome majority.[2]

On 25 June he celebrated his triumph in true Roman fashion, with a wealth of naïve symbolism, and amid scenes of remarkable enthusiasm. "His car, an antique Curricle chair, plac'd on a column—his leg, which he cannot bend,[3] supported on a kind of stool like the Fasces bound with Laurel. He sat without his hat, very pale, very handsome, very grave, and bowing to nobody ".[4] Every year a Grand Reform Dinner in Westminster commemorated the great event.

To Grey, to the Edinburgh Reviewers, to Perry of the *Morning Chronicle*, it was a challenge and an interrogation. How were the 160-odd Whig members who had survived

---

[1] Tooke, Letter to *The Times*: "Horne Tooke's Warning".

[2] Wallas, *Place*, pp. 44, 47.

[3] He had been wounded in the duel with Paull.

[4] Leveson-Gower, p. 259. Jackson gives a rather different picture : " Burdett's procession yesterday was most contemptible. Hardly one person of the character, and not one of the appearance, of a gentleman, attended it " (*Jackson Diaries*, ii. 141); *Memoirs of Burdett*, pp. 37-40, gives an account of it, with a picture. See also *Exposition of the Circumstances of Burdett's Election*, 1807, *passim*.

the election to react towards it ? The presence of Burdett
and Cochrane in the House was a perpetual reminder of
forsaken principles. Yet the Whigs made no move. The
significance of Westminster was quietly ignored. No scheme
of opposition based upon a demand for Parliamentary
Reform was determined on by the leaders. Their efforts
were to be concentrated rather on the purification of the
Governmental machinery, the abolition of sinecures, and
the further curtailment of the influence of the Crown.
After a period of complete inaction it seemed that they
were unable to take up the work of Reform where they had
dropped it in 1800 ; they must go back to the beginning,
tread once again the path that Burke had trodden, repeat
the shibboleths of the Rockinghams. It is, of course, true
that the public support for Economical Reform was considerable. Corruption is always a good cry against Ministers.
Yet the Whigs had made a beginning while they were still
in office : though their measures had altogether failed to
satisfy Cobbett or the more radical Reformers. Economical
Reform, indeed, had represented, in the very mildest form,
the concessions of the Talents to the demands of their past ;
in Opposition it became their positive programme for the
future.

(b) *Economical Reform*

The origin of this renewed attempt to subject expenditure to a more stringent control is to be found in Biddulph's
motion of 10 February 1807, for the appointment of a
Select Committee to enquire into sinecure offices.[1] Lord
Henry Petty, who spoke for the Government, showed
himself gracious and conciliatory. He had no objection to
the appointment of a Committee, but he pleaded for an
extension of the scope of its activities. He pointed out
that many sinecures had been abolished in 1783, 1786,
and 1798, and he deprecated the idea that any substantial

[1] *Parl. Deb.* viii. 703 *et seq.*

reduction was possible without danger of impairing the public dignity and compromising the public service. The prerogative might occasionally have been abused ; but that was no reason for its permanent curtailment. The position in England was in fact by no means a bad one ; customs and excise officers had been disfranchised ; many sinecures had been commuted ; and the profits of the majority of the remainder had been limited by agreement. Only two considerable offices were still held in reversion.[1] In Ireland admittedly the position was not so satisfactory ; but even there the report of the Commission which had been set up in 1804 had resulted in tangible improvements. The Talents themselves had granted no offices in reversion. On the whole, he was convinced that there was little scope for further improvement ; they could only be vigilant and see that the abuses inseparable from a large expenditure were reduced to a minimum. But though little remained to be done, yet he did not contend that that little ought to remain undone. Biddulph, therefore, was to get his Committee, but its objects were defined in Petty's amendment (to which Biddulph assented) as follows: "to examine and consider what regulations and checks have been established in order to controul the several branches of the public expenditure in Great Britain and Ireland, and how far the same have been effectual; and what further measures can be adopted for reducing any part of the said expenditure, or diminishing the amount of salaries and emoluments without detriment to the public service . . .".[2]

From this Committee sprang, directly or indirectly, nearly all the proposals for Economical Reform which were made in the ensuing five years. In the light of after-events, Petty's speech is interesting and important. The tone of

[1] Lord Arden held the office of Register of the Admiralty Court, with reversion to his brother Perceval ; George Rose held that of Clerk of the Parliament, with reversion to his son.

[2] *Parl. Deb.* viii. 712.

optimism which pervaded it, and the minimizing of such abuses as remained, were very much at variance with the opinions of his party after their fall from power. It was not the Government that had raised this question, which necessarily came home inconveniently to some of them : Biddulph was a private member ; and as a Tory later pointed out,[1] they could claim no credit as a party for having set up the Committee. The sense of the House had indeed been so strongly in favour of the Committee that it would have been unwise to make a difficulty about conceding it ; and, after all, the Whigs could cite Arden and Rose as an offset to the Grenvilles.

The Committee presented its first report, which dealt with unimportant questions concerning the Pay Office, on 22 July 1807 ; but, in the meantime, its constitution had undergone modification as a consequence of the change of Government.

Perceval's sudden dissolution was extremely galling to the Whigs. The *Morning Chronicle*, indeed, did not scruple to assert that the Tories had adopted this course only to avoid the damaging revelations which the Finance Committee was on the point of making, and even compared the situation to that of 1629.[2] But the Reports of the Commission when they eventually appeared by no means bore out this view ; for the Second Report concerned only the problems of the management of the Debt and the conduct of the Bank ; while the Third, whose findings will be examined later, contained nothing in the nature of a revelation. When Perceval returned from his victory at the polls, he very naturally desired to modify the personnel of the Committee. As originally constituted it had been predominantly Whig ; as Canning proposed to refashion it, it would have admittedly balanced the two parties. " It would almost seem ", observed Cobbett, " that the *ins* and the *outs* were litigating persons, choosing

[1] *Ibid.* ix. 207-208.   [2] *Morning Chronicle*, 27 April 1807.

arbitrators ".[1] Eleven of the old members were to be left,
and eight new men to be added. To this very fair proposal
the Whigs opposed a resistance which seems rather
unreasonable. Biddulph, however, acquiesced in the change,
though with some reluctance ; and Whitbread readily
consented to his exclusion from a Committee whose
sittings he had, as he frankly confessed, hardly attended.[2]
There is no reason to believe that the efficiency of the
Committee was in any degree impaired by the change.

On 7 July 1807, Lord Cochrane moved for an enquiry
into the sinecures and places held by members of Parliament.[3] As to the desirability of the enquiry there seems to
have been little dispute ; argument turned on the question
whether the investigation could not be left to the existing
Finance Committee. This was the line adopted by Perceval,
who possibly hoped, as the Whigs alleged, that the details
of Parliamentary sinecures would be swamped in a general
report ; and it was this policy that prevailed, by 101–60.[4]
Nevertheless, the minority included many moderate Whigs,[5]
whose views were expressed by Curwen, when he observed
that to refuse such an enquiry " would be to do the House
more mischief than all the abuse of the Corresponding
Societies could do ".[6]

The Third Report of the Committee, which appeared
on 29 June 1808, was a comprehensive analysis of extant
pensions and sinecures. The state of affairs it disclosed was

[1] *Political Register*, xii. 49.

[2] *Parl. Deb.* ix. 692 *et seq*. Biddulph tried to get Burdett on to this
Committee, but his proposal was negatived without a division, though it
was thought that from 50 to 60 would have divided in his favour.
Add. MS. 34457, f. 306. The Grenvilles had always regarded the Committee as too independent of the Whigs : see *Court and Cabinets*, iv. 132.

[3] Godwin thought Cochrane " the greatest fool he ever met with
among men ". Crabb Robinson, *MS. Diary*, ii. 28.

[4] *Parl. Deb.* ix. 745–743*.

[5] *Morning Chronicle*, 9 July 1807, for list.

[6] *Parl. Deb.* ix. 749. See also *Political Register*, xii. 97–102.

not alarming. It was shown that the King had kept within the limits of the £90,000 for Civil List pensions, prescribed by the Act of 1782. The undefined state of the reserved revenues in Scotland afforded opportunities for abuses, but it was not suggested that they had already occurred. The almost automatic grant of a pension for meritorious public services, irrespective of whether the recipient was in need of such assistance, was reprehended. And the Committee declared that " it may be expedient considerably to reduce the emoluments of some [sinecures] and to abolish others ". This declaration did not represent the original form in which it had been drafted by the Committee. As at first contemplated it had been rather more stringent, and had recommended that only those sinecures should be retained which were usually conferred to supplement the admittedly inadequate re- muneration of certain important public servants. The more conservative section of the Committee, however, had risen early one Monday morning, when a thin attendance was usual, and appearing in force had carried the milder version in spite of the protests of Bankes, who was in the chair.[1]

In 1809 the Committee was reduced in size, having proved too cumbrous for quick working ;[2] and the new Committee soon produced a supplementary report embody- ing the information which Cochrane had been demanding. From this it appeared that 76 members of Parliament held offices of some sort, to the value of over £150,000, including over £100,000 during pleasure ; and of these some 28 held sinecures or received pensions totalling £42,000.[3] Clearly the investigation had not been superfluous. On 19 March 1810 the House went into Committee to consider the Third Report of the Finance Committee, and the whole question of sinecures came under discussion. A rather vague and general resolution in favour of economy was all that Henry

---

[1] *Morning Chronicle*, 30 June 1808.
[2] *Parl. Deb.* xii. 116, 24 Jan. 1809.   [3] *Ibid.* xiii. p. cclxxxvii.

Martin (who introduced the subject) could obtain.[1] Bankes, however, pronounced himself in favour of the abolition of sinecures as soon as the interest of the present holders should terminate.[2] What provision, then, was to be made for the proper recompensing of public services if sinecures were to be done away ? Bankes was ready with his answer. On 17 May he moved to provide a fund for this purpose, simultaneously with the abolition of sinecures. He was supported by Martin, Althorpe, Whitbread, Milton, and Moore, but lost his motion by 93 votes against 99.[3] The only tangible result was the appointment of another Select Committee, this time to consider sinecures alone.[4] In due course they made their Report. They pointed out that the number of pure sinecures was really very small, and that in the majority of cases the abuse lay rather in the over-payment of the holder or the performance of the office by deputy. On the other hand, they held out hopes of saving over £80,000 by abolitions or consolidations, in addition to £20,000 by reductions of salary, and a large amount (as yet not exactly determinable) on colonial appointments.[5] These were considerable savings ; yet no action seems to have been taken in consequence of the Report. The Houses were discussing the Regency question, to the exclusion of all other topics ; and though Bankes did indeed manage to find time to have the Committee reappointed with the addition of Martin and Wilberforce,[6] it was not till May 1812 that any further move was made. In that month Bankes introduced his Sinecures Bill, to give effect to the recommendations of the Committee. It survived the Report stage by 134–123, the majority comprising Whigs of all shades, together with nearly all the Canningites and all the

---

[1] *Parl. Deb.* xvi. 13 ********

[2] *Ibid.* 26.   [3] *Ibid.* 1083-1103.

[4] *Ibid.* xvii. 226; and *ibid.* ccccxcviii, which gives the resolutions on which the Committee was to base their enquiries.

[5] *Ibid.* ccccxcviii.   [6] *Ibid.* xviii. 921-922.

" Saints " except Stephen.[1] On 17 June the third reading
was carried without a division, despite some criticism from
the Whig benches;[2] but on 3 July it met with disaster in
the Lords, being thrown out on the second reading by 8
votes to 5.[3]

So the attempt to obtain the abolition of sinecures, or
even their reduction, entirely failed.[4] How far was it a
genuine Whig policy ? The spearhead of the attack, the
chairman of the Committee, was Henry Bankes, the friend
of Thornton and Wilberforce, a member of the " Saints "
party : in no sense a Whig. It was supported also by
Canningites. The personnel of the Committee was at least
as much Tory as Whig.[5] Cobbett did not hesitate to assert
that the Whigs had more to lose by an abolition of sinecures
than had their rivals;[6] but he probably had the Grenvillites
in mind when he wrote ; and he was in any case a prejudiced witness. On the whole, the Whigs did sincerely
associate themselves with the Reformers ; though the
Edinburgh Review admitted that to do so was the shortest
cut to popularity.[7] But the days when sinecures offered a
really fruitful field to the Reformers had been over for
some time. The statistics of sinecures already abolished,
contained in the Second Report, are eloquent of this fact.
The more sober of the Whigs themselves realized that no
great saving was to be expected.[8] There were many of

---

[1] *Ibid.* xxii. 1178, 4 May 1812. Thirty-three county members voted
or paired for the Bill : *Morning Chronicle*, 7 May 1812.

[2] *Parl. Deb.* xxiii. 552.   [3] *Ibid.* 892-895.

[4] Further nugatory attempts against sinecures took place in 1813
and 1816 : see *ibid.* xxvi. 224 ; xxxiv. 807. In 1812 Wynn warned
Southey that in the state of public opinion it might not be possible
to get his sinecure renewed. Nat. Lib. Wales MS. 4814, f. 60.

[5] Though the Grenvilles thought it far too radical. Creevey, p. 127.

[6] *Political Register*, xx. 394-395.

[7] *Edinburgh Review*, xiv. 282, 284, July 1809.

[8] *Morning Chronicle*, 14 Feb. 1809 ; Petty's speech, *Parl. Deb.* xiv.
427. The *Morning Chronicle* was not always so candid. Thus on 5 May

them also—and among them Petty and Ponsonby—who
felt that sinecures were extremely convenient, and that
other methods of rewarding services might easily prove
more expensive.[1] On this point, indeed, there was a
significant difference of opinion within the party; for
the more extreme section of it—such men as William
Smith—strongly reprobated such laxity.[2] To the younger
Reformers the question was one of importance, for it
offered an easy means of sapping the Grenville alliance,
which they held to be fatal to the party's fortunes; and
it was used for that purpose quite ruthlessly by Creevey
and Folkestone, who made deliberately provocative
attacks on the sinecures of that family,[3] and succeeded
before 1812 in forming a compact anti-Grenville group
within the Whig party itself. The Grenvilles, indeed,
looked very sourly on Bankes' efforts; and one of them [4]
described the Sinecure Offices Bill as " full of absurdity
and impracticability " ; but (he added mournfully) " the
object of it was one which the House of Commons are
now wild upon ".[5] As early as 1808 the sagacity of
Thomas Grenville had discerned the temper of the times.
He warned Lord Buckingham that Bankes' Committee
was "much more popular than many people suppose it
to be"; and he argued that it would not be safe to
reckon on the new generation of Grenvilles being able,
as their fathers had been, to dispense with a regular
profession.[6]

But Thomas Grenville underrated the powers of

1812 it wrote : " Take from the Ministry only the sinecures pointed out
by name in Mr. Bankes's Bill, and the great work of reform would be
half accomplished ".

[1] See *Parl. Deb.* xiv. 947, 959.   [2] *Ibid.* 959.

[3] *Ibid.* 431 ; *Dropmore Papers*, x. 235, 237, 242, 243 (the laments of
the Grenvilles); Creevey, p. 162.

[4] W. H. Fremantle.

[5] *Court of England during the Regency*, i. 288.

[6] *Court and Cabinets of George III*, iv. 244-245.

resistance of the old order. He overlooked the great
guarantee of security furnished by the House of Lords.
How strong was the resistance they opposed to measures
of Reform even of the mildest character is admirably
illustrated by the long and uniformly unsuccessful attempts
to secure the passing of a Bill to prevent the grant of offices
in reversion.

The subject of reversions came, in fact, within the scope
of the Finance Committee, but it had, in addition, a history
of its own. It reached a critical stage on 24 March 1807,
the very last day of the Talents' Government, when
Bankes (as part of the duties of the Committee of
which he was chairman) moved, " That no office, place,
employment or salary, in any part of His Majesty's
dominions, ought to be granted hereafter in reversion ".
The resolution was carried, and Bankes, Horner, and
Sturges Bourne were appointed to bring in a Bill on the
subject. Feeling in the House was nearly unanimous in
favour of the motion, and only Yorke and that very crusted
Tory, Johnstone, opposed it.[1] On 29 June Bankes obtained
leave to bring in his Bill,[2] which passed through the
Commons without debate of any sort.

It was not apparently expected that there would be
any difficulty in putting through the Upper House a
measure upon which the Commons had shown such
remarkable unanimity of opinion ; but Perceval, as Lord
Holland remarked, " knew that in the dusk of the session,
the Lords, like a faithful Penelope, would unravel the web ";[3]
and sure enough, Lord Arden arose in haste to defend
reversions. Bolder than Perceval, he attacked the measure
as " an unnecessary and indecent attack upon the Royal
prerogative ", and succeeded in getting it rejected without

---

[1] *Parl. Deb.* ix. 178-187.   [2] *Ibid.* 669.
[3] Holland, *Memoirs of the Whig Party*, ii. p. 255.

a division [1] (4 August 1807). The Commons met this rebuff
with spirit.[2] On 10 August they carried *nem. con.* a motion
of Bankes to address the King, petitioning him to refrain
from granting any further reversions until six weeks after
the opening of the next session. Only Perceval ventured to
speak against it. His contention was, that such an Act as
was desired would be neither an attack on the prerogative
on the one hand, nor a great reform on the other. He
pointed out, quite rightly, that reversions were a cheap
and effective way of rewarding services, and in particular
pleaded the claims of needy ex-Lord Chancellors. Nevertheless he did not vote against the motion; indeed, he
had spontaneously offered to grant no reversion in the
recess.[3]

On 26 January 1808, therefore, Bankes once more
introduced his Bill; and on 1 February it passed its third
reading in the Commons.[4] On 2 March, thanks very largely
to proxies, the Lords decided to give it a first reading, by
69 votes to 61.[5] But Arden had been reserving his fire.
When the time came to go into Committee, he rallied his
forces and openly prophesied that if the Bill were carried
they would see 1641 come again. But the Whigs now
received considerable assistance from the Sidmouths, and
even from the old Pittites; and on the division they carried
their point, though the numbers on each side were equal—
84–84.[6] Arden, though worsted for the moment, was not
beaten. In Committee, Hawkesbury moved to limit the
operation of the Bill to two years, and Holland and Grey,
though they objected to this curtailment, would not have
pressed their opposition to a division, being convinced that

---

[1] *Parl. Deb.* ix. 1044 *-1049 *. The following spoke for the Bill:
Grosvenor, Lauderdale, Holland, Selkirk, Boringdon.

[2] See Vansittart's comment on the " foolishly splenetic and gratuitously unpopular " conduct of the Lords. Add. MS. 34457, f. 330.

[3] *Parl. Deb.* ix. 1158-1168. [4] *Ibid.* x. 96-100, 195.

[5] *Ibid.* 872. [6] *Ibid.* 1044-1053.

they must take what they could get. But Arden and his friends would not accept even this compromise; they insisted on a division, beat Hawkesbury's amendment and subsequently threw out the Bill by 128–48, on the third reading. The largeness of the majority is accounted for by the fact that those Tory peers who had been willing to accept the Bill with Hawkesbury's two-year clause were reduced, after that clause had been rejected, to uncompromising opposition.[1] Arden's tactics, in fact, had brilliantly succeeded. The episode is of great interest as showing very clearly the existence of a regular Court party among the peers, independent of, and often hostile to, the Tory Ministry of the day. "The Princes, four in number, came down in force with all the household troops and bishops", said Lord Grey with reference to the first reading;[2] and in that division Arden, Redesdale, Eldon, and Carlisle were found on the one side, and Hawkesbury, Harrowby, and Boringdon on the other.[3]

This situation was emphasized in the debates on the third Reversions Bill, which Bankes introduced on 28 March 1808. The new Bill was designed to comply with Hawkesbury's desire for a time-limit; but, in order to avoid the appearance of a challenge to the Lords, it was decided to suspend the grant of reversions not for two years, as Hawkesbury had suggested, but for one year from the passing of the Act, and from the close of that period to the end of six weeks from the commencement of the subsequent session of Parliament.[4] To this Perceval gave his approval, influenced perhaps by a petition in favour of the Bill, which had just been presented on behalf

---

[1] *Life and Opinions of Earl Grey*, pp. 202-206.   [2] *Ibid.* p. 205.
[3] *Parl. Deb.* x. 1053. The *Morning Chronicle* of 12 March 1808 gives the following as the " King's Party " in the Lords : the Dukes of Cumberland, York, Cambridge, Kent, Portland, and Montrose ; Redesdale, Arden ; the Archbishops of Dublin and Canterbury, and the Bishop of Durham. George Rose in the Commons.   [4] *Parl. Deb.* x. 1259.

of the City of London.[1] The Whigs, however, wanted a permanent Bill, and would have preferred to reintroduce the old Bill unaltered. Whitbread referred to " a party more powerful than the administration " ; Tierney talked of a " dark Junto " ; Taylor denounced " a compromise made with a party that nobody knew, and which that House ought not to submit to " ; and Burdett, in a long speech, attacked that " mysterious and malignant power, whose hand, felt, not seen, had stabbed the constitution to the heart ".[2] Still, it might now seem probable that the conversion of the temporary measure into a permanent Act was merely a question of time, especially as in the Third Report of the Finance Committee, which appeared in this year, the question of reversions was fully discussed. The Committee reported themselves opposed in principle to reversions, which diminished the prerogative of the Crown by taking away for another generation its power of nomination, and which frequently resulted in the appointment of unfit persons. But, on the other hand, it conceded that though many reversions ought to be abolished, still the system was cheap, and had not so far been greatly abused.[3]

Bankes brought in his fourth Reversions Bill on 31 January 1810, to make permanent the temporary measure of the previous year. Perceval, to the great indignation of the Reformers,[4] suggested that the Act should merely be continued " for a time " ; but Bankes' motion was " carried by an acclamation, in one voice, by the whole House. On the question upon the Chancellor of the Exchequer's motion, his voice and one other voice were all that could be heard." [5]

[1] *Morning Chronicle*, 1 April 1808 ; *Parl. Deb.* x. 1300-1302.
[2] *Morning Chronicle*, 29 March 1808; *Parl. Deb.* x. 1335-1336 ; xi. 18 *seq.*
[3] *Ibid.* clvii, Third Rep., Finance Committee.
[4] *Morning Chronicle*, 29 Jan. 1810.   [5] *Parl. Deb.* xv. 262.

The Lords were not impressed. They would not be parties to any irrevocable abridgment of the prerogative. When it was a question merely of suspending the grant of reversions until it should be seen which places the Finance Committee should recommend for abolition, they were willing to acquiesce ; further than that they would not go. When on 26 February 1810 Grosvenor moved the second reading, he was heavily defeated (107–67) and the Bill rejected.[1]

Faced with this insurmountable obstacle, Bankes sought to circumvent it by the method of 1807, and proposed an Address to the King. But the temper of the House was rising; and they refused to allow so pusillanimous a retreat. The Lords had cavilled at making a suspending Bill perpetual ; they must be given an entirely new Bill, to obviate the objection.[2] Bankes accordingly promised to try again ; and on 20 March obtained leave to bring in the fifth Bill.[3] This, like its predecessor, was rejected in the Lords on the second reading, this time without a division.[4] Another attempt to pass the Bill, in April 1811, was equally unfortunate.[5] At length, in February 1812, came the final failure. Bankes was beaten on the second reading in the Commons by 56–54. The minority included all the principal Whigs, and not one Whig voted in the majority. But the Commons were clearly growing tired of the project, which, as even Bankes admitted, did not promise much saving to the Exchequer, and which was embroiling them with the Lords. To temporary measures they were not averse, but, like the Lords, they were

---

[1] *Ibid.* 437, 493.   [2] *Ibid.* xvi. 12 *.

[3] *Ibid.* 18 *.

[4] *Ibid.* 1077 : on the two latter occasions there is evidence that the King interfered in favour of a suspension of reversions. Windsor Arch., George III, King to Perceval, 20 March 1810; King to Eldon, Eldon to King, 3 and 4 May.

[5] *Parl. Deb.* xix. 712 *et seq.*

beginning to look sourly on any permanent enactment.[1] So that when next the topic was raised by the unwearied Bankes (10 March), it was another temporary Act that was demanded.[2] Consistently with their previous attitude, the Lords made no difficulty about passing it, and it became law as 52 Geo. III, c. 40. It extended the period of suspension to 28 February 1814. Grosvenor had wished to extend it to 1840, but his amendment was defeated without a division.

These repeated attempts to put an end to the system of reversions illustrate the difficulties which the Whigs were liable to encounter in any scheme of Reform that they undertook. Not only were they in a decided minority in the House of Commons ; but they had to face a House of Lords which was as a rule firmly opposed to progress, and which could nearly always overwhelm Reforming opinions in a spate of proxies. The abolition of reversions was avowedly a minor reform : the saving to the nation might be £35,000 per annum. Only forty persons were involved. It was admitted on all hands that the system had its conveniences, and was not greatly abused. Why then waste so much powder and shot on a minor redoubt of the fortress of corruption ? Why strain the relations between the Houses for £35,000 ? It seems that the Whigs selected an easily practicable Reform, and encouraged themselves into thinking it important. They succeeded in convincing the Commons ; and their enthusiasm communicated itself to the politically minded outside the walls of Parliament. No doubt in principle reversions were undesirable. No doubt the Lords were mulish in suspecting an attack on the prerogative. But it does seem that Perceval was sound in his contemptuous indifference to the success or

---

[1] *Parl. Deb.* xxi. 692 : Wynn, however, strongly condemned Perceval's opposition to the Reform—a reflection perhaps on Wynn's sense of proportion, rather than on Perceval. Nat. Lib. Wales MS. 4814, f. 58.

[2] *Parl. Deb.* xxi. 1240.

failure of the measure. Ultimately even the Whigs grew
tired of it : when it came to the Lords for the last time,
Lauderdale, a staunch Whig, spoke pretty freely of the
folly of this persistence. He would vote for the Bill,
though he thought the savings which would result " a
perfect farce ", merely in order to get it through and
end these tedious and futile wrangles.[1] It was all very
well for Grey to urge that the passage of the Bill would be
the recognition of an important principle, and a gesture
of good-will towards the people ;[2] but it was the Whigs
themselves who had roused such expectations as the
people entertained. They were right in their estimate of
the hunger of Cerberus, but they wilfully exaggerated the
dimensions of the sop.

The endeavours of the Whigs to secure some measure
of Economical Reform were not confined to an attempt
to check the wasteful outpourings of the Treasury or
the Civil List. They tackled also the question of corruption. Not on their own initiative, however ; it was left to
an outsider to drag the party after him. Colonel Wardle
was the outsider, and the Duke of York was the first victim.
As early as the autumn of 1808 the *Independent Whig* had
published a leader entitled " Corruption and undue influence in the promotion of military officers the source
of national disgrace ".[3] But the main storm did not
burst until the following January. The Duke was accused
of conniving at the receipt of money by his mistress, Mrs.
Clarke, for her supposed influence in the procuring of
commissions and the hastening of promotion. At first the
Whigs would have nothing to say to Wardle, whose reputation was not of the best ; and the *Morning Chronicle* was
incredulous of the charges.[4] Both Grey and Grenville

---

[1] *Ibid.* xxii. 263-264.   [2] *Ibid.* 265 *et seq.*
[3] *Independent Whig*, 30 Oct. 1808.
[4] *Morning Chronicle*, 28 Jan. 1809.

showed a strong aversion to any attempt to make party capital out of the affair, an attitude in which they persisted, very much to their credit, throughout the investigation.[1] " It is not by such means ", wrote Grey, " that I wish to see the influence of the Crown reduced." [2] Only a few of the more radical members of the party—Madocks, Folke-stone, and Romilly in particular—began to lend their active support to " that tyresome hippocritical Col. Wardle ".[3] But public opinion soon grew greatly excited ; and either under its influence, or swayed by conviction as the revelations proceeded, a great many Whigs rallied to the side of " the Bloodhounds of St. Stephen's ".[4] As Cobbett observed :

Mr. William Smith, the famous Whig Club member, thinks it no longer necessary to *disclaim* Mr. Wardle, in the name of his party ; Mr. Whitbread is no longer in a passion at being accused of a connec-tion with the accusing member ; and the elder Sheridan talks no more of his dissuasive messages to that gentleman.[5]

The older and more sober members of the party still held aloof, " but the Whigs as a body took no distinct or manly tone whatever, on this embarrassing occasion ".[6] Indeed, even so staid a Whig as John Allen could condemn the fears and apprehensions which the aristocratic Whigs expressed in private.[7] On 11 April the Whig Club itself opened its doors, elected Wardle a member, and passed resolutions thanking those of its members who had been conspicuous in carrying on the investigation.[8] And no less

---

[1] *Dropmore Papers*, ix. 278 ; *Court and Cabinets*, iv. 327.
[2] Trevelyan, *Grey*, p. 167 ; and see Holland, *Further Memoirs*, p. 26.
[3] *Jerningham Letters*, ii. 3.
[4] Twiss, *Eldon*, ii. 71.   [5] *Political Register*, xv. 232-233.
[6] Holland, *Further Memoirs*, p. 29.
[7] *Brougham and his Early Friends*, ii. 355.
[8] *Morning Chronicle*, 12 April 1809. " It grieved me ", said Coleridge, " to see Wardle blending his yet transparent character with the muddy yet shallow stream of the Whig Club " (Stuart, *Letters of the Lake Poets*, p. 146).

than 125 Whigs, some of them as Grenvillian as C. W. Wynn, had voted for an Address to entreat the removal of the Duke from his position.[1]

Many of these men later realized that they had been too hasty in their condemnation of the Duke. There was a marked diminution in the numbers of the Opposition when the question arose of the Duke's reappointment; and it was a Whig peer—Lord Lauderdale—who was among the most zealous for his rehabilitation.[2] By the time the *Annual Register* for 1809 was published, or even before,[3] impartial opinion, swayed by the unsavoury subsequent history of Wardle and Mrs. Clarke, had swung round to a conviction of the Duke's innocence ; [4] and when Leigh Hunt came to write his *Autobiography*, he was able to make graceful, if tardy, amends for his previous attitude.[5]

But though fair-minded men revised their opinion, the country at large did not. Even so late as May 1810, over £4000 came in from all parts of the kingdom to pay Wardle's legal expenses. From Paisley 1227 subscribers

[1] *Political Register*, xv. 419, for list.   [2] Holland, *op. cit.* p. 93.
[3] *Morning Chronicle*, 30 Dec. 1809 ; Baldwin could not get the *Chronicle* to publish his defence of Wardle.
[4] *Annual Register*, 1809, p. 147.—" Never did *dirtier sticks* ascend in the *bright shape* of rockets than some of these said reformists have proved themselves to be. Cobbett is contemptible ; Wardle is in the mud ; and Burdett himself, I believe, is beginning to think that politics . . . like ' poverty brings a man acquainted with strange bed-fellows ' " (Moore, viii. 86). Wynn took a more favourable view of Wardle's character : Nat. Lib. Wales MS. 4814, f. 47. But Mrs. Clarke herself admitted frankly that no one could be so credulous as to think that she turned against the Duke of York from " pure patriotic zeal to serve the public " ; though she exonerated Whitbread, Folkestone, and Burdett from complicity (Mrs. Clarke, *The Rival Princes*, i. 72 ; ii. 117, 120). She accused the Duke of Kent of using Major Dodd to foment the agitation in order to remove the Duke of York from his position, to which the Duke of Kent aspired (*ibid.* pp. 25, 44). See Neale, *The Duke of Kent*, for his side of the case (pp. 172-186), and the chapter on the Duke of York in Fulford, *Royal Dukes*, for a convincing estimate of the affair.   [5] Leigh Hunt, *Autobiography*, p. 201.

sent £32 : 10s. ; " Twenty Citizens belonging to the Club
called ' The Convivials ', Ashby-de-la-Zouch " contributed
£1 : 0 : 0; while the " Perturbed Spirit of Allan MacLeod ",
made ghostly manifestation to the extent of a
pound.[1] A constant stream of congratulatory addresses
to Wardle and his chief associates left no doubt that
" Corruption ! " had supplanted " No Popery ! " as the
political cry of the moment. It is this fact which makes the
case so important. For the first time the Whigs were given
evidence that they had public opinion on their side, if they
would but stand by their principles. Whitbread, Folkestone,
and the young left-wing Whigs flung themselves into the
tide of popular enthusiasm ; Grey and Grenville remained
disdainfully on the bank. The one section saw only how
dirty the stream was ; the other had no eyes but for the
strength of the current. The honourable behaviour of the
Whig leaders in holding aloof did them great harm in the
country, and popular opinion applauded those Reformers
who had been most bitter in their attacks. Indeed, the most
prescient of them did not dare to do otherwise than attack
the Duke. They feared a popular outbreak if he retained
his post ; at the very least, they feared the total discrediting of Parliament, and its irrevocable branding as corrupt.[2]
" The effect which the business has produced through the
country ", wrote Wynn, " is from all accounts unprecedented, and all the old Jacobin leaven is set in ferment. . . ."[3] The more popular constituencies did not
hesitate to call their members to account if they had not
wholeheartedly supported Wardle.[4] The *Morning Chronicle*
encouraged this tendency to establish a stricter control

[1] Add. MS. 27839, f. 108.

[2] *Correspondence of . . . Lady Williams Wynn*, p. 144.

[3] *Ibid., loc. cit.*

[4] *E.g. An Account of the Proceedings of the Electors of . . . Southwark*,
12 April 1809, where Henry Thornton and Sir Thomas Turton, members
for Southwark, reviewed their conduct.

over the actions of members, and wrote : " the people now perceive what may be achieved by a bold, faithful and persevering representative and it will be their own fault if they do not *reform* the Parliament by the election of such men ".[1] The Wardle episode had lasting significance. Wardle himself might be indeed " a patriot born to scream and perish ",[2] but his work survived his reputation. " The public mind ", wrote Cartwright,[3] " seemed stricken with blindness, national patriotism to be dead, and our country left without hope. To remove this blindness, to revive this patriotism, to recal [*sic*] this hope, it pleased Providence to raise up a Wardle."

It was not long before there appeared those ambitious to imitate Providence. The Duke of York's case was followed by a period of violent attacks directed against corruption—particularly where Ministers might be supposed to have had a hand in it.[4] The case of Castlereagh and the East India Writership is a good example of the lengths to which the new-born zeal of the younger Whigs could go. A Committee on East India patronage was sitting, and in the course of the examination of Lord Castlereagh a curious story emerged. It appeared that Lord Clancarty was anxious to be in the House of Commons, and that the Government was willing to help him to get there. Castlereagh therefore gave him a Writership in the East India Company to sell to one Ogg, who was to pay £3500 for it. The money was to be given to Lord Sligo for a seat that he had at his disposal, and out of it 5 per cent. was to go to two agents, and a loan of money was promised to a Mrs. Graves. " Lord Castlereagh did not know Ogg, Lord

---

[1] *Morning Chronicle*, 20 Feb. 1809.

[2] *Patriots and Whigs*, p. 23.

[3] *Reasons for Reformation*, p. 3.

[4] " Every man that wants to make a name finds out an abuse. The Opposition are just as much alarmed at this spirit as the Ministers, and are just as unpopular with the people, at which they are quite indignant " (Moore, viii. 76).

Clancarty did not know Ogg, Lord Sligo did not know
Ogg ; but Ogg was to get the Writership, Sligo was to get
the money, and Clancarty was to get the seat." [1] In point
of fact, this nefarious triangular trade broke down, and
Clancarty did not make his appearance in the House.
Nevertheless a motion of censure was brought against
Lord Castlereagh, by Lord Archibald Hamilton, on 25
April 1809.[2] Bankes opposed this motion on the ground that
the intention, if criminal, had not been carried into effect ;
and Grattan, with great forbearance in view of his earlier
relations with Castlereagh, agreed with him.[3]

Simultaneously with the East India case, a Sales of
Offices Prevention Bill was passing through Parliament.
This was a small but effective reform undertaken by
Perceval in consequence of abuses which the East India
case had brought to light. It appeared that a firm called
Kylock & Co. carried on a thriving trade by pretending
to influence the distribution of offices in favour of those
who were foolish enough to apply to them. Perceval
proposed to make it a penal offence to solicit money for
procuring offices, or to circulate any advertisement with
that view.[4] His measure met with general approval.
Folkestone would have preferred further enquiries before
legislating, and would have wished to see the Bill's
scope extended to include specifically offices in the courts

[1] *Life of Grattan*, v. 386 ; *Parl. Deb.* xiii. pp. clxxiv-clxxviii.

[2] *Ibid.* xiv. 203.

[3] *Ibid.* 242-244, 235-237. Cf. also Windham's speech (*ibid.* 250).
". . . If he [Hamilton] meant that it should be declared criminal in any
man to endeavour to obtain a seat in that House under those circumstances with which they were all acquainted, that would embrace
much more than this motion. There was not a place in the Kingdom,
that sent members to Parliament, to which, with perhaps the exception
of Old Sarum, it would not apply. When they were called upon to
condemn so violently the noble Lord, they would do well to ask themselves the question whether they would hesitate, for the purpose of
securing an election, to recommend a friend to government."

[4] *Ibid.* xiii. 820 *et seq.*

of law ; and Creevey, in a violent speech, ridiculed these
tinkerings with the evil, and urged more radical measures ; [1]
but apart from these dissentient notes there was no
opposition, and the Bill became law as 49 Geo. III, c. 126.
It was far, however, from satisfying the more resolute
Reformers. Burdett had been ill when it was first introduced; but outside Parliament he scornfully decried it as
a " sham and idle measure ; a measure so preposterously
ridiculous, so childishly absurd, that really I am not
certain whether I could have refrained from laughing at
the proposition so pompously introduced ".[2] Of what use
was it, he demanded, to put through a Bill for preventing
trafficking in places, when at the very moment of its
passing Perceval was defending Castlereagh's conduct ? [3]

The division which was appearing between the left and
right wings of the Whig party was clearly marked in the
matter of Folkestone's motion of 17 April 1809, for a
Committee " to enquire into the existence of any corrupt
practices with regard to the disposal of offices in any
department of the State . . . and of any corrupt practices
relative to the purchase and sale of commissions in the
Army ".[4] Such a motion was too vast in its scope and too
sweeping in its implications to commend itself to any but
the most zealous. As Tierney remarked, the motion assumed
that the Government was corrupt in all its departments,
and this without pretending to state any evidence.[5] Petty
and Wynn, and Anstruther, and even Brand, were all of
the same opinion ; but Whitbread and Lord A. Hamilton
strongly supported Folkestone.[6] The minority of 30 (as
against 178) which followed Folkestone into the Lobby
contained nearly all the left-wing Whigs, together with

[1] *Ibid.* xiv. 116.
[2] *Proceedings at Westminster*, 29 March 1809, p. 13.
[3] *Meeting at the Crown and Anchor Tavern*, 1 May 1809, p. 13.
[4] *Parl. Deb.* xiv. 48 *seq.*
[5] *Ibid.* 59.   [6] *Ibid.* 51-68.

two moderates in Calcraft and Lamb.[1] But in essence majority and minority were aiming at the same goal. Each sought to maintain the prestige of the House in the eyes of the nation : the more conservative section by resisting indiscriminate attacks on public men and unjustifiable slurs on the public morality ; the more radical section by demonstrating to an irritated nation that the Commons were as eager for the reform of abuses as their constituents were. The danger of the one party was a too-convenient blindness ; and of the other, a factious pandering to a taste for popularity.

The problem recurred over Madocks' charges against Perceval and Castlereagh, which came upon the sorely tried Government this same summer, and which considerably stimulated the exertions of the Reformers.[2] Madocks alleged that a Mr. Quintin Dick had purchased a seat at Cashel through the good offices of the Treasury ; but that having determined to vote against the Government, he had been informed that he ought to resign, which he had subsequently done. There were many Whigs who entirely agreed with Perceval's contention that he was being victimized and made an example of from petty spite ; and that it would have been more candid to cast the charge in the form of a Bill for Parliamentary Reform.[3] Anstruther, Tierney, and Ponsonby all thought the accusation unfair.[4] Under the system as it then existed it was well understood that a member who voted against the opinions of the man to whom he owed his election ought at least, if he was to behave honourably, to offer his resignation. The fact that it was the Treasury, and not an individual borough owner, that was in question, could not logically be held to make

[1] *Parl. Deb.* xiv. 68.   [2] Add. MS. 27838, ff. 340-341.
[3] *Parl. Deb.* xiv. 493 *et seq.*
[4] *Ibid.* 382, 509, 518 : Wynn agreed, for apparently Dick *privately* asked Castlereagh whether he ought to resign, and Castlereagh advised that course. Nat. Lib. Wales MS. 4814, f. 50.

any difference ; for the Treasury was as regular a borough owner as Lord Lonsdale or the Duke of Bedford ; and its influence was transmitted from Government to Government. On the other hand, if the influence of the Treasury was ever to be destroyed—and to the Reformers its destruction was a capital object—this method was as good as any. Perceval's feelings could not be allowed to shelter a palpable abuse. Perhaps it was this consideration, overpowering the fear of a general blackening of the reputations of public men, which induced as many as 85 Whigs to oppose the 310 who vindicated the injured Ministers.[1] Moreover, the " Saints " deserted the Government on this issue. " All the violent or rather decided partisans, both of Government and Opposition, very strong against us, on the ground of the unfairness of censuring what we have connived at, and what is generally known to exist. Still this ought not to influence our exercise of a trust." [2] There is indeed no need to put everything down to the factious guerrilla fighting of a Folkestone or a Wardle, or to a desire to conciliate public opinion. Such a man as Romilly undoubtedly supported Madocks from the highest motives. " The decision of this night," he wrote, " coupled with some which have lately taken place, will do more towards disposing the nation in favour of a Parliamentary reform than all the speeches that have been or will be made in any popular assemblies." [3] The rank and file of the party was growing increasingly in earnest about Economical Reform ; and its ideas about what it was safe to effect were rapidly broadening. That it should desert its leaders (Ponsonby, Petty, Tierney) is not perhaps surprising in view of the chaos that prevailed in the party ; but it was significant that one of the strong men among them, and one of the most obvious candidates for the lead—Whitbread—should be invariably in favour of any measure of Economical Reform. Even though his ideas

---

[1] *Parl. Deb.* xiv. 518, 527.   [2] Wilberforce, *Life*, iii. 408.
[3] Romilly, *Memoirs*, ii. 281.

of Parliamentary Reform might not go the whole length of that for which the Burdettites clamoured, his impregnable solidity upon the question of Economical Reform offered a rallying-ground for the sincere Reformers, just as his acrid oratory attracted the factious and disappointed.

It was he who supported and directed the activities of men like Folkestone and Creevey : they were his lieutenants ; he was the directing genius. On the sinecures question, on reversions, on the attacks upon administrative scandals, it was he who was the most constant and impressive speaker on the popular side. Disappointed and sulky over his failure to secure the official headship of the party, at issue with them also over the war, it was not unnatural that he should take his own line on Economical Reform. He was singularly susceptible to flattery, and honestly desirous of pleasing : in particular he liked to please the people. He felt himself an honest tradesman in an assembly of politicians, and he was not ashamed to defend the quality of his porter in the House of Commons. He had a bourgeois delight in uncovering the scandals of High Life ; and his rather coarse-grained fibre thrilled to every skeleton in the cupboards of Government offices. He was not particularly acute nor particularly learned ; his oratory was of the bludgeoning type ; but he made his effect in the House because he was usually sincere. With Grey he was connected by marriage ; and it is said that the height of his ambition was a peerage for his wife. Despite his fine connexions, Whitbread had a business man's dislike of wasteful running. His capable management even succeeded in putting the Drury Lane Theatre on a sound basis. It is perhaps indicative at once of his exuberance and of his utilitarian leanings that he should have built his curricle on the model of a modern charabanc.[1] With a good opinion of his own ability, he combined extreme

---

[1] " Mr. Whitbread on Thursday launched a new carriage, upon a very curious plan. The body of it is near seven feet long ; it will accom-

sensitiveness to slights ; and when offended he became
sullen and violent in turns. It was his good fortune, however, that his pique rarely conflicted with the generosity
of his political principles. Thus more particularly on the
question of Economical Reform, the naturally democratic
cast of his mind and the disgust which the inefficient
leadership of Ponsonby caused him, alike led him to ally
himself with the Burdettites.

Jeffrey of the *Edinburgh Review* was on the same side.
Economical Reform might be largely a senseless clamour,
might indeed be inadequate to save the situation ; but at
least he was ready to try the expedient, to gratify the
clamour, and to curtail the expenditure. The *Morning
Chronicle* also was emphatic in its condemnation of a
House that had acquitted Perceval, and hinted plainly
that without Reform of some sort even a Whig Ministry
would be coldly received.[1] These and other supporters
of Economical Reform among the Whigs were by no
means prepared to go the whole way with Burdett. They
did not object, as he did, to the existing system as a
whole, but to the excrescences which disfigured it ; and
they were often shocked by the unbridled violence of his
language, as a curious incident in connexion with the
motion of Madocks shows. In his speech upon that motion,
Burdett remarked : " Buonaparte has a *strong ally* in this
House " :

whereupon a shout was raised from all parts of the House ; and,
after it had finished once, it began again, before he could proceed,
so loud that the boats passing upon the river (it was about seven
o'clock in the evening) lay upon their oars with surprise at the
sudden and violent burst of noise.[2]

The Whigs could feel no sympathy for such a leader.

modate fourteen persons. It is in the form of a car, and made of wicker,
painted yellow " (*Morning Chronicle*, 19 Aug. 1811).

[1] *Ibid.* 17 May 1809.
[2] Colchester, *Diary, sub* 14 May 1809.

The older and more aristocratic Whigs, in fact, looked with fear and indignation at the activities of the Burdettites ; and the majority of the party heartily agreed with them. They saw implied in the action of the Burdettites a regular system aiming at the discrediting of all public men ; the obliteration of party lines ; the bringing of the House into contempt with the nation.[1] They feared these deities of the " Crown and Anchor ", who commanded an allegiance more devoted than that they themselves enjoyed ; they mocked their stump oratory and impugned their motives, even while they availed themselves of their assistance. First the Duke, then Castlereagh, then Perceval —why not Buckingham next and Ponsonby afterwards ? Elder statesmen of unimpeachable respectability, such as Lord Hardwicke, were uneasy, and fearful of attack.[2] However sincerely such men might detest corruption, however disinterested their sentiments in prosecuting their enquiries, they could not condone inflammatory speeches. They could not dabble in anarchy. Burdett, Madocks, Wardle, and Cochrane were wholly irresponsible and potentially dangerous. It was not mere animosity that made Tierney turn so savagely against Burdett ; it was a desire to prove that a Reformer could still be conservative, and that a constitutional Puritan might still retain his sanity. Whitbread, Folkestone, and Creevey in their various ways and with varying motives elected to coöperate with the Burdettites, dared to play with fire. Their list of victims had started with Melville and Wellesley, and it was to continue with McMahon and Buckingham. In Parliament they fought their battle for Reform with no notion of giving quarter. And it was just for that reason that Grey and Grenville quarrelled so bitterly with them.

[1] *Life and Opinions of Grey*, p. 224.
[2] Add. MS. 35394, f. 17 ; Add. MS. 35648, f. 28 ; *Dropmore Papers*, ix. 289. Wardle professed to have a letter of Hardwicke offering £2500 and a place of £800 per annum for some burgage tenures.

Contemporary with the cases that we have been considering, were the great discussions on Curwen's Reform Bill. Curwen, who was the Whig member for Carlisle,[1] introduced his Bill on 4 May 1809 in a most interesting and revealing speech. Adverting to the motives which had led him to bring in the measure, he said :

> Are not the interests of the nation deeply involved in the estimation and respect in which this House stands with the people ? Could there be a greater misfortune to the country than the loss of the confidence in the House of Commons ? [2]

He felt that a change in the circumstances of the nation rendered a Reform imperative, and he laid particular stress on the growth of the influence of the Crown, and the increased weight of the House of Lords, consequent upon Pitt's large additions to the peerage. " Now, for the first time, the people call out for reform, without instigation, and purely on their own persuasion of its necessity." [3] Curwen's proposals in answer to that call were as follows. He would apply the oath against bribery and corruption to elected persons ; impose penalties for the sale of seats ; extend the bribery laws to agents and others attempting to corrupt electors during elections ; preclude electors from receiving corrupt consideration for their votes at *any* period, even after the election.[4] The measure was, as Folkestone was quick to point out,[5] and as Curwen himself admitted,[6] merely the logical corollary of Perceval's Sales of Offices Prevention Bill ; and it was calculated to renovate, not to alter, the existing Establishment.[7] He freely admitted that a general reform of the representation should precede such a measure as he was now producing, but asserted that

---

[1] Curwen was a great agriculturist, and was the father of his tenantry in every sense of the term. Lonsdale, *Curwen*, p. 96 ; Nat. Lib. Wales MS. 4814, f. 64.

[2] *Parl. Deb.* xiv. 353.
[4] *Ibid.* 358-364.
[6] *Ibid.* 358.

[3] *Ibid.* 357.
[5] *Ibid.* 370.
[7] *Ibid.* 355.

the exigencies of politics made it necessary to concentrate on the practical.[1] Moreover, the arguments used against Reform in general did not apply to measures of wise regulation.[2] His Bill would not close the door against talent ; it would not curtail the influence of the landed interest. On the other hand, as he warned the Opposition, a vote for his Bill would mean the renunciation of amiable accommodations to faithful supporters ; it would mean (for them) the end of jobbery of all kinds ; it would mean that they stood pledged as the party of purity.[3] Any future Whig Government would have to improve on the record of the Talents in these respects.

Perceval, who was not unreasonable where religion was not in question, gave a cautious assent to the first reading ; and on the Whig side Temple supported it for the characteristic reasons that it stood for the same principles as the Grenville Act of 1770, and that " it took away one of the greatest arguments in favour of Parliamentary reform. It would diffuse a salutary confidence in Parliament throughout the country." [4] Only Windham urged immediate rejection.[5] The next day, Perry gave the Bill his blessing in the *Morning Chronicle*.[6] It seemed that it would have a smooth and rapid passage.

The debate on the second reading, however, gave Perceval opportunity to produce his objections to the Bill.[7] Of these the more important were the danger of leaving the punishment of election offences to a common jury ; the difficulty of framing a satisfactory oath ; and the risks of an Act that would function both prospectively

---

[1] *Parl. Deb.* xiv. 361. [2] *Ibid.* 361. [3] *Ibid.* 362-363.
[4] *Ibid.* 374, 378. [5] *Ibid.* 367 *et seq.*
[6] *Morning Chronicle*, 5 May 1809.
[7] Curwen is said to have appeared in the House, probably on the second reading, dressed as a Cumberland labourer, in a suit of hodden grey, with clogs on, and carrying under one arm a Brown Geordie (or loaf) and under the other a Whillimer (or cheese). Lonsdale, *Curwen*, p. 58.

and retrospectively, so that no voter would be able to ask
or receive a favour from an M.P. It was around these last
two points that the struggle was to centre when the Bill
was considered in Committee. Meanwhile a division of
opinion was threatening in the Whig party, between those
who regarded the Bill as useless if it was not to lead to
further reform [1] and those who supported it as an admirable
and adequate measure.[2] The former party received rather
embarrassing support from Burdett, who left no doubt as
to his opinion of the measure. " As the laws against usury
gave the monopoly to the worst description of the people,
so this Bill would give the monopoly of the seat trade to the
Treasury."[3] It was to be an argument repeated over and
over again. Turning to the more general question of Reform
he observed with some humour that—

as to the time of reform, there were some who thought there were
two seasons improper for reform—a time of peace and a time of war.
In peace it was a pity to disturb the general tranquillity, in war
the nation had a great deal of other business on its hands.[4]

On the Tory side, Fuller, blunt and sensible as usual,
pointed out some of the difficulties of the Bill :

  . . . he did not think it could be effectual ; for there were many
things besides money which a man might give to procure votes,
such as a puncheon of rum to one, a horse to another, and a pipe of
wine to a third. He had no objection to allow the Bill to go to a
Committee ; although he did not like the administration of oaths
proposed in it, by which the Duke of Norfolk, or the Duke of

---

[1] *E.g.* William Smith. See *Parl. Deb.* xiv. 720.

[2] *E.g.* Porchester. See *Parl. Deb.* xiv. 773.

[3] *Ibid.* 729.

[4] *Ibid.* 732. Tierney, who was smarting under the reports of
Burdett's tavern oratory at the " Crown and Anchor "—oratory which
had seemed to charge him with desertion of Reform—seized the occasion
to deliver a personal attack on him, accusing him of endeavouring to
bring the House into contempt among the people, and calling him " a
political sea-gull, screaming and screeching, and sputtering about foul
weather which never arrived " (*ibid.* 773 *et seq.*).

anybody else, might be sent to Botany Bay for giving a pint of wine, and then inadvertently swearing that he had not been guilty of bribery.[1]

Still, the House had no objection to allow the Bill to go into Committee. The more zealous of the Whigs and the moderate Tories gave it their tolerance ; the conservative Whigs gave it their active support; and the " Saints " searched their hearts and found no sin in the thing.[2] So it passed, *nem. con.*, into Committee.

And in Committee the Speaker threw a bombshell.

Abbot was a Tory—he was even a Percevalian among Tories ; he was narrow, bigoted, and pedantic : but he was a Speaker whose rulings were respected, and whose considerable learning was worthily employed in the best interests of the House. His conception of his duties was lofty, his execution of them impartial. His conduct on the occasion of the impeachment of Lord Melville had commended him to the Whigs ; and even Cobbett viewed with satisfaction his re-election as Speaker in 1807.[3] None the less his speech in Committee was unexpected, and made a great impression :

The question now before us [he said] is no less than this— whether the seats in this House shall be henceforth publicly saleable? —A proposition, at the sound of which, our ancestors would have startled with indignation ; but a practice which in these days, and within these walls, in utter oblivion of every former maxim and feeling of Parliament, has been avowed and justified. . . .[4] We are now, however, come to a pass from which we have no retreat. Upon this question we must decide, Aye or No. To do nothing is to do everything. If we forbear to reprobate this traffic we give it legality and sanction. And unless we now proceed to brand and stigmatize it by a prohibitory law, I am firmly persuaded that even before the short remnant of this session is concluded, we shall see that seats in this House are advertised for sale by public auction :

[1] *Parl. Deb.* xiv. 733.   [2] *Life of Wilberforce*, iii. 408.
[3] *Political Register*, xi. 1124, 22 June 1807.   [4] By Windham.

And we shall have brought a greater scandal upon Parliament and the nation, than this country has ever known, since Parliaments have had an existence.[1]

The Speaker was not, however, prepared to accept the Bill as it stood. He was particularly opposed to the trial of election cases by the courts, and to the application of the oath to the electors, preferring that it should be tendered to the person elected.[2] But despite these qualifications, the speech did great service to the cause of Reform. So plain a declaration from one whom not even Windham could suspect of Jacobinical taint, swayed many doubtful members, and animated the friends of the measure. The *Morning Chronicle*, in a jubilant article, spoke of the " electrical effect " of the speech ;[3] and it became a regular weapon in the hand of future advocates of Reforming projects.

Subsequent discussion centred round the question of the oath, which all the Whigs demanded ; which the Tories professed to regard as impracticable ; and which the " Saints " desired should be buttressed with the penalties for perjury ;[4] and also round Perceval's amendments, which were concerned mainly with penalties. It was decided that the Act was not to extend to the sale of estates to which electoral influence was attached.[5] But a much more important point of difference began to emerge. Was the Bill to prohibit gifts of "office, place or employment " ? On the answer to that question would depend its usefulness. If it were not to include such gifts, then the frequent taunt of the Whigs that the Bill went to strengthen Treasury influence,[6] would be clearly justified. Again the Speaker intervened. " . . . unless the Bill applied to the grant of offices in return for seats in Parliament, it would be mainly deficient. It

---

[1] *Parl. Deb.* xiv. 837. [2] *Ibid.* 842.

[3] *Morning Chronicle*, 6 June 1809.

[4] *Parl. Deb.* xiv. 845, 847, 848, 904.

[5] *Ibid.* 843 *et seq.* [6] *Ibid.* 847 (Ponsonby), 848 (Tierney).

appeared that under the title of ' gift or reward ' that
application was included. . . ." [1] This pronouncement
seemed to have settled the question ; but a few days later
it appeared in a still more thorny form. There was in the
Bill a clause prohibiting " contract or agreement, *express
or implied*, to grant offices ". To this reading Perceval
objected, pointing out that if " implied " were suffered to
stand, it would be dangerous, and might prove criminal,
to give an office to a supporter who had done good service
at an election, no matter how worthy he might be to hold
it. To this the Whigs immediately made answer that no
Treasury would be so foolish as to make an " express "
contract upon such a subject.[2] On this apparently insoluble
problem, the debates of the following days turned. The
Speaker took Perceval's side, arguing that further legislation could be attempted later, and that it was well to strike
first at the more obvious abuses.[3] Among the Whigs there
was complete unanimity against Perceval ; all agreed in
thinking the " express " clause bad, but there was division
of opinion as to whether the Bill was still worth supporting.
Curwen himself, though acutely disappointed, was for
taking such reform as he could get ; and Grattan, Tierney,
and Wilberforce agreed with him. But the great majority
of important Whigs turned decidedly against the measure ;
and Romilly insisted that no such clause had previously
been inserted into an Act of Parliament.[4] On the third
reading on 12 June opposition grew even stronger, in view
of the very altered aspect which the Bill now wore on
emerging from Committee. Tierney now rejoined Whitbread
and Ponsonby in attacks upon it ; [5] and it was subjected
also to Tory cross-fire from the egregious Johnstone, who
regarded it as a mischievous tampering with a perfect
constitution.[6] Lord Grenville, too, viewed it with austere

[1] *Parl. Deb.* xiv. 849.   [2] *Ibid.* 899 *et seq.*
[3] *Ibid.* 926.   [4] *Ibid.* 957, 976, 979, 982, 986.
[5] *Ibid.* 1011-1014.   [6] *Ibid.* 991.

displeasure.[1] Only Curwen, of all the Whigs, was left to defend the merits of what had once been his measure ; which he did in a speech which bore small relation to that in which he had introduced it.[2] It had become, in fact, a semi-official Government Bill, as the division on the third reading showed. It was carried by 98–83, and the voting was upon party lines.[3] The left-wing Whigs had not yet quite finished with it, however : they had reserved a gesture till the end. For after the Bill had passed, Folkestone moved for the substitution of this preamble : " A Bill for the more effectually preventing the sale of seats in Parliament for money ; and for promoting a monopoly thereof to the Treasury, by means of Patronage ". Twenty-eight members were found to vote for this motion, including such steady and moderate Whigs as Abercromby, Milton, and Tavistock. And the *Morning Chronicle* remarked that if the faults of the measure had been merely in the nature of deficiencies, then it might have been tolerated ; but that as it was, the Bill seemed actively pernicious in principle.

It is, of course, easy to see the defects of the Bill. But Perceval's objection to " implied " was in the circumstances intelligible and almost insuperable. Until the whole system of patronage was abolished—and for that the country had to wait half a century—or until the power of the Treasury should have been submerged by wide extensions of the franchise, the dilemma remained. But the Bill had certainly many admirable features. Its legislation against bribery was unexceptionable. It went far to remedy the state of affairs against which the Speaker had inveighed. Seats were no longer advertised in the papers, no longer bought and sold in the open market.[4] And in 1812 Lord Liverpool wrote to Sir William Scott :

---

[1] *Dropmore Papers*, x. 29.   [2] *Parl. Deb.* xiv. 1004 *et seq.*

[3] *Ibid.* 1015 ; Walpole, *Perceval*, i. 334-337. It passed the Lords on 15 June, by 32–9, the minority protesting. *Lords' Protests*, ii. 423.

[4] Halévy, *History of the English People in 1815*, p. 164.

Mr. Curwen's Bill has put an end to all money transactions between Government and the supposed proprietors of boroughs. Our friends, therefore, who look for the assistance of Government must be ready to start for open boroughs, where the general influence of Government, combined with a reasonable expense on their own part, may afford them a fair chance of success.[1]

These benefits the Whigs, if they had been candid, might have admitted. The influence of the Treasury was not increased directly : it was merely that competing corrupt influences were diminished. Still, it can hardly be disputed that although the general mass of corruption grew less, the Treasury gained a relative advantage over its competitors. It was exactly on this point, moreover, that the Whigs felt most strongly the need for Reform. That there was faction in their motives need hardly be doubted ; but it is impossible to read the debates on Curwen's Bill without perceiving that a genuine desire for an extended series of Reforming measures was growing up within the party. They did not turn against the Bill because Perceval had made it his own ; they did not oppose it only because it threatened their electoral influence. The party was now awake ; its torpor had been disturbed by Wardle ; and it found itself united upon one point at least—namely, on the reduction of the influence of the Crown and the Treasury.

But though there were few Whigs who did not desire to reduce these influences, there were not many willing to follow Whitbread to the bitter end, without any sense of proportion. For he was now enthusiastically pursuing another shadow—the exclusion of the Junior Ministers from Parliament. The question of M.P.'s places had been raised once or twice

---

[1] Yonge, *Life of Lord Liverpool*, i. 444. George Eden found, too, that a borough would cost him (if he could buy one) £5000, whereas a Treasury candidate could get one for £2000 (Add. MS. 34458, f. 600). And in 1811 Ward could get nobody to take his £5000 for fear of a prosecution under the Act—or so he said : Brougham did not believe it. Brougham, *Life and Times*, i. 529.

already ; but in the course of the debates on Madocks'
charge against Perceval and Castlereagh, Whitbread gave
it a new turn. " He professed himself to be strenuously for
reform . . . as an alteration in the constitution of that
House. . . . He would not go to the same extent as the
Act of Settlement ; but he must say, that he did see
many before him holding places, who . . . he did think
ought to be excluded." [1] On 2 June, when the Third
Report of the Finance Committee came up for discussion,
he elaborated his views. He would have excluded the two
Junior Lords of the Treasury, the two Junior Lords of the
Admiralty, and all of the Board of Controul except one
member : the " Welch judges ", too, he deemed superfluous.[2] These ideas he embodied a week later in a motion
calling upon the House to take into consideration early
next session the limitation of placemen holding seats.[3]
The Whigs were, on the whole, very apathetic. Tierney,
though he supported the motion, could see no objection to
sinecurists for life retaining their places and their seats ; [4]
Ponsonby, who enjoyed a life pension as ex-Lord Chancellor
of Ireland, took the same line ; [5] and Porchester would
have nothing to do with any removal of Ministers from the
House.[6] Petty, opposing the motion, confessed that he

did not conceive that the reduction of placemen in that House
would produce much effect. The increase of the influence of
the Crown was principally from the increased patronage in the
revenue, the army, and navy, but did not appear directly upon
members of that House. Though the influence of the Crown, upon
the whole, had greatly increased, it had rather diminished in that
House.[7]

This was a damaging desertion for the Whigs, and Canning
did not fail to take advantage of it. He un-Whigged
his opponents by pleading the necessity for ministerial

---

[1] *Parl. Deb.* xiv. 387-388.   [2] *Ibid.* 876-878.   [3] *Ibid.* 934.
[4] *Ibid.* 945.   [5] *Ibid.* 947.   [6] *Ibid.* 953.   [7] *Ibid.* 946.

responsibility, and pointed out the usefulness of these minor offices in providing training for young statesmen. And, carrying the war into the enemy's country, he continued :

> There was an old philosopher, who said he would not argue with a man who had 50 legions, and for the same reason it did not become him to argue about the influence of an appointment in the Militia with a Militia Colonel [*i.e.* Colonel Whitbread]. But if this establishment of Local Militia were so very bad, and if it introduced 300 sycophants and dependants on the Crown, he would ask, was that great evil to be reduced by driving two Lords of the Admiralty out of that House ? [1]

Dialectically and logically Canning had the better of the argument. It is not surprising that the motion was rejected.[2] The idea remained, however, in the minds of advanced Whigs, and two years later the *Independent Whig* was advocating it as a useful reform ; [3] while the *Morning Chronicle* could go so far as to write :

> There is no single measure of reform that we should think more favourable to the public interests than a Bill to exclude these *underlings* of office from Parliament, whose only business there is to come down at four o'clock to make a House—and who perfectly understand when it is convenient that the House should be counted out. . . . There are about 30 such officers that ought to be disqualified from sitting in Parliament.[4]

Even the *Edinburgh Review*, which in 1807 had been of opinion that the best place for placemen was in Parliament,[5] had by 1810 completely swung over to Whitbread's point of view.[6]

(c) *Constitutional Issues*

The demands of the Whigs for a cleaning-up of the public services had not wholly been inspired by a zeal for

---

[1] *Parl. Deb.* xiv. 949-951.   [2] By 113-54. *Parl. Deb.* xiv. 957.
[3] *Independent Whig*, 5 Feb. 1811.
[4] *Morning Chronicle*, 15 March 1811.
[5] *Edinburgh Review*, x. 407.   [6] *Ibid.* xvi. 205.

economy and purity. On the contrary, they were to some
extent the result of a lingering dread of the royal prerogative. The Whigs still regarded the King much as Burke
had regarded him—as the fount of corruption ; they still
believed that the influence of the Crown had increased,
was increasing, and ought to be diminished ; and they
fancied that they detected a growth in the Crown's control
of patronage at the expense of that of the Administration.
Thus Lord Grenville wrote :

> The true economical reform which we want is a reduction of
> wasteful expense, in the Army most of all, then in the Ordnance
> and lastly in the Navy. What the public mean is something about
> places and placemen, on which head they will never be satisfied as
> long as there are persons in place and persons out of place, and as
> to which it may be right to do something for the diminution of
> the influence not of the *Government*, which is already quite small
> enough, but of the *Court*, which is paramount in this country.[1]

The Whigs usually prefaced their attacks on the Crown
with declarations that they bore no grudge to its just
prerogative.[2] To attack this, they felt, would be revolutionary, for the prerogative was a trust held by the Crown
for the benefit of the subject. This point of view—distinctly
anticipatory of future developments in constitutional
theory—was emphasized again and again by Whig speakers
in the course of the debates on the Regency.[3] The prerogative was an asset, not merely to the Crown, but to the
whole nation ; and they were far from wishing to subvert
it. The people was attached to the monarchy, and con-
spicuously so to the reigning monarch. But in the very
strength of this attachment lay danger. For the Crown,
the Whigs believed, was naturally acquisitive of power ;
and popularity was an insidious incitement to constitu-

---

[1] *Dropmore Papers*, x. 199.
[2] See *e.g.* Curwen's speech, *Parl. Deb.* xiv. 366 ; or Whitbread's,
ibid. 253 ; and Bentham, iii. 441 ; Grey, *Life and Opinions,* p. 263.
[3] Grey, *Life and Opinions*, p. 263 ; Bentham, iii. 441.

tional aggression.[1] They considered themselves, therefore, to be the guardians of the ancient fabric of the constitution, the divinely appointed pruners of despotic growths. They feared the prerogative : they watched it with the eye of jealousy ; and they succeeded in persuading themselves that the influence of the Crown was growing more formidable, and that royal corruption was poisoning the body politic as (they held) it had poisoned it in the days of Dunning.[2]

Their apprehensions are at least understandable. Their own experience in office had not been a happy one, and on the other hand the Tory Ministers who followed them were on such good terms with George III that there was not likely to be any dispute between King and Administration as to the distribution of the Treasury patronage. The King was frankly a party man, and after 1807 his party was in office. And on their side the Tories openly avowed themselves the defenders of the Crown against the assaults of Whigs and Democrats. "We are, however, bound", wrote the Duke of Richmond, " to make the best battle we can for the King. . . ." [3] Yet this harmony concealed the fact that Administration was gradually consolidating its claim to control all the patronage emanating from the Treasury. When, during the course of the restricted Regency (February 1811 to February 1812), Perceval came into conflict with the Regent over ecclesiastical appointments, it was the Prime Minister who prevailed. The projected resignation of the Household if the Whigs had obtained office in 1812 was another indication of the same tendency ; and despite the later vagaries of George IV, the end of his reign saw the question virtually settled in favour of the Government.

The Whigs did not perceive the trend of events. They

[1] See Grenville's lamentations on the nation's tolerance of Court influence, Add. MS. 34458, f. 449.

[2] Whitbread, in *Parl. Deb*. ix. 1167-1168 ; Thornton, *ibid*. xiv. 880.

[3] Add. MS. 37295, f. 399, Richmond to Perceval, 25 Sept. 1810.

saw only the great increase in the number of public servants
arising out of the increase in expenditure necessitated
by the war. It was not only the Parliamentary influence
of the King that they dreaded (though they held it to be
still dangerous); it was the spreading of that influence to
the nation at large.

If indeed [said J. W. Ward] the influence of the Crown consisted
entirely in the disposal of certain offices held by members of this
House and their connections, a Reform in Parliament (or even a
Place Bill) would prove a very effectual check to the evil. . . . But
unfortunately this influence is so extensive that it reaches not only
to the House, but to the people itself, and acts quite as powerfully on
the constituent as upon the representative body. Our establishments
are so enormous, and such a vast proportion of the whole population
of the country eat the King's bread, that there is hardly any educated person that may not hope either directly or through his connections, to become an object of royal favour.[1]

It was this contention that George Rose set himself to
refute when, in 1810, he published his pamphlet entitled
*Observations respecting the Public Expenditure and the
Influence of the Crown*. It was fundamental to the Whig
position that every public servant represented a unit of
royal influence : accepting this premise, Rose set himself,
with great ingenuity, to whittle away the undoubted growth
in the services. He stressed the effect of the Civil List Act
of 1782; he pointed out that only 40 members of Parliament
had places, as against 65 in 1781 ; and that only 63 Army
and Navy men sat in the House, as against 48.[2] The increase
in the Naval Establishment was 9, in the Barrack Establishment 184—small figures for war-time.[3] Since 1782, 217
offices—mostly mischievous sinecures—had been abolished,
at a saving of over £228,000.[4] Granted that the number of

---

[1] *Parl. Deb.* xxiii. 128 (8 May 1812) ; and see the examples of Whig
utterances on the subject given in Ranby, *An Inquiry into the supposed
Increase in the Influence of the Crown*, pp. 8-10.

[2] Rose, p. 40.   [3] *Ibid.* pp. 20, 21-23.   [4] *Ibid.* pp. 8, 13.

revenue officers had increased by 934 (a figure which for
some not very obvious reason did not include the 325
appointed to manage tobacco duties) still, the revenue
itself had increased by no less than £43,800,000.[1] In
short, Rose juggled his figures to great effect to empha-
size every saving, and minimize or disregard every large
increase.

The *Edinburgh Review* was down upon him in no time.
Rose's figures gave Brougham (the author of the review)[2]
no trouble at all. In his turn he minimized and distorted.[3]
A characteristic detail was his insistence on including the
clerks and labourers on the Barrack Establishment. Having
demolished his adversary's arithmetic, he went to the root
of the matter by asking if it were not obvious that the
increase in expenditure from 10 to 54 millions must be
followed by a corresponding increase in influence.[4] Contracts
and loans, whether the bidding were fair and open or not,
put the contractor under " attachments to the system in
general—to the government—to the Crown ".[5] As to the
Army and Navy, it was not so much the number of officers
that sat in Parliament that was in question, as the increase
of influence furnished by the enlarged scope for nomination
to the services. Patronage, he held, had become organized
and centralized, whereas formerly it had been distributed
among the various Boards :

so that he [the Minister] now, in every part of the country gives
away clerkships . . . which used formerly to be in the gift of the
chief of the particular departments. What is the consequence ? We
now see no such thing as an *opposition man* in any office :—no such
thing as an opposition member having the power to provide for a
single friend or dependant. . . . Hence the prejudice with which

[1] Rose, p. 52.

[2] *Edinburgh Review*, xvi. 187 *et seq.* Copinger, *On the Authorship of
the First Hundred Numbers of the " Edinburgh Review ",* p. 20.

[3] *Edinburgh Review*, xvi. 193-197.

[4] *Ibid.* 197.   [5] *Ibid.* 199.

all opposers of the minister are regarded in the upper and middling orders.[1]

And for this state of affairs he held the King responsible.

There are many elements of absurdity in this article. It is not easy, for instance, to see how the employment of three hundred—or three thousand—bricklayers and clerks was to increase the influence, either of King or Government.[2] There is no reason to believe that the cash nexus— plainly the only connexion between Minister and brick- layer—was strong enough to secure consistent political attachment. Presumably the bricklayer could take his trowel elsewhere. And even assuming the bricklayer fast bound in misery and economic fetters to the Government, his political influence cannot have been very considerable. Few bricklayers had votes. Few soldiers or sailors had votes; and fear of influence here can only be a survival of the Whig dread of a standing army. The only strata of society, in fact, which were likely to be of political importance, if influenced by Government, were those from which Brougham sprang, and those in which he now moved—the upper and middling classes. The Government undoubtedly could, and did, employ the necessities of the war to bind the commer- cial and sinecure-holding classes to itself: to court these classes had long been Pitt's policy. As Mr. Chesterton has said, "if ever men were responsible for handing over the country to cads, it was the party of gentlemen who waved the Union Jack after Waterloo". As uncompromising opponents of this system, the Whigs could have taken up an unassailable position. But it was by no means obvious

---

[1] *Ibid.* 203. An instance of this centralization of patronage is Perceval's revival of the " approved good practice " of using Govern- ment influence in the appointment of directors of the East India Com- pany,—a practice which had only recently been discontinued. Add. MS. 37295, f. 207.

[2] Yet many of the extreme Reformers shared Brougham's view : see Yate, *Political and Historical Arguments for Reform*, i. 55.

that the recent extensions of the system had increased the influence of the monarch. It seems unlikely that the King could, or would, have disposed of this additional patronage in opposition to the wishes of his Ministers. It was the Government, not the Crown, that reaped the main harvest, though no doubt George III gleaned a little too. And when Burdett reprobated Curwen's Bill[1] because the effect of it " would be to throw all the corrupt representation into the hands of the Treasury . . . and to render it impossible for a man of great landed property and local influence to find a person to represent that property and that influence "— then the nature of the grievance became clear. Had the Whigs been in office they would have seized only too gladly upon the additional influence which war budgets gave to Administration. Their grievance was not so much the existence of the spoils system, as the fact that they were increasingly excluded from all share in it. For their exclusion from office the King was certainly responsible, and he was therefore made the scapegoat. Brougham's article gave the game away. No Opposition men in office ! No chance to provide for friends or dependants ! Monstrous perversion of the natural order !

To meet the increasing concentration of patronage in the hands of Ministers two courses were open to the Whigs : either they might endeavour to change the whole system, or they might swamp it by an extension of the franchise. They did not heartily embrace either. The Democrats, indeed, realized that half-measures were of no use : it was not mere malice that pricked on Creevey, it was a holy hatred of jobbery, Tory or Whig ; but the main body of the party was not ready to sacrifice " influence "— it was rather jealous of it in others. And to render patronage insignificant through a reform of the representation would have demanded a wider extension of the franchise than most Whigs were prepared to contemplate. Still, those of

[1] *Parl. Deb.* xiv. 506 *et seq.*

them who supported Parliamentary Reform did hope
thereby to check corruption ; and at all events they were
less obscurantist than the Tory apologist Ranby,[1] who
held that the means used to create party attachments were
not thrown away, since (and it is to be feared that there
was no cynicism in the remark) if every M.P. were to act
upon his own honest opinion, the nation would drift into
chaos.[2]

The supposed increase of royal influence in the country
was parallelled in some Whig imaginations by a corresponding growth of the King's power in the House of Commons :
" The influence of the Crown in the House of Commons
at present is almost all-powerful ", wrote the *Morning
Chronicle*,[3] " —witness the continuance in office of the
existing administration. . . ." The conclusion was a little
naïve. A Ministry, it was argued, which is generally disapproved by the people, can only be supported by the
influence of the Crown : this Ministry is generally disapproved : therefore it is supported by the influence of the
Crown.[4] The Whigs too rashly assumed the validity of the
minor premise.[5] The Ministry could rely on the support of
moderate men in and out of Parliament, and it had, in
common with all Administrations, a control of patronage

[1] Ranby, *An Inquiry into the Supposed Increase of the Influence of
the Crown*, p. 36. He tried to show that if Government influence had
increased, Ministerial divisions would be correspondingly higher, and in
a series of interesting comparisons of maximum divisions proved that
this was not the case (pp. 24-25).

[2] Cf. Sergeant Willis' beautiful reflection :

> But then, the prospect of a lot
> Of dull M.P.'s in close proximity
> All thinking for themselves is what
> No man can face with equanimity.

[3] *Morning Chronicle*, 26 June 1810 ; and see Whitbread's speech in
Parl. Deb. xv. 389, where he calls Ministers the " tools of the Crown."

[4] See Ranby, p. 2.

[5] Even Brougham took this view : *Edinburgh Review*, xvi. 188

which exerted a strong pull on the waverers. The Whigs themselves realized the power which every Ministry held in its hands, and they were not ashamed to include it in their reckonings. Thus when, in the spring of 1811, Grenville despaired of taking on the Government unaided, Grey dissented from his judgment,

being satisfied that with our own strength, *supported by the influence of the Government*, there is a sufficient prospect of stability to impose it on us as a duty not to shrink from the task that the Prince has proposed to us. . . .[1]

There was a tacit assumption in the negotiations of May– June 1812 that whatever the personnel of the Ministry (and a wide variety was contemplated, at one time or another) it would be able to command a majority in the House of Commons. It was not merely a question of support from the Crown : Grey and Grenville can have had little hope that the Regent's influence would be put at their disposal in 1812 ; yet they counted on being able to carry on the Government. " Now the Prince Regent has made his option," wrote Bulkeley, " I take it many of the House of Commons who have been waiting for it, and not attending, will now attend under the banners of the Treasury." [2] Equally striking had been the transformation of March 1807, when, without an intervening election, Perceval's party leapt from about 100 to the neighbourhood of 250.

Ministers have a very good expectation of the House of Commons. Two hundred members have not voted at all, consequently have not committed themselves ; many will vote with the ministry to avoid a dissolution, having so recently paid the price of their seats ; many because they think the King's government must be supported.[3]

The explanation of these facts lies not so much in the corrupt influence of Government, still less in that of the

[1] Grey, *Life and Opinions*, p. 271: my italics.
[2] *Court of Regency*, i. 241.   [3] *Jackson Diaries*, ii. 91.

King, as in the strong centripetal force which every Ministry
exerted upon what was known as the "floating strength"
of the House. This floating strength was very considerable
numerically ; and, as Ranby pointed out, it acted on the
principle "that every ministry ought to be supported
until its abilities have been fairly tried, and judged insufficient ".[1] And he continued, in terms significant of the
accepted constitutional viewpoint in 1810 :

> This principle seems to me perfectly constitutional and most
> importantly beneficial ; for it secures to the King the free and
> effectual use of his prerogative of appointing his own ministers ;
> it secures to a newly appointed minister the right of appealing from
> the, perhaps prejudiced, judgment of one Parliament to the opinion
> of the nation, to be pronounced by another ; and it is a barrier to
> the interested, arrogant, and overbearing doctrine that "a minister,
> who on his first official appearance in the House has a majority
> against him, ought immediately to resign"—a doctrine, that in
> effect annuls the right of the Crown by a vote of the House of
> Commons.[2]

Another constitutional controversy of some importance
was the question of dissolution. The Whigs contended that
the right of the Minister to advise a dissolution was one
which was susceptible of grave abuses. It was a threat
that could be used against members who could not stand
the financial strain of frequent general elections. When, in
1807, Perceval's intention to dissolve became known, the
Morning Chronicle bluntly called his conduct unconstitutional, for the reasons that Perceval was dissolving with
the set purpose of securing support, and that only four
months had elapsed since the last election ;[3] and Lord
Hardwicke had a special audience with the King to attempt
to dissuade him from allowing the country to undergo "the
oppression and danger of a dissolution ".[4] No doubt the

[1] Ranby, p. 39.   [2] *Ibid.* p. 39.
[3] *Morning Chronicle*, 30 March 1807.
[4] Add. MS. 35646, f. 200 ; and see above, p. 24.

Whigs had very good reasons, then and afterwards, for
fearing a dissolution ; but they would almost seem to have
been attempting to prove the doubtful character of their
own proceedings in 1806. Again, in 1810, when a hint of a
dissolution appeared in the *Courier*, the *Morning Chronicle*
wrote :

> Ought such language to be permitted in the House of Commons ?
> Is it to be tolerated in a newspaper ? Is the prerogative of dissolving
> Parliament to be exercised, whenever that assembly expresses its
> dissatisfaction with the servants of the Crown ? . . . It is in vain for
> the Speaker of the House of Commons to demand freedom of speech
> from its members, when they vote under a menace of dissolution . . .
> it is hopeless to expect the punishment of malversation, when those
> whose business it is to prosecute public delinquents are told, that
> they shall cease to exist the moment they presume to execute their
> duty.[1]

It must be conceded that the Whigs had much right on
their side. Creevey put the case strongly from his point of
view, when, in the debate on the Sales of Offices Prevention
Bill, he said :

> It was absolute nonsense and delusion on the public, for the
> House to spend their time in considering abuses in the Commissioners
> of the Lottery, and every other minor department, when they knew,
> and when the public knew, that the greatest of all abuses was con-
> stantly practised by every Secretary of the Treasury, in buying and
> selling seats in Parliament. To talk of a dissolution of Parliament
> as an " appeal to the people " was mere mockery and imposition.
> It was perfectly well known that a dissolution of Parliament was
> not an appeal to the people, but to the Treasury. (Hear, hear !)
> Although he had great respect for the last government, and owed
> some personal favours to them, yet he must say, that their dis-
> solution of Parliament, . . . was not an appeal to the people, but
> an appeal to the Treasury.[2]

This brought up Whitbread, who could not quite swallow
such strong language, and was above all anxious to differ-
entiate between the elections of 1806 and 1807.

[1] *Morning Chronicle*, 22 Jan. 1810 ; *ibid.* 6 June 1807.
[2] *Parl. Deb.* xiv. 116. Cf. Cartwright, *The Comparison*, p. 10.

He could not help differing from his hon. friend as to a general
election being at all times an appeal to the Treasury. He believed
the Treasury did possess a most preponderating influence ; but at
the same time he knew that the people had a voice which would
be used. The infringement, therefore, on the elective right of the
people was not so great if they were not first driven mad and then
appealed to ; if they were not first driven into a state of phrenzy
and then desired to make use of their senses.[1]

Nevertheless, Creevey's uncomfortable candour gave the
gist of the matter. The power of the Government to dissolve
at will gave them an enormous advantage over their rivals.
They could organize their influence, prepare their campaign
in secret, and by a sudden dissolution catch the enemy at a
disadvantage. If they were Tories, they had the ripe
political experience of the King to aid them. In any case,
they had the resources and patronage of the Treasury.
That patronage the Whigs could not wholly consent to
abandon, so long as there remained a prospect that they
would one day be able to use it for their own purposes.

The elections of 1807 and 1812 ended, as usual, in a
victory for the Administration ; but in 1807 there were
special factors working towards that result. That election,
in England at all events, was fought upon the " No
Popery ! " issue ; and even in Scotland, where Lord Melville
recovered some ground, the cry was " King and Constitution ".[2] The Whigs accordingly revived the old cry of royal
corruption of the electorate. It was a charge very difficult
to substantiate. The secret service money and the Civil
List were strictly limited ; the Privy Purse was free from
debt and inadequate to large disbursements. Moreover, it
is unlikely that any extraordinary means were needed, for
popular sympathy seems to have been on the King's side.

[1] *Parl. Deb.* xiv. 120. The *Morning Chronicle* (17 May 1809) agreed
with Creevey.

[2] *Annual Register*, 1807, p. 235; Add. MS. 34457, ff. 287, 291; Scott,
Letters, i. 361 ; Furber, *Melville*, map at end. Melville lost ground in
the Commons, but got all his peers in.

It is certainly most improbable that the King and the
Administration should have expended anything like the
£200,000 said to have been disbursed by the rival candidates
for Yorkshire.

Still, the issue of the election of 1807 was undoubtedly
a victory for the King, as well as for the Administration.
The Portland Ministry was largely his creation, and the
Whigs made repeated but fruitless attempts to fix upon
Ministers the responsibility for those actions of the King
which had led to the fall of the Talents. They contended
that any new Ministry must be prepared to admit that by
accepting office they had also accepted responsibility for
the events which had put them in power.[1] It was a line of
argument which was not generally recognized until it was
adopted by Peel in 1834 ; against it, the Tories urged the
then accepted doctrine of the King's absolute freedom in
the choice of his Ministers. This question of the King's
freedom of choice arose again with the selection of Perceval
to be Prime Minister in 1809, when the *Morning Chronicle*
asserted that the dissolution of the Portland Ministry
should constitutionally have been followed by an application to Grey and Grenville to form a Government.[2] The
Whigs felt that the King's right of selection was an aspect
of his influence in the House of Commons : " the power of
the Crown is such as can support almost whomever the
King pleases ".[3] There is no need, however, to seek such
an explanation for Perceval's appointment and the survival
of his Ministry. The Whigs were unpopular, their leaders
irresolute and divided ; there was no other outstanding
candidate possible on the Tory side ; moderate men—the
floating strength—would give any Ministry a trial on
principle. As an anonymous pamphleteer put it, " The
matter in discussion is not now, as it used to be, whether

---

[1] See Grenville's letter to Hardwicke, 2 April 1807, in Add. MS.
35424, f. 74, which shows a remarkably sure grasp of the issues.

[2] *Morning Chronicle*, 20 Oct. 1809.   [3] Grattan, *Life*, v. 402.

the choice of the King shall be on one efficient man, or on another efficient man ; but . . . whether the King shall have any choice at all. . . ." ;[1]—and upon that question the contentions of the Whigs found little support, in theory or in practice. The Prince Regent certainly felt his choice to be quite unfettered : in February 1812 he informed Wellesley that he was still at liberty, and was resolved, to form his Cabinet according to his own views.[2] But, as the *Morning Chronicle* observed, " No Whig can consent to lodge *unnecessary* discretion in any hands "[3]—least of all the King's ; and on this question at any rate they adhered rigidly to their principles.

The Democrats as a rule divided sharply from the Whigs in their attitude towards the Crown. Hating Whigs and Tories impartially as a corrupt faction of borough-mongers, they were so far from condemning the Crown or fearing it, that they hoped to give an almost Tory basis to their reforms by reuniting King and people against the aristocratic cliques which had hitherto been exploiting both for their own narrow ends. The King, they believed, so far from extending the prerogative, was deprived of it, for he was obliged to confine its use to the balancing and conciliating of the borough-mongers.[4]

In truth [said Burdett] the borough faction have such power, that he is more like a Rope Dancer, than a King, as they make it necessary for him to be perpetually on the alert to balance himself on his slippery elevation, whilst the utmost he can do is to keep his place.[5]

The borough-mongering faction told him that the power of the King was to be dreaded by the people ; but they knew better than

---

[1] *Short Remarks on Parties at the end of the year 1809*, pp. 13-14.
[2] Add. MS. 37296, f. 204 ; and see Wilberforce, *Life*, iii. 431, regarding Perceval's selection in 1809.
[3] *Morning Chronicle*, 14 May 1810.
[4] *Reflector* (1810), i. 19. But contrast *Parl. Deb.* xiv. 1016.
[5] *Ibid.* 1052.

to be so gulled. The people had nothing to fear from the power of the King—their interests were the same.[1]

As to the influence alleged to be exerted by the Crown— he was more apprehensive of that exerted by the great landowners.[2] And Parliament, for all its constitutional prating, employed its energies, not in bridling the Crown, but in checking the people.[3] " . . . There is no question between the King and the People. The dispute is between the People and the House of Commons. . . ."[4] How far Burdett adopted this line in order to enlist the loyal masses on the side of Reform, and how far he was sincere in his belief that the Reform he contemplated would benefit the Crown,[5] is perhaps a matter for legitimate doubt. His attitude was certainly not shared by the Benthamites later on:[6] indeed, the *Independent Whig* advocated the passing of a sort of Statute of Livery, whereby the taking of royal gifts was to be made high treason.[7] Assuming, however, the sincerity of the Burdettites' declamation about the glories of the ancient constitution, their regard for the Crown becomes intelligible enough. They considered it part of a (mythical) polity, which had weakened as that polity decayed, and which should be strengthened when it was restored.

To the Whigs, on the other hand, it seemed merely that the institution which they had exploited in the first half of the eighteenth century was again threatening to burst the bonds which the Rockinghams had imposed upon it. There

[1] *Examiner* (Aug. 1810), p. 136. See also Leckie, *Essay on the . . . British Government* in *The Pamphleteer*, xi. pp. 89 *et seq.*

[2] *Parl. Deb.* xiv. 978.

[3] Burdett, *Speech*, July 1811.

[4] " Publicola ", *Letter to the Freeholders of the County of Middlesex* (in *Six Letters of Publicola on the Liberty of the Subject, and, the Privileges of the House of Commons, etc.*), p. 61.

[5] *Crown and Anchor Proceedings*, May 1809, p. 12.

[6] Bentham, iii. 441. [7] *Independent Whig*, 9 Oct. 1808.

was (it seemed to them) a danger that the Revolution Whigs, united, would not be able to tip the electoral balance against the Crown. The legend popularized by Burke was still a main tenet in their political religion ; the old suspicions and the venerable jealousies of the age of North, were still awake, and forty years of almost unbroken Opposition had merely exacerbated them. For almost the last time in English history the Crown is regarded as a great, a dangerous, political force. The mistake that the Whigs made was not so much to have opposed the influence of the Crown (for that would diminish of itself) as to have opposed to it the influence of landed property. " You cannot tell the people ", as Thomas Grenville remarked, " that the influence of what they call corruption is, for practical purposes, too small rather than too great." [1] It was partly because the Whigs felt the reign of property threatened by taxation that they were whetted to prosecute economies ; and because they felt their own power in the land growing less, that they assumed the King's to be growing greater.

... it will not be imputed to the Whigs [wrote the *Morning Chronicle*] that they are enemies to our establishments ; or to the illustrious family whom they seated on the throne. But when by the growing pressure of our burthens it is seen, that almost all the middle ranks of our gentry are forced away from their paternal seats, and are crowded together in Bath, or Brighton, or some such place, for the purpose of retrenchment, it is a mortifying thing to see the manner in which patronage is distributed, and all reform of expenditure is opposed.[2]

It would be unfair to the Whigs to attribute all their Reforming zeal to jealousy of the King, or dread of the miseries of Bath and Brighton. A considerable section of the party, at all events, prosecuted Economical Reform from motives of the highest patriotism. They performed a

[1] *Dropmore Papers*, ix. 296.
[2] *Morning Chronicle*, 31 Jan. 1809.

public service which needed performing, and as to which many Tories regretted Perceval's obstinate lack of sympathy. If they did not diminish the number, at least they checked the increase of sinecures. They temporarily arrested the granting of reversions. They made the " corruption-eaters " walk more warily for the future. They brought administrative scandals to the knowledge of the nation at large.[1] They made a real attempt to secure, if not perfect purity, at least relative cleanliness at elections. Startled into life by popular excitement over the Wardle case, they gradually lost unity of action and purpose, until at the end of the period they were divided into two or three well-marked sections, each in its way aiming at the same general goal, but quarrelling bitterly as to *tempo*, method, and deportment. As Parliamentary Reform came to the front, their interest in Economical Reform grew less. From the point of view of party unity it was a dangerous topic. The principal interest of such efforts as were made in 1812 (apart from the campaign against reversions) lay in the fact that they were deliberate attempts by the extremists, such as Creevey and Folkestone, to irritate, and if possible to alienate, the Grenvilles, or to annoy the Prince.

The movement for Economical Reform was not initiated or directed by the nominal leaders of the Whig party. Ponsonby, Tierney, and Petty remained decently in the background while Whitbread held the stage. Yet a very considerable proportion of the party was actively concerned in the movement. Analysis of seven fairly characteristic divisions gives a list of about 80 Whigs who, at one time or another, were prepared to take a strong line in favour of Economical Reform.[2] If only

---

[1] See petition from weavers of Chorley, 1812, where accurate knowledge of the gains of the principal sinecurists is displayed. *Parl. Deb.* xxii. 1156-1158.

[2] Divisions on Folkestone's motion, 17 April 1809 ; Folkestone's

those are taken who voted in three or more of these
divisions, there remain 27 names: Althorpe, Brand,
Burdett, Calvert, Coke, Combe, Creevey, Curwen, Folkestone, Grattan, Hibbert, Horner, Hutchinson, Lyttelton,
Madocks, Martin, Milton, P. Moore, Ossulston, Parnell,
St. Aubyn, W. Smith, Tracey, Wardle, Western, Whitbread, and C. W. W. Wynn.[1]

There are obvious omissions from this list. The accident
of absence prevents Cochrane's name from being there,
and probably Romilly's. If those were included who voted
in only two of the divisions, a further 28 names would
have to be added. The 27 given above are not exactly
identical with the strongest champions of Parliamentary
Reform. Still, the list gives a good idea of the more energetic
and determined section of the party. Ponsonby appears
only once ; [2] Tierney and Petty not at all.

The fact that 80 members of the party, which rarely
mustered 150 votes in the House, should have been found
to commit themselves to stringent measures of Economical
Reform is evidence of the change that had come over it
since 1806. That change will become more apparent in
considering Parliamentary Reform.

(d) Parliamentary Reform

(1) *The First Efforts.*—The agitation for Parliamentary
Reform started, as far as the Whig party was concerned,
rather later than that for Economical Reform : indeed, the
one was stimulated by the other. After the Talents had
silently allowed Parliamentary Reform to drop out of their

---

amendment, 12 June 1809 ; reappointment of Duke of York, 6 June
1811 ; McMahon's sinecure, 22 Feb. 1812 ; Madocks' motion, 11 May
1809 ; Wynn's Bribery Bill, 25 March 1811 ; pension to Lord Lake's
family, 28 Feb. 1808.

[1] I have in all cases omitted the "Saints".

[2] On Wynn's Bribery Bill.

programme, it was some time before any official Whig
ventured to introduce it again. The country was apathetic
—no petitions for Reform were presented to Parliament ;
the only persons who still seemed to have a lively enthusiasm
for it were Burdett, Cobbett, and Gale Jones—men with
whom the Whigs had no desire to associate themselves.
Indeed, the Whigs lost no opportunity of publicly dis-
avowing all connexion with Sir Francis and his principles,[1]
and openly mocked his demand for annual parliaments
and universal suffrage. Cobbett, the former friend of
Windham, became particularly obnoxious to them when
his *Political Register* took a radical turn.[2] The period
immediately after 1807, seems to be a time of aberra-
tion, or at least of gross distortion of former principles.
Reform now must by no means endanger the nation's
habit of following its natural leaders among the aristocracy :
if this leadership is to be called in question, then Reform
must be opposed. But if Reform was to make no difference
to the personnel of the rulers, why trouble with it at all ?
The balance of the constitution, that beautiful Whig fiction,
became the shadow of a shade when they professed to see
it existing in a House of Commons where King and Lords
each had equal weight.[3] The fact was, they were alarmed
by the nabobs and stockjobbers of Pitt :[4] they abandoned
their democratic propensities without difficulty when
they felt their grip on the constituencies threatened.
Even the Treasury and the Crown, which they were soon
to attack so bitterly, seemed preferable to the City man
and the East India magnate. The sacred influence of
Property—and by Property they meant landed property—
must at all hazards be preserved. In many ways their
instinct was a just one. The struggle of the Land against
the City, of agriculturist against trader, was then, as it

[1] *E.g.* Grey in *Parl. Deb.* ix. 714.
[2] *Edinburgh Review*, x. 399 (1807).
[3] *Ibid.* 412-413.   [4] *Ibid.* 417.

has always been, a party affair. The Tories, the original advocates of a Land Bank, were now the party of trade; the Whigs, who were later to make *laissez-faire* their own, were for the moment the party of agriculture.[1]

The arguments of those who rallied to the monopoly of the land were reinforced by the perennial consideration of expediency. It was not an argument without weight, certainly. The " hurricane season " was still prevailing; indeed, to the normal stormy conditions an " economic blizzard " was shortly to be added. To the Grenvilles, for instance, practical patriotism would always take precedence over idealistic legislation. Grey, too, was undoubtedly moved by these considerations. In 1808 we embarked upon the Peninsular war, a contest which, as the *Edinburgh Review* itself perceived, was likely to be a long and taxing one. In the excitement over Vimeiro, Cintra, and Coruña, Reform dropped rather into the background even for zealous Reformers. Yet Cartwright's mind did not shift from the groove in which it had been running for years. He still believed that Grey was the man of 1797 ; but he watched him with misgiving pursuing the " ignis fatuus of expediency " through the underwood of party tactics to the swamps of political impotence.[2] Cartwright was soon to supplement

[1] See *Independent Whig*, 31 July 1808, where influence of Stock Exchange and Lloyds' is feared. On the other hand, the paper opposed the *Morning Chronicle* (23 March 1811) over distilling from sugar, holding that cheap bread and favour to colonies were preferable to high prices for farmers (30 Nov. 1811). See Galpin, *Grain supply of England in Napoleonic Wars*, pp. 42-73, for this controversy. Prohibition of distillation from grain was a Tory policy. Creevey thought all great agriculturists beneficial, and usually Reformers : Burdett did not (Creevey, p. 94). In 1812 the *Morning Chronicle* expressed its contempt for Liverpool's Administration in these significant terms : " The whole body of the men in whose hands the reins of Administration are placed, do not possess, of hereditary stake in the country, the moiety of the interest of only one member of the Opposition " (*Morning Chronicle*, 21 Aug. 1812).

[2] *Life of Cartwright*, i. 358, 13 June 1808.

oratory by action, or rather to combine them, by reviving Reform Dinners ; but the time for these was not to come until 1809.[1] Meanwhile, the Whig opposition to Reform was breaking down. A sign here and a sign there proved that if an occasion were to come to them there were Whigs who would take up the Reforming cause. Lord Folkestone could be seen exchanging amenities and even visits with Cobbett ;[2] and in the pages of the *Independent Whig* (less responsible but more enterprising than the *Morning Chronicle*) was to be found an occasional sneer at the House of Commons as then constituted, and a bold mention of Parliamentary Reform in its programme for Utopia.[3] The publication of the famous " Don Cevallos " article in the *Edinburgh Review* of October 1808 was, moreover, a portent which alarmed the more nervous of the Tories, for it applied the parable of Spain to the situation of England. " It is as absurd as Sir F. Burdett, and as blackguard as Cobbett ", wrote one of them ;[4] and another felt spurred on to produce (under a pseudonym) a famous pamphlet on *The Dangers of the Edinburgh Review*, wherein he charged it with " *Infidelity* in religion; *Licentiousness* in morals; ... *Seditious and Revolutionary Principles* in politicks ".[5] A much more serious affair was the case of the Duke of York. This episode, indeed, is the real source of the revival of interest in Parliamentary Reform. It acted powerfully on a public opinion already agitated by the Spanish revolt. The Duke had not been condemned by the House of Commons : the nation believed him guilty. *Ergo* the House of Commons did not represent the people. " The old Jacobin leaven "[6] was

---

[1] *Life of Cartwright*, i. 384, 10 Dec. 1808.

[2] *Life and Letters of Cobbett*, ii. 19.

[3] *Independent Whig*, 11 Sept. 1808. The leading Whigs had indeed remained sufficiently true to the memory of past convictions to continue to support Godwin with very handsome financial assistance. See the list in Paul, *Godwin*, ii. 161.   [4] *Milne Home Papers*, p. 140.

[5] " Mentor ", *Dangers of the Edinburgh Review*, p. 4.

[6] *Letters of Lady Williams Wynn*, p. 144.

again set in a ferment ; the wearisome party strife of 1808 was replaced by contentions over things that were really of importance ; and among the Whigs there were found some who were not insensible to the change.[1]

In March of this year a meeting was held in Westminster to vote thanks to those who had assisted Wardle in his attacks on the Duke. It comprised most of the prominent Westminster Reformers ; but only two members of Parliament attended. They were, Burdett and Whitbread. To find Whitbread among the Burdettites is at first rather surprising ; but just at this time he was cutting himself off from the main body of the party, in disgust at intrigues for the leadership which seemed to settle nothing, except that he should not have it.[2] His attendance at the Westminster meeting was probably at once a gesture of defiance and a reconnaissance for possible allies.

Burdett's speech was a good sample of his Reforming eloquence, and was particularly trenchant in its treatment of the House of Commons, which was (he said) " So far from representing the sense of the people of England, I have ever found, since I have been a member of the House of Commons, that the most popular sentiment which can be expressed in that place, is a sentiment of contempt for the people of England, whose representatives they still profess to be. I do believe that the House of Commons is the only spot in all the world where the people of England are spoken of with contempt."[3]

Whitbread, who followed him, was wise enough not to commit himself to the extreme doctrines of his companion.

---

[1] See also, *Jackson Diaries*, ii. 420, for an account of the effects of the case. And compare Wishart's speech at the Westminster meeting on 24 March : " The result of these investigations must have proved, to every sensible and constitutional mind, the necessity of a reform in Parliament, more than a hundred volumes had been written in its favour " (*Full Report of the Proceedings at Westminster*, p. 9).

[2] *Dropmore Papers*, ix. 285 ; *infra*, p. 314.

[3] *Proceedings . . . at Westminster*, pp. 14-15.

There was no windy declamation, and no abuse of the
House of Commons. Instead, there was a definite pronouncement in favour of some measure of Parliamentary
Reform. He was convinced, however, that if such a reform
were to be carried, it must be as the result of a great
popular movement. He had the good sense to realize that
until the nation was enlisted on his side, Parliamentary
campaigns were of slight value. Unlike the rest of his
party, he did not quietly abandon the cause with the
explanation that he would be willing to take it up again
when the people should show that they desired it. He did
not by indifference damp the interest of the nation, and
then charge his timidity on its apathy. On the contrary,
he urged the people to become vocal, to agitate, to petition.

What I *now* hope is, that the *People* will be thoroughly convinced of the necessity of Parliamentary reform, and that they will
express that conviction as clearly and decidedly, and with the same
temper and firmness, that [*sic*] they have conducted themselves
during the last six important weeks—without tumult, without
violence, without threat. Under this system of temperate conduct,
I am of opinion that *the measure of Parliamentary reform would be
carried.*[1]

This speech is of great importance. It did not commit
Whitbread to a definite programme, which he might later
be forced to modify ; it did not necessarily involve him
with the Burdettites and their precious constitutional
nonsense ; but it was an earnest of good intentions—a
gesture towards the people—an attempt to win back
popularity for the Whigs. Not that it was in any way a
straining of the speaker's conscience. Whitbread was an
honest Foxite, who considered himself heir to Fox's
principles : he was, indeed, more Foxite than Fox, as his
discontent with the proceedings of the Talents proves.
But he was the first Whig at that time who dared—or

[1] *Proceedings . . . at Westminster*, pp. 30-31.

cared—to go to a public meeting and incite the people to demand Reform. Many were prepared, as the *Independent Whig* was prepared, to lament the Pittish proclivities of the Whigs, and their remissness in office ;[1] and there were those who were only waiting for a lead—such as W. Smith ; but only Whitbread came forward to give that lead. If any one day were to be selected for the beginning of that movement which came to fruition in 1832, it might well be that day in March 1809 when Whitbread went down to Westminster, and spoke hearteningly to the people of England.

The sudden jolt to men's political complacency, which the egregious Wardle had administered, brought into the foreground other controversies. Not only did men ask again whether a more equitable representation of the nation was not desirable ; they demanded (less radically) whether such representation as they had, was working well. That the Duke of York should have been virtually acquitted by the Commons argued that members could not be trusted to reflect even the opinions of that small section of the nation that had sent them there. Was the M.P. to be allowed to remain irresponsible to his constituents ? Were his constituents to be prevented from seeing that he faithfully discharged the trust reposed in him ? To such questions as these, the Whig papers answered with a decisive No. With a rashness which only extreme public excitement can explain, they pronounced unequivocally for the delegate as against the plenipotentiary.[2] The feeling was not only expressed in newspaper leaders : it took shape also in action, when the borough of Southwark called a public meeting to demand from its members an account of their conduct, and obtained from them not only explanations, but assurances (rather vague, however)

[1] *Independent Whig*, 1 Jan. 1809.
[2] *Morning Chronicle*, 8 March 1809 ; *Independent Whig*, 19 March 1809.

of support for Parliamentary Reform.[1] And a little later W. Smith maintained in Parliament that the essence of Reform was that the member of Parliament should be quite independent of all except his constituents.[2] The Burdettites clung persistently to this idea ; and when, in 1811, Cartwright was endeavouring to induce Romilly to stand for Middlesex as his candidate he presented him with a declaration (which Romilly refused to sign) which would have bound him to carry out the policy of his constituents.[3]

Such aims, which the complication of Parliamentary business was already making hopeless and anachronistic, had obvious repercussions on the Reform movement. They lent great force to all demands for the shortening of the duration of parliaments, whether to one year or three ; and they whetted the popular appetite for Economical Reform. All these considerations reacting upon and strengthening one another undoubtedly produced, in the early summer of 1809, a movement for Reform which however superficial and transitory in the majority of cases, may justifiably be described as general.[4] " The present cry for reform ", said the *Morning Chronicle*,[5] " comes from the most respectable part of the elective Body of the United Kingdom—the yeomanry, the house-keepers, and the middle ranks of society, who have been goaded into clamour by the ingenious torture of the assessed taxes, the vexatious inquisition of which is more unbearable than the amount of the duty itself." [6] The movement had, in particular,

---

[1] *An Account of the Proceedings of the Electors of . . . Southwark,* 12 April 1809, pp. 22-25.

[2] *Parl. Deb.* xiv. 377 (4 May 1809).

[3] Romilly, *Memoirs,* ii. 415.

[4] *Morning Chronicle,* 20 April ; *Parl. Deb.* xiv. 62.

[5] 17 April 1809.

[6] See *Parl. Deb.* xiv. 364, where Curwen says : " Simplify the system ; levy a few efficient taxes : do not by means of multifarious unintelligible laws inflict on the people constant vexation. Do not

taken hold of the City. To the Livery Dinner on 22 April,
twelve M.P.'s were invited—namely, Whitbread, Folkestone, Ossulston, Hamilton, Moseley, Wardle, Coke,
Curwen, Byng, (Anthony) Brown, Tracey, and Brand. It
was apparent that the acceptance of Parliamentary Reform
as an immediate programme was spreading in the House
of Commons. Folkestone at the dinner openly declared for
it ; Wardle, as his manner was, followed in a flamboyant
speech ; and Whitbread himself upheld Reform in a lengthy
address "abounding with every liberal and noble sentiment,
which a luminous view of the nature of political institution
could suggest ".[1] In short, as Burdett and Whitbread agreed,
when discussing the charge against Castlereagh and the East
India Company, " The converts of Parliamentary reform
were now " (in their opinion) " numerous in every part of
the country ".[2] As to plan, it was true that they had for
the moment none that was clear or coherent. They agreed
as yet in vagueness and optimism, for they were still
coöperators, rather than rivals.

What did the Whig leaders think of all this ?

Lord Grey was undoubtedly annoyed at what he
considered the excesses of Whitbread. That his brother-in-
law should have so far forgotten himself as to appear, and—
worse—speak, at a Westminster Hall meeting, was to him a
matter of great regret and some irritation. Even so warm
a supporter of Whitbread as the Duke of Bedford felt
himself a little shaken by such rashness ; and the Grenvilles
made no attempt to disguise their satisfaction that he
should have committed himself to demagogic courses.[3]
The Grenvilles had no real liking for Parliamentary Reform,

summons a whole country to know who keeps a dog ; or whether the
petty farmer who curries his own horse and plants his own cabbage, is
to be surcharged with a groom and a gardener."

[1] *Morning Chronicle*, 22 April 1809.
[2] *Parl. Deb.* xiv. 253, 248.
[3] *Dropmore Papers*, ix. 286-289.

which was just as odious to the controllers of six seats as
Economical Reform was to the beneficiaries of so many
sinecures. They were wary and acute politicians, however,
and they were not blind to the strength of the popular
demand for some sort of reform. They made up their
minds that it would be foolish to oppose a rigid resistance
to this demand. They would bend, rather than be broken.
Moreover, there was the alliance with Grey to be considered ; and they were not prepared to endanger that for
want of a few democratic phrases which need not mean
very much.[1] It seemed unlikely that Grey would be very
exacting about it. It was no wonder, then, that they
viewed Whitbread's conduct with malicious satisfaction,
and waited confidently for the moderates to take fright.[2]

No doubt they hoped that Grey, too, would be led to
abandon so disreputable a cause. If so, they were disappointed. Grey was certainly alarmed at the violence of
the House of Commons ; he lamented the persistent attacks
on public men ; he feared that the party was getting out
of hand.[3] But he did not allow himself to be frightened
into abandoning Reform. He seems to have felt, however,
that it would be well to define his attitude to the question—
to assure Reformers that he was still on their side ; and on
21 April, in the course of a debate on the war, he suddenly
made the following avowal.

To the principles of reform—to a temperate, intelligible, and
definite reform—I have always been, and still continue, a friend. To
promote that desirable object was, I contend, the study of the last
Administration ; and I can answer for it, that no man is more
friendly to such an object than my noble friend near me. It was in
our endeavours to attain that end that we incurred the reproaches
of those who covered their censure under the specious phrases of
a sordid economy and want of vigour.[4]

There is no need to doubt the sincerity of this statement.

---

[1] *Dropmore Papers*, ix. 292.   [2] *Ibid*. 286.
[3] Trevelyan, *Grey*, p. 168.   [4] *Morning Chronicle*, 27 April 1809.

Indeed, its very vagueness and lukewarmness tally with what is known of Grey's opinions at this time. A Reformer, yes : but a Reformer content to wait for Reform to come of its own accord. Grey saw clearly enough that the first era of Reform was dead ; what he did not see was that the second era was beginning. He was convinced that no good result could come from the methods which Whitbread was using, and the persons with whom he was associating. He equated the new Reformers with the violent revolutionaries whom the Friends of the People themselves had disavowed :

I was quite as much at war with the Patriots of this class in 1792 as I am now, and equally denounced by them : . . . in the very speech and, I believe, the very sentence to which Waithman alludes as you probably may remember [that of 21 April] I professed the same attachment to the cause of moderate and constitutional reform which I had always manifested ; and censured only the fashionable cant . . . that there is no difference in public men, and no advantage to be expected from any change of ministers.[1]

Grey's speech was received only with modified rapture by his followers. The *Morning Chronicle*, it is true, wrote a week later, " When Lord Grey declares himself a friend to a temperate, intelligible, and definite reform, he, in fact, says all we want him to say " ; [2] but it was not slow to point out that the Talents had fallen from power because they had refrained from actively prosecuting any measure of Parliamentary Reform—because they had in fact (though the *Morning Chronicle* left this to be inferred) taken up precisely the attitude that Grey was now adopting. It was no theoretical perfection that the *Morning Chronicle* was advocating ; no daring and violent innovation ; no invasion of the legitimate rights of Monarchy and Aristocracy : it was a restoration of the balance of the constitution by the concession to the democratical part of it, of that

---

[1] *Life and Times of Brougham*, i. 485.
[2] *Morning Chronicle*, 27 April 1809.

share in Government which was its just portion.[1] The *Morning Chronicle* here fused two ancient conceptions : that of Reform as a renovation rather than an innovation ; and that of balance in the constitution. Neither was very vital or fresh at this date ; for the one was being made ludicrous by Cartwright and Wardle, and the other was the common property of men of all shades of opinion.[2]

One thing, then, was clear in the summer of 1809, and that was, that Grey could not be counted upon to push forward the cause of Reform. In these circumstances, the leadership fell into other hands. There was in the City of London a considerable body of men who were keenly desirous of promoting the movement : some of them were on the Common Council, and nearly all of them were men of some consideration.[3] In the main, they were enthusiastic followers of Burdett. About this time, they approached the little group of Reforming M.P.s and, with their collaboration, decided to hold a grand Reform Dinner at the Crown and Anchor Tavern on 1 May. Their list of stewards was a long one, and included, besides eight members, many provincial Reformers.[4] On the appointed day the dinner was duly held, with Burdett in the chair, and Wardle, Byng, Brand, Madocks, Lord Cochrane, and William Smith representing the Parliamentary movement. France Place, Capel Lofft, Cartwright, Hare Townsend,

---

[1] *Morning Chronicle, loc. cit.*

[2] *E.g.* in rather protean form, in Wordsworth, Grosart, i. 248, 257 ; *Letters of the Wordsworth Family*, ii. 110.

[3] *E.g.* Matthew Wood, S. Goodbehere, Sir W. Rawlins, Waithman, Favel, and Miller. Crabb Robinson knew some of them, and wrote : " Waithman talks emphatically, but is not guilty of long speeches. An inclination to indulge in egotism, but not offensively. He is a sound-headed man, with[out] the ornaments of a learned education, and without affecting either to possess or despise them. Goodbeheere and Favel are both inferior in power but superior in manner " (*MS. Diary*, i. 106).

[4] *Crown and Anchor Proceedings*, 1809, p. 1.

Bosville, and 1200 other friends of liberty and enemies of corruption, assisted.[1]

The meeting was not an unqualified success.[2] After Burdett had made his usual speech, Smith, the member for Norwich and a Reformer of thirty years' standing, rose to deliver his sentiments. They proved by no means to the liking of his audience. He pointed out that Reform was not to be carried by isolated meetings of this kind, however enthusiastic. As a former member of the Society for Constitutional Information and, later, of the Friends of the People, he had learnt by bitter experience how small a proportion of the nation was actively interested in Reform ; he had learnt the power of the hostility of the corrupt voter ; and, more important than all, he had learnt that there could be opposition to Reform on a basis of honest conviction, from men who were certainly not corrupt. He had no doubt that there were grave difficulties in the path of the Reformers : as an instance, he cited the present apathy of Yorkshire, which was vouched for by no less a person than Wyvill himself. He warned them, therefore, against over-confidence and impatience.[3]

This speech provoked a bitter attack from Waithman. He denounced the treacherous pusillanimity of the Friends of the People, of whom Smith was a typical example ; and continued :

Here I cannot but observe, that I really and firmly do believe, that, however the great leaders of the party to which I have alluded, may, at times, have spoken on the subject of Parliamentary reform,

---

[1] *Ibid.* ; *Life of Cartwright*, i. 392. Wynn was invited to go, but declined to dine with " such redhot radical reformers " (Nat. Lib. Wales MS. 2791, C. Wynn to H. Wynn, 14 May 1809).

[2] Crabb Robinson, who was present, gives an amusing description of Capel Lofft's being howled down by intoxicated members of the general company. Crabb was disgusted. Crabb Robinson, *MS. Reminiscences*, i. 418.

[3] *Crown and Anchor Proceedings*, pp. 22-24.

they only supported that measure inasmuch as it was an annoyance to the existing Administration.[1]

After this, there could be no permanent coöperation between the Burdettites and any who still clung to the name of Whig. Burdett and his followers showed, over and over again, that they distrusted the Whigs completely. However much, therefore, the Whigs might desire Reform; however far they might be prepared to go in support of Burdett's schemes ; they could not be expected to regard him and his party with any great favour. Despite their intestine quarrels, the Whigs believed in Whiggism ; despite Whitbread's disappointment he could not and would not cut himself off from the Whig party. Was he not heir to the true tradition of Fox ? Although he had not been present at the meeting, he had entirely approved the Reforming sentiments that had been expressed there, and had even induced the Whig Club to declare for Parliamentary Reform on the principles of 1793.[2] But, by the very mention of those principles, he put a barrier between himself and the Burdettites ; for 1793 meant the Friends of the People, meant a continuation of the Whig tradition which Grey was allowing to lie dormant, but which Waithman declared had been a sham from the start. There could, in fact, have been no real return to 1793 ; the thread of continuity was of a gossamer lightness ; the ideas behind the movement, though hardly yet formulated, were different from the ideas of 1793. But there is no doubt that Whitbread and Smith were aiming at making Reform a *Whig* policy. They were not content to see the movement in the hands of Burdett and Waithman : they were anxious to capture the leadership for themselves.

To that end, Whitbread did not scruple to associate with Burdettites, to speak at crowded tavern meetings,

---

[1] *Crown and Anchor Proceedings*, pp. 36-38.
[2] *Morning Chronicle*, 3 May 1809.

to court the City—in short, to play the demagogue. He felt it imperatively necessary to show that an undoubted Whig was not afraid to do these things, and could match Burdett on his own ground. Not unnaturally, his conduct was misconstrued and disapproved by his leaders, and, indeed, by the bulk of the party, who felt that by degrading himself to Burdett's level Whitbread was forfeiting his claims to serious consideration as a statesman. They put it down to faction ; or to pique ; to anything, in short, but the real cause. Many of them—for instance, Curwen and Tierney—doubted whether the time was ripe for Parliamentary Reform ;[1] others, such as Temple, bluntly declared themselves hostile to it.[2] Even from those who had favoured it, there were doubts and criticisms as to the wisdom of indiscriminate tavern oratory ; and when Smith began a sentence " And now, Gentlemen ", the House roared with delight.[3] It seemed likely that the question would resolve itself into that of the respectability or otherwise of the " Crown and Anchor " ; particularly when Curwen observed that " It was not to the inflammatory proceedings of a drunken meeting in a tavern that he looked for the opinion of the people. He abhorred such meetings, and he lamented that men of character, talents and respectability should be found to countenance them." [4] But Whitbread in his reply on the following day not merely defended taverns, but spoke to the general issue as well. He readily avowed, that during the whole of his political life, he had been in the habit of attending meetings of the people.[5] For this amiable weakness he declined to apologize. As to Reform itself, he conceived it to be

the greatest good the country could experience, and therefore he sought for it. He thought it necessary in order to prevent convulsion ; but he never did think, nor did he ever say, that it would operate

---

[1] *Parl. Deb.* xiv. 505, 509.   [2] *Ibid.* 378.
[3] *Ibid.* 377, 4 May 1809.   [4] *Ibid.* 379.   [5] *Ibid.* 385 *et seq.*

like enchantment, as a panacea for all evils.[1] He never was deluded by theories, but looked for that reform only which was sought for by so many great men, by Mr. Blackstone, by Dr. Paley, by Mr. Fox, by Mr. Pitt, and many others.[2]

Why, he concluded, was there a popular sentiment for Parliamentary Reform in the country at that moment? It was because of the acquittal of the Duke of York, the rejection of the Reversions Bill, the exoneration of Lord Castlereagh.[3]

It cannot have escaped observation how vague and intangible the Whig proposals have hitherto appeared. Beyond the mere statement of their will to reform, they have hardly given any indication of how far they may be prepared to go. But in the *Morning Chronicle* of 17 May 1809, there is a definition of what the paper does not want, from which we can make shift to infer, what it does. " We do not wish for universal suffrage, or annual Parliaments, because we think that property, whether in lands, money, or talents, ought to be the basis of all representation." If only these elements are all adequately represented, annual parliaments, for which the Burdettites are clamouring, will become unnecessary. Its object is to make the House more dependent upon the constituencies. To that end, therefore, it is willing that parliaments should be more frequent. It approaches Parliamentary Reform, not from any basis of political theory, but from the point of view of expediency. Economical Reform is the taking-off ground. It is to check corruption, as much as for any other reason, that it urges Parliamentary Reform ; and even as it urges it, it warns the reader not to expect a Utopia. There will be no relief from taxation, and but little from public burdens ; but at least the taxpayer will know where his money is going. It attributes the disunion between the

---

[1] Cf. Lord Cochrane's speech, *Parl. Deb.* xiv. 518.
[2] *Ibid.* 513.   [3] *Ibid.* 515.

Houses and the nation—a disunion which it deplores—
not so much to the lack of a democratic franchise, as to the
fact that property is represented *capriciously*. That representation should be based upon property it has no doubt.
" Property and power ", said Davies Giddy, " should
invariably be connected together, for without that connection, no peace could be maintained in society." [1] The Whigs
did not doubt it. They drew a distinction, however, between
the " fair and inseparable " influence of property and the
corrupt influence of money given for the purchase of votes.[2]
With the system of small borough representation they had
little fault to find : it afforded an easy entry into the House
for the talented nobleman, and the impecunious genius ;
and, as a Whig speaker pointed out, a considerable number
of members for boroughs was always to be found voting
on the popular side.[3] They resented, however, the irruption
into their aristocratic pale of men whose only property
was money, and whose influence was derived, not from
legitimate primacy in the locality, but merely from the
banknotes they brought in their pockets. If these men
were given adequate representation, they would not be
driven to attack constituencies in which they had no concern. Landed property would resume its rights when the
moneyed men were given theirs. The country was conceived
as divisible into spheres of influence : what was needed was
the creation of new districts in which the newly rich could
develop their own politics. Rotten boroughs, whose representation was purely a monetary transaction, might
advantageously be disfranchised ;[4] and wealthy copy- and
leaseholders be given the vote to balance the " lawyers and
adventurers " whom Burdett so disliked.[5] The Whigs had,
indeed, no desire at all to change the nature of the personnel
of the House ; on the contrary, they were prepared to resist

[1] *Ibid.* 723.　　　　　[2] *Ibid.* 778 (Curwen).
[3] *Ibid.* 722 (Smith).　　[4] *Ibid.* 620 (Lockhart).
[5] *Ibid.* 726 ; Nat. Lib. of Wales MS. 4814, f. 61.

bitterly any serious alteration of this nature.[1] The *Edinburgh Review* of this period aimed rather at reducing inequalities in the franchise, than at eliminating them; and in return would have raised the qualification of electors.[2] To all schemes of a Burdettite nature it was inflexibly opposed, deeming them " by far the greatest calamity that can be inflicted upon us by our own hands ".[3]

When these were the theories that were current, is it any wonder that a sincere Reformer like Sir Thomas Turton could remark that he was sure that " universal representation was universal nonsense " ? [4] An unwieldy electorate, besides being dangerous, is imperfectly amenable to the wishes of its natural leaders.

This moderate position was by no means destined to represent the permanent Whig view on Parliamentary Reform; but for the whole of this period it was the view of most of the conservative members of the party, though the extreme left wing advanced a good deal beyond it. It was held, for instance, by Horner, who was equally disgusted by the excesses of the Patriots (*i.e.* Whitbread's group) and the apathy of the Whig leaders.[5] Thus he writes :

I would give members to some important classes of the population who can scarcely be said to be represented. It is at the same time a perilous thing, either to change the qualification, or to take away the franchise, or by compensations, to recognize the principle of the acquisition of that kind of property.[6]

For the moment, however, Burdett's plan of Parliamentary Reform, which he produced on 15 June 1809, offered a sort of touchstone to try Reformers. His motion was, to take into consideration the necessity for a reform of Parliament early in the next session. It was seconded

[1] *Edinburgh Review*, xiv. 300, July 1809.
[2] *Ibid.* 298. [3] *Ibid.* 302.
[4] *Parl. Deb.* xiv. 991.
[5] Horner, *Memoirs*, i. 461. [6] *Ibid.* 463.

by Madocks. In his speech proposing it, Burdett expounded
many of his favourite ideas. The remedy for diseases of
the body politic was for him always the same—a return
to the ancient purity of the true constitution ; his method
—" To reunite the King and people by the constitutional
bond of allegiance on the one hand and protection on the
other ". In more concrete form, his proposals were as
follows :

   (1) That freeholders, householders, and others subject to direct
       taxation in support of the Poor, the Church, and the State
       [*i.e.* all of them] be required [N.B.] to elect members to serve
       in Parliament.
   (2) That each county be subdivided according to its taxed male
       population, and each subdivision required to elect one
       representative.
   (3) That the votes be taken in each parish by the parish officers ;
       and that all elections be finished in one and the same day.
   (4) That the parish officers make their returns to the Sheriff's
       Court, to be held for that purpose at stated periods.
   (5) And that Parliaments be brought back to a constitutional
       duration.[1]

And when this remarkable re-creation of (an imaginary)
Anglo-Saxon polity should have been achieved ; when the
King and the people should have sealed their alliance so ;
what a prospect opened before the eyes of the Reformer !
" No bribery, perjury, drunkenness, nor riot ; no ' Wealthy
Brewer ' [? Whitbread] who, disappointed of a job takes,
in consequence, the independent line and bawls out against
corruption. . . . " ;[2] best of all, no Burdett ! " If I *am* a
demagogue, I am as complete a *felo de se* as can well be
imagined." [3]

   Madocks, seconding the motion, further explained the
principles of the Burdettites, and took obvious pains to
conciliate moderate opinion. " With respect to property,"

---

[1] *Parl. Deb.* xiv. 1053 ; see also the pamphlet *A Plan of Reform.*
[2] *Plan of Reform,* p. 18.   [3] *Ibid.* p. 19.

he said, " undoubtedly he admitted, or rather, was as anxious as any man to assert, that property was the only true and legitimate basis of representation, and it was because that property was not the basis of representation at present, that he wished the present system to be altered."[1] What could be so ridiculous, he urged, as to deny the vote to a £1000 copyholder or leaseholder, and give it to the stones of Old Sarum ? Not that he would advocate any drastic extension of the franchise : " he wished distinctly to state that nothing in his opinion was so absurd, as the notion of universal suffrage ; an idea he believed universally exploded ".[2] On the whole, however, few Whigs were conciliated, and the motion was beaten by 74 votes to 15—a thin House, as usually happened (so the *Morning Chronicle* bitterly remarked)[3] when questions of reform were under discussion.

When we come to examine the 15, we find very few pure Burdettites. The list was as follows : Adams, Burdett, General Campbell, Cuthbert, Hutchinson, Knapp, Lefevre, Maxwell, Moore, Thornton, Wardle, Western, Tracey, Turton, Wharton (J.) ; Combe and Madocks were Tellers. Add to these Lord Cochrane, accidentally absent, and Lyttelton, who paired. Now of these Hutchinson, Turton, and Western expressly disclaimed support of Burdett's plan in particular : they voted merely for a pledge to some kind of reform.[4] Thornton and Turton, it is almost certain, voted to satisfy their constituents, who had just extracted a promise to support Reform.[5] Cuthbert, who sat for Appleby, a borough controlled by Lord Lonsdale and Lord Thanet, could hardly have retained his seat if he had been a Burdettite ; and one suspects that Campbell

---

[1] *Parl. Deb.* xiv. 1061.　　　　　　　　[2] *Ibid., loc. cit.*
[3] *Morning Chronicle,* 16 June 1809.
[4] *Parl. Deb.* xiv. 1064, 1070, 1068.
[5] *An Account of the Proceedings of the Electors of . . . Southwark,* 1809.

and Maxwell, neither of whom was at all important,
voted with reservations resembling Hutchinson's. Whitbread was unable to be present ; and he suspected that the
motion had been suddenly made so as to make it impossible
for him to get up to London in time.[1] It is possible that
this was so ; for Burdett may have felt him to be a rival
for popular favour. It is undeniable that the insulting
allusion to the " wealthy brewer " could only be meant for
Whitbread ; for the only other man in Parliament to whom
the whole passage could apply—H. C. Combe—acted as
Teller for the motion.[2] Whitbread, however, seems to have
borne no malice ; for a year later he declared that if he had
been present upon this occasion, he would have voted for
the motion.[3]

Burdett's programme claimed the Whigs' attention on
the strongest grounds ; for it bore a striking resemblance
to Grey's plan of 1797. That scheme also had provided
for the subdivision of the counties ; for the copyhold and
leasehold vote in the counties, and the household vote in
the towns ; it too had sought to regulate and shorten the
mode of conducting elections ; and lastly, it too had aimed
at a reduction in the duration of parliaments—in this case,
to three years.[4] That scheme obtained 93 votes : Burdett's
only 15. For the difference in these figures, several explanations are possible. Burdett was certainly mistrusted, and
probably with justice, for his head was easily turned by the
favour of the mob. The Whigs may have been jealous that
their measure should have been brought forward by any
one else than they. But the essential reason was that there
was no real continuity connecting the two occasions. The
persons were the same ; the plans were the same : but the
ideas and the movement were different.

[1] *Tierney MSS.* Whitbread to Tierney, 15 June 1809.
[2] See *Public Characters*, 1806, for article on Combe.
[3] *Parl. Deb.* xvii. 147.
[4] Meadley, *ap.* Bentham, iii. 555-556.

Burdett's motion, in fact, should have made it clear that the radicals could not march with the Whigs—however "left" those Whigs might be. Whitbread and his group, who were trying to save the Whigs from themselves by adopting a popular programme; Holland, who had all Fox's vague liberalism; and Brand, who was soon to launch his own type of "moderate Reform", were none of them prepared to admit into the party the dissolute and vapouring Burdett, the grimly purposive Place, or the preposterously peripatetic Cartwright. Wardle had been forced on them; he was enough to discredit any party; they were glad to be able to drop him next year. The Whigs were not, as the *Morning Chronicle* pointed out with some disdain, of Cobbett's order of Reformers.[1] Cartwright's gift of his published works drew from Whitbread a message of thanks which was no more than coldly polite;[2] and Cartwright, on his side, had no hopes of the "hollow Whigs", who were even prepared to compromise with corruption by proposing *Triennials*; when every true Reformer knew that only annuals could save the country.[3] Cartwright, however, was indomitably confident. Ninety addresses to Wardle, but not one imploring the dissolution of Parliament: plainly the people knew that these Parliamentary parties had, from the common blackness of their corruption, become indistinguishable.[4]

This was perhaps susceptible of another explanation; but certainly it had the effect of stirring up the Whigs. Oblivious, apparently, of the *démarches* of Whitbread and Smith, Jeffrey of the *Edinburgh Review* suddenly took fright; and in the autumn and winter of 1809 wrote at length to Horner, in a high state of agitation. He fears the stiffness of the aristocracy in the contest with democracy which grows more serious every hour; he fears it, for it

[1] *Morning Chronicle*, 21 Nov. 1809.
[2] *Life of Cartwright*, i. 395-402.
[3] *Ibid.* 391.   [4] *Ibid., loc. cit.*

may lead to a catastrophe. Grey and Grenville, however well-meaning, are too unbending, " too aristocratical, and consequently likely to be inefficient " (what a confession for a Whig to make !). Admirable as hauteur is with the King, it will hardly do for the people.[1] For Jeffrey, from the Olympus of Calton Hill, has a sudden flash of supernatural vision. He sees—and apparently he was the only important Whig at that time to do so [2]—that there is something more than the desire for political equality behind the Reform agitation ; something more even than indignation at administrative scandals. He sees, in short, that a new ally has been given to the Reformers—an ally who may sweep all others from the field—an ally whose names are distress, economic oppression, squalor, starvation. *That*, among other things, made 1797 seem mere doctrinairism ; made it clear how essentially the first Reform movement was a summing up of the eighteenth century, rather than an anticipation of the nineteenth.

You ask too much of the people [he says], when you ask them to have great indulgence for the ornaments and weaknesses of refined life. You should consider what a burdensome thing government has grown ; and into what dangers and difficulties they have been led by trusting implicitly to those refined rulers. As long as they are suffering and angry, they will have no indulgence for these things ; and every attempt to justify and uphold them will be felt as an insult.[3]

Two months later, stung by the Walcheren disaster, he bursts out again :

Do, for Heaven's sake, let your Whigs do something popular and effective this session in Parliament. Cry aloud, and spare not, against Walcheren ; push Ireland down the throats of the Court and the country ; and do not let us be lost without something like a generous effort, in council as well as in the field. You must lay aside a

[1] Cockburn, *Life of Jeffrey*, pp. 195-197.
[2] Brougham perhaps excepted—he was not yet in Parliament. The *Independent Whig* is remarkable for an almost anti-capitalistic tone.
[3] Cockburn, *Life of Jeffrey*, p. 196.

great part of your aristocratical feelings, and side with the most respectable and sane of the democrats; by so doing, you will enlighten and restrain them; and add tenfold to the power of your reason, and the honour of your cause. Do you not see that the whole nation is now divided into *two*, and only two, parties— the timid, sordid, selfish worshippers of power, and adherents of the Court; and the dangerous, discontented, half noble, half mischievous advocates for reform and innovation ? *Between* these stand the Whigs, without popularity, power or consequence of any sort; with great talents and virtues; but utterly inefficient, and incapable of ever becoming efficient, if they will still maintain themselves at an equal distance from both the prevailing parties. . . . Is this a time to stand upon scruples, and dignities ? Join the popular party; which is every day growing stronger and more formidable. Set yourselves openly against the base Court party; bring the greatest delinquents to serious and exemplary punishment; patronize a reform in parliament; and gratify what may be a senseless clamour, by retrenching some unnecessary expenditure. I doubt whether all this can now save us; but I think it quite certain that we shall have rebellion, as it will be called, as well as invasion, unless something be done upon a great generous system. Cobbett and Sir F. Burdett will soon be able to take the field against the King and his favourites; and when it comes to that, it will be hard to say which we should wish to prevail.[1]

Jeffrey's remedy, therefore, is an alliance, for the sake of saving Whiggism, with the Reformers. There is something of Whitbread's policy about this; but the emphasis is distinctly different. Whitbread was as earnest about Reform at this time as Burdett was: Jeffrey was disposed for embracing it only as a manœuvre which need not mean very much. Like Whitbread, he wished to make the Whigs popular : unlike him, he did not care very much at this time about the means to be used, for he believed that the public was the victim of a delusion, and he hoped very much that it would soon regain a Whiggish normality.

Summing up this Reform movement at the end of

[1] Horner, *Memoirs*, ii. 12-13. See also *Edinburgh Review*, xv. 504 *et seq.*, for an almost literal reproduction of these passages.

1809 : the regular leaders of the Whigs are apathetic, and
the majority of their followers equally so ; but new leaders
have arisen who are drawing the young men increasingly
to their side, and, assisted by the journalism of the
Morning Chronicle, are soon to enlist the *Edinburgh
Review* also. Parallel with, and distinct from, the Parliamentary agitation, is a popular movement, centring in
Westminster, but having considerable ramifications in the
country. The supporters of this movement look usually to
Burdett and his friends for leadership : only a few as yet
are followers of Whitbread. But the country, as a whole, is
more awake to the possibility of Reform than at any time
in the previous ten years ; and " alarmist " or " reformer "
seem likely to drive " Ministerialist " and " Oppositionist "
out of fashion.[1]

(2) *Bentham.*—At this point, however, there came to
the Reformers a new accession of strength, which was to
have a permanent influence on their fortunes. In 1809
Bentham joined the movement. It was in 1808 that
Bentham first met James Mill, and it was through him
that he first became acquainted with the Westminster
Reformers. By a sort of free trade in opinions, Mill accepted
Bentham's philosophy, and Bentham broke away from the
conservative feelings of a lifetime to embrace the cause of
radical Reform.[2] Bentham's *volte-face* had for some time been
preparing itself. The hopes of a reform of the Scotch law
which he had entertained had been dashed by the fall of
the Talents.[3] He was annoyed that his own schemes, and
the efforts of his friend Romilly, for legal reform in England
should have met with such poor success.[4] He was, too, at

[1] *Lyttelton Correspondence*, p. 69 ; Bagot, *Canning*, i. 307.
[2] Halévy, *Radicalisme philosophique*, ii. 196 ; Bain, *Life of James Mill*, p. 72.   [3] Bentham, *Works*, x. 423, 432, etc.
[4] Stephen, *English Utilitarians*, i. 207 ; Halévy, *op. cit.* ii. 198, 193 :
" La réforme juridique suppose accomplie la réforme politique. . . ."
" Ses déceptions, ses misères, font de lui un démocrate. . . ."

home in the liberal atmosphere of the best Whig society ;
Shelburne had long been his patron, and with Holland he
was on terms of some familiarity.[1] He had, moreover, been
drawn into liberal courses by his interest in the Spanish
patriots, for whom he was anxious to provide a constitution.[2] It was perhaps not very surprising, therefore, that
he should have swung so easily to the side of the radical
Reformers. Not that he was unconscious of their failings :
he discerned the shallowness and potential mischievousness
of Burdett, though he approved the work that he was
doing.[3]

The Reformers had certainly caught a man worth
having. As early as 1809 Bentham was placing his pen at
the service of the cause ; and in that year he poured out
his excitement in two pamphlets of great importance. One
of them, the *Elements of Packing*, dealt with the supposed
abuses in the constitution of special juries, and was so
violently phrased that Romilly (who was consulted) persuaded him not to publish it. A few privately printed
copies, however, went round the Benthamite circle.[4] The
other was the famous *Parliamentary Reform Catechism.*
This work, whose vivid and hard-hitting style comes as a
surprise to the reader, was not published until 1817, when
it appeared with many revisions and alterations.[5] It
becomes no easy matter, therefore, to decide how far the
version of 1809 went ; and it is very much to be regretted
that Cobbett should have hesitated, and lost the chance of
securing it for his *Political Register* at that time.[6]

The plan itself differs little from that outlined by

[1] Bentham, *Works*, x. 439.   [2] *Ibid.* 433.
[3] *Ibid.* 471.   [4] Bain, *Mill*, pp. 99-102 ; Halévy, ii. 198.
[5] Bentham, iii. 435. On 29 Sept. 1809 Bentham writes to his brother :
" *Parliamentary Reform* is grown into a capital, constitutional work : the
particulars of the reforms proposed have been long ago settled, and
reduced to the form of a Table " (Add. MS. 36524, f. 27). And see Add.
MS. 34079, f. 83, which shows that Bentham read Roscoe's work on
the subject.   [6] Bentham, *Works*, x. 459.

Burdett in his 1809 motion, or from Grey's scheme of 1797. Equal electoral districts ; annual parliaments ; household franchise—or a franchise based on the value of taxes paid ; reform of electoral procedure—all these are here. In addition, there are characteristically Benthamite features : placemen are to be excluded ; correct reporting of speeches in Parliament is to be ensured ; and attendance at the House is to be enforced.[1] The principles on which these reforms are based are given by Bentham a little earlier. As regarding the elector, they are, that the suffrage should be as widely distributed as good sense will allow, and that its exercise should be pure, untrammelled, and easy. As regarding the elected person, the goals to be aimed at are his due dependence on his constituents and his proper independence in Parliament : these are to be obtained, the one by the member's sense of his own impermanence, the other by the exclusion of placemen.[2]

The importance of this scheme lies neither in its radical nature nor in its novelty : it seemed much too mild to Bentham, eight years later ; and, as he confessed, many of its provisions had been anticipated by Cartwright. Its importance lay rather in the vigour and clarity with which it urged its conclusions, and the keen logic by which it arrived at them. The Reformers had been in the unhappy position of not having brains enough for their programme. Bentham supplied them. He classified and (inevitably) systematized the vapourings of Burdett and the nebulous projects of Cartwright. Bentham took the Burdettite catchwords of the day and gave them meaning : he redeemed the cause of democracy by providing it with a basis of reasoned theory.[3] The sole clue to political conduct,

---

[1] *Ibid.* iii. 540. I have omitted the more radical proposals, which almost certainly belong to 1817.   [2] *Ibid.* 451-458.

[3] Yet it is surely too much to say, with Halévy (*op. cit.* ii. 202-204), that the *Catechism* was a purely philosophical essay. It had, and was intended to have, practical application.

he held, was Interest. What wonder, then, if Whigs and
Tories were indistinguishable, since their interests were
identical ? [1] The country was being governed by a minority
for the partial interests of a minority : was not that the
very definition of corruption ? Corruption was not merely
a matter of petty pilferings or sordid sinecures : it was a
system, it was a political theory, it was the whole government of England. Aristocracy as a form of government
was itself an intolerable grievance—

> Without any outward and visible change in the forms of the
> constitution [*i.e.* merely by corruption] . . . have the two separate,
> partial and sinister interests—viz. the *monarchical* and the *aristo-
> cratical*, obtained over the *democratical* interest (which is no other
> than the *universal* interest) not only an *ascendency* [*sic*]—but an
> ascendency so complete, that under the outside show of a mixed
> and limited monarchy, a monarchy virtually and substantially
> absolute is the result.[2]

The " democratical, which is the universal interest "—
here is the core of it all. How aptly it fits into the Utilitarian
philosophy ; how inevitably is that philosophy henceforth
linked with Reform ! Not that he is satisfied with a mixed
Government : inasmuch as it *is* mixed, by so much is it
less than perfect.[3] He claims not equality for the people,
but predominance.[4] " What—what could man ever find to
say in behalf of *monarchy* but that monarchy is *legitimacy* ?
—or in behalf of *aristocracy*, but that *property is virtue* ?
Fair questions these :—should any man feel disposed to
answer them, let the answers be so too : and let them not
—oh ! let them not ! be either imprisonment or death ! "[5]
One by one the cherished idols of the moderate Reformers
are swept aside by his invective. The judicious sobriety
of such as talk (as the *Morning Chronicle* had talked) of
the balance of the constitution is altogether too much for
him :

[1] Bentham, *Works*, iii. 526.   [2] *Ibid.* 446.
[3] *Ibid.* 450.   [4] *Ibid.* 451.   [5] *Ibid.* 451.

Talk of *balance* : never will it do : leave that to Mother Goose and Mother Blackstone ! *Balance ! Balance !* Politicians upon roses, to whom to save the toil of thinking—on questions most wide in extent, and most high in importance,—an allusion—an emblem— an anything—so as it has been accepted by others, is accepted as conclusive evidence . . . what mean ye by this your *balance* ? Know ye not, that in a machine of any kind, when forces *balance* each other, the machine is at a stand ? [1]

The *Edinburgh Review*, the influence of property, the eighteenth century itself, all swept away in one condemna- tory paragraph. One lapse into the *naïveté* of Cartwrightism he has, one joint in the armour of his omniscience : he believes in renovation, as against innovation.[2] But even here he avoids the attitude of Burdett. Not for him the union of King and People : not for him the Patriot King of the *Independent Whig*.[3] Eschewing equally the mysticism of the neo-Burkeians, and the constitutional fallacies of the Burdettites, he plumps for a restoration of *democracy*. Did he mean the folkmoot or the Mayfield ? It hardly matters. As constitutional history it was equally non- sensical with Burdett's theories : but it was—and this is important—purely democratic. Burdett used the King as a cry to rally loyalty against aristocracy. Bentham dis- dained such devices. He based his democracy not on political considerations, but on the fundamental tag of the " greatest happiness of the greatest number ". He gave Reform an irresistible catchword : he opened up a new and unimpugnable line of argument. The tough captious mentality of Place was conquered : the philosophers were enlisted in the faith their fathers had resisted. While Byron and Shelley in their day were to be essentially anachronistic, Bentham was fresh, devastatingly up to date. The poets of the new generation, like Walt Whitman in Mr. Beerbohm's cartoon, incited the bird of freedom to

[1] *Ibid*. 450.   [2] *Ibid*. 446.
[3] See *Independent Whig*, 12 Feb. 1809.

flap its wings and soar ; they preached the doctrine that
Southey and Wordsworth had tried and found wanting.
They preached the gospel of Greece, 'the sentimental
nobility of 1848. They were far more relevant on the
Continent than at home. But Bentham was the prophet,
not of 1830, but of 1832. He was, perhaps unconsciously,
the philosopher of the Industrial Revolution, and the
Industrial Revolution was rapidly becoming a factor in
politics. That he influenced the Westminster Reformers
is undeniable : that the Westminster Reformers were in
the vanguard of the Parliamentary Reform movement is
equally so. The ideology of the intelligent Reformer of 1810
was fundamentally different from that of his fellow of
1793.[1] The first Reform movement, which finished in 1800,
was essentially of the eighteenth century. There was no
real spiritual connexion between the Duke of Richmond
and the Chartists. Price and Mackintosh had little influence
on Brougham and Lambton. As to Fox, Bentham was
acute enough to realize the insignificance of his Reforming
activity.[2] Benthamism may have over-simplified and over-
systematized, but as an intellectual influence it was seminal,
and it is apparent even where it is not acknowledged. By
the power of his logic, and the intellectual eminence of his

---

[1] Stephen (op. cit. i. 289) regards Bentham as largely a revival of the
school of Horne Tooke : " The Utilitarians were the reformers on the
old lines ; and their philosophy meant simply a desire to systematize the
ordinary common-sense arguments ". But in doing so they provided a
new argument. As he points out, Bentham rejected the doctrine of
abstract rights, and regarded the Declaration of Independence as
" jargon ". Bentham may have founded " not a doctrine but a method ",
but it was the popularizing of the method until it became a doctrine
that made it so great a force.

[2] Bentham, Works, x. 428-429 : " My expectations of him were never
very sanguine. He was a consummate party leader : greedy of power
. . . but . . . destitute of any fixed intellectual principles, such as would
have been necessary to enable him to make, to any considerable extent,
a beneficial use of it. . . . Pitt, or anybody else in power, might have
made him oppose anything by adopting it."

personal circle, Bentham gave the Reform movement a much-needed intellectual fillip. Through Mill, in the *Edinburgh Review*, he reached the genteel establishments : through Place, he stiffened the people.

(3) *The Burdett Riots and Brand's first Reform Bill.*   On 19 February 1810 the British Forum, a London debating society conducted by John Gale Jones, advertised the following subject for discussion : " Which was the greater outrage on public feeling, Mr. Yorke's enforcement of the Standing Order to exclude strangers from the House of Commons, or Mr. Windham's recent attack upon the liberty of the press ? " At Yorke's instance Gale Jones was haled to the bar of the Commons, and on 21 February committed to Newgate for contempt. Burdett saw the opportunity, and took it. In a letter to the *Political Register* of 24 March he attacked the action of the House, and denied its power to imprison the free Britons who had elected it. Rather unwisely, the Government decided to take notice of this letter, and on 5 April ordered Burdett to be committed to the Tower. Burdett refused to surrender to the Speaker's warrant, and prepared to stand a siege in his house. The Serjeant-at-Arms eventually broke through his defences, to find Sir Francis gravely instructing his family in the constitutional mysteries of Magna Carta. Unmoved by this affecting tableau, he removed his prisoner and lodged him in the Tower. The London Reformists thereupon seized the occasion to stir up the London mob to riot with a violence little inferior to that of the No-Popery rabble that had followed Lord George Gordon.

To the Reformers of Westminster it was an opportunity of which they were not slow to avail themselves. It was, in fact, the best thing that had happened to them since the case of the Duke of York—and, indeed, it was better than that, for it gave them a martyr, which they had previously lacked. To the Whigs, however, and particularly to the

Reforming Whigs, it was rather a source of embarrassment.
The popular cry in Westminster was now directed against
those privileges of the House which had secured the
imprisonment of the people's idol, and the Burdettites lost
no opportunity of attacking the tyrannous laws which
allowed such despotic action on the part of an assembly
notoriously corrupt. The Whigs were in their usual dilemma,
only that this time it was in an acute form. The majority
no doubt agreed in censuring the levity with which Burdett
had precipitated a riot ; [1] but on the question of principle
they were not so clear. Did they believe in the sovereignty
of the people, or the sovereignty of Parliament ? It put
them at a serious disadvantage as against the Burdettites,
who had clearly made up their minds upon the question.
The Whigs had certainly not done that : and on the one
hand Wynn, by a motion in the House and a learned
pamphlet on constitutional history, sought to tighten up
and reinforce the privileges of Parliament ; [2] on the other,
Creevey, at a Livery Dinner, publicly denounced and
abandoned them.[3] Faced with excited mobs which menaced
their personal safety,[4] the Whigs wavered in their support
of Parliamentary privilege. A meeting of the Opposition
peers was called to Camelford House to decide on a common
course of action ; but it seems that they were unable to
reach a decision.[5] Grey and Grenville, indeed, held stoutly

[1] *Letter to Sir Francis Burdett from a Country Gentleman*, p. 9 ;
Creevey's Life and Times, p. 47.

[2] *Morning Chronicle*, 22 May 1810. He obtained only 16 votes (*Parl.
Deb.* xvii. 513-527) ; *Argument upon the Jurisdiction of the House of
Commons to commit in Cases of Breach of Privilege*, by C. W. W. Wynn.

[3] *Morning Chronicle*, 20 April 1810.

[4] " Little O[ssulston] was obliged to explain his politics to the mob,
who were going to swallow him, I believe. He is so factious that if he
was not so small and inarticulate he might some day or other get into
mischief. As it is he is never heard and scarcely seen. So *passe, passe,
petit bonhomme*, very harmless and very ridiculous " (*Letters of Harriet,
Countess Granville*, i. 3).   [5] Add. MS. 35648, f. 364.

to the Government side : in their opinion Burdett richly
deserved imprisonment ; but the general line of moderate
men, as exemplified by Lord Holland,[1] was that while
Burdett was undoubtedly in the wrong, still, the privileges
of Parliament were certainly capable of odious extensions,
which might become inimical to liberty. They feared that
the privileges which their fathers had wrested from the
Crown were being perverted to subserve Tory ends.[2]
Whitbread and Smith took much the same view of the
case : " privilege ", said Whitbread, " was given to that
House [of Commons] for the people's protection, and it
ceased to be applied beneficially whenever it was used
against them " ; yet he pleaded for the retention of Parliamentary privileges,[3] and Smith agreed with him.[4] Perhaps
they had found the solution to the Whig dilemma : perhaps
they realized that with a really democratic franchise the
dilemma vanishes. When the privileges of Parliament
should become, as the royal prerogative was to become,
the privileges of the people, then they would be really
valuable ; and since Whitbread believed that sooner or
later democracy must triumph, it was both reasonable and
adroit to invite the people not to curtail the inheritance
which must soon be theirs.

The House's vigorous assertion of its privileges was
very galling to the nation. Popular feeling strongly condemned Burdett's imprisonment ; and it seemed that by
its own action the House had brought upon itself the
hatred which it always charged him with fomenting. At
all events, there can be no doubt that its unpopularity was
such as to give real cause for alarm. A deluge of petitions
demanding the release of Burdett descended upon the

[1] *Early Correspondence of Lord John Russell*, i. 138.
[2] *Morning Chronicle*, 9 April 1810 ; Sydney Smith, *Letters*, p. 73 ;
even Southey took Burdett's part : Nat. Lib. Wales MS. 4812, f. 223.
[3] *Morning Chronicle*, 20 April 1810.
[4] *Parl. Deb.* xvi. 805.

House, and much time was taken in discussing whether they should be received or no. The petitioners soon left the particular grievance of Burdett's imprisonment—a grievance which the end of the session was soon automatically to remove—and entered upon the broader question of Reform. All sorts of demands appeared in these petitions : some were for a purely Economical Reform ; [1] some lamented the estrangement of the House from the nation ; [2] some recapitulated Grey's petition of 1793 ; [3] some sought to re-establish the balance of the constitution. [4] On the whole, however, the House could no longer remain in any doubt as to the sentiments of a certain section of the public, where Parliamentary Reform was concerned. A round dozen of petitions had demanded it : and they had originated not merely in the metropolis, but in towns as widely separated as Rochester, Hull, Carmarthen, and Worcester; [5] and in the rising industrial centres such as Liverpool and Nottingham. [6] A dozen petitions for Parliamentary Reform may not seem very impressive ; but when compared with the previous paucity, or even total absence, of such petitions, it was startling. It is true that there was little that was extreme in most of them, for when it came to suggesting remedies they had a tendency to take refuge in generalities ; but the Middlesex petition, for instance, reproduced Grey's statistics of pocket-boroughs, and protested against septennial parliaments for the interesting reason that seven years was just half the probable expectation of life at the most favourable age. [7] Special mention must also be made of Cartwright's petition. This great document, drawn with all Cartwright's merciless verbosity,

---

[1] *Parl. Deb.* xvii. 201* (Berwick).   [2] *Ibid.* xvi. 951 (Reading).

[3] *Ibid.* xv. 363 (Westminster).

[4] *Ibid.* 354 (Middlesex) ; *ibid.* xvi. 951 (Reading).

[5] Worcester, however, also sent an Address against Reform. *Ibid.* xvii. 604.

[6] *Morning Chronicle*, 5 June 1810.   [7] *Parl. Deb.* xv. 354.

throws no new light on him or his associates, but it helped
to keep alight in Parliament the little fire which Burdett
had kindled in the preceding year. It was presented by
Whitbread, and was sober and decent in its language ; but
even so, the House, which was in an irritated state, refused
to receive it, by 91 votes to 32. Whitbread and Brand
voted in the minority.[1] By doing so they did not associate
themselves necessarily with Cartwright's point of view ;
indeed, they explicitly stated that they would not give his
proposals their unreserved support.[2] They backed up
Cartwright's petition because they were anxious to protect
the right to petition, and because they were anxious to
assist any effort to strengthen the cause of Reform. It did
not matter that they disagreed with Cartwright over
details : it did not matter very much that they were rivals
for the confidence of the people ; but it was very serious
that the country at large should regard the House,
which was supposed to represent it, with contemptuous
hatred. That was the real significance of this sudden burst
of petitions, a significance which few of these petitions
failed to convey. Instead of taking warning from these
portents, the House of Commons made the breach between
itself and the nation wider by refusing to receive many
of the petitions that were forwarded to it. It was no wonder
that a second Middlesex petition (rejected, like the first)
should have extracted from Smith the gloomy admission
that " the House had lost much of its weight and respectability in the public estimation, and through its own conduct . . . ".[3] An outrageous petition from the City of
London, rejected without a division on 13 July, was

---

[1] *Ibid.* xvi. 1020-1031. Cartwright had already endeavoured to present a petition directly to George III ; who commented : " His Majesty
conceives that the impertinent attempts of such individuals as Major
Cartwright cannot be too positively checked " (Windsor Arch., George
III, 20 Jan. 1810). A little earlier he had tried the Prince of Wales,
with similar success : Windsor Arch., George IV, 20 April 1809.

[2] *Parl. Deb.* xvi. 1031, 1020   [3] *Ibid.* 805.

only the climax of a menacing movement.[1] In the pages
of the *Examiner* a correspondent was to be found advocating mass petitioning ; [2] and with this foreshadowing of the
Chartists we feel that we are in the nineteenth century
indeed.

The Whigs were undoubtedly alarmed at the strength
and suddenness of the movement ; and in their alarm they
reacted in two opposite ways. On the one hand, they desired
more than ever to propitiate the people ; and on the other,
they developed a sincere dread of violent innovations. The
more courageous of them urged the definite abandonment
of the policy of moderation ; [3] and a few frankly recognized
the validity of the sharp criticisms which had been levelled
at the House.[4] They saw, these wiser ones, that it was by
no means wholly a case of the instigation of the mob by
ill-disposed persons ; that, on the contrary, there was in
many parts of the country something like a spontaneous
movement. They grasped the fact that this movement was
largely the result of the prevailing distress : where they
erred was in ascribing the distress to the pressure of
taxation. It was just the moment when the Continental
System was nearest success ; when South America was
becoming glutted with our goods ; when the licences to
neutrals touched their peak, and when, in consequence, the
distress of our shipping industry touched its peak likewise.
It is hardly surprising, therefore, that discontent should have
become vocal, particularly when the House of Commons
by its own actions had presented so easy and so obvious a
mark. Nevertheless, though the agitation was natural, it
was not pleasant ; and the *Morning Chronicle*, for instance,
was far from easy about it. It could not see the public

[1] *Parl. Deb.* xvii. 601 ; Add. MS. 27839, ff. 104-105.

[2] *Examiner*, No. 131, 1 July 1810.

[3] *E.g.* Byng at a Middlesex meeting (egged on, perhaps, by the rival
presence of Hare Townsend) : *Morning Chronicle*, 27, 28 April 1810.

[4] *E.g.* Peter Moore. *Parl. Deb.* xvi. 1100.

confidence in Parliament, " our only sheet-anchor ",[1] turn
to hatred, without misgiving. Declamation against revolution and innovation began to appear in its columns,[2] and
though it quoted the resolution of the Whig Club in 1795,
in justification of the petitioners,[3] it by no means warmly
embraced their policies. Faced with a real agitation for a
real Reform, the moderate Whigs wavered and turned pale;
and with reprehensible timidity ran for shelter to the
aegis of Grey and Grenville. Grey's declaration of 1809 was
now their watchword, nor could they be persuaded to
advance further. They would " repair the injuries of time ",
but " God forbid that more should be attempted ".[4] It was
in a similar temper that Grey in June 1810 made the
declaration he had long contemplated,[5] on the subject of
Reform. He affirmed that he stood fast by the " fixed
principles of the constitution ", and in the light of those
principles (which had, moreover, been Fox's guiding beacon
too) he would endeavour to correct abuses when they were
felt to produce an admitted inconvenience. His attitude to
the extremists now, he claimed, was precisely what it had
been in 1792. As then, he now disavowed Cartwright and
his disciples.

The path they are treading is dangerous in the extreme, and
demands the most vigilant caution to prevent it from leading to a
fatal termination. Whenever this great question shall be taken up
by the people of England seriously and affectionately,—(for, not-
withstanding all we everyday hear, I doubt whether there exists a
very general disposition in favour of this measure)—there will then

---

[1] Add. MS. 34458, f. 238, Grenville to Auckland.

[2] " We wish reform, and not Revolution ; the repair and cleansing
of what we have already ; we want nothing new, either in mode or
substance " [could Eldon have said more ?] ; " we will send nothing to
the crucible, though almost everything to the cleanser. We want no
Corresponding Societies—no surrounding the Parliament House . . . "
(*Morning Chronicle*, 20 April 1810).

[3] *Ibid.* 14 May 1810.

[4] *Ibid.* 8 May 1810. [5] *Dropmore Papers*, x. 29, 30, 44.

be a fair prospect of accomplishing it, in a manner consistent with the security of the constitution . . . to the success of a temperate reform, no impediment is calculated to have a more hostile influence than the attempt to force a reform by public clamour.[1]

Grey's speech reflected the general feeling of alarm. The Burdett riots had revealed the depth of the popular dislike of Parliament. All through the eighteenth century the London mob had been a lurking danger, liable to break out into terrible and irrational violence. But the Burdett riots were the beginning of a new kind of mob ; they mark the watershed between the unintelligible fury over the Excise Bill, and the intelligible hatred expressed by the cheers at Castlereagh's funeral. There was more of real distress, and less of mere villainous ebullience; there was, also, a reasonable and important political motive.[2]

This sharp reaction from the Reforming zeal of the preceding year was, however, neither permanent nor universal. It was the expression of alarm at the excesses of the Burdett riots ; when the memory of the riots had died away, and when Burdett had made his followers ridiculous by his discreet avoidance of their celebrations for his enlargement, moderate men forgot their fears and resumed their interest in Reform. Indeed, even before the *Morning Chronicle* had got well over its nervousness, the Parliamentary Whigs had shown, by another important effort, that they were not disposed to be frightened into dropping the subject.

On the contrary, on 21 May 1810 Brand produced the first comprehensive *Whig* plan of Reform since 1797. The speech in which he introduced his scheme was distinguished alike by its good sense, its moderation, and its total absence of original ideas. Moderation was indeed its keynote : so much so, that adherents to Brand's particular kind of

[1] *Parl. Deb.* xvii. 565.

[2] There is an excellent account of the Burdett riots in *The Bland Burgess Papers*, pp. 316-317.

reform were immediately distinguished as " moderate Reformers ". His views proved to be decently conservative. He professed himself an adherent to the " renovation " school of constitutional history ; but offset this Burdettite conviction by his soundness on the necessary influence of property—an influence which it must, inevitably, possess, " in spite of the theory of the philosopher, or the violence of the people ".[1] But where the property was concentrated into the hand of one elector, there he would disfranchise. Rotten and pocket boroughs—both should go. As to compensation, though no legal claim could be substantiated, still he would allow it, as an eventual saving to the country. This was remarkably intelligent, from a member of a party which had opposed the principle of compensation for the last twenty-five years. For the rest, his proposals were informed with the spirit of compromise. Rejecting septennials and annuals as equally undesirable, he suggested a return to triennial parliaments. The franchise was to be extended to copyholders in the counties, and in the boroughs to householders paying " parochial and other taxes " ; but the large extensions which this vagueness might seem to admit were certainly not part of his intention : property was still to retain its supremacy. Lastly, as to electoral procedure, he decisively rejected the plan of equal electoral districts, which would throw political predominance into the hands of the large towns ; but on the other hand, he was in favour of the creation of polling districts.[2] " He was aware ", as he modestly remarked, " that this plan had not any of the ostentatious parade of theory, or the affectation of being rendered such as to be intelligible to even the meanest capacity ; but it was all of pure English growth, and on that account principally he was inclined to prefer it." [3]

The whole scheme was typical of the Whig Reformers of that time. With the traces of the old traditional Whiggism

[1] *Parl. Deb.* xvii. 127.   [2] *Ibid.* 123-134.   [3] *Ibid.* 128.

still clinging to it, with the caution which a distrust of anything of a Burdettite cast inspired, it displayed a new breadth of outlook, and a disposition to experiment with new methods. It was, in fact, a skilful blending of the appeal to conservatism, the appeal to expediency and the appeal to democracy. It was not very surprising that it should have obtained the very large number of 115 votes as against 234.[1] It was, therefore, a pretty full House—in itself a hopeful sign.

Whig opinion of the motion fell into three clearly marked divisions. First there were the extremists like Wardle, who were willing to vote for the Committee, but much preferred Burdett's plan, and were particularly anxious for annual parliaments ;[2] these were few, and can hardly now be reckoned as true Whigs. Then there were the Whigs for whom the scheme was too radical : Lord Milton was the chief spokesman of this group. He made much play with the fallacy of " restoration ", and strongly attacked the delegate theory of representation.[3] That Milton should have opposed the motion was not, perhaps, very remarkable, for he had already declared, in 1809, his fixed aversion for all such measures ;[4] but it was note-worthy that Lord Porchester and Charles Wynn should have agreed with him, for they were both ardent Eco-nomical Reformers.[5] Lastly, the main body of Whigs who voted for the motion. Conspicuous among them was Whitbread. By supporting Brand's motion, and by con-curring in his plans for Reform, Whitbread drew a clear line between himself and the Burdettites. He declared for

[1] *Parl. Deb.* xvii. 164. Wilberforce and Henry Thornton were the only non-Whigs in the minority.

[2] The following is typical of Wardle's constitutional history : " By an act of Edward 3, parliaments were ordered to be holden every year, and oftener if necessary. This rule was strictly observed from the 18th Richard 2nd, and was first infringed in the reign of Charles I. . . ." (*Parl. Deb.* xvii. 144).   [3] *Ibid.* 137-139.

[4] 11 May 1809.   [5] *Parl. Deb.* xvii. 165.

triennials, as against their annuals : he declared against the delegate theory. Convinced as he was that Reform was *urgent*, he was perhaps more enthusiastic and more radical than many who voted on the same side ; but it was strictly in consonance with his policy to support the motion. The scheme was practical, and it was Whig : if it passed it would go far to ingratiate the Whigs with the people ; while if it were beaten, *a fortiori* Burdett's schemes would be beaten too. By discarding delegacy and annuals, he sacrificed a little popularity to common sense : it was a sacrifice which would have to be made sooner or later.[1]

Ponsonby was for once on the same side as Whitbread ; [2] and Tierney, supporting the motion, considered that Brand's scheme would " render that House what it ought to be—a constitutional check upon the power of the Crown, and a sparing dispenser of the money of the people ".[3] Such a remark gives us a sharp flash of insight into what the older Whigs might mean by Reform. The House of Commons was to them a check first and foremost : its constructive possibilities were almost ignored. To check the Crown, they believed, by keeping a vigilant eye upon public expenditure, was all that the nation could ask of them. This function the unreformed Parliament had in some sort performed : but the extension of royal influence which (they held) was the result of the war ; the scandals which the Economical Reform campaign had brought to light ; their own inability to effect anything while in hopeless opposition—all had led them to consider whether the people should not be called upon (in a cautious way) to assist them in their task. It is not suggested that this motive actuated a majority of the 115, or even a very large number of them ; but there can be no doubt that it actuated some.

Nevertheless, 115 Whig members had voted for a Reform Bill, a thing which would have been considered

---

[1] *Ibid.* 147-151.   [2] *Ibid.* 162-165.   [3] *Ibid., loc. cit.*

impossible in 1808. Divergent as they were in motives and
outlook, the Whigs had made an important step forward.
In 1809 the Reform movement had gripped the City, and
even extended into the country : in 1810 it fastened on the
Whigs. A view of the Whig position at the end of the
session of 1810, and of the evidences from the politically
empty months of the summer and autumn, shows how
variegated were the sentiments which the revival of Reform
had stirred up. But one feeling was common to all ; the
feeling that the House did not represent the will of the
people. The great defeat on Porchester's vote of censure
on the Walcheren fiasco became the text for all future
Whig homilies on Reform. The *Edinburgh Review*, for
instance, had been particularly explicit. If Ministers were
acquitted on the Walcheren enquiry, then Parliament
would stand condemned before the nation.[1] Lord Holland
echoed the sentiment.[2] The *Edinburgh Review*'s article on
the " State of Parties " in its issue of January 1810 repeated
the exhortations of Jeffrey's letter to Horner of the
previous December. It urged a union with the Reformers ;
but it urged it in terms which left no doubt that it was to
be a *mariage de convenance*. There was no suggestion of
real democratic conviction. It was a remedy for the
"State of Parties" ; it was a *move* to rehabilitate Whiggism.
But what else was Whitbread's policy than that ? To this
it may be answered that Whitbread wished to gain for
the Whigs the credit of leading a movement which he
(and most of his immediate followers) would have supported in any event ; whereas the *Edinburgh Review*
seemed to be prescribing a sacrifice of present inclination
for the sake of future gain. It is possible, perhaps, to
classify the Whigs at this time somewhat as follows : first,
the anti-Reform section (Grey, Milton, Porchester, Wynn,

[1] See *Political Register*, xvii. 518 ; *Life and Times of Brougham*,
i. 504.

[2] Holland, *Further Memoirs of the Whig Party*, p. 47.

etc.) ; secondly, the moderates ; thirdly, the ardent Reformers (Whitbread, Smith, Coke, Creevey, etc.). The
moderates comprised those who, like the *Edinburgh Review*, sought Reform for party advantage ; those, who, like
Tierney, sought it as a help against the Crown; and those,
like Brand, who, while actuated by Whitbread's motives,
were yet more cautious and dilatory in their procedure.

The moderate Reformers are, in fact, the really interesting figures just at this time. They represent, on the one
hand, the actualization of the principles of Reform to which
in the abstract Grey still adhered ; and, on the other, the
shrewd calculations of political tactics. Honourably distinguished among them was the *Morning Chronicle*, which
seems to have abandoned its rash adherence to the delegate
theory and become a convinced supporter of cautious
policies. It undertook once again the defence of Grey
against radical attacks,[1] and it entirely abandoned the
note of urgency which had distinguished it in 1809.
Education and social amelioration were now counted upon,
quite in the manner of Southey, to relieve the distresses
of the people ; and most significant of all, it expressly declared its desire that Reform should take place "in parts
and piecemeal".[2] There was no suggestion, however, of
courting the popular approval. Romilly, too, occupied a
middle position. He was convinced that some measure of
reform was necessary, and might, in fact, be easily adopted ;
but it must be moderate, if it were not to be accompanied
by "such convulsions as every honest man must contemplate with horror".[3]

Equally typical of the moderates is Lord Holland,
though his accent is more aristocratic, and though he is
perhaps more of a *politique*.[4] He takes his stand on Grey's

---

[1] *Morning Chronicle*, 29 June 1810.
[2] *Ibid.* 13 June 1810.   [3] Romilly, *Memoirs*, ii. 339-340.
[4] Wynn was afraid that he might be lured away by the *enragés* :
Nat. Lib. Wales MS. 2791, C. Wynn to H. Wynn, 9 May 1809.

speech of 1809, and, like him, declares for a definite, intelligible, and moderate Reform. But 'though he would abolish the rotten boroughs he deplores abuse of the borough-mongers, for (and the eternal justification follows) " the influence of property *must* exist ". Sinecures to him are odious; but they are not pernicious. Economical Reform, indeed, no matter how desirable in itself, is not a characteristically Whig policy. From a Whig something more is expected—" A certain disposition to reform of Parliament, and no alarm at it if the present mode be found to be inadequate to ensure the confidence and enforce the will of the people, I allow to be essential in a Good Whig ".[1] This does not go very far; and, unhappily, this solicitude for the enforcement of the will of the people is contradicted by a more convincing passage a little earlier. " The only reason ", he says, " for which I wish for a reform is because the House of Commons has lost *its influence* with the people, not because I think a new mode of chusing them either wiser, better, or more independent. . . ."[2] Here is the weak point of men like Holland. They view Reform almost entirely from the standpoint of their own class. They are influenced neither by the old revolutionary democracy, nor by the new *égalité* of Utilitarianism. Holland wished to restore the influence of the House of Commons on the people : Burdett wished to assert the influence of the people on the House of Commons. Each recognized the breach between House and nation. Burdett sought to widen it, in order to promote a general political reconstruction ; Holland sought by modest and timely Reform to re-establish the predominance of the upper classes ; but Whitbread sought to close the breach by extending the franchise in accordance with the dictates of equity and the qualifications of common sense. At this moment the future was in Whitbread's hands. If he had

[1] *Early correspondence of Lord John Russell,* i. 135–139.
[2] *Ibid., loc. cit.*

continued resolutely in his efforts to gather round him a body of young Whig Reformers ; if he had provided them with a coherent programme of Reform which should have been at once popular and effective ; if, in short, he had pushed on where Brand's scheme pointed the way, then the subsequent history of the Reform movement might have been very different. But, as the future was to show, he faltered at the critical moment, and left it to other men to achieve what should have been his work.

(4) *The attempt to radicalize the Whigs.*—The reception which the Burdettites had given to Brand's measure sufficiently indicated their position. Though they were probably jealous of the considerable success it had enjoyed, they no doubt honestly regarded it as a quite unsatisfactory compromise. Cartwright, for instance, found it desirable to re-state the true faith in one of the ablest and most celebrated of his pamphlets—*The Comparison.* The comparison, of course, was between " true reform, half reform, and mock reform ". He implored Brand and his followers not to be content with being half honest, particularly as they were the only section of the Whig party which seemed to have some glimmerings of good sense.[1] Grey's hints of Reform were " so delicate, so faint, so evanescent, so equivocal, a man must have good eyes and close attention to find them out. . . ."[2] Nor was the current enthusiasm for Economical Reform, as it had been manifested in Brougham's *Edinburgh Review* article on Rose's pamphlet, very much better.[3] To Cartwright the influence of the Crown was the effect, not the cause, of borough corruption.[4] But he was not minded to waste his time on

[1] *Comparison*, p. 83.   [2] *Ibid.* p. 22.

[3] *Ibid.* p. 22 ; *supra*, p. 222. Brougham wrote a revised edition of the article which was surreptitiously published without his leave as *An Epistle to the Caledonians.* He got an injunction restraining further publication. I have not been able to find a copy.

[4] *Comparison*, p. 35.

Grey and the *Edinburgh Review*, holding it more important
to reclaim Brand. He particularly reprobated piecemeal
Reform :

> All experience shows that a nation's expiring liberties were
> never recovered "*piecemeal* "; a lost constitution never was so re-
> covered. It must be done—it always has been done "at a heat ",
> either by such a reformation, as that called the Revolution, in 1688 ;
> or by such a struggle as established American independence on
> English principle. . . .[1]

The history of the Reform movement showed him to have
been right in holding that Reform must be done "at a
heat ". Cartwright tried to generate that heat ; Brand, to
avoid doing so. Cartwright also objected to the suggestion
that any measure of reform should be accompanied by dis-
franchisement, whether of rotten boroughs or (as a result
of that) of former voters. "Disfranchising . . .! Good
God ! The very term is revolting. . . ." It would prove, as
he foresaw, an apple of discord among the Reformers. He
desired also—what Brand had made no provision for—
that when the larger boroughs should be enfranchised,
they should not be forced to content themselves with the
same number of representatives as some small country
town. And lastly, he joined issue on the question of annuals
versus triennials.[2]

The whole pamphlet, though it contains a good deal of
the same sort of constitutional nonsense about the "County
Power " as had appeared five years before in *England's
Aegis*, is a fair criticism of Brand's proposals. Granting the
point of view—that half reform is no reform—its arguments
have weight ; but they become less persuasive in the face
of Cartwright's own admission that the country was not in
1810 ready for the sweeping measure which he could alone
consider satisfactory.[3]

Nevertheless, in the summer of 1810 it is plain that the

---

[1] *Comparison*, p. 39.　　[2] *Ibid*. pp. 87-92.　　[3] *Ibid*. p. 92 *et seq.*

Burdettites were winning much more support than ever before, not merely from the mob, but both from the educated and literary community and from the daily press. In 1807, when Burdett was a candidate for Westminster, he had been opposed by the full power of the press, Cobbett and White only excepted.[1] In 1810, in his contest with the House of Commons, he received support at one time or another from *The Times*, the *Alfred*, the *Statesman*, the *Morning Chronicle*, the *Independent Whig*, the *British Press*, the *Evening Star*.[2] Not all of these were papers of importance; and, indeed, we may say that the less important they were, the more likely they were to have extremist leanings. But it is worth while to distinguish the *Alfred and Westminster Gazette*, which became one of the most considerable organs on the popular side. The editor of the *Alfred* had previously conducted the *Statesman*, and had as late as 1809 given that paper a Foxite tone ; but he found, what is hardly surprising, that to be a Foxite involved some pecuniary sacrifice ; so in 1810 he changed his politics with his paper, and no doubt made a much better thing of it.[3] Curiously enough, the *Statesman*, too, turned Burdettite after his departure. More reputable journals than these began to take the same line. The *Reflector*, for instance, a half-literary, half-learned review put out by John Hunt in this year, damned the Grenvilles and the *Edinburgh* through four numbers.[4] More important than the staid and short-lived *Reflector* was the sprightly *Examiner*, a Sunday paper which John Hunt had started in 1808, and which gave full scope for the brilliant humanity of his brother Leigh. In 1810 its influence was already considerable. It had survived a prosecution for libel in 1809, and was soon to lay itself open to a more successful one by its article on military floggings. Its literary criticism and theatrical reports were capital, and

[1] Add. MS. 27838 *passim*.   [2] Add. MS. 27839.
[3] Add. MS. 35648, f. 17.   [4] *e.g. Reflector*, i. 17.

its politics had Cobbett's pungency with an extra polish of their own.[1] " It disclaimed ", said Leigh Hunt in his *Autobiography*, " all knowledge of statistics, and the rest of its politics were rather a sentiment, or a matter of general training, than founded upon any particular political reflection ". At first, in consonance with this amiable empiricism, it had no party, " but Reform soon gave it one " ; and its editors were soon on good terms with Brougham and Bentham.[2] Leigh Hunt's warm-heartedness led him inevitably to embrace the cause of the Burdettites, though it was for the sake of liberty rather than of demo-cracy that he did so. " Sir Francis, though he was for a long time our hero, we never exchanged a word with ; and Cobbett and Henry Hunt . . . we never beheld. . . ." How-ever that may have been, the Burdettite cause got its best support in these months from the Hunts.[3] And not content with the peppery paragraphs of the *Examiner*, Leigh Hunt produced in this year his *Reformist's Answer to the Article entitled " The State of Parties " in the last " Edinburgh Review "*.

The *Reformist's Answer* is an admirable attack on the self-righteous *Edinburgh* and its English counterpart, the Holland House clique. The picture which the reviewer had drawn of the political situation—half the nation courtiers, half revolutionaries, with " a small, but most respectable band " of old Whigs alone retaining their political sanity—Hunt briskly dismissed as nonsense. The Holland House party in the character of the Sabine women parting the combatants aroused his mirth rather than his sympathy.[4] " The people must be the keepers of their own freedom.

---

[1] Murray even asked Leigh to write an article on the contemporary drama for the *Quarterly* in 1809. Add. MS. 38523, f. 8.

[2] Add. MS. 38523, f. 11 ; Add. MS. 38108, ff. 40-60.

[3] Hunt, *Autobiography*, p. 172 ; Blunden, *Life of Leigh Hunt*, ch. v ; Blunden, *The Examiner Examined*, pp. 3-30.

[4] *Reformist's Answer*, pp. 12, 27-28.

Nobody else can or will keep it for them " ; not even the
" small but most respectable band ", not even the *Edinburgh Review*, from which this very quotation was taken.[1]
The Whigs might use the Reform cry at elections, but they
never raised it in the House ; they considered themselves the
party of the people, but not unless the people put itself
under their tutelage. And their leaders were so unpre-
possessing ! Grenville—the prince of sinecurists ; Grey the
apostate, "whose first proceeding, after the Duke of
York's expulsion from office, was to go and take a pathetic
chop with him" ; Windham, the "*preux chevalier* of in-
consistencies—opponent of Curwen's Bill ".[2] What wonder
that the friends of freedom preferred Burdett, and that
the nation in general preferred the Tories. The Whigs,
as he unkindly told them, were not fit to form a government.[3] His own programme was simple. He was not so
foolish as to be a Republican : he asked only for retrenchment of expenditure, responsibility of Ministers, and reform
in Parliament. A vague programme, as well as a simple
one : how did Hunt propose to realize it ? He had his
scheme ready. He recommended a union between Whitbread, Curwen, Coke, Wilberforce, Granville Sharpe,
Burdett, Romilly, and Cartwright.[4] Apart from Sharpe,
who seems of minor importance in this connexion,[5] and
from Wilberforce, whose inclusion is plainly a miscalcula-
tion,[6] the list is a good one ; and to Hunt there seemed no
objection to the alliance of " that old constitutional Whig "

[1] *Ibid.* p. 27.

[2] *Ibid.* pp. 31-32. I have dealt more particularly with Leigh Hunt's
place in the Reform movement in the *Review of English Studies* for
Jan. 1935.

[3] *Ibid.* pp. 6-7.   [4] *Ibid.* pp. 12, 44.

[5] Sharpe was a prominent Abolitionist. He had, however, circulated
petitions for annual parliaments in 1779. Paul, *Shorter Parliaments*,
p. 142.

[6] See *Life of Wilberforce*, iii. 451-453, where his reasons for opposing
Brand's motion are noted.

(Whitbread), with one " who though old and little rooted
to the world, stands fixed in the public estimation by the
weight of his character, like the ancient oak in his native
field " (*i.e.* Cartwright).[1] Hunt, in fact, by a very remarkable
exercise of political prescience, or by a still more remarkable
guess, had suggested the policy which in 1812 was to come
to fruition in the foundation of the Hampden Club. At the
time at which he wrote, it was a solution far from obvious.
The Reformists and the left-wing Whigs were divided on
many points, and embittered on some. It was but slowly
that a spirit of mutual conciliation prevailed. Hunt's
scheme remained for nearly two years a prophecy unlikely
of fulfilment.

For Whitbread was not ready in 1810 to renounce the
name of Whig, nor could he avoid in his dealings with
the Burdettites that appearance of condescension which
so irritated Hunt. Moreover, there was no denying that
Brand's Bill had been the best blow struck for Reform so
far : the Burdettites had nothing to show against it. The
best criticism of Brand's proposals had come, not from
Cartwright and the Burdettites, but from the moderate
Whig John Coker, whose admirable pamphlet not merely
exposed the historical and practical weaknesses of the
Reformers' programme, but showed a Southeyan modernity
in urging that the way to purity of election lay through
the education of the electors, and the appeal to their sense
of citizenship.[2] Moreover, the old argument against
alliance with persons of so ambiguous a character as some
of the Burdettites was at this time very strong. Cobbett
was in prison for libel, and he had compromised himself,
even if he had not disgraced himself, by vacillations which
seemed to imply a desire to be bought by the Government.
Burdett had damped the ardour of his supporters by his

---

[1] *Reformist's Answer*, pp. 12, 44.

[2] Coker, *Letter to the Hon. Thomas Brand, upon the Subject of Parliamentary Reform*, pp. 6, 15-20, etc.

apparent timidity in avoiding their celebrations of his release ; and already the private lives of himself, Wardle, and Cobbett were affording material for an intensive propaganda which did something to discredit his party.[1]

The political conjunctions, also, did not seem to be favourable to any new coalition. At the very moment when Brand's motion was under discussion, the expiring charter of Maldon was renewed, and a close borough thus perpetuated ;[2] and such minor reforms as the Government put in hand served only to give Leigh Hunt the opportunity for heavy sarcasm in the *Examiner*.[3] At the end of the year the madness of the King engrossed the attention of politicians ; and all of them who had pretensions to constitutional learning, besides many who had not, plunged into the interminable wrangles over the Regency Bill. And when the Bill was at length passed, the crisis of February 1811 left behind it a feeling of flatness and uncertainty which adversely affected the cause of Reform. These factors, and the impossibility of always maintaining enthusiasm at fever-heat, made it seem that in the first half of 1811 the country had become apathetic.[4] It was at

---

[1] See (*inter alia*) *The Faction Detected and Despised* (1810) ; *Adultery and Patriotism* (1811).

[2] *Morning Chronicle*, 25 May 1810.

[3] " Reform.—Ministers have at length commenced that *moderate* and judicious reform, for which they so loudly professed their friendship. In all the public offices, the consumption of sealing-wax, quills, pen-knives, paper, almanacs, and court-calendars is to be considerably reduced. One almanac and one court-calendar only are to be allowed in each office ; and newspapers are no longer to be read at the public charge. . . . Here's economy for you ! Not even a single sheet of paper is now to be unprofitably employed ; no amorous clerk must now breathe forth his vows upon superfine wove gilt, or stamp a bleeding heart on the best Dutch wax, unless he has recourse to the Privy Purse . . . " (*Examiner*, 9 Sept. 1810). A Royal Commission at this time was appointed to investigate the possibility of a reform of the constitution of Jersey : *Morning Chronicle*, 4 Jan. 1812.

[4] Francis to Cartwright, 2 April 1811. *Life of Cartwright*, ii. 4.

this time, however, that Crabb Robinson's " Academy " turned its ripe judgment to the problem;[1] and it was at this time also that Roscoe, in his *Letter to Brougham*, condemned the moderate Reformers (of whom Brougham at that time was one) and advocated thorough and immediate Reform.[2]

Cartwright and his friends, moreover, were awake and zealous ; and towards the end of March 1811, they made a move of great significance. They decided to try the policy of union with the moderate Reformers which Leigh Hunt had advocated. Hitherto there had been little love lost between Whigs and Burdettites ; such association as there had been between them had been either tinged with Whig condescension or fostered by Whitbread and his friends for their own ends. Now for the first time the " Reformists " (as some of them preferred to be called, not choosing to commit themselves to being known as Burdettites) took the initiative and made the advances. The surprising volume of support for Brand's motion was an attraction to a party which felt the lack of Parliamentary advocates. Already in the later numbers of the *Reflector* there had been indications of a more tolerant attitude, distinction being drawn between the " time-serving part of the Foxites, the Greys and Ponsonbys ; and the philosophical and public-spirited part of them, the Hollands and Whitbreads ", who were held to be moving leftward, and to be not much inferior in " staunchness " to the true Reformists.[3] The petition of the Hertfordshire county

[1] Crabb Robinson, *MS. Diary*, i. 36.

[2] Roscoe, *Letter to Brougham*, pp. 8-12. It was written, however, in May 1810, and was in reply to a letter of Brougham's. In the *Edinburgh Review*, xx. art. viii, Roscoe's work is reviewed and his controversy with Brougham surveyed—the writer being Brougham himself ! *Life of Roscoe*, ii. 9-10 ; Aspinall, *Brougham and the Whig Party*, p. 27.

[3] *Reflector*, i. 460. Compare John Russell's view that Holland was the only true Whig left in England—an opinion which drew a mild reproach from Bedford : *Early Correspondence of Lord John Russell*, i. 156.

meeting, moreover, showed that moderate Reform was not without a following in the country.[1]

On 30 March 1811, therefore, a meeting was held between the leading men of the two parties. With Brand came Byng, Halsey, Sir G. Heathcote, C. H. Hutchinson, and Hanbury Tracey—all M.P.s ; while on Burdett's side appeared his brother, Jones Burdett, with Cartwright, Fawkes, Northmore, and Strickland—all well-known metropolitan Reformers. Between the two stood Madocks. The meeting showed remarkable harmony and circumspection in drafting bases of doctrine to be common to both sides. With discreet vagueness they decided (i) that the Commons did not speak the sense of the nation ; (ii) that Reform of the Commons was equally necessary to the independence of the Crown and the liberties of the people ; (iii) that at the proposed general meeting no specific plan should be brought forward. They thus not merely burked the main issue of the nature of the reform to be attempted, but further resolved to avoid the question at their next meeting. Still, if unity could have been patched up for a little, perhaps some compromise on principle might have been arrived at ; but their harmony was interrupted before their principles had had a chance to come into conflict.

It appears that it had been agreed that each side should bring recruits to the next meeting, and Brand is said to have promised thirty. He found it impossible to fulfil his promise. When they reassembled on 6 April, it was Cartwright who had produced thirty, while Brand could find only three. Chagrin at this result, reinforced by the threat of his Parliamentary friends to desert him unless he dropped his connexion with Burdett, led him to withdraw from the meeting, together with most of his friends. The projected alliance had broken down on the intractability of the Parliamentary Whigs.

It is much to be regretted that the Whigs should have

[1] *Morning Chronicle*, 18 Feb. 1811 ; *Parl. Deb.* xix. 690.

thrown away this opportunity. The process of *radicalizing* the party, which was to be the work of the next two decades, might well have begun at this date. Madocks, Tracey, and Halsey, however, refused to follow Brand, and with Burdett and Cartwright continued their preparations for a great Reform meeting in June. A list of stewards was secured, 265 in number ; Sir John Throckmorton was to take the chair ; and 300 members of Parliament were asked for their support, not one of whom consented to give it.[1]

The meeting, which the *Morning Chronicle* described as " the most respectable meeting for Parliamentary Reform that ever took place ", was held on 10 June.[2] It was indeed a respectable meeting which included an Earl of Oxford, a Scudamore, a Honeywood, and a Wolseley. Cartwright boasted with justice of the large number of country gentlemen who had consented to act as stewards. Lord Cochrane represented the Services, Coke and Western the agriculturists, Combe the brewing interest, Cobbett the Radical press. Of all the leading Reformers, only Place, as usual, remained quietly in the background.[3] With some courage, Perry too presented himself to a crowd which was almost certain to be hostile to his party. Apart from Perry, only Byng, of all the moderate Reformers who had followed Brand, cared to face the reception of the company and the reproaches of their friends.

The speeches of the Burdettites were of the usual vigorous type, and expounded the regular Burdettite programme, with pointed references to the principles of

[1] Cartwright, *Letters to Lord Tavistock*, pp. 3-5, 15, for the above account. The breach does not seem to have been complete, however, for on 3 May there was a Livery Dinner at which Waithman, Brand, Ossulston, Combe, Wardle, W. Smith, Hutchinson, Cartwright, and Goodbehere were present, and at which Whitbread's health was drunk : *Morning Chronicle*, 4 May 1811.

[2] *Ibid.* 10 June 1811.

　　Cf. Add. MS. 27839, ff. 193-194.

1793. Byng was not dismayed. In a speech which was received with marked disapprobation, he declared his adherence to those principles, and declared that he had supported Brand's scheme not as a *ne plus ultra* but as a practical instalment. He deprecated calumnies and insults, but concluded that "As a Whig, it was his duty to be forgiving". Perry was more pugnacious. "The Whigs of England", he said, "had but one feeling, that of maintaining every branch of the constitution in its place." Their remedies changed with the disease : what that disease was, he indicated by his references to increased expenditure. Government influence, not the electoral system, was to him the real danger. And he spoke up with all the conviction of a Rockingham Whig for the party system which the Burdettites were attacking.[1] He elaborated his position two days later in the *Morning Chronicle*, in the course of an article defending the reputations of the former "Friends of the People" :

We are confident that there is not an altered, or even a luke-warm heart, in the whole body of men distinguished by the name of Whigs, in the cause of that degree of reform which may be safely tried, and which is applicable to the present condition of the country. . . . Shortening the duration of Parliament, and lessening the expense of elections, are obviously prudent and safe expedients. . . . There are other and minor modes of reform to which this would lead. . . . And if all the genuine friends of reform, the many country gentlemen who have given their names to the cause, and pledged themselves to its promotion, would concur in this scheme, and make a solemn declaration, each in his district, that he would oppose all advances beyond this, can it be doubted that by a universal canvass at the general election, the object would be obtained in the next Parliament ? [2]

It was no wonder that Cartwright distrusted the Whigs. The *Morning Chronicle*, which in spite of Perry's diplomatic

[1] *Morning Chronicle*, 11 June 1811.
[2] *Ibid.* 12 June 1811.

denials was indeed their official organ, had receded very far from its outburst of democratic enthusiasm of 1809 ; and so, it is fair to suppose, had the men it represented. It took two features of Brand's 1810 scheme—triennials and purity of election—and to obtain these was ready not merely to abandon all future change but specifically to oppose it. In view of these facts it is impossible to credit the Whig argument that their reform was really as radical as that of Burdett, and infinitely more practical.[1]

Had it appeared from the grand meeting at the Freemasons' Hall, that any greater success was to be anticipated in less official circles ? From the point of view of immediate effect the meeting was only a qualified success. By no means so many attended as had been hoped and expected.[2] The resolutions passed were not very constructive. " No fixed or predetermined plan was proposed—no systematic resolutions were offered for their consideration, but all met together to offer their own sentiments upon the birthrights of Englishmen, and to vote according to the dictates of their own honest hearts."[3] Yet though these results did not appear to be very tangible, the meeting was in fact extremely useful and important. It led directly to the formation of the Society of the Friends to Parliamentary Reform—which was the first society of its type since the old revolutionary societies had perished at the turn of the century ; and this in turn led to the founding of the Hampden Club in the next year. It organized national opinion ; and by drawing its stewards from every part of

---

[1] Cartwright, *Letters to Tavistock*, p. 13. The first attempt to alter the Septennial Act was in 1734 : Paul, *Shorter Parliaments*, p. 102.

[2] *The Statesman*, 11 June 1811, *ap.* Add. MS. 27839. " It was a subject of amusement to us moderate men that the red-hot patriots appear to have made so miserable a business of their meeting. They allowed none to be present but those who took a ticket for dinner 15/- in consequence there were hardly 200 persons prest. scarcely the number of the conveners."—Crabb Robinson, *MS. Diary*, i. 167.

[3] *Sunday Review*, 16 June 1811.

the kingdom it made Reform no longer the affair merely of the Home Counties and the metropolis.[1]

The regression of the official Whigs from a position to which in 1809 popular excitement and political disappointment had driven them must undoubtedly be attributed to the prospect of office which opened to them in 1811. They had no desire to commit themselves either to hasty reform or to unbending opposition to it : they took a middle course, which they hoped would conciliate as many followers as possible. They had sufficient personal and political divisions as it was. It seems certain that it was these considerations that sufficed to gag Whitbread. His ambition was whetted by the prospect of Cabinet rank, and to attain it he sacrificed his projects of reform. Accordingly he vanishes from sight just now, and the leadership of the little party he had formed passes to Brand, whom no one for a moment considered for inclusion in the Ministry.

The very fact that he had no real chance of a lucrative post was one reason why Brand should not give up the hope of a *rapprochement* with the Reformers. While the more important Whigs were squabbling over their shadowy Cabinets, Brand and his men clung to their tenets, and Leigh Hunt began to have good hope of seeing the programme of the *Reformist's Answer* realized.[2] Cartwright, therefore, took heart to make fresh advances to the Whigs. Early in 1812 the Society of Friends to Parliamentary Reform was modified, and took the new title of the Union for Parliamentary Reform according to the Constitution. There were other changes also. The society became more metropolitan, and less Parliamentary in tone—that is, if

---

[1] A meeting at Bodmin (of all unlikely places) was soon to endorse the Burdettite policy. *Morning Chronicle*, 16 July 1811.

[2] *Examiner*, 12 Jan., 16 Feb., 31 May 1812 : and see *Morning Chronicle*, 2 Jan. 1812, for a letter of Montague Burgoyne appealing for the coöperation of the Whig and independent interests in the county of Essex.

we may judge from its committee : of the 15 M.P.s who had been stewards of the meeting of June 1811, only 3 remained. Moreover, a new constitution was drawn up, which embodied a fairly extensive reform, including annual parliaments, and the extension of the suffrage until it was coincident with direct taxation.[1] No doubt some of the earlier members were excluded by that article which ordained that no person holding office of profit under the Crown was to be eligible for membership.[2] The subscription was fixed at £1 : 1s., and the administration of the monthly meetings and other activities was in the hands of a committee of consultation. Very soon it prepared a petition in which an attack on the income tax was skilfully blent with Parliamentary Reform ; while it made its existence known to the masses by its *Appeal to the Nation*.[3] In appearance this reconstitution of the Society was a move hostile to the Whigs ; but it seems in fact to have been part of a plan whereby the more hot-headed of the Reformers were to be shepherded together into a society where they might air their views without embarrassing their leaders. These latter meanwhile were trying to catch the Whigs with the Hampden Club. The Hampden Club, which was founded at the Thatched House Tavern on 20 April 1812, included some members of the Union, but was in general much more representative and Whiggish in tone. The list of founders gives the impression that there was an attempt to include men of weight from all districts and of many callings.[4] Among them were Honeywood the Kentish, and Maule the Scottish Whig, and—most significant— Perry. It is not easy to keep pace with Perry's vacillations in these years, but at least it may be said that his adhesion

---

[1] *Life of Cartwright*, ii. 377 ; *Institution of the Union for Parliamentary Reform.*

[2] *Institution of the Union*, art. 5.   [3] Add. MS. 27839, f. 229.

[4] Veitch, *Genesis of Parliamentary Reform*, pp. 344-345 ; *Life of Cartwright*, ii. 380.

was a sign that the hope of attracting the Whigs was not
illusory. All members were required to be men of substance
—they were to draw at least £300 per annum from land—
and the annual subscription was to be £2. It is noteworthy
that Wardle, Henry Hunt, and Cobbett were not members,
and it appears that even Cartwright found it advisable to
absent himself for a time, for fear of alarming the staider
of his allies.[1] The objects of the society were vaguely
reforming, though its programme eschewed precision,
and it sought to attain them by meeting twice a year to
dine.[2] Such a club could hardly be expected to do much
active work, and it does not seem that Cartwright had
at first any very great hopes of it.[3] But it was, in fact,
of quite extraordinary importance. It achieved the union,
imperfect and jealous though it was, of the adjacent wings
of the Whigs and Reformers. It gave hope that the Whig
party might one day be educated. It brought the Whigs
into touch with the people—at any rate vicariously. It
ultimately made it possible for Brougham to remain a
Whig, and for Grey to take command in 1830. The Hampden
Club is the analogue of the Society of the Friends of the
People. It is true that the Hampden Club had a short life,

---

[1] Veitch, pp. 344-345.

[2] The first dinner of the Hampden Club was held on 11 May, and
was reported in the *Morning Chronicle* of the following day. Unfortunately, all available space was taken up with accounts of Perceval's
assassination, and only a meagre report is given, in which Fawkes, the
Chairman, confines himself to generalities. Later in the year he replied
to Lord Milton, but again without entering into details of his reforming
programme. He regarded the extant state of affairs as a violation of
the rights of property, which often paid taxes without being represented;
and added : " Your Lordship has often demanded of the friends of
Reform, to what period they would revert to seek for the constitution
of England. The Reformers, my Lord, will make answer, and tell you
that the real constitution, only with a much greater latitude of suffrage
than is now sought for, existed from the earliest times to the famous
disfranchising Act of the 8th of Henry VI " (*Morning Chronicle*,
13 Nov. 1812).   [3] *Life of Cartwright*, ii. 36.

and that as the Hampden Club movement spread the nature of the clubs changed. But that did not affect the fact that for a moment Whig reform and popular reform were brought into proximity and proved not incompatible. The foundation of the Hampden Club was the culmination of a period of five years of continuous agitation in and out of Parliament—a period which is really the seed-time of nineteenth-century Reform.

Cartwright seized the golden moment in his usual way, and in the summer of 1812 poured out *Six Letters to Lord Tavistock*. They were essentially an earnest appeal to the Whigs to unite with the popular leaders. As usual, they iterated and reiterated the familiar points of the more radical programme ; but it is for the urgency with which they appeal to the Whigs that they are chiefly remarkable. It is as though Cartwright had seen the magnitude of the opportunity. Why, however, were they addressed to Lord Tavistock ? Partly because he was the rising hope of the Russells, a family honourably distinguished for its zeal for Reform,[1] but more particularly because of his conduct over Brand's second Reform motion.

This Bill, which Brand introduced in a thin House on 8 May 1812, did not profess to be more than a partial measure. It was, in fact, to be considered in conjunction with a Bill which Tavistock had just obtained leave to introduce, and which was to reduce the expenses of county elections (and, consequently, the opportunities for corruption) by providing local polling booths.[2] Brand's speech was a curious attempt to trim between the people and the proprietors. He found a happy compromise in attacking the nabobs—an old gambit, but, as usual, a successful one. " It was ", he remarked, " a question between a disgusted aristocracy and a borough faction " ; and he added that though 182 persons returned 326 members, he regarded that fact (such was his belief in the legitimate influence of

[1] Cartwright, *Tavistock*, pp. 5-10.   [2] *Parl. Deb.* xxiii. 89.

property) " more as a matter of curiosity than anything else ". His proposals were as follows : (i) the vote to copy-holders ; (ii) abolition of the right of nomination. The seats to be obtained were to be given to the more populous counties. Whatever Brand might say about the necessary and permanent influence of property, it was not possible to persuade the House that such a proposal left that influence intact. Tavistock in seconding the motion made an attempt to conciliate moderate Reformers by promising that if this Bill were passed he would introduce a triennial Act ; but J. W. Ward seized the occasion to make a set speech against Reform, and the motion was lost by 215–88. The minority was, perhaps, larger than might have been expected, considering the much more radical nature of the proposals compared with those of Brand's previous Bill, and it included Burdett, Romilly, Whitbread, and even Ponsonby.[1]

(5) *The position in 1812.*—With the defeat of Brand's Reform Bill we reach a clearly marked stage in the Reform movement. Not for another five years was the subject raised again in Parliament. Sinecures and reversions agitated the House of Lords now and then (though always ineffectually), but neither of Tavistock nor Brand nor Whitbread was any more heard in a Reforming connexion. This is the end of the prelude, the end of the continuous Parliamentary action which had begun with Burdett's motion in 1809. The five years from 1807 to 1812 form, indeed, a well-defined and quite distinctive period. The movement springs from the revived agitation for Economi-cal Reform ; receives a powerful fillip from the case of the Duke of York ; is led in Parliament by Whitbread and Smith, and out of it by Burdett and the City Reformers. A Whig Reform Bill obtains 115 votes. Then follows reaction and timidity : the Burdett riots and the prospect of office

[1] *Ibid.* 100-106, 113 *et seq.*, 161.

frighten the Whigs ; Whitbread fails them in the crisis ;
and there is a disposition to return to the safer policies of
Grey. Finally, under the undistinguished leadership of
Brand, the younger and more progressive Whigs at last
make a serious, and a not unsuccessful, effort to regain
their popularity by going to the people. For the next five
years the political education of the party was to come from
outside Parliament. Whitbread had indeed missed his
chance ; and he spent the last years of his life dabbling in
the futilities of the Princess of Wales' affairs, cut off from
his party and not invariably followed by his fellow free-
lances.[1] Brougham, now on the threshold of his work, could
afford to meddle with the Princess' affairs, for, after all, he
was her legal adviser ; but he did not thereby lose his grip
on politics. As convinced a Reformer as Whitbread, he
stepped later on into the place which Brand had uncon-
vincingly filled when Whitbread deserted. He became, as
Whitbread might have become, the educator of his party—
the liaison officer between two worlds.

In 1812, too, occurred another event of importance, for
in that year Place was introduced to Bentham by Mill.[2]
Henceforward the influence of Benthamism on the Westminster Reformers was to be even stronger, because more
direct, than it had been since 1809. Already Leigh Hunt
was " trumpeting " Bentham in the *Examiner* ; and soon
Tavistock and Lansdowne were to be in correspondence
with young John Cam Hobhouse, with a view to obtaining
a seat for him in Parliament.[3] The familiar history of
Westminster politics was preparing—or rather, it had been
prepared in the years we have just been considering. The
Reform movement was, in fact, on the brink of a great
popular extension : it was about to harness the forces of
unrest to the triumphal chariot of Westminster. Burdett,

[1] Creevey, p. 181 ; Nat. Lib. Wales MS. 2791.
[2] Add. MS. 35147, f. 70.
[3] Bentham, x. 471 ; Add. MS. 36456, f. 103.

indeed, was still unconscious of the new power at his disposal. Fundamentally aristocratic, he included in his portentous list of popular grievances none that a well-bred man could not reckon as within his own experience.[1] He had no idea that of the men whom he proposed to enfranchise there were many to whom life itself was a grievance. Radical theory was, indeed, very static in the hands of men like Burdett, Wardle, and Combe, for it corresponded with their views of constitutional history, which were always fixed and often erroneous.[2] But the men in touch with reality—Cobbett in the country, and Place in the city—they realized what forces were preparing on their side. Even Jeffrey saw the danger.[3] And Cartwright, old as he was, was yet, perhaps, the first to make capital out of the new conditions. As early as 1812—long before the extension of the Hampden Club movement—he was using the Union for Parliamentary Reform to turn the agitation in the disturbed districts into profitable channels.[4] By the end of the year he had held meetings for Parliamentary Reform in Manchester, at which the Hampden Club had been toasted ;[5] and a little later he drew out a Form of Petition in order to facilitate mass petitioning.[6] The connexion between distress and reform was becoming

[1] Burdett, *Letter from Oxford*, : "£900,000,000 of debt ; inland fortresses under the name of barracks ; an army of German and other foreign mercenaries ; an army of spies and informers ; of Tax and Excise agents ; an Inquisition of private property ; a Phantom for a King ; a degraded aristocracy ; an oppressed People ; a confiding Parliament ; irresponsible Ministers ; a corrupt and intimidated Press ; pensioned justices ; packed juries ; vague and sanguinary laws . . . which, together with a host of failures of foreign expeditions, and the present crushing burden of taxation, are some of the bitter fruits of corruption in the House of Commons."

[2] *E.g.* the fact that the provisions in the Act of Settlement had been altered by the Act of 1705, as concerned placemen, came as a surprise to the Reformers : Add. MS. 27838, f. 242. And see p. 274, note 2 above.

[3] See above, pp. 256-258.   [4] *Life of Cartwright*, ii. 31.

[5] *Morning Chronicle*, 8 Sept. 1812. [6] *Ibid.* 28 Dec. 1812.

rapidly obvious. In petitions to Parliament this year it is clearly put forward ;[1] and John Knight summed up the workers' case when he wrote :

I have been informed that a prejudice exists against us, in the minds of some responsible persons, . . . on account of the lower classes interfering in political affairs. The poor, I am persuaded, feel no wish to usurp the place of their superiors, in an expression of their political sentiments ; but so acute, so long continued, and so severe have been their sufferings, that the apathy and indifference of the middle and higher classes, on subjects of the most vital importance to their welfare, and even existence, have rendered it imperiously necessary for them to come forwards.[2]

The whole Luddite movement was inextricably tangled up with a genuine, serious, moderate movement to petition Parliament for Reform. It appears most clearly, from the famous *Trial of Thirty-eight Men*, that the capital object for which they met together was really Parliamentary Reform. It was the activities of the ill-disposed and the *agents-provocateurs* that turned it into a revolutionary movement. In Yorkshire this Reforming element was, perhaps, less noticeable ;[3] but in Lancashire it was dominant, and it was expressed intelligibly in Knight's resolutions of 26 May 1812.[4] Even in the violently revolutionary movement the Reforming element was never obscured. Stones, the spy, told the Lancashire Luddites that Cochrane, Burdett, and Whitbread would join them ; and among the pseudonyms adopted by the conspirators were Grey, Grenville (!), Whitbread, and Wardle.[5] After the great riot

[1] See, *e.g.* that from Bolton, *Parl. Deb.* xxii. 29-30, 18 March 1812.
[2] *Trial of Thirty-eight Men*, p. viii.
[3] Peel, *Risings of the Luddites*, has little to say about Reform.
[4] *Trial of Thirty-eight Men*, pp. 94-99, for these resolutions, which, in addition to demanding franchise coincident with taxation, and annual parliaments, touched on prevailing distress, informations for libel, paper currency, the Combination Acts, foreign troops in barracks, and sinecures.
[5] Hammond, *Skilled Labourer*, pp. 278-280.

of 8 April there were no more " Church and King ! " mobs
in Manchester: henceforward they shouted for Reform.[1]
It was, perhaps, these facts that made the Whigs oppose
such measures as the Frame-breaking Bill and the Preservation of the Peace Bill ; for there is no sign that the
Whigs possessed sufficient social conscience to care much
about the industrial North for any other reason, and the
minorities against these Bills, though small, were consistently formed of just those members who were most in
earnest about Reform, together with a few non-party
humanitarians like Babington.[2] It is, perhaps, not without
significance that Brougham was one of the counsel for the
defence of the Thirty-eight. His experiences on the northern
circuit might well account for the sudden sharpening of his
Reforming zeal, so noticeable in 1813.[3]

In 1812, too, there was published an important work on
Reform, by Walter Honeywood Yate, which may be taken
to sum up the political theory of the Burdettites at this
date. There is no need to recapitulate his familiar arguments
for annual parliaments, responsibility of members to their
constituents, franchise coincident with direct taxation, and
so forth. He borrows his notion of the " County Power "
from Cartwright, and his tolerant attitude to the Crown
from Burdett. But he goes further in his demands than was
usual at that time. Like Bentham he claims dominance,
not equality, for the people. He would take away the veto
from the Lords. He would fine absentees from the House.
He would exclude one-third of the members in rotation
from re-election to his annual parliaments. Not that he is a
champion of the proletariat. When he claims that the
people are the fountain of authority, he is careful to add,

[1] Prentice, *Manchester*, p. 48.
[2] *Parl. Deb.* xxi. 1084, 965 *et seq.*, 840 ; xxiii. 962, 999, 1056, 1060,
1099 ; *Morning Chronicle*, 18 Feb. 1812.
[3] Hammond, *Skilled Labourer*, p. 299. But Brougham did not mention Reform at the Liverpool election. Brougham, *Liverpool Speeches*.

" I do not mean the illiterate rabble, who have neither
capacity for judging of matters of government, nor property
to be concerned for ". Property for him meant something
very different from the property whose rights Brand was
concerned to defend ; for Yate demanded representation
for the moneyed interests—the very interests which the
Government had captured, and against which the Whigs
declaimed. Yate seems, in fact, to have been the precursor
of the prosperous, violent, middle-class radical who was to
be so common a figure in the middle years of the century.
His attack on the nobility is quite ferocious : " jockies,
rooks, gamblers, blasphemers, Sabbath-breakers, adulterers,
corrupters, election jobbers ", he calls them. And if he
envisaged the aristocracy as so many Sir Mulberry Hawkes,
he denounced vengeance on them with the eloquence of the
Watertoast Association :

> British Lion ! Where dost thou crouch ? Rouse thy wraths :
> utter thy tremendous roar. The slavish and enslaving junto will
> tremble at the glare of thine eye. Genius of England ! ever formid-
> able to tyranny, awake ! Guardian angel of these favoured realms !
> save thy important charge ! [1]

That such stuff should come not from a Carlile or Hone,
but from a gentleman of good family (though possibly of
reduced circumstances) was, perhaps, a sign of changing
times.[2]

To sum up : the Reform movement had arrived at a
moment of transition, and was soon to take upon itself a
new and more popular complexion. It was emphatically a
going concern, which paid its way not only in popularity
but in actual money ; [3] and it was to be the endeavour of

---

[1] Yate, *Political and Historical Arguments for Reform* ; i. 9, 12, 14,
18, 22, 27, 36-37, 55 ; ii. 4-5, 139, 335-337 ; for the above account.

[2] Cobbett, *Rural Rides*, pp. 431, 1051, where there is a short biographical note of him by the editors, G. D. H. and M. Cole.

[3] Add. MS. 27838, ff. 42-43, for the financial accounts of the movement.

the next five years to secure for the Whigs some share of the political profits, when it should at length be in a position to declare a dividend. Unfortunately the divisions in their party made such endeavours for the moment fruitless.

A Reformer [said Hazlitt] is necessarily and naturally a marplot, for . . . the following reasons. First, he does not know very well what he would be at. Secondly, if he did, he does not care very much about it. Thirdly, he is governed habitually by a spirit of contradiction, and is always wise beyond what is practicable. . . . Let him have the plaything of his fancy, and he will spoil it. . . . Give him one thing, and he asks for another. . . . He would rather have slavery than liberty, unless it is a liberty precisely after his own fashion.[1]

There is no critic so harsh as a disillusioned member of one's own party ; and, perhaps Hazlitt, who liked to hurt, was too severe. But his words were the result of his contemplation of the history of the Reform movement in the period immediately following that with which we are dealing, and they were prompted by the notorious squabbles between the Reformers. The Whigs could not agree with the Burdettites ; and the Burdettites could hardly agree among themselves. The unity of which the Hampden Club was the symbol did not endure. The Parliamentary Whig party relaxed its efforts. Brougham was at first no substitute for Whitbread, for he was too unreliable and too radical ; Brand lacked weight and energy. Even the most enthusiastic Reformer felt in 1814 and 1815 that the times were unpropitious for activity. Moreover, the great effort which Whitbread and his friends and successors had made, between 1809 and 1812, to bind the Whigs as a party to Reform, had not been successful. They had drawn but a small section to them. Even moderates like Milton held aloof, and confessed Reformers like Lord Holland clung obstinately to a policy of inactivity. Grey remained as

[1] Hazlitt, *Works*, vii. 14-15.

ever unconvinced of the necessity of any step that would inconvenience him. The Grenvilles, in spite of some tactical concessions, were honestly too sure of their value to the country to dream of sharing its government with any one else. The year 1812 is a great year in the history of Reform —marks, indeed, the first climax of the new movement— but it is not a great year in the history of *Whig* reform. The very success of the temporary union with the Reformists was an indication of this fact. The Hampden Club was the farthest possible point of Whig advance ; and it was joined only by a pitiable fragment of the party. So that though the period ends on a note of triumphant expectation, it ends also with the promise of a speedy anticlimax, and a further period of futility. And this because quarrels, largely personal, divided Whitbread and his lieutenants from the main body of the party. Their attacks on the Grenvilles, however logical and laudable, alarmed the moderate. But when the Grenvilles cut adrift —and their doing so coincided with the revival of Reform— then the value and significance of the gallant efforts of Whitbread and Brand were clearly seen; for then, too, Brougham returned from the wilderness of radical faction to find a place once more within the foremost ranks of the true Whigs.

CHAPTER IV

THE LEADERSHIP IN THE COMMONS

The unpopularity and disunion of the Whigs, in consequence of their attitude to the major problems of the day, were not the only factors which contributed to weaken their position. For there were occasions when their forces equalled or exceeded those of the Government.[1] The system of small personal groups, which had, since the deaths of Pitt and Fox, taken the place of more organized parties, and the large "floating strength" which stood outside these groups, facilitated opposition, because they often provided purely fortuitous allies. Yet even under these conditions, and with a normal voting strength of about 150–170 in the Commons, the Whigs made but a poor showing. The true explanation of this state of affairs lies in the difficulties which the party experienced in finding a suitable leader in the House of Commons.

It was a real disaster for them when Lord Howick was removed to the Lords by the death of his father in November 1807 ; for Howick, though lazy and not very efficient, was, at least, generally accepted. As Tierney wrote mournfully to the new peer :

The hour that made you an Earl made the power of the Crown during the present reign at least, absolute, for it set the House of Commons adrift. If that blow had come upon us in office, office might have enabled us to weather the storm, as it is I quite despair and look upon the party of the late Administration as split or soon about to be split into a thousand pieces.[2]

[1] *E.g.* on the Walcheren enquiry, 23 Jan. 1810 ; *Parl. Deb.* xv. 161-210 ; Creevey, p. 124.

[2] *Tierney MSS.* Tierney to Grey, 26 Nov. 1807.

The choice of a successor was, indeed, very difficult. It was necessary to get some one who would be agreeable to either wing of the party ; and since the only topics upon which Grey and Grenville thought alike were Catholic Emancipation and the conduct of the war, it seemed likely that a leader of no very decided views would be essential. The candidates were numerous, but, on the whole, unsuitable. Windham, for instance, had recently quarrelled with the Grenvilles and attached himself to Grey, so that to choose him would have been to invite a breach between them ; moreover, he was himself, despite the wishes of his friends, unwilling to take the lead.[1] Tierney, another possibility, was perhaps better fitted to be a whip than a leader. He had a sound business head, and was a good debater ; but he was not habitually able to take a broad and statesmanlike view of policy. Organization and intrigue were, perhaps, his true *métier*. In any case, his unpopularity was very great among the Democrats, where, from being an idol, he was regarded as an apostate ; and even by the moderates of his party he was viewed with a certain suspicion.[2] Sheridan was hardly now a serious candidate. His ignominious defeat at Westminster in 1807, his untrustworthy character, his lack of money, and his friendship for the Prince of Wales were all valid arguments against him.[3] Lord Henry Petty was a more likely choice, for he had shown some ingenuity in his handling of the finances as Chancellor of the Exchequer in the last Government, and he would perhaps have been the choice of the

[1] Add. MS. 37887, f. 179 ; Add. MS. 37906, f. 285 ; Holland, *Memoirs of the Whig Party*, ii. 205 ; Trevelyan, *Lord Grey of the Reform Bill*, p. 142.

[2] Barnes, *Parliamentary Portraits*, p. 59 ; Creevey, p. 327 ; Gale Jones, *Five Letters to G. Tierney, passim* ; S. F. Waddington, *Three Letters to Tierney, passim* ; *A Letter to His Majesty*, p. 24, speaks of " the ponderous, drowsy Tierney . . . his very breath is somniferous ".

[3] *Tierney MSS.* Grey to Tierney, 20 Dec. 1807 ; J. W. Ward, *Letters to " Ivy "*, p. 63.

bulk of the party, if there had been a vote upon it.[1] He
was young, intelligent, and conciliatory ; but he had no
desire for the leadership, for he was apathetic about partisan
warfare.[2] This could never be said of Whitbread, who was,
perhaps, the most likely candidate in the field. Whitbread
was courageous, tenacious, and inflexibly honest in dis-
charging unpleasant duties. He was an adept at harrying
Ministers, and insatiable in the discovery of abuses. He
regarded himself as the spiritual heir of Fox ; [3] and hating
the Grenvilles, was hated by them in return. If the Whigs
had been willing or able to cut the Grenville connexion,
Whitbread might have been their choice ; though his
arrogance disgusted many of his party, and a certain
irresponsibility alarmed others.[4] He was, perhaps, more
ignorant than a man should be who aspires to lead his
party : in foreign affairs certainly he was so. But he had
wealth, he had a purposeful sincerity and he had the
friendship of the Hollands and Russells. These things,
however, could not offset the inconvenience of his advanced
Reforming opinions, his unreasoning pacifism, and, most
fatal of all, his quarrel with his brother-in-law, Grey.

Whitbread had considered himself entitled to office in
the Ministry of All the Talents ; but through some misunderstanding of his attitude he was passed over, and he had
never forgiven Grey. Thenceforward he became a man with
a grievance ; and he was inclined to think that it was Grey's
fault that he was not now invited to succeed him in the lead,
though in reality, as Tierney explained to him quite frankly,
the reason lay in the fact that his opinions differed so widely
from those of the bulk of the party that the majority of

[1] *Tierney MSS.* Tierney to Grey, 7 Dec. 1807 ; Tierney to Grey,
19 Dec. 1807.
[2] For an analysis of his finance see *Edinburgh Review,* x. 74 *et seq.*
[3] See his speech, *Parl. Deb.* x. 853.
[4] *E.g.* Brougham : Creevey, p. 181 ; and Horner, *Memoirs of Francis
Horner,* ii. 260-261.

them would not consider him.[1] Tierney made great efforts to reconcile the two ; but Whitbread was too sore to be propitiated. It was in vain that Grey wrote graciously of Whitbread's services, of the certainty of his inclusion in the Cabinet if the Talents' Government had gone on,[2] and of his own endeavours to push him forward.[3] Whitbread complained of Grey's "mysterious superiority" of manner;[4] and on Christmas Day 1807 poured out his mortified pride in an extraordinary outburst :

My dear Tierney,

I have received your letter, and am highly gratified by the friendly disposition you manifest towards me, and the pains you take to smooth the little political roughnesses there are between me and Grey. As to personal differences there can be none, for I have the greatest possible affection and respect for him, and so I am sure has he for me. What I complain of is that he does not understand my feelings upon subjects of this sort, and of course cannot enter into them. I want not to be the Leader of his party—if he in the warmth of his heart, and an estimation of my fitness far different from what he has, had pressed upon me to take his place, and pressed upon his friends my adoption ; I am so well aware of the sort of reasons which prevail against me, and of the difficulties attending upon the situation itself, that I declare to God I would not have accepted it, if indeed there is anything to accept. But I am mortified in supposing, that he, above all other persons, questions my capacity ; and I am disappointed because he does not show at any time (except in very particular emergencies) any belief that I could assist him. I cannot have a stronger proof of his misconception of my feelings than his letter to you furnishes. He imagines I want him to *push me forward*. I neither wish him to do it, nor has he the

[1] *Tierney MSS.* Tierney to Whitbread (draft), 24 Dec. 1807 : " I told you frankly that I had heard many object to your having the lead, and that I was convinced that such a measure could not at present be carried, but I also told you . . . that the specific objections if there were any had not come to my knowledge except in so far as related to your conduct on the negotiation for peace. . . ."

[2] Tierney suppressed this information when passing the letter on to Whitbread.　　　　[3] *Tierney MSS.* Grey to Tierney, 20 Dec. 1807.

[4] *Tierney MSS.* Whitbread to Tierney, 21 Dec. 1807.

power. I shall find my level and always have found it without his assistance, and my estimation with the country I would not change for his : however I may, and do acknowledge his superiority in many respects to be very very great.

I need not elucidate my meaning to you ; when you know that he thought a peerage would be an acceptable thing to me : and he was so good as to say that he had talked to Fox about it, and that in time after the impeachment [of Melville] it might be managed. I could not but be indignant at the offer especially so made : and I was immediately convinced that as an active friend he could have no opinion of me at all, or he would not have dreamt of disabling me, and disgracing me. . . . His manner too has always been so unlike poor Fox's. . . .

Grey talks at a distance about stern virtue and disregard of great political obligations and so forth which I cannot but suppose means to glance at me. But in truth I have no political obligations to any person. I have some disobligation to most of the late Cabinet personally ; for having acquitted Melville, which they did by abandoning the trial. . . .[1]

It is plain, that whatever leader Grey and Grenville might ultimately choose, he would not find it easy to manage such a subordinate as Whitbread.

It was unfortunate, therefore, that they should have now concentrated on the candidature of George Ponsonby. On 19 November 1807, only five days after the death of Grey's father, his name was put forward by Thomas Grenville.[2] Among the Irish members Ponsonby was popular, and he was the uncle of Grey's wife ; but he had not otherwise many claims to the leadership. A sort of dogged ambition drove him on, and gave him courage to endure slights which would have disheartened a weaker man, or a more sensitive one ; but he had no real aptitude for politics. Dignified but dull as a speaker, he was judged even by his friends to be superficial in his learning, and by his enemies was considered to be intellectually only fitted to the hunting field. Among the English members he had no

---

[1] *Tierney MSS.* Whitbread to Tierney, 25 Dec. 1807.
[2] *Dropmore Papers*, ix. 147.

personal following at all.[1] Perhaps it was his very obscurity
that led to his being put forward, for his elevation by the
combined exertions of Grey and Grenville would be likely
to bind him to their joint policy (in so far as they had one)
and there would be little danger of his setting up a standard
of his own. The suggestion was by no means well received
at first. Both Lord Holland and Lord Grenville would have
preferred Petty ; and it is clear that Thomas Grenville only
persisted in the proposal in the belief that it would be
gratifying to Lord Grey, and not offensive to his own group.[2]
There was a feeling, which Thomas Grenville strongly
combated, that it would be better to do without a definite
leader for some time. As Lord Grenville put it : " I do not
feel sure enough that our army is a united army, to think
things ripe to proceed to the choice of a new general ".[3]

These and other representations had their effect ; and
for the moment Thomas Grenville gave way. Ponsonby
had made the mistake of alienating the Duke of Bedford,
who had spontaneously offered to bring him in to Parliament for Tavistock, a seat which was being kept warm for
Lord Tavistock. Ponsonby had neglected to return any
answer to this invitation, and the Duke was annoyed.[4]

---

[1] Grattan, *Life and Times of Henry Grattan*, v. 140-141 ; Barnes,
Parliamentary Portraits, art. Ponsonby ; O'Flanagan, *Lives of the Lord
Chancellors of Ireland*, art. Ponsonby ; *A Vindication of the Conduct of
the Irish Catholics*, by " A Protestant Barrister ", p. 22 ; Holland,
Memoirs of the Whig Party, ii. 168 ; Wellington, *Civil Correspondence,
Ireland*, p. 546, for one of Ponsonby's indiscretions.

[2] *Dropmore Papers*, ix. 148-149 ; *Tierney MSS.* Tierney to Grey,
7 Dec. 1807.

[3] Duke of Buckingham, *Memoirs of the Court and Cabinets of
George III*, iv. 209.

[4] Add. MS. 37888, f. 120 ; *Tierney MSS.* Tierney to Grey, 19 Dec.
1807 : " The D. of Bedford told Tierney that P. was unpopular in
Ireland, and that his brother Lord W[illiam] had said that P. would
not do here ; Anstruther attacked Tierney on the same subject, and
said, ' The man is a perfect stranger '. If these objections spread it will
become impossible " (*Dropmore Papers*, ix. 159).

Little by little, however, Ponsonby's cause gained ground. He succeeded in reconciling himself with the Russells.[1] Moreover, it became plain that nothing was to be expected from Lord Henry Petty, who was " desperately in love and just going to be married to a sister of Lord Ilchester's ".[2] It was, further, considered extremely important that some decision should be taken before the beginning of the session ; and as it was already December, there was no time to be lost.[3] On 7 December Tierney wrote at length to Grey, weighing the arguments on either side ; and though he did not conceal from himself the disadvantages of Ponsonby's leadership, he inclined towards it for Grey's sake.[4] The determining factor in the ultimate selection of Ponsonby was the fact that Tierney was able to extract from Whitbread a promise of qualified support for him : that is, he reserved the right to express his own sentiments on points upon which his opinions were fixed, but promised general coöperation.[5] This was not much, but it was more than had been expected ; and for the rest, Grey, Grenville,

[1] *Tierney MSS.* Tierney to Grey, 19 Dec. 1807.

[2] Add. MS. 37887, f. 186 ; *Court and Cabinets*, iv. 216-218.

[3] *Tierney MSS.* Tierney to Grey, 19 Dec. 1807.

[4] *Tierney MSS.* Tierney to Grey, 7 Dec. 1807 : " The advantages of G. P. [*sic*] are his talents and his age, his parliamentary experience, and his connection with you, the Cavendishes, and Lord Fitzwilliam, and as I must presume his being acceptable to Lord G. . . . His disadvantages are that he is an Irishman, little known in Parliament, and scarcely acquainted with a large proportion of the present opposition. . . . Do you believe that our other candidates will not feel additional mortification at being superseded by one whom they will describe as a stranger ? Will our English country gentlemen . . . be satisfied ? May there not be particular Irish jealousies ? Will it not be expected that a Leader should be constantly resident in England ? I honestly confess I have great fears that G. P. will not do. . . . As for general approbation that is more than can be expected. . . . I shall be satisfied with a reasonable expression of good-will and acquiescence."

[5] *Tierney MSS.* Tierney to Grey, 19 Dec. 1807 ; Tierney to Whitbread, 24 Dec. 1807 ; see also Add. MS. 37887, ff. 185-186 (Grenville to Windham).

Holland, Bedford, and Fitzwilliam concurred in preferring Ponsonby to any other. The *Morning Chronicle* gave cautious approval, and the rank and file submitted in astonishment.[1]

Fox's friends are indifferent since his death. Petty is reasonable as usual, and Whitbread, goaded by a scribbling gazetteer of the name of Belsham, submits with a thousand reservations, each more hostile than the last.[2]

Ponsonby, characteristically, stayed in Ireland.[3]

It now remained to be seen whether Ponsonby would justify Thomas Grenville's estimate of him " as a handy man in Parliament ". It is not easy to guess from the reports of his speeches at his success in the House, for there is a family likeness in all Parliamentary speeches at this time which submerges personal peculiarities ; still, speeches of his which Palmerston considered " dull and heavy " were qualified by the *Morning Chronicle* as " animated and logical ".[4] He was to be seen occasionally addressing the members in the lobby, and endeavouring to secure a good attendance for important divisions.[5] But on the whole, there is no doubt that he quite failed to control his men, or to enforce a definite line of opposition to the Government. There were indeed wranglings and recriminations in plenty, and the public found them tedious ; [6] but the Chief Secretary summed up the situation when he wrote :

We are opposed by the most active and the most persevering, though not the most able and judicious opposition that ever existed in England. I agree very much in opinion with you respecting their leader, who never appeared to me to have a sufficiency of general

---

[1] *Tierney MSS.* Tierney to Whitbread, 16 Dec. 1807 ; *Morning Chronicle*, 17 Dec. 1807.

[2] Lady Holland, *Journals*, pp. 235-236.

[3] *Tierney MSS.* Tierney to Whitbread, 28 Dec. 1807.

[4] Bulwer, *Life of Palmerston*, i. 80 ; *Morning Chronicle*, 4 Feb. 1808.

[5] *The Melbourne Papers*, p. 47.

[6] See an anonymous pamphlet entitled *Public Spirit*, pp. 69-71.

knowledge for the situation in which he has been placed, or the head of a statesman.[1]

The one important personal contribution which Ponsonby made to the session—the introduction of the veto question—ended in bitterness and futility, largely through his fault. The party gradually fell to pieces, and Ponsonby was apparently incapable of holding it together.[2] On the other hand, whatever Ponsonby's failings as a leader, it must be admitted that he had had to contend with disloyalty, petty squabbles, and unsatisfied ambitions. As early as February 1808 there was bad feeling between Tierney and Whitbread, who seems to have been particularly irritable about this time.[3] And Ponsonby might well have complained also of the slackness of Grey himself. Long before Lady Grey's confinement he was making it an excuse for his reluctance to leave Howick ; and when the governess of his children left him suddenly, that was quite sufficient to keep him away from the House. Nor was Grenville much better. It consequently happened that when the Convention of Cintra afforded a favourable opportunity of concerting measures against the Government, Grey was secluded in Northumberland, and Grenville inaccessible at Boconnoc.[4]

Tierney realized that some attempt at greater efficiency

[1] Wellington, *Civil Correspondence*, p. 344 ; to the Bishop of Meath.

[2] Windsor Arch., George IV, 7 Feb. 1808, the Duke of Northumberland to McMahon : " Pray how do such persons as Mr. Coke, and other independent country gentlemen, relish the self-appointment of Mr. Ponsonby to be manager and Director of the Party in the Hᵉ of Commons ? I should imagine to many of them, as well as to myself, he was totally unknown, and I can hardly suppose such persons would submit to be led by anybody that Lord Grey chose to set up to govern them. This would be bowing to the golden image that Nebuchadnezzar had set up, with a vengeance."

[3] Trevelyan, *Grey*, p. 165.

[4] *Dropmore Papers*, ix. 197 ; *Court and Cabinets*, iv. 274 ; *Tierney MSS.* Grey to Tierney, 20 Dec. 1807 ; *Creevey's Life and Times*, p. 40.

must be made before the session of 1809. He " had a great horror " of the " loose practice of the last session ", and he had already remonstrated forcibly with Grey on his continued absenteeism.[1] He now took the lead in instituting a series of party conferences, which took place towards the end of December 1808, and to which Ponsonby was not invited. Tierney, Grey, Grenville, Petty, and Thomas Grenville formed the committee. They took the gloomiest view of the situation of the party, and seriously contemplated secession from the House. Undeterred by the experience of a former experiment of this sort, Grey and the Grenvilles anxiously balanced the relative merits of a " declaration of *mitigated attendance* " and of a " *mitigated secession* ", finally deciding in favour of the former. Petty condemned either policy ; and Tierney, though he accepted mitigated attendance, did so explicitly on the ground that by breaking up the party such policy would give them all a better chance of reuniting later.

The truth is [wrote Thomas Grenville] that Tierney is so desirous of seeing this division of the party, that he almost openly professes it ; while to me it appears that we should be found doing what is right, but with every desire and attention to keep the party together as much as possible.[2]

Tierney's common sense had in fact seized on the essential instability of the Grey–Grenville coalition. He realized that it was precisely because their union was so artificial, because they had so little in common in their programmes, that the position of Ponsonby was impossible, even when his personal inefficiency had been discounted. Ponsonby could hardly move without offending one or other section of the party : therefore he remained torpid. There was also the problem of Whitbread, whose enthusiasm

---

[1] Trevelyan, *Grey*, p. 164 ; *Dropmore Papers*, ix. 250 ; and see Tierney's later protest, *Tierney MSS.* 3 Oct. 1809.

[2] *Dropmore Papers*, ix. 254 ; Brougham's vigorous disapproval of secession in *Creevey's Life and Times*, p. 40.

for immediate Reform was shared by no other prominent man in the party. Even if he were to choke down his disappointed ambition, his political convictions must lead him into courses which the Grenvilles would consider factious. And in fact Whitbread was too proud and sensitive to submit to the mediocrity for whom Grey had passed him over. His liberalism and his ambition were thus interdependent and mutually sustaining. The best thing that could have happened to the Whigs would have been a split so serious as to force Grey to separate from the crypto-Tory Grenvilles and reunite with Whitbread and his group, but such a disruption would clearly not suit those—the majority of the party—who hoped to climb back to power by a steady adherence to the coalition of 1806. Ponsonby, perfunctorily consulted as to his views on the situation, appeared embarrassed, and conscious of the delicacy of his position ; but he was able to bring himself to agree that any serious Parliamentary effort must be wasted. The body of the party, however, would have none of the proposed declaration of mitigated attendance ; and when Parliament met, nothing had been decided.[1] The party meeting on the first night of the session was held at Ponsonby's house, but the fact of his leadership was not otherwise perceptible.[2] Whitbread, who had been particularly disgusted at the talk of secession, and was still very disgruntled, began to take an independent line, and it soon became apparent that a section of the party was prepared to follow him in it.[3] As Lord Bulkeley observed, " Ponsonby, or Lord H. Petty, or Tierney, or whoever leads the Constitutional Opposition ", was indeed " confoundedly embarrassed how to act with Whitbread and the *enragés* ".[4] And in February, during the debates on the Duke of York's affair, the impotence

[1] *Dropmore Papers*, ix. 254, 266-267.
[2] *Morning Chronicle*, 19 Jan. 1809.
[3] Creevey, p. 92 ; *Court and Cabinets*, iv. 300.
[4] *Ibid.* 304-305.

and divided counsels of the party were plain for all to
see. As Lord Holland put it :

> . . . the Whigs as a body took no distinct or manly tone whatever
> upon this embarrassing occasion. The different sides they espoused
> proved that no leader had any authority over them, and perhaps the
> violence of some and the irresolution of others proved as clearly
> that not one of them had the qualities requisite to assume it. Mr.
> Ponsonby sunk in the estimation of the party, and the party sunk
> yet more in the estimation of the public.[1]

Under the influence of this chaotic state of affairs, a
resolute effort was made in March 1809 to end the difficulty
by putting pressure on Ponsonby to retire. It was hoped
that this would be sufficient to conciliate Whitbread ; for
it was not intended that he should be offered the lead.
That was to fall to Petty, who was safer and less extreme
than Whitbread, and consequently less obnoxious to the
Grenvilles. He had not compromised himself, as Whitbread
had, by associating with Wardle and Burdett, nor spoken
from the tables of the Crown and Anchor Tavern.[2] Petty
himself was to approach Whitbread, with a view to reunion ; while Grattan and Lord Ponsonby were left to deal
with the leader. The project collapsed at both ends. Whitbread told Petty plainly that he would no longer consider
himself a member of the party. There should be no public
explanation, no deliberate attempt to embarrass the Whigs ;
but, since he considered the party as having no leader, he
should govern his conduct henceforward " solely by the
opinions of Samuel Whitbread ".[3] Two days later (that is,
on 30 March 1809), Ponsonby was equally decided in
refusing to retire from the leadership, pointing out with
some show of reason, that since most of his embarrassments
had proceeded from the presence of Whitbread in the
party, there was every reason to expect better times now

---

[1] Holland, *Further Memoirs of the Whig Party*, p. 28.

[2] *Proceedings . . . at Westminster*, March 1809 ; *Letters of Lady
Williams Wynn*, p. 144.   [3] *Dropmore Papers*, ix. 283.

he had seceded.[1] The only perceptible result, therefore, of this attempt to retrieve the mistake of 1807, was to make definite the breach with Whitbread, and to fix more firmly in his seat a leader who was incapable of leading.

The alienation of Whitbread was more serious than the Whigs imagined ; for it did not merely involve a coolness between them and his friend Lord Holland, or the loss of the dozen or so of " Insurgents " whose commander he was. It was really a victory for the Grenvilles over the Foxites. It meant that Reform would be more than ever pushed into the background. At this moment, the Duke of York's case had given rise to a large number of enquiries into abuses ; the case of Castlereagh and the East India writership, the case of Mr. Quintin Dick, Lord Folkestone's motion for a general investigation into corrupt practices, and Curwen's Reform Bill all showed the strength and direction of the popular current. Whitbread was clearly emerging as the one man inside the Whig party who could control this current and turn it into useful channels. By a judicious playing of the demagogue he was trying to steal Burdett's reputation for the Whigs ; he was trying to radicalize the party from within. The Reform movement, which had been quite dead since 1800, was reviving ; Economical Reform first, Parliamentary Reform afterwards. If Whitbread had been given the lead, no doubt the edge of his ardour would have been blunted ; but it is extremely probable that he would have adopted something in the nature of that " Moderate Reform " which Thomas Brand propounded from 1810 to 1812. Its chances of success would have been much improved by the substitution of Whitbread for Brand, the leader for the private individual. But as long as the coalition with Grenville lasted it was almost impossible for Whitbread to lead the party, even if he were reconciled to Grey. Thomas Grenville apparently imagined that it was only wounded pride that had driven

[1] *Ibid.* 286.

Whitbread into " factious " courses. Lord Grenville judged more truly. He saw that in Whitbread lay principles hostile to the whole Grenville system. He rejoiced in the breach which had opened between them.

What you will see of the Westminster Hall language will certainly lead you to feel pleasure in learning, that on a full explanation which Lord Grey and Lord Henry Petty have separately had with Whitbread it has been distinctly understood that their party-connection with him is at an end. This separation has, as you well know, existed in fact from the very moment the last government was formed—but it is useful to have it at last explained and avowed that the fact is so.[1]

From a Parliamentary point of view the result of all this was anarchy. At Brookes' itself Coke was to be heard denouncing his leaders, and young Whigs previously thought to be " safe " were exhibiting disquieting tendencies.[2] The division on Madocks' motion of 11 May demonstrated the condition of the party. The question was the sale of seats by the Treasury, with reference to the case of Mr. Quintin Dick ; and in the division every member of the Talents' Government, with the solitary exception of Romilly, voted with Ministers against their own man, Madocks ; yet in spite of this no less than 85 Whigs—a good deal more than half their normal strength on a division—voted against their leaders.[3]

. . . The truth is [wrote Lord Grenville], that while we are disputing whether the ship be well steered or not, others are at work to destroy its whole frame ; and it is very difficult to resist the blunders of the pilot, without assisting the mutinous part of the crew.[4]

At the end of the session Tierney and Grey exchanged surveys of the situation and found themselves in gloomy

[1] Add. MS. 34457, ff. 510-511.
[2] *Dropmore Papers*, ix. 285-286.
[3] *Parl. Deb.* xiv. 527 ; Romilly, *Memoirs*, ii. 280 ; Wilberforce, *Life of Wilberforce*, ii. 408.   [4] Add. MS. 34457, f. 512.

agreement;[1] and Tierney in a long letter to Ponsonby
told him that he considered the party dissolved, that he
could no longer be responsible for the attendance of
members, and that for the future he (Ponsonby) must
fend for himself as best he might.[2] To many it seemed
probable that a new Opposition would be formed by
Whitbread out of the old Whig left wing.[3]

In September, however, the Portland Ministry fell
owing to the dissensions of its members, and there appeared
to be a chance of the Whigs' coming in. It soon became
clear that Perceval was not prepared to offer to retire in
favour of Grey and Grenville, and that they in their turn
were not prepared to give him the opportunity of proposing even the most reasonable compromise. On the other
hand, no one had the least confidence in Perceval's ability
to survive for very long ; and as neither Canning, nor
Wellesley, nor Sidmouth was capable of forming a Government, it behoved the Whigs to think of how they should
fill up their Cabinet. In these circumstances, it occurred
to Tierney that it would be better to have Whitbread with
them than against them. Once again, therefore, he opened
negotiations in the hope of reconciling him with Grey, and
in an endeavour to induce him to return to the Whig fold.
In this he was fairly successful : cordial letters were
exchanged between Whitbread and Grey, and Whitbread
admitted that he would not be unwilling to take office.[4]
The question of leadership, however, still rankled, and
made it very difficult to reach a satisfactory settlement.
Tierney again suggested Petty, or failing him, Lord George

[1] *Tierney MSS.* Grey to Tierney, 27 June 1809 ; Tierney to Grey
[June 1809] : " whether anything, and what, can be made out of the
remnants, time alone can show, but I am too old to take much interest
in distant prospects ".

[2] *Tierney MSS.* Tierney to Grey [n.d.—about 26 Sept. 1809] quotes
this.   [3] Ward, *Letters to " Ivy "*, p. 76.

[4] Creevey, pp. 109-112 ; *Tierney MSS.* Whitbread to Tierney,
27 Sept. 1809.

Cavendish. Cavendish was a complete nonentity, and
Whitbread suspected that he was put forward so that
Tierney himself could exercise the real control.[1] To Creevey,
Whitbread expressed his private indignation at these
proposals,[2] and to Tierney he wrote disclaiming responsibility for the break-up of the party, pointing out that
Petty was no debater, and that Tierney himself had
admitted that he had no very high opinion of Petty's
abilities. As to the events of the last session, if Ponsonby
had been equal to his situation, a difference of opinion on
a particular point would not have been " an inexpiable
offence ".[3] However, the Duke of Bedford, Lord Carrington,
and other magnates were brought to bear ;[4] Tierney used
a little flattery ;[5] and Whitbread was, for the moment,
regained, though the question of the lead still remained
open.[6]

Just when there seemed to be a prospect of reuniting
the party, perhaps under the leadership of Petty, the death
of Lord Lansdowne on 15 November 1809 threw everything
again into confusion. " It will cause a world of vexation

---

[1] Creevey, pp. 112, 100.

[2] *Ibid.* p. 100 : " Should I not lose all power in one way, and gain
nothing in the other ? Should I not bind myself to a compact that I could
not keep ? Should I not at every turn be said to be endeavouring to
outstrip my leader ? and would it not be confusion worse confounded ?
Yet I suppose these are the only nostrums recommended. I cannot take
them—this is between ourselves. . . ."

[3] *Tierney MSS.* Whitbread to Tierney, 13 Nov. 1809.

[4] Creevey, p. 111 ; *Tierney MSS.* Tierney to Whitbread (draft),
18 Nov. 1809.

[5] *Creevey's Life and Times,* p. 44 : Tierney to Whitbread : " I did
not know you were in Town or I should not have omitted to pay my
respects to you as a mark of proper attention to the Leader of the
Opposition ".

[6] Whitbread's health at this time was not good. " He has a heaviness
in his head and a degree of languor which is very unpleasant ", perhaps
the beginnings of the disease which caused his suicide ? (*Tierney MSS.*
Tierney to Grey, 28 Nov. [1809]).

and trouble ", wrote Tierney,[1] and so it proved ; for with
the removal of Petty to the Lords the only likely substitute for Ponsonby vanished, and the Whigs were left to
choose between the ineptitudes of Cavendish and the
enthusiasms of Whitbread.[2] Ministers realized very well the
extent of their good fortune ; for, as Palmerston observed,
it was not so much that Petty had been formidable personally, as that he had been potentially dangerous as a leader
who might have given strength and unity to the Opposition.[3] The only remaining candidate who had not yet been
suggested was—Tierney himself.

> Ponsonby's incapacity is admitted on all hands. Whitbread takes
> a line of his own, and is determined to ride the popular horse as
> far as it will carry him . . .'so that unless some distinguished recruit
> can be raised, Tierney—Citizen the Right Honourable George
> Tierney—will become the principal person on the front bench. . . .[4]

Tierney realized that his chances were now much improved :

> Since the removal of Petty and the failure of G. Ponsonby it
> would be an affectation in me to pretend that I did not perceive
> an opinion beginning to prevail that I am in the next Session to be
> looked up to as Leader.[5]

On second thoughts he deleted that passage from his letter ;
and a week later, after thinking it over, he took his decision
to adhere to his refusal to serve. He knew the Grenvilles

---

[1] *Tierney MSS.* Tierney to Grey, 4 Dec. [1809].

[2] Grey's comment is typical : " Petty will undoubtedly be a great
loss in the House of Commons ; but it would be very selfish on that
account to regret his succeeding to a great fortune. To me personally
this is by no means an undesirable event, as I may now be permitted to
stay here [Howick] as long as I please, without anybody being able to
pretend that there can be any want of my exertions in the House of
Lords." (*Tierney MSS.* Grey to Tierney, 18 Nov. 1809).

[3] Bulwer, *Palmerston*, i. 111 ; even Wellington in Spain commented
on the importance of this event : *Despatches*, v. 318.

[4] Ward, *Letters to " Ivy "*, p. 82.

[5] *Tierney MSS.* Tierney to Grey, 28 Nov. 1809, deleted passage.

thought him unfit for the office ;[1] he was, as he frequently
remarked, growing old ; perhaps he was lazy, perhaps he
disliked the prospect of bringing order out of the anarchy
Ponsonby had left behind him. At all events, he was firm
in his refusal.

I know what is expected of me [he wrote], and I feel that non-
compliance on my part will make me be held up as the cause of all
the confusion that may arise among us. I cannot however help it.
The most I can do is to take the post Old Nicholls assigned to me
some years ago and play the part of Berthier, and even that in the
present state of things I would much rather let alone.[2]

Whoever might succeed to the leadership, it was felt
to be urgently necessary to extract a definite abdication
from Ponsonby ; for if, as seemed not improbable, the
Whigs were to be offered the Government, it would be very
awkward for them if Ponsonby were still nominally at the
head of their forces in the House of Commons. In such a
case he could clearly expect to retain his situation ; and,
though, as Thomas Grenville remarked, he might serve at
a pinch as leader of the Opposition, he was inconceivable
as leader of the House.[3] Grey had foreseeen this, and had
already written to Ponsonby suggesting that, if they came
in, he might like to return to his old office of Lord Chancellor
of Ireland. But Ponsonby, though he pointed out that the
matter did not seem to be of pressing importance, made it
clear that he was not to be so easily disposed of : if the
Whigs came in under his leadership, they must continue
under it.[4] This rebuff disconcerted Grey. But presently a
report began to get about that, after all, Ponsonby wished
to retire ; and as the source of it was Lord Ponsonby, the
leader's nephew, it was generally believed. There was a
flutter of correspondence between the Grenvilles ; Tierney

[1] *Dropmore Papers*, ix. 385.
[2] *Tierney MSS.* Tierney to Grey, 4 Dec. [1809].
[3] *Dropmore Papers*, ix. 425, 426.
[4] *Tierney MSS.* 30 Nov. 1809 ; *Dropmore Papers*, ix. 401, 431.

and Grey were consulted; and it really seemed as though they were going to get rid of him.[1] Unfortunately, the report proved to have been a fiction, or at least a gross exaggeration, fabricated by Lord Ponsonby himself, who does not seem to have been very straightforward in his dealings with his uncle.[2] Ponsonby remained aloof in Ireland, apparently indifferent to the agitation at Stowe and Dropmore, and fully determined to appear again as leader in January. The Whig magnates were mortified when this became apparent to them: " all this looked damned unpleasant, as if he meant to come back "; [3] but as they were wholly incapable of agreeing on a supplanter, they could do nothing. And when the session opened, there was Ponsonby, " sprung up in Arlington Street, with his sceptre in his hands, which he is ready to lay across the shoulders of any man who shall withhold all due allegiance ".[4]

The magnates, after a little hesitation, were forced to admit defeat. They could console themselves with the reflection that they had avoided the fresh difficulties and dissensions which the choice of a new leader would have involved; and the Grenvilles, for their part, had agreed privately to reconsider the question of allowing Ponsonby to lead the House, if they should accept office.[5] The opposition to Ponsonby was, indeed, still formidable: " Tierney quotes Anstruther as vehement against Ponsonby, and Adam and Abercrombie and a whole host of young ones "; [6]

---

[1] *Ibid.* 385; *Tierney MSS.* Grey to Tierney, 25 Aug. 1809.

[2] *Tierney MSS.* Tierney to Grey, 4 Dec. [1809]: " It is true [Lord] Ponsonby told me that I might rely upon it his uncle had distinctly declared his intention to withdraw, but it is equally true that Lord Grenville told me the reverse and they both spoke on the authority of conversations they held with him, Lord G's being the latest ". Both Creevey and Lady Holland disliked Lord Ponsonby: Creevey, p. 110; Lady Holland, *Journals*, p. 269.

[3] *Dropmore Papers*, ix. 401. Tierney, quoted by Thomas Grenville.

[4] *Court and Cabinets*, iv. 418.

[5] *Dropmore Papers*, ix. 437-438.   [6] *Ibid.* x. 5.

and the Hollands, newly returned out of Spain, and not very familiar, therefore, with the political situation, were inclined to press Whitbread's claims. Nevertheless on 20 January 1810 Grey, Lansdowne, and the Grenvilles agreed on the formal acknowledgment of Ponsonby ; and on the following day the revival of the old order was inaugurated by a general meeting of the party at his house, attended even by such Whigs of the " left " as Fergusson, Coke, and Creevey. Whitbread, however, stayed away.[1] For the present he maintained an attitude of reserve, though he was consulted by the party as to the form of the amendment to the Address.[2]

The session of 1810 was not so unsuccessful or chaotic, from the Whig point of view, as those that had preceded it. The party acted better together, and Fremantle (a Grenvillite) considered that they showed " the greatest harmony and zeal ".[3] The extravagances of Burdett, and his committal by the House in April, gave the party a chance of proving its conservatism, and Ponsonby an opportunity of distinguishing himself, in the defence of Parliamentary privilege, an opportunity which he used well enough to bring down upon him the especial reprobation of the popular press.[4] He was less successful in debates on the Walcheren expedition. He did try to rally his men in the lobby, and he certainly spoke at length ; but it was thought by many Whigs, that if he had spoken less, and allowed Brougham to speak more, the result of the crucial divisions might have been in their favour. Cobbett, moreover, succeeded in making his oratory appear ridiculous.[5] But the Whigs were in fact predestined to fail on this question,

---

[1] Creevey, p. 122 ; *Dropmore Papers*, x. 7.   [2] *Ibid.* 20.

[3] *Court and Cabinets*, iv. 421.

[4] *Sunday Review*, 27 May 1810 ; and see newspapers in Add. MS. 27839.

[5] Ward, *Letters to " Ivy "*, p. 98 ; Holland, *Further Memoirs*, p. 46 ; *Morning Chronicle*, 31 March 1810 ; Cobbett, *Political Register*, xvii. 515.

which would have involved the fall of Perceval's Government if it had been carried. The majority in Parliament which supported Perceval was not disposed to trust the conduct of the war to a party so disorganized and so ill-led, so long as there was any reasonable alternative. The Walcheren vote was a vote not so much in favour of the Tories as against the Whigs. Still, as far as Ponsonby was concerned, the session was a happier one, and he had his revenge on Milner in the debate on the Catholic petition ; so that the Grenvilles were able to congratulate themselves that he was " stouter " than hitherto. He was perhaps stouter than they cared about when he supported Brand's motion for Parliamentary Reform on 21 May, and took 115 members with him into the lobby.[1] Whitbread still remained rather independent, and continued to shock the Whigs by his indiscretions. Wardle and Madocks had fortunately retired again into obscurity, so that there was no temptation for him in that direction ; but he ran counter to the official Whig attitude towards the privileges of Parliament, which he aspersed at a Livery Dinner in April. His speech caused much irritation :

> Lord Grey, Sir A. Lauderdale, Piggott, Morpeth and Tierney [wrote Thomas Grenville] all concur in opinion that it is utterly impossible to go on with Whitbread upon these terms ; Lord Grey says that he had rather support any Ministers than do so, and Tierney is talking of making his farewell speech to Parliament ; the evil is quite incurable [2]—

but they managed to finish the session without an open breach. In September there was another attempt to persuade Tierney to take the lead. Holland and Grattan approached him through Lord Duncannon with an offer, which seems to have been accepted.[3] But there is no trace

---

[1] *Court and Cabinets,* iv. 445 ; *Parl. Deb.* xvii. 161, 164.

[2] *Dropmore Papers,* x. 26 ; *Morning Chronicle,* 20 April 1810, for his speech.

[3] Grattan, *Life and Times of Grattan,* v. 418 (the only authority).

of it to be found in the correspondence of the Grenvilles, nor among the *Tierney MSS.* ; and it does not seem that anything ever came of it. It seems likely that Tierney withdrew his consent when he realized that Grenville and Grey were not aware of the proposal ; or perhaps the crisis caused by the King's illness and the prospect of a Regency (and hence, perhaps, of office) made it seem advisable to leave matters as they stood. For the Regency certainly united the Whigs as no leader had been able to do ; and even Ponsonby made a good speech on the Regency resolutions.[1] The prospect of office, moreover, made Whitbread more tractable, and his ambition began to get the better of his principles. He stopped his visits to the " Crown and Anchor ", abandoned the lead of the Reforming Whigs to Brand, and so threw away his true career and prepared for himself the tragic futility of the last three years of his life.[2]

If the Whigs had come in (as they expected to do) in February 1811, it is not quite clear who would have had the lead of the House. Their arrangements provided for only three Cabinet Ministers in the Commons, of whom (as an adversary unkindly said) " Whitbread was too impracticable, Ponsonby incapable, and Tierney lazy ".[3] It seems, however, that Ponsonby was to have been Home Secretary, Whitbread Secretary for War, and Tierney Chancellor of the Exchequer, so that perhaps Tierney would have been the choice.[4] The Marquis of Buckingham, indeed, was afraid that the real power would centre in Whitbread, in which case he felt alarm for the safety of Grenvillite principles.[5] In the event, the Queen, or Sir

[1] Grattan, *Life and Times*, v. 425.

[2] See *Dropmore Papers*, x. 110, for his improved relations with the Grenvilles.   [3] R. Plumer Ward, *Memoirs*, i. 384.

[4] Nat. Lib. of Wales MSS., Williams Wynn Papers, 2719 (unfoliated). C. W. Wynn to Henry Wynn, 13 Feb. 1811. In an earlier list Whitbread was to have had the Admiralty. *Dropmore Papers*, x. 98.

[5] *Ibid.* 98, 9 Jan. 1811 : " I could not be brought to enrol my family flag and friends under Mr. Whitbread's standard ".

Henry Halford, or the filial sense of the Prince of Wales,
or all three, made their calculations superfluous. The
Whigs were to wait a year, at least ; and as it turned out,
they were even then to be disappointed. Matters within
the party, therefore, resumed their normal aspect of
anarchy. Attendance at the House was slack, Ponsonby
was often absent, Tierney alone made some show of
efficiency ; and though Whitbread was more circumspect,
he was still hostile to Ponsonby.[1] Discipline was entirely
absent ; and Ponsonby was quite unable to check the indiscretions of Sheridan.[2] The Tories could taunt the Whigs
with having no leader,[3] and even J. W. Ward (still a Whig)
admitted that they had " no man that is at all a match for
little Perceval ".[4] When party policy was settled at the
beginning of the session of 1812, it was settled by Grey,
Grenville, Lansdowne, and Holland ; and though during the
crisis of May–June 1812 there was, indeed, a meeting of 70
selected commoners at Ponsonby's house, the real business
was done by the meeting of peers which assembled
simultaneously at Lord Grenville's.[5]

The formation of Lord Liverpool's Government relegated
the expectations of office to the remote future : Whitbread,
therefore, broke out again into faction, and joined himself
to the " Mountain ", lately known as the " Insurgents ".
He was no longer formidable, however, for he was losing
his sense of proportion ; and the violence with which he
embraced the cause of the Princess of Wales disgusted many
of his former followers. He had lost his chance of becoming
what Brougham afterwards became, the educator and
radicalizer of his party. His final severance from the Whigs

[1] Add. MS. 34458, f. 335 ; Buckingham, *Memoirs of the Court of the
Regency*, i. 368.

[2] See *Dropmore Papers*, x. 141.

[3] *Parl. Deb.* xxi. 1015 ; speech of Mr. Matthew Montague.

[4] Ward, *Letters to " Ivy "*, p. 151.

[5] Add. MS. 34458, f. 313 ; *Bath Archives*, i. 384.

took place in 1813, to the Grenvilles' undisguised satisfaction ; and in 1815 he committed suicide.[1] Ponsonby survived till 1817, calmly presiding over the misfortunes of his
party, occasionally even presiding over their meetings.[2] The
discipline of the party did not much improve. The *Morning
Chronicle* on 30 November 1812 lamented that no amendment to the Address had been prepared, " as was always
practised in the best times of Parliamentary discussion " ; [3]
and a year later Ward gives a pathetic picture of Ponsonby,
excluded from the meetings of the magnates, yet bound to
carry out the policy on which they had determined :

... about five minutes before the debate began, Snouch [Ponsonby]
crossed the House and showed him [Canning] the long rigmarole you
saw (or did not see, for I am not sure it was inserted in them) in
the papers, as the address which, by order of his superiors, he was
about instantly to move, whether Canning liked it or no.[4] He apolo-
gised to Canning, however, for not having shown it him sooner, by
saying that the Lords who had drawn it up (the great boys that
had given him his exercise) had not been able to meet till that
very day, and had not finished their work till 5 o'clock—*i.e.* till
an hour after the Speaker had taken the chair. Indeed the very
appearance of the paper they at last handed down to their unfortunate underling sufficiently indicated the circumstances under which
it had been drawn up. It was scribbled over hastily, and so blotted
and interlined that poor Snouch blundered in every other sentence
as he read it, and the Speaker himself, though his eyesight and
understanding are both a good deal sharper, made frequent pauses.[5]

And he adds, " Snouch was duller and feebler than ever ".
Under the circumstances, it was hardly surprising.

Grattan summed up the qualities required by the leader
of a party thus :

[1] Nat. Lib. Wales MS. 2791, C. Wynn to H. Wynn, 7 July 1812 ;
Nat. Lib. Wales MS. 4814, f. 66, C. Wynn to Southey ; Add. MS.
34458, ff. 429, 479.
[2] *E.g.* Add. MS. 37297, f. 205.
[3] *Morning Chronicle*, 30 Nov. 1812.
[4] The Whigs were coöperating with Canning at this time (June 1813).
[5] Ward, *Letters to " Ivy "*, pp. 206-207.

He must be affable in manner, generous in disposition, have a ready hand, an open house, and a full purse. He must be grave and gay, lively and severe. He must have a good cook for the English members, fine words and fair promises for the Irish, and sober calculations for the Scotch. He must sacrifice time, and temper, and fortune ; his private affairs, his health, and his constitution.[1]

Poor Snouch did not come very near to this ideal. He is said to have sacrificed his fortune ; and on one occasion he rose from his bed at four o'clock in the morning, with a broken rib, to vote for his party.[2] Yet it is rare to read of dinners at his house. The fashionable intelligence of the *Morning Chronicle* announces occasionally that he is about to depart for, or is just arrived from, Ireland : [3] otherwise it is silent as to his activities. Among the Irish members he may have been popular : among the English it is clear that he was not so. But his main defect lay not so much in his lack of the social graces, nor in his ineffectiveness as a speaker, as in his irresolution, torpor, and lack of the ability to inspire others, or even to unite them. A couple of instances will demonstrate his inability to control the party.

On 29 February 1808 Whitbread brought forward three motions condemning the rejection by Ministers of the recently proffered mediation of Russia and Austria. At a conference before the debate, it had been arranged that the first two of these motions should be supported, while the third should be opposed. But Ponsonby failed to convey any clear intimation of this decision to the bulk of the party, who were surprised and irritated when he spoke in opposition to Whitbread. The divisions tell their own tale : that on the first resolution was 70–210 ; that on the third, 58–217. Only about a dozen Whigs, therefore, were prepared to follow their nominal leader.[4]

[1] Grattan, *Life and Times*, v. 417.
[2] *Ibid.* 140-141 ; Plumer Ward, *Memoirs*, i. 450.
[3] *E.g. Morning Chronicle*, 2 Jan. 1812.
[4] *Parl. Deb.* x. 870 ; Grey, *Life and Opinions of Earl Grey*, pp. 181-183.

On 1 February 1810 there was a similar incident. The question was the vote of thanks to Wellington for Talavera. Before the debate it had been decided that there should be a division, and notes were sent to members of the Opposition to that effect. At the last moment these were cancelled, without explanation ; in reality because the Grenvilles were disinclined to vote against their old friends the Wellesleys. The younger members of the party, led by Lord Folkestone, Lord John Townshend, and Creevey, refused to obey, and pressed for a division. They did not get it, but they had the satisfaction of seeing Ponsonby give way and speak on their side.[1]

As Charles Wynn remarked, both Ponsonby and Tierney were " destitute of that courage and energy which enables men to take a resolution upon the sudden, and instead of *leading* are always anxious to be *led* by the wishes of the party ".[2] Yet Ponsonby was not regarded by any one section of the party as particularly belonging to them. He was neither Grenvillite, Foxite, nor Holland House man. It was this neutrality of hue that made them tolerate him for so long ; for though he was feeble, he did not actively offend. The Grenville alliance made reasonable political development impossible. Ponsonby was the symbol of this sterility. The Whigs tried to make of him the sort of leader that the Tories afterwards made of Liverpool ; they failed, not only because Ponsonby had not Liverpool's knack of managing men, but because he was the link between two parties, rather than between two sections of the same party. The trouble over the leadership is the essential, significant fact in the history of the Whigs in these years, and if the amount of space it occupies in their correspondence be a criterion, they realized this. The true policy for the true Whigs was to

[1] *Parl. Deb.* xv. 277-302 ; Creevey, pp. 124-127 ; *Court and Cabinets,* iv. 421.

[2] Nat. Lib. Wales MS. 2791, C. Wynn to H. Wynn, 7 July 1812.

have chosen Whitbread, and sloughed off the Grenvilles. Failing that, neither Petty, nor Tierney, nor Cavendish could have effected any lasting improvement. So Ponsonby became a source of contention and wrangling, quite as much as an acceptable compromise. They did not remove him, because they knew that they would never agree on his successor. Until the party should be united Ponsonby was safe : until Ponsonby was removed, real unity was impossible.

CHAPTER V

IN OR OUT ?

(a) *Possible Allies*

THE disability which the leadership of Ponsonby brought upon the Whig party might to a certain extent have been mitigated if they had been able to find in the House of Commons allies who would unite with them to turn out the Tories, or collaborate with them in forming a Government. The prospects of obtaining such assistance seemed in 1807 to be by no means unpromising. The two-party system, which had enjoyed a false dawn in the days of Fox and Pitt, had vanished with their deaths. The force of their personalities had been able to separate politicians into two main groups, and had thus simplified and solidified politics. After they were gone, the process of disintegration was rapid. A chaos of personal groups, with a great " floating strength " not permanently attached to any of them, took the place of " Foxites " and " Pittites ". The process of confusion had been in action since 1801 ; but it was not until the Talents fell in 1807 that it reached its climax.[1] Yet though Fox and Pitt were gone, the

---

[1] C. Wynn wrote to Southey, 22 Feb. 1812 : " Now usually since I have been in the House there have been but three parties, the Ins, the Outs, and the Independents ; and the existence of so many distinct bodies at present proceeds only from the want of distinguished men in the House of Commons to two of whom we all should naturally look up as leaders and in whose ranks all the minor squads would unite. The real grievance at present is the great increase of the mercantile men in the House of Commons above all former precedent, and their having become from the circumstances of the war and the new commercial system more entirely in the power of the government than ever—these

attachment to their names remained. Even after 1807 there were some who contended that " Pittite " and " Foxite " were perhaps more familiar party titles than " Tory " and " Whig ".[1] The Pittites were a miscellaneous, scattered, and divided body. In 1807, of those who had at one time or another been Pitt's adherents, Grenville, Windham, and Sidmouth were in opposition ; Wellesley, Melville, and Wilberforce were neutral ; while Pitt's young

therefore with a certain number of county gentlemen who in order to obtain the local patronage of excisemen, etc. support every minister constitute a floating transferable body so powerful as to enable the Crown to give a majority to any minister however small may be the number of his adherents . . ." (Nat. Lib. of Wales MS. 4814, f. 58).

[1] " . . . In truth, party names have latterly lost a good deal of their application, on all sides. Whiggism and Toryism, which in the moderate sense meant a leaning to the popular and a leaning to the regal part of the Constitution, and in their extreme sense, Republicanism and Despotism, have long been applicable to none but individual theories. It is a singular instance of what the personal weakness of our later princes has effected in spite of the increase of the Crown's influence, that the decided Tory has utterly vanished, and the name itself been discontinued by universal consent, even by those who chose to retain the appellation of Whigs. Whig itself has long ceased to mean any particular contrast of opinion, as opposed to that of the Pittites . . . " (*Reflector*, i. 464). " There are men who are in place, and others who, upon all occasions, whether right or wrong, censure the measures of Ministers, with the sole view of supplanting them. But in any other sense, the word party has now no more meaning than has the word *Tory* which no man has any longer the impudence to use " (*Political Register*, xv. 355). " . . . Opposition have pressed so long against the Ministry without effect, that being the softer substance . . . they have been moulded into their image and super-scription, spelt backwards, and they differ as concave and convex. . . ." (Hazlitt, *Works*, vii. 20.) But these are " No-party " views, and a little prejudiced therefore. There are many instances to the contrary, *e.g.* a correspondent in *Morning Chronicle*, 7 Nov. 1808, writes : " Tho' I am a Tory, I am an honest man ", and Sydney Smith, *Letters*, p. 48 (Dec. 1808) : " Do not listen to anything that is written to you about a change of administration. There may be a change from one Tory to another, but there is not the slightest chance for the Whigs." Yet we find one who was certainly not an extremist referring to " my friends the Outs " —not the *Whigs*. (*Paget Papers*, ii. 364).

men—Perceval, Castlereagh, Canning—were superficially
united in office under a renegade Whig. In 1809 there is a
shuffling of positions. Canning and Castlereagh go out,
Wellesley comes in. In 1812 there is a further shuffling.
And all the time there is a perfect maze of intrigue, since
both Ins and Outs try to attract the neutrals to their side.
Yet two main principles of politics pervade the period.
On the one hand is the effort towards a reintegration of
the Pitt party ; and on the other, the effort for an *épuration*
of the Fox party. In their best days, when the quarrel
with Pitt had really concerned *principle*, the Foxites had
always been rather a small minority ; and the desire to
purge the party of irrelevant accretions was a harking
back to the 'nineties. A powerful Whig party could only
be built up on the old basis—not indeed on the same
principles, for times were changed, but upon the same
rocklike foundation of intellectual agreement. Shoddy
coalitions would never serve. The Insurgents in the Whig
camp, who professed this view, aimed therefore at continuing
the Foxite tradition of opposition to a point at which Fox
himself would certainly have balked. It is plain, then, that
between the effort to reunite the Pittites and the effort to
purge the Foxites the Whig party would sustain a double
injury : the delicate equipoise of agreement upon which
the Grey-Grenville coalition rested would be threatened,
and the search for allies would be made more difficult by
internal and external obstacles.

The allies that the Whigs might look for were men whose
strength rested rather in their name and reputation, than
in the numbers of their adherents. The group system of
politics did not tend to large parties. A personal following
of a dozen was a considerable force. Canning or Sidmouth
might have so many, but Lowther had not, and he was a
great political power. Ministries were built upon personalities rather than upon numbers : the numbers came
afterwards of themselves. Thus the Whigs sought for

assistance, not because this or that group could of itself
turn a division,[1] but because the great mass of waverers
would tend to swing away from Government if all the men
of mettle seemed to support Opposition. The remnants of the
two great parties did indeed remain. The Foxites, even after
1807, reckoned over 150 members [2] (the Grenvilles hardly
added a dozen) ; [3] and the Pittites had perhaps as many.
But there were nearly 300 members who were permanently
unattached to any political party.[4] They served the

[1] Though this sometimes happened. Thus Castlereagh and four
friends beat Perceval, 26 Jan. 1810; and Canning's eleven turned
the scale against Government, 9 Jan. 1811. Creevey, p. 124 ; Bagot,
i. 368.

[2] *Morning Chronicle*, 29 June 1807 : " A Minority of 157 persons of
the first consideration in point of landed property, as well as of political
talents, embodied at the commencement of a Parliament is a tremendous
thing, unprecedented in the history of our country. . . ." Add. MS. 34457,
ff. 302-303 (Grenville's estimate—210–220). The question involves the
difficult point of the election of 1807, a critical examination of the returns
for which would probably show that the Whigs were right in contending
that it was nothing like the disaster that later historians have considered
it. They lost the floating strength ; but contests were few, and their own
losses small. The damage was done *before* the election.

[3] " The *condottieri* of the Grenvilles—for they have no political
principles, and therefore no political *party*, detached from their immense
influence over individuals " (Scott, *Letters*, ii. 267). The following may
be reckoned Grenvillites : T. Grenville, Newport, Temple, the Wynn
brothers, Lords Kensington and Althorpe, King, Plunket, Horner,
Fremantle, and (after 1810) Anstruther. About five peers.

[4] Ranby, *Inquiry into the Supposed Increase of the Influence of the
Crown* (1811), pp. 46-49. On the principle that the true strength of a
Ministry is seen in its last desperate division, he gives North 243,
Shelburne 190, Addington 240, and Perceval (taking the Walcheren vote)
about 240. He reckons auxiliaries of Ministers as equal to their highest
division *minus* their true strength ; in Perceval's case, 350 – 240 = 110.
He estimates absentees at about 150, even on important divisions ; puts
Whig extremists at about 50 or 60 (surely a high figure ?), adds 25
conscientious waverers, and arrives thus at 88 true Whigs in Opposition.
If we add the extremists to this, we get very near 150 Whigs. The figure
for Perceval's supporters seems too high : Zachary Macaulay speaks of
the two parties as " equally poised " (*Life*, p. 276).

Government of the day because they thought that the King's Government should be supported as far as possible, and also because in that course lay their best hope of favour and emolument.[1] Of these 300, nearly half were absentees at division time,[2] a signal of the fact that they were in reality independent members, and not placemen owing attendance at divisions in return for Ministerial favour. Pitt in his day had come near to making *them* Pittites too ; but after he died Perceval was not able to hold them.

The sources from which the Whigs in 1807 might hope to recruit allies included the "Saints", the Wellesleys, the Sidmouths (or Doctors), and the Carlton House party. The "Saints" were a small force, with a bare half-dozen of M.P.s, but they had a considerable following outside the House. They had been prominent Abolitionists, and had on that account supported the Talents; so that it was hoped that gratitude would keep them firm on the Whig side. The *Morning Chronicle* tried to put upon the Tories the stigma of endeavouring to re-establish the Trade, and ridiculed the suggestion that Wilberforce would support them.[3] Yet the "Saints" were drawn irresistibly to the Tory side. Had not the S.P.C.K. entered the field for Perceval at the election of 1807 ? [4] And was not Perceval a man after their own heart—a man so religious that on one occasion he deferred the meeting of Parliament for a day so that members should not be obliged to break the Sabbath by travelling up to Town ? The "Saints" were at least determined to give the new Government a fair trial.[5] Wilberforce, the Grants, Zachary Macaulay, and Bowdler were all more or less Tory

[1] Mr. G. Johnstone on 11 June 1812 clearly enunciated this principle : " he deemed it his duty to support any government. The representatives of large commercial bodies must and would support government " (*Parl. Deb.* xxiii. 414-415).   [2] Ranby, *op. cit., loc. cit.*

[3] *Morning Chronicle*, 22 May, 18 June 1807.

[4] *Ibid.* 8 May 1807.   [5] Wilberforce, *Life*, iii. 308.

by prejudice,[1] and even Bankes and H. Thornton were not really in sympathy with the Opposition on general principles. Still, the "Saints" remained independent. Bankes was zealous for Economical Reform; and Babington's name is to be found in minorities which are otherwise quite radical in appearance. Thornton, as member for Southwark, could not afford to neglect popular opinion. Upon some great questions, such as that of the Duke of York, the "Saints" were prominent on the Whig side; upon others—as that of Copenhagen—on the Tory side. Since they were guided only by moral criteria, it was natural that politically they should be incalculable. The conscience which had broken Pitt's heart by voting against Melville naturally demanded a vote against Perceval and Castlereagh on Madocks' motion in 1809. Yet, on the other hand, Stephen was a close friend of Perceval, and partially responsible for the more stringent Orders in Council. From the "Saints", therefore, the Whigs could upon the whole hope little; and their hopes grew less rather than greater, as gratitude for Abolition faded.

The Wellesleys were at one time a more probable speculation. They had always been on good terms with the Grenvilles, and they continued to be so even under the strain of disagreement over the Peninsular war. In 1807 Hawkesbury and Canning had made great efforts, when forming the Government, to induce Wellesley to come in as Foreign Secretary; but he had not allowed himself to be persuaded.[2] But though he kept aloof himself, he allowed his brother Henry to be one of the Secretaries to the Treasury, and his brother Arthur to be Chief Secretary in Ireland; and the *Morning Chronicle* considered the Government to be emphatically of a Wellesley complexion.[3]

---

[1] *Life and Letters of Zachary Macaulay*, p. 277.

[2] Windsor Arch., George III, Hawkesbury to King, 23 March 1807; Add. MS. 37295, f. 107, Wellesley to Canning, 22 March 1807; Add. MS. 37309, f. 170.   [3] *Morning Chronicle*, 29 Nov. 1808.

There were persistent rumours that Wellesley was to take
the place of the inefficient Portland as Prime Minister.[1]
Wellesley had in fact his grievance against the Talents. He
was deeply wounded by their failure to stop the attacks
made by the young extremists upon his achievements in
India, and he was disappointed at not having been offered
the Garter.[2] It is true that some of his followers—*e.g.*
Anstruther—usually voted with the Opposition;[3] and in
1808 there were certainly negotiations going forward whose
object was to attach him to the Grenvilles;[4] but upon the
whole, from 1807 to 1809, he drifted towards the Govern-

[1] *Tierney MSS.* Tierney to Gen. Maitland, Sept. 1807 ; *Morning
Chronicle*, 23 Sept. 1807. Portland is not known ever to have attended a
debate while he was Prime Minister. *Memoirs of Lord Liverpool*, p. 303.
The following squib appeared in the *Morning Chronicle*, 31 March 1807:

> Full well I know the people say
>   That " P——d's Duke has had his day,
>   He totters on a crutch ;
> His brain, by sickness long depressed
> Has lost the sense it once possessed
>   Though that's not losing much ".
>
> · · · ·
>
> But, spite of all the world can say,
> My talents yet feel no decay,
>   They're what they were before ;
> And now, at sixty-nine, I still
> Can fold my paper, point my quill,
>   And when did I do more ?
>
> Large parties, too, I still invite,
> Nor these as services too slight,
>   Ye Tory friends, contemn ;
> The Whigs, those Whigs who knew me well
> For thirty tedious years, can tell
>   I did no more for them.
>
> · · · ·

[2] Add. MS. 37295, ff. 101 *et seq*. Yet he had given advice to the
Talents when they asked for it. *Tierney MSS.* Wellesley to Tierney,
27 Feb. 1807.

[3] Add. MS. 37295, f. 173. He later turned Grenvillite : see note 3
on p. 333 above.   [4] *Court and Cabinets*, iv. 256.

ment. In July 1809 Canning tried to introduce him into
the Ministry ; and though the King would not hear of that,[1]
he was forced to allow him to go to Spain as our representative to the Junta. So that Wellesley's acceptance of
Perceval's offer of the Foreign Seals in the autumn of 1809
was not really unexpected.[2]

The party of the Prince of Wales was not a large one.
Moira and Erskine were its leading members in the Lords,
and Adam and Sheridan its most prominent M.P.s. The
Prince could, however, influence men indirectly through
such friends as the Duke of Northumberland, who boasted
of having eight votes at his disposal.[3] The majority of his
friends continued to be attached to the party of Fox ;
and Adam and Sheridan were for all normal purposes certain votes on the Whig side. Moira, Erskine, and McMahon
were Whiggish too. Unfortunately the Prince himself was
a doubtful quantity. In 1807 he drew up a well-known
letter to Lord Moira, declaring that he would for the
future take no part in politics ;[4] and at the same time he
made an attempt to effect a reconciliation with his father.[5]
He was offended that the Whigs had neglected to consult
him when they were in office ; and the result of his displeasure was seen in the sudden resolution of the Duke of
Northumberland to contest the county at the election of
1807, so that Howick was driven to a pocket-borough.[6]
Towards the end of 1807, indeed, Portland was anticipating
a formal offer from Carlton House ;[7] but the Prince remained

[1] Windsor Arch., George III, Portland to King, 21 July 1809.

[2] *Correspondence of . . . Lady Williams Wynn*, p. 147.

[3] Windsor Arch., George IV, Northumberland to McMahon, 3 Nov.
1807.

[4] Add. MS. 38242, ff. 55-57 (copy). The Prince's decision was not
popular with Adam and McMahon : Windsor Arch., George IV, Adam
to McMahon, 3 April 1807.

[5] Windsor Arch., George IV, Northumberland to McMahon, 3 Nov.
1807.

[6] Add. MS. 34457, f. 296.   [7] Add. MS. 38191, f. 247.

true to his policy of neutrality, and even refused his assistance to those desirous of using his influence to obtain sinecures.[1] When Erskine and Moira informed him with indignation of the bombardment of Copenhagen, they were disconcerted to find that he totally disagreed with their opinion of that measure.[2] The influence of Lady Hertford, however, was already suspected of pushing him towards the Tories,[3] and he advanced a further stage in that direction by his behaviour at the time of the Ministerial crisis of 1809. The Whigs took particular pains at that time to keep him informed of all their actions, and gave him copies of their letters to Perceval, hoping, no doubt, that this sign of confidence would breed confidence in return.[4] The Prince did in fact show himself "exceedingly gracious" to the Whig leaders ; but he was none the less playing a double game with them. To the King he renewed his protestations of neutrality and dutifulness, and assured him that he had no intention of interfering in politics.[5] The King was much pleased, and something of a reconciliation took place between them. The Tory Ministers were pleased too, since it had been the Prince who had urged Wellesley to accept office under Perceval.[6] Yet he still kept up a connexion with Canning and the Whigs ;[7] and it was no doubt in accordance with his wishes that the Duke of Northumberland declined to accede to Perceval's pressing request for his support.[8] It was plain, however,

[1] Windsor Arch., George IV, Prince of Wales to Lord Darnley, 20 May 1808.

[2] *Diaries of Lord Glenbervie*, ii. 12.   [3] *Dropmore Papers*, ix. 129.

[4] Windsor Arch., George IV, Grenville to Prince, 25 Sept. 1809 ; Moira to McMahon, 28 Sept. ; Add. MS. 37847, f. 233.

[5] Windsor Arch., George IV, Prince to King, 30 Sept. 1809 ; George III (Private), King to Prince, 30 Sept. 1809.

[6] Rose, ii. 404 ; Twiss, *Eldon*, ii. 103.

[7] Windsor Arch., George IV, Canning to Sheridan, 30 Sept. 1809.

[8] Windsor Arch., George IV, Perceval to Northumberland, 26 Oct. 1809, Northumberland to Perceval, 30 Oct. 1809.

to the discerning eye of Thomas Grenville, that the Prince
was not greatly to be relied upon.[1] As an ally he was uncertain ; and the Regency was to prove that he could be
faithless as a master.

There remained the Sidmouths. The Sidmouths had
been an important component of the Administration of all
the Talents, but towards the end of it they had been
anything but happy with their colleagues. The Catholic
question, as it had been handled by Grenville and Howick,
had driven them, willy-nilly, to part company with the
Whigs. But, on the other hand, they were not willing to
unite with the Tories.[2] Sidmouth and Canning were
polarizing agents in politics. The inclusion of the one or
the other of them in a Cabinet determined its general
character ; and the feud between them prevented their
ever acting together. One of the causes of Sidmouth's
coolness to the Talents had been Grenville's scheme for the
inclusion of Canning in the Government.[3] One of the reasons
for Sidmouth's aloofness to the Portland Ministry was that
Canning was a member of it. The Sidmouths were a
numerous group—probably over twenty [4]—and they kept
well together. They had in Vansittart and Bragge Bathurst
a pair of steady and reliable workers ; and, on the whole,
their personnel was rather above the mediocre. Yet there
was an aura of unpopularity which clung fatally about

[1] " I know there are difficulties all round, but I know of none greater
than a confidential intercourse where you cannot place confidence "
(*Dropmore Papers*, ix. 329).

[2] Pellew, *Sidmouth*, ii. 468 ; *Bathurst Papers*, p. 62.

[3] *Dropmore Papers*, ix. 67 ; *Court and Cabinets*, iv. 125-128 ; Holland,
Memoirs of the Whig Party, ii. 196.

[4] Grenville estimated them at rather under 50 : *Tierney MSS.*
Grenville to Tierney, 20 May 1807 ; but C. W. Wynn, writing to Southey
on 22 Feb. 1812, put them at "about a dozen ": Nat. Lib. Wales MS.
4814, f. 58. The most prominent members of the party were : Lords
Powis, Buckinghamshire, Ellenborough, and De Dunstanville ; Vansittart, Bragge Bathurst, Hatsell, Adams, Bond, and Hiley Addington.

them, and which explains how it came about that no
party was particularly anxious to avail itself of the advantages which an alliance with them might be thought to have
brought with it.[1] Appearances were against Sidmouth. It
seemed as though he had betrayed Pitt, and he was suspected of having betrayed the Talents. His narrow Anglican-
ism—more intolerant and less discreet even than Perceval's
or Eldon's—was liable to burst out awkwardly ; and his
bourgeois origin subjected him to much the same disabilities
as Tierney and Whitbread experienced. Sidmouth therefore
remained in Opposition, though he did not always vote
against the Government. Copenhagen shocked his conscience, but *per contra* he was for vigorous measures in the
Peninsula. The resignation of Canning in 1809 made the
prospects of a revival of the alliance with the Whigs still
more unpromising, for there now remained few points
upon which Perceval and Sidmouth were not in agreement.
Perceval's tactlessness, however, postponed their union, for
he did not ask Sidmouth himself to join his Government,
but invited him to allow his followers to do so.[2] So invidious
an offer could hardly be expected to meet with success,
and in fact it resulted in Sidmouth's reacting towards Grey
and Grenville. There were serious efforts made, in October
1809, to renew the former alliance with them, and much
correspondence was exchanged ; but the old difficulty of
the Catholic question proved insuperable. Sidmouth demanded some explanation or formula which should set the
King's mind at rest, but Grenville stood firm in his refusal
to give what he considered to be an unconstitutional
pledge ; and on this point the conversation terminated.[3] It

---

[1] Colchester, ii. 216 ; *Huskisson Papers*, p. 64.

[2] Windsor Arch., George III, Perceval to King, 9 Oct. 1809 ; *Memoir
of Herries*, i. 12 ; Holland, *Further Memoirs*, p. 40.

[3] Add. MS. 37888, f. 192, Sidmouth to Windham, 18 Oct. 1809 :
" Can it be consistent with public duty, when the country is in
danger of falling to pieces, that those who are confessedly best able to
keep it together, should withhold the certain and positive good they are

was the last chance the Whigs were to have of saving the
Sidmouths from falling to their rivals. In the division upon
the Address at the beginning of the session of 1810 they
supported the Government,[1] and they were suspected of a
desire to unite with Wellesley, who had for the moment
got rid of Canning ; [2] but their Parliamentary attitude was
still one of ostentatious neutrality. " Measures not men "
became avowedly their watchword.[3] In reality they moved
steadily towards the Tories : 1810 marks the end of the
career of the Addington who had won the applause of the
Whigs by the Peace of Amiens, and the beginning of the
new career of Lord Sidmouth, unkindly remembered by
posterity for the employment of Oliver. For the next two
years Perceval vainly endeavoured to secure his formal
adhesion to the Government. In October 1810 there were
rumours that he was to come in as President of the Council,
but they proved to be false.[4] He supported the Ministers
upon the Regency question, however, and this encouraged
Perceval to make another attempt at an understanding.
The personal harmony between them was complete, but
the negotiation itself broke down, probably because
Wellesley was by then too firmly attached to Canning to
please Sidmouth.[5] In the spring of 1812 the offers were
repeated, at first to Bragge and Vansittart alone, later also
to Sidmouth, and this time they were accepted.[6] The Prince
Regent, however, disliked Lord Sidmouth, and it was not

capable of rendering, for the sake of pursuing an object which some of
themselves consider as of doubtful benefit . . . ? " ; *Dropmore Papers*,
ix. 354; Pellew, iii. 10-12 ; Add. MS. 34457, f. 553; Plumer Ward,
i. 248.

[1] *Hastings Papers*, iii. 277.
[2] *Bath Archives*, i. 85-86, 94 ; *Morning Chronicle*, 22 March 1810.
[3] Pellew, iii. 17, 20-23.
[4] *Morning Chronicle*, 29 Oct. 1810.
[5] *Supplementary Despatches*, vi. 647 ; Add. MS. 35649, f. 120 ;
Memoirs of Court of Regency, i. 51.
[6] *Ibid.* 182 ; Pellew, iii. 73.

until May that he permitted him to enter the Ministry as President of the Council.[1]

Thus, of the groups which were independent in 1807 there was not one that did not tend by force of circumstance rather away from the Whigs than in their direction. For some one particular division they might be able to count upon a little external assistance from this group or that, but there was a diminishing chance of a permanent or solid union. The Cabinet crisis of 1809, however, made it appear more than possible that assistance might be available from the *disjecta membra* of the Tories, and in particular from the Canningites. Canning had been on the very brink of office when the Talents fell, for Grenville hoped to find in him the successor to Thomas Grenville as the family's representative in the Commons. He had not been happy in Portland's Government, and in the months preceding its collapse had made, among other manœuvres, some which seemed to indicate a desire for union with portions of the old Ministry of the Talents. Twice he took the Speaker into his confidence and adumbrated schemes for a union with Tierney, Vansittart, and Bathurst—all ex-members of Addington's Ministry, which Canning had so enjoyed attacking.[2] It seems extremely improbable that these projects were more than delicate hints to Portland and Perceval that he did not lack the power to do them a mischief. When the Ministry went to pieces, Canning was left in Opposition with only his dozen or so supporters.[3] Unlike Melville, he was not prepared

[1] *Court of Regency*, i. 219.

[2] Colchester, 30 April, 11 May 1809 ; *Political Register*, xiv. 4, 98.

[3] The Canningite party in the Parliament of 1807 comprised the following : Bagot, Lord Binning, Blachford, Sturges Bourne, Col. George Canning, Dent, Ellis, Lord Fitzharris, Greenough, Huskisson, Joliffe, Holt Leigh, Lord Granville Leveson Gower, Sir Henry Mildmay, R. P. Milnes, W. Taylor, Wilbraham—17 in all. By 1812 the number was reduced to 15 : Aspinall, *The Canningite Party*, pp. 222-223. Wellesley was said in Sept. 1812 to have had 11 followers : *Court of Regency*, i.

to retire from the battle, or indicate his displeasure with
Perceval merely by negative action ; nor was he, as Melville
was, an object of irreconcilable hatred to his former political
adversaries.[1] So it was natural to expect that he would
sooner or later drift into some sort of alliance with his
companions on the Opposition benches, particularly as
he was still on good terms with the Grenvilles. Lady
Holland, moreover, took him into favour about this time.[2]
The Foxite wing of the Whig party was seriously alarmed.
Brougham and Grey feared that an alliance with Canning
would mean subjection to Canning.[3] Whitbread was
violently hostile to him, and would certainly secede if he
were taken in. There were Sidmouth's feelings to be considered. Besides, although Canning's explanation of the
causes of the duel had first appeared in the *Morning
Chronicle*, he had been severely handled by that paper, a
few days afterwards,[4] and his reputation as a public man
had certainly suffered. Canning on his side was not anxious
to be a mere auxiliary.[5] The " flirtation " therefore (to
use Cobbett's phrase) for the moment came to an end.[6]

The year 1810 was notable in party politics for a most
persistent effort to reunite the old followers of Pitt. In this

405. Canning, however, referred to himself in Feb. 1812 as " an individual standing almost alone, unbacked by any party " (*Parl. Deb.*
xxi. 1035).

[1] For Melville's attitude to Government, *Milne Home Papers*, p. 140;
Furber, *Henry Dundas*, pp. 283-286 ; Matheson, *Melville*, pp. 395-397 ;
Add. MS. 37295, f. 272 ; Scott, *Letters*, ii. 249 ; Windsor Arch., George IV,
Moira to McMahon, 12 Oct. 1809. For suspicion of his motives, *Inde-
pendent Whig*, 15 Jan. 1809, 29 April 1807.

[2] Brougham, *Life and Times*, i. 462.

[3] Various views on probable results of Whig–Canning alliance in
Scott, *Letters*, ii. 267 ; *Dropmore Papers*, ix. 334, 321 ; Creevey, pp. 108
et seq.; Brougham, *op. cit.* i. 462-475.

[4] *Morning Chronicle*, 28 Nov., 1 Dec. 1809 ; *Political Register*,
xvi. 612.

[5] Bagot, i. 346, 336 ; Malmesbury, ii. 188.

[6] *Political Register*, xvi. 626.

Wellesley was the leading spirit, for he felt that the Government must be strengthened in order to ensure adequate support for his brother in the Peninsula.[1] The idea was by no means a new one. In 1807 Lord Lonsdale had insisted on inviting Grenville to join Portland's Government on this basis ;[2] and in the autumn of 1809 there had been similar speculations in the air.[3] Perhaps it was an idea which appealed most strongly to men who were not really at the centre of politics,[4] and it was probably taken up by Wellesley solely with the idea of regaining Canning. In his memorandum of 13 March 1810 he was careful to propose simultaneous approaches to Canning, Castlereagh, and Sidmouth.[5] There are also signs that Windham was sounded.[6] But the personal antagonism between Canning and Sidmouth, and Canning and Castlereagh, were too serious for easy reconciliation ; and it became increasingly obvious in the course of the year that Wellesley was indisposed for any but Canningite accessions to the Cabinet.[7] All through the summer and early autumn negotiations were going forward between Perceval and the three group-leaders ;[8] and it was even stated in September that an arrangement had been arrived at ;[9] but in the end animosity proved stronger than loyalty to the memory of Pitt. Wellesley was much irritated at the failure of his scheme, and was only prevented from resigning by the madness of the King.[10]

[1] Wellington, *Despatches*, v. 523-524 ; vi. 11-12, 165, etc.

[2] *Lonsdale Papers*, p. 231.

[3] Scott, *Letters*, ii. 268, 312 ; and see below, p. 347.

[4] *E.g.* Scott in particular.

[5] Add. MS. 37295, ff. 244-250, 282.   [6] Add. MS. 37849, f. 314.

[7] See Windsor Arch., George III, Perceval to King, 26 April 1810, for the best statement of the principle of the negotiation ; contrast Add. MS. 37295, f. 282 ; *Supplementary Despatches*, vii. 261.

[8] Add. MS. 37295, ff. 348, 364, 382, 403, 409, etc.

[9] *Morning Chronicle*, 28 Sept. 1810.

[10] *Supplementary Despatches*, vii. 267.

At the beginning of 1811, indeed, Canning seemed to turn a little against the Government. He was much courted by the Grenvilles, and was also in good odour at Carlton House.[1] There can be little doubt that he was not averse to office ; and had it not been for the irreconcilable hostility of Grey and Whitbread he might have obtained it. But he was not even then prepared to abandon his former principles, and when Romilly attacked Pitt's memory, Canning gave him sharp chastisement.[2] When the Whig hopes of office were disappointed in February 1811, the last serious chance of a union with Canning vanished.[3] Henceforward he united himself still more closely to Wellesley, and when that Minister resigned a year later, all differences of opinion between them were at an end. On some points, it is true— *e.g.* upon Catholic Emancipation—Canning came round to a Whig way of thinking ; but he never had adequate common ground with them upon which to base a junction, and in the tangled negotiations of May–June 1812, both he and Wellesley seemed clearly to prefer to treat with Liverpool.

It is plain, therefore, that the political currents were running against the Whigs. Integration was succeeding differentiation, to the advantage of their rivals. By 1812 Liverpool had to a great extent reconstituted the Pitt party.[4] The death of Perceval removed one of the com-

[1] See below, p. 362 ; Add. MS. 38738, f. 50, for offers to Huskisson.

[2] Wilberforce, *Life*, iii. 490 : " sad quarrelling work " ; *Morning Chronicle*, 4 Jan. 1811 ; see Add. MS. 38738, ff. 57-58, for Canning's alleged reluctance to join the Whigs.

[3] Both Canning and the Grenvilles now recoiled from the prospect of an alliance ; Add. MS. 38738, f. 92 ; *Court of Regency*, i. 103. There were, however, some shadowy negotiations in the weeks before Perceval's murder. *Court of Regency*, i. 291.

[4] The group principle was still felt after Castlereagh and Sidmouth had joined the Government. When on 12 May the Speaker asked " some Parliamentary persons of all descriptions " to confer with him about the vote to Perceval's family, the committee was Castlereagh and Ryder ; Ponsonby and Whitbread ; Bathurst and Vansittart ; Bankes and Wilberforce ; Sir Wm. Grant and Scott. Wilberforce, *Life*, iv. 24-25.

petitors for Pitt's inheritance ; Castlereagh, Sidmouth, and
the Dundases were all regained ; Windham was dead ; the
Saints were upon the whole reliable. Only Grenville,
Canning, and Wellesley remained outside. Wellesley was
broken in fortune and reputation, and soon retired into
pompous obscurity ; Canning significantly enough dis-
banded his following in 1813 ; [1] and within five years even
the Grenvilles were to move once more towards the
Tories.

It was natural that these groups should gravitate
towards the Tories rather than towards the Whigs.[2] Some
of them were after all mere slivers of the main Tory trunk.
They could all appreciate and approve the essentials of
Tory policy. They knew that the Tories, if they differed,
differed mostly in degree ; whereas the dissensions among
the Whigs touched fundamentals. They could see that the
Tories had after 1809 but one leader, and he a man of
capacity. And finally, the Regent's invention of *laissez-faire*
upon the Catholic question gave ease to unquiet con-
sciences. The Whigs on their side quarrelled with the
Carlton House party upon household influence ; with the
Sidmouths upon Catholic Emancipation ; with the Yorkes
and Dundases upon Reform ; with the Wellesleys upon the
war. Over Canning they quarrelled among themselves ;
while their reactions to the Burdettites ranged from abhorrence to encomium. Had they been less Puritanical in
their intellectual honesty, they might have patched up an
alliance with one or other of these groups ; but in truth
alliance with the Whigs offered too few attractions to make
any statesman seek it very earnestly.

[1] Much to the disgust of the Whigs, who felt it to be a blow at the
ideal of party-connexion. *Court of Regency*, ii. 37, 38.

[2] Tierney did not think so. He wrote to Grey [n.d.—Oct. 1809] :
" The means of forming a regular opposition undoubtedly exist and
very ample means too after allowing for a falling-off of a great
number amongst those who were accustomed to act with us " (*Tierney
MSS.*).

(b) *The Four Crises*

(1) *September 1809.*—At the beginning of September 1809 the Portland Ministry was nearing dissolution. Its head was mortally ill, and its members had no health in them. The great quarrel between Castlereagh and Canning, which had been banking up all the summer, was now to break out openly and to bring the Government to the ground. Canning's demand for Castlereagh's dismissal, which the Duke had deferred as long as he could, had now become insistent, for it was plain that Walcheren was a failure, and probably a disaster. Portland was at length induced to resign ; and Castlereagh, informed thereby of the intrigues which had been making against him, followed his example (10 September).[1] For the moment Canning stayed in. He had good hopes of obtaining the reversion to the premiership, and he had sufficient friends among the Ministers to make these hopes not unreasonable, apart from the assistance which he expected from Wellesley. In his way, however, stood Perceval, his rival for the inheritance of Pitt, and undoubtedly the leading spirit in the late Government. As Chancellor of the Exchequer and Leader of the House, Perceval's claims to the premiership were strong. Canning recognized this ; but he was not prepared to subordinate himself to a man of whose talents he had no very high opinion ; nor on the other hand would he accept Perceval's suggestion that they should compromise by serving together under a Prime Minister in the Lords.[2] All hope of patching

---

[1] Windsor Arch., George III, 9 Sept. 1809, has Castlereagh's resignation, which became public on the 10th. The King was aware that Camden had refused to tell Castlereagh of Canning's demands, and he refused to undertake the task himself. He told Portland that he must find some other substitute, as for his part, he would rather Castlereagh remained in office. Windsor Arch., George III, King to Portland, 7 Aug. 1809.

[2] Windsor Arch., George III, Canning to Portland, 12 Sept. 1809. Canning's insistence on the principle that the Premier must be in the

together the old Government was therefore at an end. In these circumstances Perceval and the Ministers who adhered to him held a Cabinet on 18 September, at which they reviewed the situation. In the minute sent to George III, they avowed their conviction that their weakness in the House of Commons was such that without fresh blood they could not hope to hold their own. They had already in vain urged office on the Speaker ; they considered acceptance by Lord Hardwicke and his friends unlikely ; and they thought the Dundases inadequate, even if favourably disposed. Lord Wellesley was far away in Spain. Lord Sidmouth was certainly a possibility ; but the numbers of his party were not large enough to outweigh the fact that he was himself unpopular with many Tories on account of his attitude to Pitt in 1803. There remained two possibilities. Either the King could venture to test Canning's conviction that he could form a Government of his own—and as to this Perceval was frankly sceptical ; or he could commission Perceval to approach Grey and Grenville. Perceval made it clear that it would be of no use to make overtures to Grey or Grenville separately : such a manœuvre would at once wreck the negotiation ; and, moreover, they could neither of them, if separated, attract the weight of numbers that the Government so urgently required. It was thus proposed to make " a direct communication to Lord Grey and Lord Grenville, with a view to their uniting . . . in forming an extended and combined administration ".[1] On the 19th Perceval went down to Windsor and talked the matter over with the King. He found him very reluctant to agree to any approach to the Whigs. George was afraid that they would give trouble to him on the Catholic question, and he particularly disliked Lord Grenville. However, he promised to let

House of Commons was not calculated to conciliate his ally Wellesley. See Add. MS. 37295, f. 113.

[1] Windsor Arch., George III, Cabinet minute, 18 Sept. 1809.

Perceval have his decision in the course of a few days.[1]
Before it arrived, Castlereagh and Canning had fought their
duel, and it now became more than ever unlikely that
Canning would succeed in forming a Government. So on
22 September the King returned his answer ; and, with
many reservations upon the Catholic question, gave permission to Perceval to communicate with the two Lords.
This Perceval did immediately, sending to Howick and
Boconnoc identical notes which ran as follows :

> The Duke of Portland having signified to His Majesty his inten-
> tion of retiring from His Majesty's service, in consequence of the
> state of his Grace's health, His Majesty has authorised Lord Liver-
> pool, in conjunction with myself, to communicate with your Lordship
> and Lord Grenville for the purpose of forming an extended and
> combined administration. I hope therefore that your Lordship, in
> consequence of this communication, will come to town in order that
> as little time as possible may be lost in forwarding this important
> object, and that you will have the goodness to inform me of your
> arrival.[2]

The inconveniences of a duumvirate whose heads were at
some 400 miles distance from each other were now clearly
seen. Grenville lost no time in coming to London ; but
Grey declined to budge from Howick, and returned a
refusal (as he would have phrased it) *in limine.*

> Had His Majesty been pleased to signify that he had any com-
> mands for me personally, I should not have lost a moment in showing
> my duty and obedience by a prompt attendance on his Royal pleasure.
> But, when it is proposed to me to communicate with His Majesty's
> present Ministers, for the purpose of forming a combined administra-
> tion with them, I feel that I should be wanting both in duty to His
> Majesty and in fairness to them, if I did not frankly and at once
> declare that such an union is, with respect to me, under the present
> circumstances impossible. This being the answer I find myself under
> the necessity of giving, my appearance in London would be of no
> advantage, and might possibly, at a moment like the present, be
> attended with inconvenience.[3]

---

[1] Walpole, *Life of Perceval*, ii. 23.   [2] *Ibid.* 31.   [3] *Ibid.* 31-32.

Grenville arrived in town to find that his partner had taken a course differing from his own : he therefore lost no time in bringing himself into line ; and on 29 September he wrote to Perceval declining his offer :

Having last night arrived here, in humble obedience to His Majesty's commands, I think it now my duty to lose no time in expressing to you the necessity, under which I feel myself, of declining the communication proposed in your letter ; being satisfied that it could not, under the circumstances there mentioned, be productive of any public advantage.

I trust I need not say that this opinion is neither founded in any sentiment of personal hostility, nor in a desire of unnecessarily prolonging political difficulties.

To compose, not to inflame, the divisions of the Empire, has always been my anxious wish, and is now more than ever the duty of every loyal subject.—But my accession to the existing Administration could, I am confident, in no respect contribute to this object, nor could it I think be considered in any other light than as a dereliction of public principle.

This answer which I must have given to any such proposal, if made while the Government was yet entire, cannot be varied by the retreat of some of its members. My objections are not personal ; they apply to the principle of the Government itself, and to the circumstances which attended its appointment.[1]

The negotiation was over ; and Perceval was left to form his Cabinet as best he might from the ruins of the Tory party.

It is clear that Grenville was driven into a peremptory rejection of the proposal by the precipitate action of Grey. It is also clear that he would have been prepared to negotiate, or otherwise he would not have come up to London. Now Grey had already for some weeks made up his mind that he did not like the idea of taking office. Letters written in June and July show that even then, when the rumours of the approaching dissolution of the Ministry were but rumours, Grey had set his face against

[1] Walpole, *Perceval*, ii. 32 ; Add. MS. 38243, ff. 210-211.

coming in, and that Tierney had agreed with him.[1] On
18 September Grey had written to Tierney : " I can assure
you most unaffectedly that whatever removes me from the
possibility of engaging in the government under circumstances which appal me even as a spectator will be most
agreeable to me".[2] And in a revealing letter to Windham of
26 September 1809, he debates, as though soliloquizing, as
to whether or no he has done right in returning such an
answer to Perceval. But he also makes it very plain that
even if the King had given him *carte blanche* as to the
Catholics he would have hesitated, and probably refused,
in the face of the dangers threatening the country, and the
difficulties of forming a Government.[3] From some conversation which Grey had had with J. Willoughby Gordon,
Perceval certainly concluded that he was not averse to
the idea of office ;[4] but the event showed that either
Perceval or Gordon was mistaken. There seems to be no
doubt that Grey had resolved to decline any offer that
might be made to him, from sheer laziness and pusillanimity.

With Grenville the case was rather different. He by
no means gave up the negotiation as hopeless, until con-
strained by the intelligence of Grey's letter. His second
letter to Perceval, following upon the promise of his first,
needed, therefore, some explanation ; and the explanation
he gave turned upon the Catholic question. Grey and
Tierney both lamented that this matter had been dragged
forward ; and it is obvious that to them, at any rate, the
negotiations did not seem to have been broken off upon

[1] *Tierney MSS.* Grey to Tierney, 23 June, 27 July ; Tierney to Grey,
n.d. ; Tierney to Grey [21-25 Sept.]. Holland is reported by Tierney as
being in favour of " making the King eat humble Pye ".

[2] *Tierney MSS.* Grey to Tierney, 18 Sept. Compare Windham's remark, " I have not virtue enough to wish the ministers out, at the risk
of being one of those, who may be called upon to succeed them "
(*Windham Papers*, ii. 353).

[3] Add. MS. 37847, ff. 265-267.

[4] Walpole, *Perceval*, ii. 25.

the question of Emancipation.¹ It is not so easy, however, to arrive at Grenville's position. Did he bring in the Catholic question as an excuse—the only one that lay ready to hand—for the discrepancy between his two letters ? Or was it the real reason for his refusal ? The Grenvilles had certainly looked at the prospect of an offer with apprehension, for, unlike Grey, they felt that they owed it to the country at least to entertain it ; and they feared that the King might contrive to put forward conditions which they could neither accept with honour nor reject without odium.² They did not feel themselves at liberty to refuse *in limine*, though they had not the least confidence that the proposal would be such as they could accede to with safety. Lord Hardwicke wrote to Grenville expressing his hope that he would accept office if possible ; and the *Morning Chronicle* was of the same way of thinking.³ Thomas Grenville and Auckland, too, had faint hopes that they might effect some good by joining Perceval ; but Lord Buckingham foresaw that it would not do.

The great management [he wrote] will be to put yourself on good grounds, and not to let the King . . . break off on the *Catholic* question: which I know he is prepared to do *in the present moment*.⁴

Grenville himself was suspicious of the King's *bona fides* :

Should it [an offer] really come it would not be very uncharitable to believe that it has no other object than to involve Grey and myself in a discussion which may be broken off on the alledged extravagance of our demands, and an appeal then made to the country to support the Protestant religion.⁵

---

¹ *Tierney MSS.* Grey to Tierney, 2 Oct. ; Tierney to Grey, 6 Oct. Grey, unlike Grenville, did feel " personal objections " to the late Ministers, " who lacked even good faith and common decency to one another ".

² *Dropmore Papers*, ix. 319-320.

³ Add. MS. 35648, f. 156 ; *Morning Chronicle*, 25 Sept. 1809.

⁴ *Dropmore Papers*, ix. 325.

⁵ *Tierney MSS.* Grenville to Tierney, 22 Sept. 1809.

The resentment at the defeat of 1807 was still strong.
Grenville certainly inclined to be very stiff upon the
Catholic question in any negotiation into which he might
enter. Indeed, the political situation made it by no means
impossible that he might win a partial victory over the
King ; since it seemed certain that Perceval could not long
survive, unaided. Grenville, at this time, was not eager for
hasty, partial legislation in favour of the Catholics, particularly as he could not obtain from them the " securities "
he desired : if he could get the King to accept him without
the demand for a pledge, honour would be satisfied, and
wounded pride assuaged. " It seems to be fully understood
on the part of Lord Grenville", wrote Marsden to Hardwicke,
" that he did not mean to press the Catholic question on
the King."[1] Yet he had determined, as he explained to
Grey, never to take office again without a distinct explanation upon that point.[2] Moreover, as he pointed out when
justifying the allusion to the question in his reply to
Perceval, it would have been just there that the negotiations, if they had gone on, would probably have broken
down ; and the allusion, in support of a refusal already
determined upon, was at least a sop to the Catholics.[3]

Grenville's refusal, however, couched in this form, was
extraordinarily irritating to the King. George now hated
Grenville almost more than he had hated Fox ; for Grenville added to his other delinquencies the damning sin of
desertion. It was for this reason that the King had tried
to persuade Perceval to approach Grey separately. His
comment on Grenville's refusal was typical of his attitude.

Lord Grenville speaks of his junction with the present Government as of a dereliction of principle. He states that his objections
apply to the principle of the Government itself, and to the circum-

[1] Add. MS. 35648, f. 216, 10 Nov. 1809.
[2] *Dropmore Papers*, ix. 335.
[3] *Ibid.* 335 ; Add. MS. 35648, ff. 167-169 : Grenville was piqued at
being approached through Perceval, and not directly.

stances which attended its formation. It is impossible to misconceive such a declaration after what passed upon that occasion ; it is avowing the intention of bringing forward the Catholic question whenever he shall have the means of so doing, and the question is therefore whether the Sovereign shall be guilty of a dereliction of principles to which he has steadily adhered during fifty years, to which he is bound by his Coronation Oath, or whether Lord Grenville shall abandon a principle which he has constituted at option, and assumed within these last few years.[1]

Now what, in point of fact, was Perceval going to propose when Lord Grey so rudely cut him short ? Would Grenville's stickling on the Catholic question in any case have ensured the failure of the negotiation ? " The proposal ", said Romilly charitably, " was probably not intended as an insult to Lord Grenville and Lord Grey." [2] Indeed it was not. Nothing can be more certain than that Perceval and his colleagues were thoroughly in earnest in their desire to secure an alliance with the Whig leaders. Arbuthnot, one of the Tory Secretaries to the Treasury, on 12 and 14 September foreshadowed an offer to them ; on the 16th Sydenham reported to Lord Wellesley their intention ; on the 18th it was strongly urged in a Cabinet minute ; on the 19th Perceval pressed it in private conversation with the King.[3] The very fact that Perceval insisted on an offer to them jointly demonstrates his sincerity. And Lord Lonsdale had demanded, as the price of his support, that no attempt should be made to continue as a purely Tory Government, until a serious effort to secure Grey and Grenville had failed.[4] It was certainly in contemplation to give them a generous share in the more important offices of Government. Many Tory Ministers were prepared, and

[1] Windsor Arch., George III, King to Perceval, 30 Sept. 1809.

[2] Romilly, *Memoirs*, ii. 295.

[3] Add. MS. 38737, ff. 331, 334 ; 37295, f. 114.

[4] Twiss, *Eldon*, ii. 101 ; Add. MS. 38737, ff. 358-359 ; Scott, *Letters*, ii. 212. *Tierney MSS.* Grey to Tierney, 2 Oct., where Lonsdale seems, perhaps, to be playing Perceval false.

several offered, to resign their offices for the sake of facili-
tating an arrangement. It was calculated that, besides the
two Secretaryships, no less than seven posts would be
vacant, including the Exchequer, the India Board, the
Privy Seal, and the Secretaryship at War.[1] It seemed to
some Tories that it would be less an offer of alliance, than
a surrender at discretion.[2] " If they come in ", wrote Henry
Wellesley, " I fear there is an end of Pitt's friends, for the
division of offices and of power will be the *partage du lion*." [3]

All this, however, would be of no avail, if a demand for
a pledge on the model of 1807 were to be put forward by
the King. There is no doubt that George III would have
much preferred to take this course. In his view there must
be an express renunciation of Emancipatory legislation.
Perceval saw that no appeal to Grey and Grenville on that
basis could possibly succeed ; and in the interview of 19th
he had persuaded the King to be content with an implied
renunciation which would not conflict with an honourable
adhesion to former opinions.[4] But the King, when author-
izing his Ministers to open the negotiations, made it clear
that he expected the Whigs to recognize the implication.
Perceval certainly realized that Grey and Grenville were
not at this time at all likely to give trouble about Catholic
Emancipation ; and there is no doubt that he was trying
to " gloze over " the subject.[5] Indeed, in his reply to
Grenville's letter of refusal, he said expressly that " no
idea existed in our minds of the necessity of any dereliction
of public principle on either side ".[6] It was to be a tacit
compromise of the sort with which Grey and Grenville were
only too familiar. At the worst, the Government could have

[1] Rose, *Diaries*, ii. 381-397.
[2] Malmesbury, *Letters*, ii. 133-134.
[3] *Wellesley Papers*, i. 268. Only Westmorland remarked " what an
escape the country has had ! " Holland, *Further Memoirs*, p. 38.
[4] Walpole, *Perceval*, ii. 24-25.
[5] Plumer Ward, i. 255-256.
[6] Windsor Arch., George III, Perceval to Grenville, 29 Sept. 1809.

jogged on upon the *laissez-faire* principle afterwards hit upon by the Regent ; and Harrowby, at least, seems to have hoped for this.

If it [the offer] is met in the spirit in which it is made, I trust it will be successful. Whatever we may be *driven to do* if they shut their ears to the proposal of an extended and combined administration we shall not, in my opinion, have been justified in our own eyes, or in those of the country, if any party feelings prevented us from endeavouring *bona fide* to form such a government as may both protect the King [from a pure Whig administration], and be fit for these times. They are, I believe, as little able to form a separate Government as ourselves, unless they mean to reunite themselves with those at whose proceedings they were evidently so alarmed last year [*i.e.* the Burdettites]. If they come in alone by force, they will have the Catholic question as a millstone round their necks. The very fact of an union with us who are known to entertain a decidedly opposite opinion upon that question (some of us for ever, and all during the King's life) would enable them to get rid of it for the present, as, without any pledge, which after all that has passed, could be neither asked nor given, that question could never be made a Government question without the immediate dissolution of the Administration.[1]

This was Perceval's argument also. If the Whigs showed signs of breaking out into Emancipation, the Tory Ministers would wreck the Government.[2] Perceval, indeed, hoped to build a golden bridge for Grenville, along which he might retire honourably from his quarrel with the King. Writing to Wellesley after the formation of his Government, he refers to " that question concerning the Roman Catholics from which we had hoped to furnish his Lordship his best retreat by giving him the opportunity of forming an united administration with ourselves ".[3] The idea of Grenville's returning to the Tory fold was not so fantastic as might appear. The Archbishop of York, J. Willoughby Gordon, and Sir Walter Scott all toyed with the notion ;

[1] *Private Papers of William Wilberforce*, p. 141.
[2] Walpole, *Perceval*, ii. 24-25.   [3] Add. MS. 37295, f. 135.

and all considered it within the bounds of possibility that
Grenville might rally the old Pittites once more under his
standard. The Oxford election in the autumn, too, encouraged such views.[1]

Thus the fiasco of 1809 was the result of the interaction
of three causes. First, the incompetence of the Whigs with
regard to the war. Grey was afraid to take office because
the difficulties of the situation were more than he cared to
face, and because he had no intelligible policy—or at all
events, could not agree upon one with his partner. Secondly,
the survival of the rancours of 1807. The Catholic question,
even though it never got to the stage of discussion, certainly
poisoned the political atmosphere, and destroyed trust in
the good faith of the King and his Ministers. Thirdly, the
hatred of coalitions, which led the bulk of the party to
applaud Grey's curt refusal and to reprobate Grenville's
reply.[2] There was resentment, too, at the idea of being
tacked on to an already existing Government. The crisis
proved that Catholic Emancipation was a question upon
which the Whigs still felt that they had not the body of
the nation behind them. It proved, too, that the facts of
geography might impose upon the precarious alliance of
Grey and Grenville a strain which was too severe to be
often repeated. No doubt the fact that the crisis occurred
in the vacation took them at a disadvantage ; but the
lack of coördination in 1809 was a valid argument for
Grey's more regular attendance in London, or at least
within easy reach of Stowe and Dropmore. The absence
of the Whig leaders at Howick and Boconnoc meant a

[1] *Harcourt Papers*, xii. 152 ; *Tierney MSS.* Gordon to Tierney,
25 Oct. ; Scott, *Letters*, ii. 268.

[2] *Tierney MSS.* Whitbread to Tierney, 29 Sept. ; Grey, *Life and
Opinions*, p. 231 ; *Morning Chronicle*, 3 Nov. ; Brougham, *Life and
Times*, i. 469 ; Horner, i. 469 : " For God's sake, let us have no more
coalitions ; and then, either victory upon the Catholic question, or a
resolute prosecution of it, may help us again up hill ". Cf. Wilberforce,
Life, iii. 428.

week's delay in what was really a national emergency ; and a week's delay meant still heavier losses on Walcheren.

The Whig leaders do not emerge with much credit from this crisis. The Government, without them, could hardly be expected to survive. It was improbable, in view of the dislike with which many of them regarded Canning, that the Whigs would be able to make a Government of their own.[1] Yet they allowed Perceval's Government to go on, at a time when Parliamentary crises were above all things to be avoided—a time when the most trenchant Administrative action was needed to save the wrecks of Walcheren, and support the Wellesleys in the Peninsula. With their views on the foreign policy of the country, the Whigs should have seized the opportunity to get in, and correct or mitigate the errors of the previous Ministry. But their views were too negative, and above all, too divided, for such a policy to be possible. After the negotiations were over, Grey wrote, as if to justify himself, to Auckland ; and after expatiating on the risk of taking office, he continued :

a sense of duty might compel me to incur that risk, if a fair hope were presented to me of rendering my services useful to the country. Such a hope did not offer itself in the proposed junction. . . .[2]

If this had been written after a long and fruitless negotiation, there would have been no difficulty in accepting it as an honest, if mistaken, opinion. But it was written after the instantaneous rejection of an offer the real purport of which Grey never took the trouble to learn. The Whigs, in fact, were well content to leave Perceval to flounder on in office—to allow him to carry on the government of the

[1] Sydney Smith, *Letters*, p. 63 : " I have no doubt that the country would rather submit to Masséna than to Whitbread. If the King were to give the opposition *carte blanche* tomorrow, I cannot see that they could form an administration in the House of Commons " (22 Nov. 1809). Cf. Harrowby's opinion on p. 356 above.

[2] *Auckland Correspondence*, iv. 326.

country at a very critical moment of the war, with the assistance of such incompetents as Ryder, Westmorland, and Mulgrave—and to supplement purely destructive criticism by a stiff intractability in negotiation.

So, belike [wrote Cobbett], the Whigs, the *haughty* Whigs, who licked the shoes of the Grenvilles, will leave us to perish in the hands of the Walcherers, as a just punishment for our blindness in not being able to discover their superior patriotism.[1]

(2) *January–February 1811.*—The illness of the King in the autumn of 1810 made the situation very uncertain for Perceval's Government. Everything depended upon the expectation of his recovery. The King was old, but he was exceptionally strong and healthy, and it was not for some weeks anticipated that the disease would prove incurable. But as Christmas approached it became clear that a Regency was necessary ; and with the prospect of a Regency Whig hopes grew buoyant. There was, perhaps, hardly a man on either side who doubted that if the Prince were installed as permanent Regent, he would change his Ministers to suit his predilections. When Perceval, too literally following in the footsteps of his master Pitt, introduced a Regency Bill which would require a " phantom " to give assent to it, and which in the expectation of the King's early recovery limited the exercise of the royal prerogatives, the Whigs were true to the Foxite faith, and opposed it systematically in both Houses. Grenville, indeed, stood by his attitude of 1788, but he managed to do so without ostentation or offence, and his relations with Grey remained unimpaired.[2] The Whigs were disappointed that their fight against the restrictions won so little recognition

[1] *Political Register*, xvi. 755.
[2] Grey was prepared to split with Grenville, if necessary, on the Regency question. Grey, *Life and Opinions*, p. 262. For Whig views on the Bill, and Grenville's part in it, see *Morning Chronicle*, 2, 7, 11, 18, and 21 Jan. 1811.

or support from the Prince ;[1] but later they had the
gratification of knowing that he had personally urged his
royal brothers to sign the Protest against the Bill.[2] Still,
Thomas Grenville was inclined to be irritable at the reserve
which the Prince continued to maintain towards them. But
the Whigs recognized that the Prince must at all costs
avoid the imputation of haste ; and at the end of 1810 a
few royally tactful words to Lord Grenville had made
all smooth again.[3] It was, therefore, with the highest hopes
that the Whigs entered upon the new year ; while for the
Tories it was a period correspondingly depressing. "We are,
I think, all", said Palmerston, "on the *kick and the go*. . . ."[4]
Liverpool, reporting on the situation to Wellington in
Spain, told him plainly that the Government did not
possess the Prince's confidence.[5] Many of the Irish supporters of the Government were deserting—no doubt
because they hoped for some concession to the Catholics
of that country. The Prince, as his Ministers realized, was
in constant consultation with the Opposition, and they had
now no hope of the King's recovering in time to come to
their rescue.[6] The Whigs were already celebrating their
triumph, by anticipation ;[7] the old Duke of Gloucester was

---

[1] Windsor Arch., George IV, Robert Adair to Prince, 13 Dec. 1810,
reporting the Duke of Bedford.

[2] Windsor Arch., George IV, 28 Dec. 1810.

[3] *Dropmore Papers*, x. 62, 84.

[4] Bulwer, *Palmerston*, i. 121.   [5] Grattan, v. 427.

[6] Perceval and Eldon were said to have seen the King and to have
been detected turning their backs upon him ; upon which this squib
appeared :

> " The people have heard, with delight and surprize,
>   That his Ministers' conduct has op'd the K——'s eyes ;
> With just indignation his royal breast burned,
>   When he thought he saw Per——l's back on him turned ;
> Exclaiming, ' Thank G-d ! I've recovered my sight,
>   For I now see you, Sir, in your own proper light ! ' "

Ashton, *Regency*, p. 22.

[7] Scott, *Letters*, ii. 432.

writing to Grenville to ask for the post of Master General
of the Ordnance;[1] and in Scotland Fox's birthday was
observed with an exuberance inspired by the prospect of
victory.[2] " We will let you have the felicity of procuring
the supplies ", remarked Lord Porchester to the Tory
Plumer Ward, " and, after the Budget and the Mutiny
Acts, will change places."[3] The Whig leaders were busily
constructing Cabinets; and Lauderdale was said by Sydney
Smith not to have taken off his clothes for six weeks.[4]
Grey, indeed, was as nonchalant as ever, and annoyed his
colleagues by proposing to shoot pheasants instead of
attending party conferences ;[5] but in spite of this obstacle
some progress was made towards determining on a Ministry.
In the first suggestions for the Cabinet, there was a large
preponderance of Foxites ; and the Grenville party was
represented only by Lord Grenville (Prime Minister), and
by Auckland, with possible support from Lord Hardwicke.
To such a distribution, the Grenville family felt they could
not agree, particularly in view of the projected inclusion of
Whitbread at the Admiralty. Canning, or Perceval, "or even
. . . that contemptible animal Lord Sidmouth " would be
preferable.[6] They feared that in any such arrangement Grey
might tend to support Whitbread's point of view, rather
than theirs. But later suggestions did not remove their
objections. In every project for an Administration that has
been preserved Whitbread appears in the Cabinet. On this
point the Grenvilles were beaten, and Creevey and his
friends were elated.[7] The struggle had involved more than
the inclusion or rejection of Whitbread. It was obvious
that if Whitbread were not given Cabinet office, the

[1] *Hastings Papers*, iii. 287.   [2] Bain, *Mill*, p. 116.
[3] Plumer Ward, *Memoirs*, i. 304.
[4] Sydney Smith, *Letters*, p. 85.
[5] *Dropmore Papers*, x. 113.   [6] *Ibid.* 98-99.
[7] Creevey, p. 137 ; for other Cabinet projects, Grattan, v. 429 n.
Bath Archives, i. 207 ; Wilberforce, *Life*, iii. 492.

disappointment, coming on top of his neglect in 1806, would drive him into opposition. The Grenvilles had proposed to discount this possibility by coöpting Canning, and they had made serious overtures to Huskisson through the medium of Willoughby Gordon.[1] The quarrel over the composition of the Government was, in fact, one between the partisans of Canning and the partisans of Whitbread, and it was only Grenville's desire to subordinate all other considerations to the formation of a strong Government that induced him to acquiesce in Whitbread's inclusion.[2] The victory of Whitbread's supporters was important, because it possibly compromised them with the Prince, who had supported Canning and was disappointed when Grey refused to accept him.[3] And, on the other hand, Grenville had offended the Prince by his steady opposition to the immediate reappointment of the Duke of York as Commander-in-Chief—a measure which was favoured by Lauderdale and Grey. Grenville, moreover, was a little unpopular with his party at this moment, from his stubbornness in refusing, as Auditor of the Exchequer, to issue moneys which had already been voted by Parliament, contending that the Lords Commissioners, in issuing the warrant, had acted *ultra vires*. The Whigs were irritated, too, by his declared intention of retaining the Auditorship upon his accession to office as First Lord of the Treasury, in accordance with his own precedent of 1806. Such a combination of offices would put him technically, if not practically, in the position of auditing his own accounts, and it had been already unfavourably commented upon by the zealots for Economical Reform.[4] To persist in this intention would

---

[1] Add. MS. 38738, f. 50, Gordon to Huskisson, 19 Jan. ; *Dropmore Papers*, x. 104 ; Plumer Ward, ii. 330 ; Holland, *Further Memoirs*, p. 87 ; Lady Holland, *Journal*, p. 285.   [2] *Dropmore Papers*, x. 110.

[3] Add. MS. 38738, f. 62 ; Holland, *Further Memoirs*, pp. 80-82. As late as 30 Jan. the Prince supported Canning.

[4] Grenville was prepared to give up the Auditorship if he were made

be to expose the Whigs to the taunts of the Tories. Perhaps as a measure for soothing these irritations the suggestion was put forward that the premiership should be offered either to Lord Holland or to Lord Fitzwilliam.[1]

A much more serious matter than any of these was the question of the reply which the Regent was to make to the Address of Parliament. The Prince asked Grey and Grenville to draw up this document for him, but characteristically suggested that they should consult upon it with his friend Lord Moira. This they refused to do, and the paper which they eventually produced was entirely their own work. It was a cautiously phrased document which, while showing that the limitations had not the Prince's approval, yet maintained a tone conciliatory to Parliament.[2] But the Whigs had reckoned without the wounded susceptibilities of Sheridan, who was willing enough that his old friend Grey should form a Ministry, but who heartily disliked Grenville, who, he felt, had slighted him.[3] Sheridan thought that he detected in the reply an attempt to cover the difference known to exist between the two Lords on the principle of the Regency Bill ; and when the draft arrived at Carlton House, he criticized it so artfully that the Prince was persuaded into believing that he had himself made the objections which Sheridan had brought forward. In the end,

---

Home Secretary, but not if he were to be Premier, because of the expense to which that office would put him. Hence he suggested another Premier. *Dropmore Papers*, x. 101, 110 ; Plumer Ward, i. 314-318 ; *Morning Chronicle*, 5 Jan. 1811, defending Grenville ; Leigh Hunt, *Reformist's Answer*, pp. 31-32.

[1] Colchester, *Diary*, ii. 307 ; Plumer Ward, i. 342.

[2] *Dropmore Papers*, x. 97.

[3] Sichel, *Sheridan*, ii. 343 ; Holland wrote (*Further Memoirs*, p. 72) : " The good-will of a man alike brilliant in society and in Parliament, and very formidable at Court, might have been . . . purchased at a very cheap rate, without any sacrifice of principle or any surrender of dignity. . . . But Lord Grenville never saw him, and Lord Grey was hardly civil to him when he did. . . ."

the Whig draft was dropped and a new version was produced
by Sheridan which expressed more decidedly the Prince's
resentment at the restrictions to which he had been subjected.[1] The indignation of Grey and Grenville was intelligible, but their expression of it was certainly indiscreet.
On 10 January they forwarded a long remonstrance to the
Prince, protesting in the strongest terms against the secret
influence which had been employed against them, and
plainly intimating that if they came into office they would
expect to be secured against a repetition of such incidents.[2]
Sheridan, of course, averred that he had acted from no other
motive than a desire to secure the best possible speech for
the Regent ; and in a letter to Lord Holland he referred to
Grey and Grenville as " those distinguished characters,
whom His Royal Highness appears to destine to those
responsible situations which must in all public matters
entitle them to His exclusive confidence ".[3] Sheridan's letter
is endorsed " read and approved by the Prince ", so that it
is possible that the affair did little to prejudice the Whigs'
chances. It is more probable, though, that the Prince was
dissimulating his annoyance. On the day that Sheridan
wrote to Holland, the Duke of Northumberland received
a letter from McMahon in which the Prince was reported

[1] Moore, *Sheridan*, ii. 388 ; Grey, *Life and Opinions*, p. 267.

[2] *Dropmore Papers*, x. 103-104 ; Grey, *Life and Opinions*, p. 437.

[3] Windsor Arch., George IV, Sheridan to Holland, 15 Jan. The best
reply Sheridan could make ran as follows :

" *An Address to the Prince : 1811*

With all humility we crave
Our Regent may become our slave,
And being so, we trust that he
Will thank us for our loyalty.
Then if he'll help us to pull down
His father's dignity and Crown,
We'll make him, in some time to come
The greatest prince in Christendom."

Memoirs of Regency, i. 28.

as having determined to take the Whigs into office *if necessary* ;[1] and it seems very unlikely that a man so sensitive to personal slights, and so devoted to the idea of a Government of his own servants, could have easily forgiven such a remonstrance. Lord Holland certainly regretted that it had been sent, and thought that it had told against his party; remarking ruefully that " the passion for pen and ink was strong upon Lord Grenville during the whole of that season ".[2]

Everything now depended upon the health of the King ; and of that it was not easy to get trustworthy report. Grenville had, in the early days of his illness, maintained an elaborate spy system, having its headquarters at Eton, with Fremantle, Tyrwhitt, and (it is said) Cumberland as his scouts ;[3] but towards the end of January he was certainly in the dark. About 20 January, just when the Whigs were settling the minor offices of their Government, the Prince wrote to Grey and Grenville, to ask their advice as to the course he ought to pursue. Their reply was frank and honourable. They recommended him, if there should be a prospect of the King's recovery within a few weeks, to avoid a change of Government which would only involve the affairs of the nation in needless confusion. If on the other there should be no such prospect, they had no hesitation in advising a new Ministry.[4] On 30 January, at the Prince's request, Dr. Willis, representing all the King's physicians, was examined at Carlton House. His replies to the questions that were put to him certainly gave the Whigs good reason to suppose that the Regency would not be a short one. He was, in general, quite confident of the King's recovery, but affirmed that he was at the moment

[1] Windsor Arch., George IV, Northumberland to McMahon, 18 Jan. 1811.   [2] Holland, *Further Memoirs*, p. 85.
[3] *Bathurst Papers*, pp. 151-152 ; Glenbervie, *Diaries*, ii. 112.
[4] Windsor Arch., George IV, Grey and Grenville to the Prince, 21 Jan. 1811.

unfit to transact business ; and he would hold out no expectation of his recovery within a limited time.[1] In view of this report, which was communicated to Grey and Grenville, they had some ground to hope for office. The Tories were for their part quite certain that they were to be dismissed ; and on 1 February Creevey was debating what office he should take in the new Administration.[2] But though the Prince saw the Whig leaders on the 30th, he was reported by Willoughby Gordon to be still uncertain ;[3] and on 2 February a rumour began to gain ground that he would change his mind and not his Ministers. The Whigs decided to risk all on a bold stroke. They drew up a letter to the Prince which was nothing less than an ultimatum. The time was arrived, they pointed out, when the Prince must take his decision. The Regency Bill would shortly be passed ; whereupon the Prince would have to take the necessary oaths, meet his Privy Council, adjourn or prorogue Parliament, and deliver various speeches, all of which would require the assistance of responsible advisers.

If therefore your Royal Highness shall determine to continue the King's present servants in their offices, it is due to them that they should be apprised of this intention, so as to be prepared with such advice as they may wish to offer on these subjects.

If, on the contrary, your Royal Highness should determine to resort to other counsels, some intermediate discussion of the arrangements and other details for giving effect to that resolution will evidently be necessary. Nor would it be possible without the utmost embarrassment to your Royal Highness' affairs, that the time either for declaring or for acting upon it should be deferred beyond the day of the first Privy Council.[4]

All this was no doubt true, though it was not calculated to propitiate a man who was wrestling with a difficult

[1] *Dropmore Papers*, x. 113-115.

[2] Plumer Ward, i. 372 ; Creevey, pp. 142, 143 ; Campbell, *Life*, ii. 201 ; Wilberforce, *Life*, iii. 493-494.

[3] Add. MS. 38738, f. 61, Gordon to Huskisson, 30 Jan. 1811.

[4] *Dropmore Papers*, x. 117.

decision. But in fact, the letter never reached the Prince. He was too quick for them. On the morning of 3 February, as the Whig leaders sat in conclave, a message came from Carlton House, announcing that the Government of Perceval would be continued in office. The effect of this unexpected announcement was considerable.

Shoals of public men of all parties beset the Palace, where a thousand inquiries were making after the King, and the whole of Pall Mall was crowded with knots of opposition, who had either been, or were, conferring with those who had been at Carlton House. The result is that they are all in very bad humour; they said (in particular Fremantle) " that he (the Prince) adhered to his resolution ", a sign that they had endeavoured to shake it.[1]

It was true that they had remonstrated ; and in their remonstrances even the Prince's peculiar friends had joined.

Lord Moira told him he would lose Ireland. Sheridan told him he would lose his Crown, and all told him that his character would be wholly gone. . . . Young Lord Devonshire spoke to him very strongly ; Lord Thanet, who demanded an audience, perhaps more so. Lord T. told me himself what he said to the Prince ; representing to him that the determination he had made to continue the same Ministers was the greatest calamity that had happened to the country since the death of Mr. Fox. The Prince spoke of his strong attachment to that great man, he begged Lord T. would suspend his judgment for a few weeks. . . . Lord T. left him, pitying him but not blaming him, unless for want of firmness, for he totally acquits him of any deceit whatever. . . .[2]

The rank and file of the party were bitterly disappointed. Only the Grenvilles retained an unruffled equanimity ; for to them office would bring no increase in their income that was not offset by increased outlay ; and it would burden them with responsibilities of which they were not sorry to be quit. It was no wonder, therefore, if " Lord Grenville

---

[1] Plumer Ward, i. 377.

[2] Sterling, *Coke of Norfolk*, ii. 96-97, Roger Wilbraham to Coke.

went down to Dropmore as lightsome as a bird ".[1] But the *Morning Chronicle* did not find it easy to explain away its previous triumphant anticipations of victory. Its explanation that the decision had been taken on the advice of the Whigs made no impression on the country, and still less on its old adversary the *Courier*, whose editor seized the occasion to deliver an attack upon it which Cobbett admiringly called a " *Stinger* ".[2] Cobbett had his own theory of the late events :

The *real* cause of the change in the Prince's intentions was, the inability to *go on* with the proposed ministry. . . . A ministry without Lord Grenville, a ministry that would have, at once, dashed at *Parliamentary Reform*, would have gone on ; . . . .[3]

Cobbett's explanation was wildly wrong. The immediate cause of the Prince's decision was undoubtedly a letter from his mother, of which the original is preserved at Windsor. At the critical moment, on 29 January, the Queen wrote to the Prince :

You will I am sure be glad to hear my dearest son that Mr. Perceval has seen the King & communicated the state of public business pending in the two Houses of Parliament. His Majesty gave perfect attention to his report, & was particularly desirous to know how you had conducted yourself, which Mr. Perceval answered to have been in the most respectful, most prudent, & affectionate manner. I send my Servant on purpose with this account as it will I am sure give You as much satisfaction as it has given to
　　　　　　　　　Your ever affectionate Mother
　　　　　　　　　　& friend,
　　　　　　　　　　　　　　　　　CHARLOTTE [4]

On the following day the examination of Willis gave a

---

[1] Nat. Lib. Wales MS. 2791, Charlotte Wynn to H. Wynn, 9 Feb. 1811.

[2] *Morning Chronicle*, 4 Feb. ; *Political Register*, xix. 225, 302.

[3] *Ibid.* 324.

[4] Windsor Arch., Queen Charlotte, 29 Jan. 1811. Plumer Ward (i. 376) in his version of the letter makes the Queen specifically urge the Prince not to change the Government.

much less favourable report—indeed flatly contradicted the
Queen in stating that the King was not well enough to do
business. Yet it was common knowledge that the King
feared and hated Willis, and had, after a previous attack,
made his family promise that Willis should never be called
in again. The King, no doubt, appeared at his worst in
Willis' presence, and at his best in that of persons whom
he liked and trusted, e.g. Perceval. No wonder, then, that
on 30 January the Prince was "very uncertain". His
position would be most invidious if the King were to recover
within a month or so, and find a Whig Government in
office. This might even induce another attack of madness.
Could the Prince, who had no illusions as to his unpopularity
as compared with the popularity of his father, afford to
risk the charge that his unfilial conduct had blighted the
King's hopes of recovery ? It is arguable that the Queen's
message was to be discounted as the result of her pathetic
optimism,[1] or possibly, as Plumer Ward seems to have
imagined, as a deliberate attempt to prevent a Whig
Ministry. The Queen does not appear as a very vehement
partisan in her correspondence, but she would naturally
support the party that the King had supported, and,
moreover, the Whigs had opposed the arrangements for her
Household, as being too expensive.[2] The Whigs always
considered that Sir Henry Halford had had a hand in their
disappointment.[3] Wilberforce, with his mild zest for tittle-
tattle, imported Mrs. Fitzherbert and "Lady H." as the
Regent's advisers at the crisis.[4] But these suggestions were
beside the point. If the Queen's information was false, why

---

[1] As early as December, before he began to mend, she had had
"not the smallest doubt of his perfect recovery" (*Harcourt Papers*,
vi. 98).

[2] *Morning Chronicle*, 23 Jan. 1811.

[3] Romilly, ii. 360 ; Grey, *Life and Opinions*, p. 276 ; Holland,
Further Memoirs, p. 90. Munk, *Life of Halford*, has nothing on this point.
Some even suspected Willis : *Autobiography of Cornelia Knight*, ii. 273.

[4] Wilberforce, *Life*, iii. 494.

did she drag in Perceval, who was an honourable man, and would have denied her story if it had been untrue ? [1] And, whether false or true, the effect on the Prince was the same. It led him to decide, probably correctly, that a Whig Government was a risk which he ought not to take ; [2] and the very rapid improvement in the King's health in the succeeding two months seemed to justify his decision. The final relapse of the early summer was unexpected by all parties.

It is probable, then, that the quarrels about the answer to the Address and the inclusion of Canning made little difference to the final issue. The Prince in his letters and behaviour to Perceval was studiously offensive—no doubt with a view to propitiating the men he had disappointed.[3] Yet it is difficult to believe that the Regent forgot or forgave the ultimatum of 2 February—of which he must have been cognisant through Adam, to whom it was sent; or that Sheridan forgave Grenville for the letter of 11 January. The Regent and his friends began to feel the irritation of having the Whigs' claims pressed upon them as matters of right, rather than of grace ; and they resented this veiled truculence. Their resentment grew steadily

---

[1] Holland's argument (*Further Memoirs*, p. 89) that the legal phrase " business *pending* in the two Houses " proved that the letter was dictated by Perceval, does not seem to have much weight; though it is true that he asserts that the Prince himself was " diverted " by the " artifice ". Holland was writing some years after these events.

[2] Even a Whig like General Fitzpatrick could agree in this. See his letter to Lord Ossory [n.d.—early Feb. 1811] quoted by Holland in *Further Memoirs*, pp. 95-97.

[3] See his letter retaining Perceval, in *Dropmore Papers*, x. 118-119. H. G. Bennet's lost MS. diary gives a good account of his first council, cited in Torrens, *Wellesley*, p. 452 : " The Prince kept the Council waiting two hours : the King never detained anybody a minute. He was very civil to some and very rude to others, particularly to the Speaker Abbott, and to Perceval, turning his head away while they kissed his hand. He had brought into the Council Room that morning the busts of Mr. Fox and the Duke of Bedford, and they were placed at the head of the table." *Morning Chronicle*, 8 Feb., confirms this last detail.

throughout the year of the Regency restrictions, and in 1812 it became a matter of importance.

(3) *February 1812.*—The restrictions which the Regency Act had imposed upon the Prince were to expire on 18 February 1812. As it became plain that little hope remained of the King's recovery, the expectations of both parties were concentrated upon the steps which the Regent might take when he should be at length free to act, unrestrained by the fear of offending his father. The events of February 1811, however, had taught the Whigs not to be too confident. They no longer entirely reckoned on the Prince. From Grey and Grenville, indeed, his parting had been cordial ; but the rank and file of the party, which judged him only by his overt acts, were embittered and suspicious. The more charitable held that he did not know his own mind ; [1] the more censorious, that he designed to play off the one party against the other, to his own profit.[2]

The Prince's conduct in the twelve months preceding his letter to the Duke of York of February 1812 makes it clear that he had definite, fixed views as to the end to be pursued : it was as to the means to be adopted that he wavered. His object was the formation of a strong Government, comprising his personal friends and as wide a selection of moderate men as possible, which should carry on the war with vigour, and, if it were feasible, defer the consideration of the Catholic question. A sentimental loyalty to old associations drove him to make repeated efforts to include some of the Whigs in this arrangement, and blinded him to the fact that they did not really accord well with it. In the same way, he deceived himself into thinking that he was, as in the old days, in favour of

[1] Add. MS. 38738, f. 118, Willoughby Gordon to Huskisson, 21 Aug. 1811 ; 35649, f. 302, Lady Anne Barnard to Hardwicke, 17 Nov. 1811.
[2] Quoted as A. Baring's opinion in *The Farington Diary*, vii. 74 ; Scott, *Letters*, ii. 537.

Catholic Emancipation, if only the Catholics would be quiet for a little, and give him time. The secret negotiations of 1811 amply corroborate these conclusions. In appearance, they are chaotic ; in reality, they are governed by a steadily pursued policy. Thus on 23 May, Moira was allowed to approach Grey with an offer to discuss the possibility of a union between them, with perhaps the addition of some of the extant Government. Grey refused at once. He would not even discuss the matter. The Grenvilles, among themselves, blamed him for this refusal, which they considered marked a very unjustifiable repetition of his attitude in 1809. They felt, even more strongly than at that time, that, for the country's sake, they should, if it were at all possible, accede to the Government ; and they would not agree to a Government formed upon a principle of exclusion.[1] But, though the Grenvilles did not know it, the offer was probably not intended to include them. They were too extreme in their opinions about the war and the Catholics to suit the Regent ; and they were not, as Grey was, of the friends of his youth. Nor had their belated support of the Duke of York's restoration propitiated him.

It does not seem that Grey's refusal put him out of favour with the Regent. He certainly had good hopes of office at this time, for he drew up a careful definition of policy and sent it to Grenville for comments.[2] On 24 June he had the honour of entertaining the Prince to a dinner at which a select company of old Foxites was present ; and even if it is apparent that McMahon considered this by no means an instance of favour, but perhaps rather the contrary, it was offset by the Regent's dining with Perceval on 18 July.[3] The Regent, however, having

[1] *Dropmore Papers*, x. 136-139.

[2] *Ibid.* 151-152. No new principle was brought forward. The main points were Ireland, paper money, the war, and Economical Reform.

[3] Windsor Arch., George IV, 25 June, 13 July ; *Morning Chronicle*, 25 June, 18 July 1811.

found Grey intractable, was quietly swinging round to
another possibility. The intention now was to reunite old
Foxites like Holland and Bedford with the Prince's own
party ; and in the course of the summer these two noblemen
were sounded by Sheridan, but gave him no encouragement.[1] The Regent still kept Grey skilfully in play, with
the prospect of a Ministry not founded upon an objectionable coalition ;[2] but he turned in the early autumn to yet
another quarter. As his dislike of Perceval was apparently
not much diminished, it was perhaps natural that he
should be drawn to Perceval's particular enemy, Wellesley.
Wellesley was one of a number of politicians who felt their
talents to be superior to those of the Prime Minister, and
under the influence of that delusion considered themselves
justified in making themselves impossible to their colleagues
in the Cabinet. He undoubtedly hoped, by negotiations with
the Prince's party, either to put himself at the head of a
coalition Ministry, or to be the controlling force in a Cabinet
with a *fainéant* at its head.[3] To the Regent also the prospect
was not unattractive. Wellesley had been much with him
during his stay at Oatlands, on the business of the Household Bill—which meant in fact the Prince's debts—and he
had indoctrinated him with a good deal of his enthusiasm
for the war.[4] A union with the Whigs of the Holland school
certainly appeared to be a possibility. Wellesley was, outside the camps of the two main parties, the only man of
sufficient weight to hold a Ministry together, and he was

[1] Holland, *Further Memoirs*, pp. 108-109.
[2] *Dropmore Papers*, x. 168.
[3] Wellington, *Supplementary Despatches*, vii. 269. Wellesley said :
" Grenville and Grey will certainly not offer me any situation I could
take. My best chance would be in his retaining the present Government
with an admixture of his personal friends ... with, probably, the Duke
of Norfolk at the head. This seems to be the scheme that is floating in
his mind, but he appears to have nothing fixed as yet, except that ...
Mr. Perceval must make way for some friend of his."
[4] Torrens, *Wellesley*, pp. 460-461.

the only man who could have held a balance between
them.[1] There were rumours that he was to head a Government established on a warlike bottom, with Perceval safely
removed to the Lords ; and the Percies and Cavendishes,
besides the Duke of Norfolk, were reported to have been
won over to this project.[2] The Regent certainly told
Wellesley that he had no intention of retaining Perceval in
his service.[3] Yet signs to the contrary were not lacking.
Yarmouth had been forced to admit that Perceval could
get the Household Bill through the Houses better than
anybody else.[4] His prestige in the House was very great,
and his authority in it was compared by Liverpool to that
of Pitt.[5] The Scottish appointments, after a prolonged
delay, had gone, not to the Prince's particular friends the
Scottish Whigs, but to Perceval's men; and Moira saw in
this the beginning of the end.[6] Wellesley Pole had been
suffered to pursue his policy under the aegis of the Regent ;
and a follower of Perceval had filled the vacancy in the
Irish representative peerage. The influence of the Dukes of
York and Cumberland, which grew stronger while the
Prince was laid up at Oatlands, was working in the same
direction, as was that of the Hertford family. To the
Regent the choice must have seemed to lie between Lord
Moira and Catholic Emancipation, on the one hand, and
the Peninsular war and Lady Hertford on the other. He
felt the difficulties of his situation acutely; and in December
1811 his mental agitation combined with the pain from his

---

[1] Wellington, *Supplementary Despatches*, vii. 269 : " The Prince . . .
seemed to wish to put an end to the distinction between the Pitt and
Fox parties, and was continually saying ' In God's name, is it not time
·to leave at rest the ashes of the two great men now no more, who are
quoted at every step ? ' "

[2] *Memoirs of Regency*, i. 127.

[3] Wellington, *Supplementary Despatches*, vii. 269.   [4] *Ibid.* 271.

[5] *Ibid.* 102, Liverpool to Wellington, 11 April 1811.

[6] Scott, *Letters*, ii. 520 ; Ward, *Letters to " Ivy "*, p. 146, for the
Prince's Scottish friends.

injured ankle to reduce him to a condition really alarming. It was widely believed that he was insane;[1] and he certainly lay on his stomach at Oatlands and refused to do business, so that some thought him to be malingering.[2]

In January, though his health improved, his political activities became more feverish. Every kind of solution was tried. An attempted reconciliation between Wellesley and Grenville broke down through Grenville's attacks on the war.[3] There were strong rumours of an overture to Whitbread, for a junction with the Prince's friends, to be sealed by a peerage for his wife.[4] Wellesley was still the centre of every project, even after his suspensive resignation of 17 January.[5] Grey came again into favour, while Grenville was increasingly ignored.[6] At the close of the month, with only three weeks to run to the end of the restrictions, Grenville reviewed the position.

I do not believe [he wrote] we can carry the P. with us in such a system of public measures decidedly announced and *resolutely persevered in*, as can alone save the country ; and if he lets us for a time make the experiment I should expect to see a fresh change on the very first appearance of the innumerable difficulties and

---

[1] Wilberforce, *Life*, iii. 559 ; " Prince's health said to be bad—he is very nervous. It is reported that he is insane, and many well-informed people seem half to suspect it. Sir W[illiam] Scott looked significantly at Stephen, and said, ' He certainly has done no business for some time.' " Cf. *Milne Home Papers*, p. 150 : " The Prince Regent has been in a very dangerous state, his leg and thigh perfectly black, and the physicians had ordered him so much opium, he had no passage for some days ".

[2] The *Independent Whig* of 23 Nov. suggested that the Regent's ankle was of inferior public importance in comparison with the starvation and riots in Nottinghamshire, but the *Morning Chronicle* does not seem to have taken this view.

[3] *Memoirs of Regency*, i. 193.

[4] *Dropmore Papers*, x. 193-194.

[5] Windsor Arch., George IV, Wellesley to McMahon, 14 Jan. 1812; Add. MS. 37296, f. 175; *Supplementary Despatches*, vii. 256; *Dropmore Papers*, x. 190-206.

[6] *Memoirs of Regency*, i. 179 ; *Bath Archives*, i. 316.

discontents which such measures must infallibly produce among friends as well as enemies.[1]

The overture, if it came, would, he felt, be " of the *hollowest* description "; and he was afraid that the Prince might try to curtail their right to patronage, a thing to which he could never consent.[2] At last, on 13 February the long-expected offer arrived. It took the form of a letter from the Prince to the Duke of York, who was authorized to communicate its contents to Grey. It had been a common rumour for some days previously, that when the offer came it would come through this channel.[3] After an extended preamble, canvassing the motives for his actions since his accession to the Regency, explaining that he now felt it incumbent upon him to come to some decision, and asserting that he had deferred it in order not to prejudice the debates on the Catholic question, the Regent passed to the congenial theme of the glories of the Peninsular war, and proceeded :

In the critical situation of the war in the Peninsula I shall be most anxious to avoid any measure which can lead my allies to suppose that I mean to depart from the present system. Perseverance alone can achieve the great object in question, and I cannot withhold my approbation from those who have honourably distinguished themselves in support of it. I have no predilections to indulge, no resentments to gratify, no objects to attain but such as are common to the whole empire. If such is the leading principle of my conduct . . . I flatter myself I shall meet with the support of Parliament and of a candid and enlightened nation.

Having made this communication of my sentiments on this new and extraordinary crisis of our affairs, I cannot conclude without expressing the gratification I should feel if some of those persons, with whom the early habits of my public life were formed, would strengthen my hands and constitute a part of my Government. With such support, and aided by a vigorous and united Administration

---

[1] *Dropmore Papers*, x. 197.
[2] *Ibid.* 205-206 ; *Memoirs of Regency*, i. 222.
[3] *Dropmore Papers*, x. 205-206.

formed on the most liberal basis, I shall look with additional confidence to a prosperous issue of the most arduous contest in which
Great Britain was ever engaged.

You are authorized to communicate these sentiments to Lord
Grey, who I have no doubt will make them known to Lord Grenville.

P.S. I shall send a copy of this letter immediately to Mr.
Perceval.[1]

[1] *Ibid.* 212-213 : the version sent to Perceval is not quite identical :
Windsor Arch., George IV, [13 Feb. 1812]. Moore's parody, *R——l
Consistency*, has some good hits :
Pp. 5-6 :
" At length, dearest Freddy, the moment is nigh
  When, with P-rc-v-l's leave, I may throw my chains by ;
  And, as time now is precious, the first thing I do
  Is to sit down and write a wise letter to you.
  I meant before now to have sent you this letter,
  But Y-rm—th and I thought perhaps 'twould be better
  To wait till the Irish affairs were decided—
  That is, till both Houses had prosed and divided,
  With all due appearance of thought and digestion ;
  For though H—rt—rd House had long settled the question
  I thought it but decent, between me and you,
  That the OTHER two Houses should settle it too.

     *   *   *   *

P. 8 :
  You know, my dear Freddy, how oft, if I WOULD,
  By the law of last Session, I might have done good . . .
  I might have told Ireland I pitied her lot,
  Might have sooth'd her with hope—but you know I did not :
  And my wish is, in truth, that the best of old fellows,
  Should not, on recov'ring, have cause to be jealous—
  But find that, while he has been laid on the shelf,
  We've been, all of us, near as * * * as himself.

     *   *   *   *   *

Pp. 11-12 :
  It is true we are bankrupts in commerce and riches,
  But think how we furnish our allies with breeches ;
  We've lost the warm hearts of the Irish, it's granted ;
  But then we've got Java, an island much wanted
  To put the last lingering few who remain
  Of the Walcheren warriors out of their pain.
  Then how Wellington fights ! and how squabbles his brother !

This remarkable letter was hardly calculated to propitiate. Grenville wrote to Hardwicke : " I certainly never read a paper drawn in terms less conciliatory, or to speak more properly, I never saw one so highly offensive ".[1] It was indeed designed to wound the Whigs at their tenderest points. The emphatic commendation of Perceval's war policy ; the vague reference to Ireland, pointed by the selection of that strong Protestant the Duke of York as messenger ; the palpable attempt to divide Grey from Grenville—were all extraordinarily ill-judged if the offer was meant to be accepted. The Whigs believed that it was so intended, that it was in fact the offer of 1809 repeated ; and certainly there is a good deal of evidence that the Prince entertained this idea—among others—before the letter was sent. Yet on the whole it seems more likely that it was not sent with the expectation of being taken seriously. The original draft of the letter was the work of Perceval, and its wording makes it clear that the Regent had instructed him to produce reasons for not making an offer to the Whigs rather than suggestions for a union. It was in fact, as Perceval drew it, a simple statement of the Regent's decision to retain his present Ministry, with an explanation that the decision was based on the necessarily unsatisfactory nature of any coalition in which the views of Ministers conflicted upon the Catholic question. In other respects it was very like the letter that was actually sent,

> For Papists the one, and with Papists the other ;
> One crushing Napoleon by taking a city,
> While t'other lays waste a whole Cath'lic committee !
> Oh, deeds of renown !—shall I boggle or flinch
> With such prospects before me ? by Jove, not an inch.
> No—let England's affairs go to rack, if they will,
> We'll look after th'affairs of the Continent still,
> And with too much at home of starvation and riot,
> Find Lisbon in Bread, and keep Sicily quiet."

The last line contains a *canard* that made Wellington very angry. See p. 166 above.   [1] Add. MS. 35424, f. 92.

though its phraseology was not so flamboyant. And it
bears corrections in pencil in the hand of the Duke of
York.[1] The Regent, provided with this frank but not
insulting declaration, wavered in the very moment of
decision. He could not bear to have it said that he had
ratted ; he must leave a way open to his old friends, if they
would take it. He therefore re-wrote the letter. His belief
in his old friends was not sufficient to induce him to leave
a path that was practicable, or even honourable. But it
could not be said, now, that he had shut them out. His
conscience was satisfied. He would make it up to them by
damning Perceval, and he would protest all the time that
it was not his fault, that he had always hoped that they
would come in and help him, that they were too absolute,
too hasty, too uncharitable. The Archbishop of York—a
Grenvillite—was selected to be the recipient of the Prince's
simple-minded casuistry, and drew up a lengthy memorandum of what must have been a very tedious interview.[2]

The Whigs appear at their best in the reply to the
Regent's letter. Grey had refused to allow the Duke to
read the letter to him unless Grenville were present ;[3] and
after they had heard it, they declined to give an immediate
answer. On 15 February they sent in their refusal. It was a
dignified document from which all suspicion of resentment
was carefully excluded.

All personal exclusions we entirely disclaim ; we rest on public
measures, and it is on this ground alone that we must express
without reserve the impossibility of our uniting with the present
Government.

They referred to their conduct in 1809 and 1811, and
avowed that the reasons which had then led them to hold

[1] Windsor Arch., George IV, [13 Feb. 1812]. Perceval was confident of retaining office. See his reply to Curwen on 13 Feb. *Parl.
Deb.* xxi. 782.

[2] *Dropmore Papers*, x. 220-222.

[3] Windsor Arch., George IV, Duke of York to Regent, 13 Feb. 1812.

aloof from coalitions had now, in their opinion, still greater
force. They differed from Ministers on " almost all the
leading features of the present policy of the empire ", and
in particular on the affairs of Ireland. They laid it down
emphatically that, if they were to come into office, they
must be at liberty to recommend immediate measures to
remove the civil disabilities of the Catholics of that
country.[1]

There can be no doubt that the Whigs were right to
reject an offer so made, and so expressed. In a subsequent
debate in the House of Lords they elaborated—super-
fluously—their reasons for refusal.[2] From their expressions
upon that occasion, and from their private correspondence
in the days immediately preceding the offer, it seems very
likely that they would have refused any proposition,
however tactfully worded, which implied a coalition with
Perceval, or the possibility of compromise upon the
Catholic question. The Whigs justly felt that the Catholic
question was their strongest point. On that, at least, Grey
and Grenville were in absolute agreement. And with the
tide beginning to set in favour of the Catholics, it would be
folly to sacrifice their reputations for the doubtful benefits
of a probably unstable arrangement. Thomas Grenville,
however, with characteristic straightforwardness, was afraid
that they might, by insisting too much upon this ground
for refusal, suppress the unpopular fact of their resolute
opposition to the war : it would be more open and manly,
he felt, to put their cards on the table, even if it emerged
that in this matter they were not in perfect agreement
among themselves.[3]

The indignation of Wellesley at this unexpected
termination of his hopes of placing himself at the head of
a great coalition Ministry of moderate men led him to

[1] *Dropmore Papers*, x. 213-215.
[2] *Parl. Deb.* xxii. 36 *et seq.*
[3] *Dropmore Papers*, x. 212.

carry into effect the resignation which he had been defer-
ring since January.[1] Yet his surprise was a little naïve. The
Regent had done no more than pursue the course long
prophesied for him. As early as July 1811 Canning and
Willoughby Gordon had foretold what would happen, with
complete accuracy.[2] Moreover, the Regent's letter, whatever
its defects, was politically sound as concerned the retention
of Perceval. The Prince perhaps realized that Wellesley's
threatened resignation was a matter of pique and personal
jealousy for which differences with Perceval about the
Peninsular war were only an excuse. Wellington was
reasonably satisfied with the behaviour of the Ministry,
and that was sufficient. Besides, it seemed doubtful whether
Wellesley was suited by temperament to be the head of a
solid Ministry. English politics were too small an arena
for one who had been accustomed to the grandeur and
subservience of the East. As a possible rallying-point for
the coalition Government he appeared perhaps hardly so
suitable as the Prince had at first imagined. Still more
important, it began to be doubtful whether the " Prince's
party " would any longer follow the Prince. Moira was
alienated ; Hutchinson and Donoughmore were openly vitu-
perative ; and the Scottish Whigs were disappointed. An
immediate, wholesale concession to the Catholics might win
them back ; but the Regent was disinclined for that. He
dared not have an all-Whig Ministry, for Spain's sake. So
he went about the matter of strengthening the Government
in a different way. He kept Perceval, made the Whigs shut
themselves out, and then forced on the Tories the *laissez-
faire* solution of the Catholic question, and by that means
secured Castlereagh's support. He now had almost exactly
what he wanted—a vigorous prosecution of the war, with
a postponement, not a rejection, of the Catholic claims.
And the whole time he kept up a network of intrigue to

---

[1] Windsor Arch., George IV, Wellesley to Regent, 17 and 18 Feb.
1812.   [2] Add. MS. 38738, ff. 100-103.

give the impression that he preferred any one to the Ministers actually in office. In this net the unfortunate Wellesley had been caught, and was to be caught again. If only the Prince had his own friends carrying out these policies, or helping to carry them out, or if a more tractable Premier could be substituted for Perceval, so that he himself might feel the pulse of Government more perceptibly, it would be perfect. For three months he fretted at this blemish, until the tragic death of Perceval gave him once more an opportunity to attempt to remove it.

(4) *May–June* 1812.—By his " Letter to the Duke of York ", of February 1812, the Prince had effectively severed his connexion with the Whigs. The Carlton House party was indignant at his conduct. Though Northumberland's devotion remained unaltered,[1] Lords Donoughmore and Hutchinson were already alienated from the Prince.[2] The Duke of Norfolk rejected his overtures. Lord Moira declined the Garter in a letter which showed that he was, not angry, indeed, but grieved at his aberrations.[3] Perceval's death, therefore, placed the Regent in a most difficult situation. The Government had been weak before that event : after it, the weakness proved mortal. As Northumberland observed, " nothing could possibly have happened, which would have embarrassed His Royal Highness so much ".[4]

[1] Windsor Arch., George IV, Northumberland to McMahon, 21 Feb. : " We shall again hear the Arrogance of Disappointment talk of storming the Closet ".

[2] *Court of Regency*, i. 180, 240 ; Holland, *Further Memoirs of the Whig Party*, p. 125 : and see Donoughmore's speech attacking Lady Hertford in *Parl. Deb.* xxii. 524.

[3] *Morning Chronicle*, 19 Feb. ; Windsor Arch., George IV, Moira to Regent, 28 Feb. ; Nat. Lib. Wales MS. 2791, C. Wynn to H. Wynn, 24 Feb.

[4] Windsor Arch., George IV, Northumberland to McMahon, 15 May. Wynn remarked of Perceval's Government : " In the whole of the list, there is not one man of old property, weight, and influence in the country but that ideot Lord Westmorland ". Nat. Lib. Wales MS. 4814, f. 58.

Yet the Ministers, under the acting-captaincy of Lord Liverpool, did not immediately give up hope ; and when the Regent consulted them as to whether they could go on, they held a Cabinet on 13 May to review their chances. In the minute of the meeting which Eldon drew up, they admitted that their prospects were gloomy, but they professed themselves willing to make the attempt, if the Regent were prepared to support them.[1] It was, therefore, agreed that the Government should make offers to Wellesley, Canning, and their followers. The Regent, however, seems to have felt that some reinforcement would probably be necessary, and he got in personal touch with Canning.[2] Liverpool opened formal negotiations with them, which continued from 17 May to 20 May. Wellesley and Canning, though they would have preferred to form a Government of their own, were not disposed for an immediate rejection of this offer, if its terms should suit them ; but they by no means considered Liverpool's attitude to the Catholic claims to be satisfactory. Canning may have been jealous of Castlereagh, who would have had the lead in the new arrangement, and he certainly disliked the prospect of serving with Lord Sidmouth.[3] The negotiation, therefore, which all the world had considered as successfully concluded, was broken off ; but not before Lord Liverpool in a letter of explanation had promised liberty of action upon the Catholic question.[4]

The Regent's expedient had thus failed ; but there was still hope that Liverpool could hold his ground alone.

[1] Windsor Arch., George IV, Eldon to Regent, 13 May.

[2] Windsor Arch., George IV, Canning to Regent, 13 (or 18) May.

[3] Windsor Arch., George IV, Arbuthnot to McMahon, 18 May; Bagot, *Canning*, i. 387; Pearce, *Wellesley*, iii. 213-240 ; Add. MS. 37296, ff. 326-374; Wilberforce, *Life of Wilberforce*, iv. 29 ; *Parl. Deb.* xxiii. App. i-xix.

[4] Add. MS. 38247, ff. 277, 287-291; *Parl. Deb.* xxiii. App. xii; *Dropmore Papers*, x. 255-265 ; W. A. Miles, *Correspondence*, ii. 379; *Diary of a Lady in Waiting*, i. 94-95.

At all events, Vansittart was made Chancellor of the Exchequer on 20 May, as though the Government were contemplating an extended lease of life.[1] A single day was sufficient to dispel such illusions. On 21 May Stuart Wortley carried by a majority of four an Address to the Regent, praying him to take immediate steps to secure an efficient Administration.[2] Wortley was a follower of Perceval,[3] but a considerable proportion of the majority was of the same faction ; for it was considered that the late Government had depended so much upon the Administrative ability and Parliamentary talents of that Minister that any attempt to carry it on after his death must necessarily be futile, if not presumptuous.[4] Liverpool's Administration accordingly resigned on 22 May,[5] and the Regent turned to Lord Wellesley for assistance. But he did not immediately authorize him to form a Government. He was simply to ascertain the possibilities, and to draw up the plan of an Administration, upon which the Regent would then pronounce an opinion.[6] The intention, no doubt, was to renew the negotiations with Liverpool upon terms more acceptable to the Wellesleys ; for the Prince had already warned Wellesley not to have anything to do with the Whigs.[7] Unfortunately the situation had changed since 20 May ; for on 21 May Wellesley had published his correspondence with Liverpool, without Liverpool's explanatory letter upon the Catholic question ; and the Tories attributed the defeat upon Wortley's motion in part to that fact. They were in any case angry that their private correspondence should so soon have been published to the world.[8]

---

[1] Wilberforce, *Life*, iv. 30.   [2] *Parl. Deb.* xxiii. 281.

[3] There seems to be some doubt as to Wortley's precise position at this time. As he does not appear in Mr. Aspinall's lists of Canningites in 1807 and 1812, he has been counted a Percevalian.

[4] *Parl. Deb.* xxiii. 284-286.

[5] Windsor Arch., George IV, Cabinet minute, 22 May.

[6] Add. MS. 38738, f. 229.   [7] *Dropmore Papers*, x. 265.

[8] *Bathurst Papers*, p. 174 ; Windsor Arch., Queen Charlotte, Queen to

An even more serious ground of difference was a "Statement" of the reasons for Wellesley's resignation from Perceval's Government, drawn in terms extraordinarily wounding to the feelings of his colleagues, and reflecting most odiously upon the abilities of Perceval. This appeared on 22 May, at the very moment (as Harrowby observed) when Perceval's friends were but just returned from following his hearse.[1] To Liverpool and his colleagues it seemed a deliberate insult. The "Statement" was in reality the work of T. Sydenham, one of Wellesley's followers; but Wellesley was cognizant of it, and made no attempt to disavow it until he was forced to do so upon 8 June.[2] It was consequently in vain that Canning approached Liverpool with proposals for a union based upon the immediate consideration of the Catholic question, and the prosecution of the war in the Peninsula with the utmost vigour.[3] Melville indeed expressed his concurrence in these principles, and Liverpool treated Canning with cordiality; but they all refused to serve in a Cabinet with Lord Wellesley.[4]

In the meantime Wellesley had been sounding Grey

Regent, 21 May; Add. MS. 38738, f. 229; *Parl. Deb.* xxiii. 365; Holland, *Further Memoirs*, pp. 135-136. Liverpool told Holland that he read Wellesley's last letter to him in *The Times* before receiving, or at least before opening, the original.

[1] *Parl. Deb.* xxiii. 366; Add. MS. 38247, f. 275, has a draft reply from Liverpool to Wellesley, apparently never sent, in which the attack on Perceval is plainly stated as the reason for refusal. Grey later remarked with some effrontery: "It is painful to be convinced that personal animosity, in times like these, can be found to agitate any bosom". *Parl. Deb.* xxiii. 373.

[2] Wellington, *Supplementary Despatches*, vii. 279; *Parl. Deb.* xxiii. 370.

[3] *Ibid.* App. xix-xx. There was a simultaneous proposal from William Dundas for a reunion of Pittites. Add. MS. 37296, ff. 402 *et seq.*

[4] Windsor Arch., George IV, Melville to Canning, 23 May; Pearce, iii. 242; Add. MS. 38247, ff. 321-323; Moira too concurred in Wellesley's principles: Windsor Arch., George IV, Moira to Wellesley, 23 May.

and Grenville, who, after an interval for consultation, had returned him the following answer :

Lord Wellesley has selected two among the many important subjects which must engage the attention of any men who could in such circumstances be called upon to consider of the acceptance of stations of public trust. On these two points our explanation shall be as distinct as it is in our power to make it.

On the first [*i.e.* the Catholic claims], indeed, our opinion is too well known and has been too recently expressed to need repetition.

As to the second point, no person feels more strongly than we do the advantages which would result from a successful termination to the present contest in Spain. But we are of the opinion that the direction of military operations are questions not of principles but of policy, to be regulated by circumstances. . . . On such questions therefore no public men . . . can undertake for more than a deliberate and dispassionate consideration according to the circumstances of the case. . . . But we cannot in sincerity conceal from Lord Wellesley that, in the present state of the finances, we entertain the strongest doubts of the practicability of an increase in any branch of the public expenditure.[1]

This relatively conciliatory reply gave good grounds for hope. Grenville had been for some days of opinion that it would be difficult to oppose a Wellesley–Canning Government ;[2] and though Grey had been apprehensive of Wellesley's violence on the question of the war,[3] it was now felt that he was, perhaps, more conciliatory than

[1] Windsor Arch., George IV, Grey and Grenville to Wellesley, 24 May ; *Dropmore Papers*, x. 271-272 ; Add. MS. 35424, ff. 103-104. The above is a much abbreviated version, for these documents have been often printed, and are to be found, in various degrees of completeness, in most of the large MS. collections. None of the MS. versions differ materially from the printed versions. The most convenient collection is in the Appendix to vol. xxiii. of the *Parliamentary Debates*.

[2] *Dropmore Papers*, x. 246.

[3] *Ibid.* 263 : " Our ultimate agreement with Wellesley, if he persist in his romantic notions with regard to the war in the Peninsula, seems nearly impossible ".

Canning.[1] At all events they could concur verbally in the principles that had been enunciated.[2]

The Prince viewed this result with consternation. He had not anticipated that Wellesley and Grenville could come to an agreement about the Peninsular war. It was said that when Wellesley returned with the Whigs' answer, the Prince exclaimed, without reading it, " What ! a refusal ? "[3] Even when he had read it, he neglected to give Wellesley any authority to proceed to the formation of an Administration. On the contrary, he resurrected the Liverpool Government, and urged them to consider Wellesley's two principles once more, and, if it were possible, to sink their personal feelings in an alliance with him.[4] Enquiries by Canning elicited the information that Wellesley's commission was now considered to be at an end, although Liverpool still regarded himself merely as a stop-gap.[5] So that, when, on 27 May Liverpool and his colleagues again declined coöperation with Wellesley, the Regent had again to decide what course he should pursue.[6] He had already on 26 May had a maudlin reconciliation with Moira ; and if another resort to Wellesley proved fruitless, he had now the hope of an acceptable alternative.[7] For on one thing he seems to have been determined : that

---

[1] Holland, *Further Memoirs*, p. 135.

[2] There was a trivial discrepancy in the wording of Canning's and Wellesley's offers which caused a futile correspondence with the Whigs between 27 and 29 May. *Parl. Deb.* xxiii. App. xxvi-xxxi.

[3] Holland, *Further Memoirs*, p. 138.

[4] Add. MS. 38247, f. 328 ; Regent to Liverpool (copy).

[5] Windsor Arch., George IV, Memorandum by Canning, 26 May ; reply by Melville, 27 May ; Add. MS. 38738, ff. 231-233.

[6] Windsor Arch., George IV, Cabinet minutes, 27 May. They agreed that a union with Wellesley would be a source of weakness, not strength. Camden and Castlereagh absent by their own desire.

[7] Windsor Arch., George IV, Moira to McMahon, 26 May ; Add. MS. 37297, f. 25. Holland states that between 25 and 31 May, Moira was asked to form a Government, but declined. I can find no clear confirmation of this. *Further Memoirs*, p. 139 ; Creevey, pp. 157-158.

he would not send for the Whigs while he could avoid it.[1] During the entire crisis neither Grey nor Grenville was favoured with an audience ; and such offers as were made to them were made through an intermediary.

For three days the Prince revolved the problem in his mind, without apparently getting any nearer to a solution of it, although the country was without a Government, and the Treasury nearly empty. As usual with him when he was in a difficulty, he allowed his irritation to verge on insanity, and Liverpool in alarm fetched the Duke of York to talk to him.[2] Both the Duke and McMahon advised recourse to Grey and Grenville, and were sharply snubbed for their pains.[3] The Prince was still smarting under a speech which Grey had made upon the Irish question in March, in which his treatment of the Catholics had been animadverted upon with some severity. Moira now attempted to remove this obstacle. He succeeded in getting from Grey an explanation of his speech which, it was hoped, would be satisfactory.[4] Whether it was so is uncertain ; but on the following day, 1 June, the Prince at last made up his mind to renew the commission to Wellesley. This time he was given full powers to form an Administration.[5] He at once approached Grey and Grenville, and offered them a share in the Government, upon the following terms : there were to be no exclusions ; any person who could subscribe to the principles of the Administration was to be eligible for office ; those principles were to be as already enunciated in the earlier negotiations ; by

[1] Cf. *The Bath Archives*, i. 377 : " Of the Grenvilles nobody seems to think, but to exclude them ".

[2] *Dropmore Papers*, x. 275.

[3] Add. MS. 38738, ff. 234-235 ; *Dropmore Papers*, x. 276.

[4] *Court of Regency*, i. 300 ; Grey, *Life and Opinions of Earl Grey*, p. 293 ; Windsor Arch., George IV, Moira to McMahon [30 May] ; *Parl. Deb.* xxiii. App. xlii-xliii. Sichel (*Sheridan*, ii. 359) calls Canning the " coadjutor " of Grey and Grenville. I can find no evidence of this.

[5] Pearce, *Wellesley*, iii. 260.

the Prince's desire, Wellesley was to be Prime Minister, and Canning, Moira, and Erskine were to be given places in the Cabinet ; and lastly, the Whigs were to nominate four members, if the Cabinet consisted of twelve in all, and five if it consisted of thirteen.[1] After taking some time for consideration, the Whigs refused this offer.

We are invited [they wrote] not to discuss with your Lordship or with any other public men, according to the usual practice in such cases, the various and important considerations both of measures and arrangements which belong to the formation of a new Government in all its branches, but to recommend to his Royal Highness a number, limited by previous stipulation, of persons willing to be included in a Cabinet of which the outlines are already definitely arranged.

To this proposal we could not accede without the sacrifice of that very object which the House of Commons has recommended, the formation of a strong and efficient Government. We enter not into the examination of the relative proportions or of the particular ar-rangments which it has been judged necessary thus previously to establish. It is to the principle of disunion and jealousy that we object ; to the supposed balance of contending interests in a Cabinet so measured out by preliminary stipulation. The times imperiously require an Administration united in principle and strong in mutual reliance, possessing also the confidence of the Crown. . . . No such hope is presented to us by this project, which appears to us equally new in practice and objectionable in principle. It tends, as we think, to establish within the Cabinet itself a system of counter-action inconsistent with the prosecution of any uniform and beneficial course of policy.[2]

It must be a matter of opinion as to whether the Whigs were right to decline this offer. On Wellesley's behalf it was reiterated that the Government was never intended to have been formed upon any principle of exclusion.[3] Moira even went beyond the facts in asserting that the Prince had made no stipulation as to the filling of any

[1] *Dropmore Papers*, x. 276-277.
[2] *Ibid.* 279-280.   [3] *Parl. Deb.* xxiii. 360.

office ; [1] and in a letter to Grey of 3 June he denied that the Whigs would have been fettered in any way.[2] Wellesley himself fully concurred in this view.[3] Canning for his part contended that the Whigs would in any case have had a majority of one in the Cabinet, since it was well known that Erskine and Moira shared their views, even if they were not officially of their party.[4] It was obvious that the Prince would wish to have his interests represented in the Government : were they not getting off cheaply with Moira and Erskine, the one personally acceptable to them, the other their own Lord Chancellor ? Since the Government was to be avowedly a coalition, the exclusion of Wellesley's ally, Canning, was hardly to be expected ; nor could it with propriety be made a matter of objection that Wellesley, who was forming the Administration, should take the leading place in it. As for a mutual sacrifice of principles, or a balance of interests within the Cabinet, was such a state of affairs unknown to the Talents ? But indeed, would any such sacrifice have been necessary ? Had they not concurred in Wellesley's principles hardly a week previously ? [5]

Against these arguments may be set others not without cogency. Creevey expressed the opinions of many of his party when he wrote :

[1] *Parl. Deb.* xxiii. 339 ; Grey's reply, 343.

[2] *Ibid.* App. xxxiv-xxxvi.

[3] *Ibid.* App. xxxvi.

[4] *Ibid.* xxiii. 345 (Moira) ; 450 (Canning) ; Add. MS. 38738, ff. 236-242, Arbuthnot to Huskisson [c. 1 June]. Arbuthnot thought that the Whigs would swamp Wellesley in the Cabinet. Richmond wrote from Ireland on 7 June: "If their wish is to do good, it ought to have satisfied them, but as their object is power it will not. . . .". *Bathurst Papers*, p. 178.

[5] " Tierney has often assured me that the cause of many of the Opposition holding back was their doubt of the Prince Regent's sincerity towards Lord Wellesley, and that they would have acted differently if they had seen the Treasurer's staff in his hands " (Wellington *Supplementary Despatches*, vii. 283).

". . . The high and honourable conduct of Wellesley and Canning throughout the whole of the business." This was the language of our friends. . . . This is capital, two fellows without an acre of land between them, the one an actual beggar, both bankrupt in character, one entirely without parliamentary followers, the other with scarce a dozen. These two bucks I say in the abundance of their high honour and character condescend to offer to Earl Grey of spotless character, followed by the Russells and the Cavendishes, by all the ancient nobility and all the great property of the realm and by an unshaken phalanx of 150 of the best men in parliament, these honourable worthies offer Earl Grey, so circumstanced, four seats in the Cabinet to him and his friends.[1]

And if the offer had been meagre, that was not the worst. In his verbal communications with the Whig lords, Wellesley had mentioned Melville and even Eldon as possible members of his Cabinet.[2] The Orders in Council were soon to be considered : was there any guarantee of unity upon that question ? The principle of " casuistry ", upon the question of the war (*i.e.* the judging of each case for action according to the circumstances of the moment)—such a principle was too vague to leave room for hope that an assent to it would secure harmony. The problem of paper money was at this time agitating the public mind, in consequence of the provocative action of the bullionist landlord, Lord King ; [3] and upon that the Whigs held decided views. There was the eternal problem of the Prince and his private friends, and the well-founded suspicion of his motives which the experience of the past eighteen months had engendered. The Whigs were now the strongest single party in the House : why had they not been approached directly ? Yet, if the Whigs considered it

[1] *Creevey's Life and Times*, ed. Gore, p. 55.

[2] *Dropmore Papers*, x. 278. Melville was certainly willing to join. Windsor Arch., George IV, Arbuthnot to McMahon [31 May] ; Holland, *Further Memoirs*, p. 140.

[3] Lord King had refused to accept payment of his rents in paper money.

to be a moment of national emergency, they might surely have been prepared to compromise ; and if they were to compromise at all, they could hardly expect to do so upon terms more favourable than those offered by Wellesley, which Canning described as " generous, . . . liberal, and even rash ".[1] Certainly it seemed that the measure of relief to the Catholics which they had been urging for so long might be carried, even though they declined part in the Administration ; and it was at least questionable whether they would be able to carry their war policy, if they came in. But it is undeniable that many Whigs thought that their leaders had made the wrong decision.[2] Sydney Smith, for instance, condemned them in the *Edinburgh Review* :

> We cannot at all understand [he wrote] why an arrangement, in itself good, should be rejected, because those to whom it is tendered have not assisted at its maturation.[3]

Sydney Smith considered that the offer had been frank and honourable : he was disposed to give the Regent credit for a sincere effort to make a strong Government. But this appears to be more than questionable. When Wellesley was explaining to the House of Lords how it was that his negotiation had failed, he let slip the remark that it had been wrecked by "dreadful personal animosities".[4] Peers of every party successively disclaimed animosity of any sort ; and it was only when it seemed likely that the imputation would be attached to the Regent, in default of any one else to whom to apply it, that Wellesley explained that he had referred to Liverpool and his colleagues.[5] It is remarkable that nobody enquired how Liverpool's resentment could

---

[1] *Parl. Deb.* xxiii. 450.

[2] The *Morning Chronicle* (30 May) had hoped for a junction with Wellesley ; though on 4 June it applauded the rejection of his offer.

[3] *Edinburgh Review*, xx. 31-37 ; Add. MS. 34458, f. 377, for proof of Sydney Smith's authorship.

[4] *Parl. Deb.* xxiii. 333.

[5] *Ibid.* 334-336, 338-350, 360.

have affected Wellesley's negotiation with Grey and Grenville. Either Wellesley had originally meant to refer to the
Regent's dislike of Grey,[1] and was now trying to cover his
mistake by reviving his quarrel with Liverpool; or, if he
had really referred to Liverpool in the first instance, it was
plain that he had attached more importance to a junction
with him, than to a junction with Grey and Grenville.
Having regard to the negotiations which had been going
forward since 16 May, the latter explanation appears the
more probable. Certainly, a union of Wellesley with the
Whigs would have represented a surrender to circumstances
on the part of the Regent. The offer to Grey and Grenville,
indeed, bears every indication of having been a trap, carefully baited by the Regent. It was by his desire, as Wellesley
clearly stated, that the stipulation for the inclusion of
Canning, Erskine, and Moira was included in the offer. The
Prince was gambling on the Whigs' justifiable suspicion of
his motives. He put forward a plan to which no reasonable
man could object, because he knew that in such a matter
the Whigs would not behave like reasonable men. The
Whigs took the bait; and by rejecting Wellesley's offer
alienated many moderates in their own ranks. That was a
clear gain to the Prince. Wellesley had now served his
purpose, and he was not allowed to continue the negotiation. The Regent had already passed on to his next
expedient, Lord Moira.

Lord Moira had taken the Wellesley negotiation at its
face value. He considered it most unfortunate that the
Whigs had put an end to it so abruptly, and he showed by
his explanations in Parliament that he thought they had
done so without good reason.[2] But he was honestly anxious
to clear away misunderstandings; he was convinced that
he could form an Administration of adequate strength;
and he came forward, full of chivalrous loyalty to the

---

[1] As Creevey assumed ; Creevey, p. 164.
[2] *Parl. Deb.* xxiii. 335.

Prince, to take up the threads where they had broken, and give the country a settled Government. Twice he attempted to renew negotiations with Grey and Grenville ; but they were not to be induced to enter into informal discussions, and declined to see him unless he could produce the Prince's authority to treat.[1] On 6 June, therefore, he obtained the Prince's consent, and went to interview the Whig lords. Their conversation was a short one. They found themselves in general agreement upon political principles ; but before they could come to details Grey and Grenville enquired whether the Household would resign if they took office. To this Moira replied that he considered it highly inexpedient that they should do so. The Whigs then declined to pursue the conversation further, and the interview came to an end.[2]

Such was Lord Moira's negotiation, as it appears from the printed documents which were published after its conclusion. If the question were merely whether the Whigs were justified in breaking off upon the Household, when (as they knew) everything else was to be conceded to them, when it was not even stipulated that Moira should be Prime Minister, when there were to be no exclusions and no reservations, it would not be difficult to decide that the point was not of sufficient importance to justify refusal. All the features to which they had objected in Wellesley's negotiation had disappeared : only the Household stood between them and office. It is true, that the removal of certain Household officials at a change of Government had been customary for the last thirty or forty years ;[3] but Moira admitted that the Whigs had the right to demand such dismissals : he merely contended that it was inexpedient to exercise it at this particular moment,

[1] *Parl. Deb.* xiii., App. xxxv-xxxix.
[2] *Ibid.* App. xli-xlii; *Court of Regency,* i. 355; Windsor Arch., George IV, Moira to Grey and Grenville, 6 June.
[3] *Parl. Deb.* xxiii. 432, 413.

since it would seem to put a slight upon the Prince, and
to confirm the calumnies as to the strength of " secret
influence " at Carlton House.[1] In the face of such an
admission, the Whigs might well have been for the moment
content to come into a Cabinet where all the weight would
have been upon their side.

The printed documents, however, do not by any means
give an accurate impression of Moira's negotiation. There
are circumstances yet to be considered which make it
very difficult to condemn the Whigs upon this occasion,
and which involve a blot on the career of Sheridan which
his biographers, from Tom Moore onwards, have lamented
without being able satisfactorily to explain.

In the Commons debate upon the negotiations of
Wellesley and Moira, Lord Yarmouth confounded the
Whigs by mentioning that he, and all the other members
of the Household, had for some time been determined to
resign if the Whigs came in. He added that he had himself
informed Sheridan of this fact, from which he inferred
that the Whigs must have been cognizant of it at the time
of their negotiation with Moira, and must therefore have
adopted a rigid attitude only in order to humiliate the
Regent.[2] This brought up Tierney, who denied that they
knew anything of the matter. On the contrary, Sheridan
had, in conversation with him, expressly denied that the
Household was to retire, and had offered to bet him five
hundred guineas that no such step was in contemplation.[3]
This was awkward for Sheridan, who was, of course,
immediately accused of suppressing Yarmouth's information from malicious motives, and of direct falsehood in his
conversation with Tierney, as well as in other similar conversations with Ponsonby. Now in spite of Sheridan's
anguished appeal to the Prince,[4] every effort was made,

---

[1] *Ibid.* 453.   [2] *Ibid.* 423.   [3] *Ibid.* 456-457.
[4] Windsor Arch., George IV, Sheridan to McMahon, 16 June. See
Appendix B, No. XIII.

by Moira and the Prince's friends, to prevent his coming down to the House to vindicate himself.[1] Sheridan did at last have his way, on the understanding that his explanation was to be short and discreet.[2] He was really much too ill to appear in public ; but he went down to the House to try to exculpate himself. It was a painful scene : no one believed his explanations ; his voice faltered and grew weaker ; and at last he was obliged to sit down.[3] Two days later, he had recovered a little, and could meet the charges more successfully. He showed that so far from being the enemy of the Whigs, he had done everything to facilitate their accession to office. He had congratulated the Regent, when at last he allowed Wellesley to make an offer to them.[4] He had encouraged Moira to persevere in his attempts to treat ; and, with Erskine and Whitbread (whom he had summoned from the country specially to that end), had persuaded him to apply to the Regent for full powers to open a negotiation.[5] As to the bet, he admitted it, but most positively averred that he meant it only as an emphatic figure of speech. He denied that he had ever been given a *message* by Lord Yarmouth, and asserted that he had dissuaded him from resignation by representing to him that to do so would be tacitly to admit the justice of the charges that were levelled at the Household. Finally, as to his denial that the Household was to resign, he said : " I knew that resignation was contingent

---

[1] Windsor Arch., George IV, Moira to McMahon, 14 June. See Appendix B, No. XII.   [2] *Ibid.*

[3] *Parl. Deb.* xxiii. 558. See the description of his distressing state in Fitzgerald, *George IV*, ii. 105.

[4] Windsor Arch., George IV, Sheridan to Regent, 1 June. See Appendix B, No. I.

[5] Fitzgerald, *Lives of the Sheridans*, ii. 176, cites the lost MS. diary of H. G. Bennet for 17 June : " Whitbread told me that Lord Moira told him that Sheridan had been working night and day for weeks to remove the impression that existed in the Regent's mind against Grey, pressing that he should be Prime Minister "

upon a circumstance which, at the moment of the bet, was more remote from taking place than ever ".[1] What was this circumstance ?

In an earlier debate Canning had produced a very curious account of the conclusion of Moira's negotiation, which, he said, he was " authorized to state particularly ". He affirmed that, after the negotiations had been broken off and the minute of the conversation drawn up, Moira returned to Carlton House and asked the Prince if he were prepared, if he advised it, to surrender the Household. To which the Prince simply answered, " I am ". Whereupon Moira replied, " Then your Royal Highness shall not part with one of them ".[2] As Tierney remarked, it must have been a theatrical scene : [3] it would have been more rational to have announced the failure of the negotiations, or even read the minute of the meeting. Such an account presupposes that Moira and the Regent were ignorant of each other's views on the Household question. But Moira's attitude was perfectly well known. He had been for years opposed on principle to such changes.[4] His views were public property ; and the Whigs had indeed only been led to bring forward the question so soon " from excess of candour ", because they knew his opinions were so fixed upon it.[5] It is most unlikely that he should have been permitted to begin negotiations without a distinct understanding with the Prince upon this point, and still more unlikely that the Prince should meekly have answered, " I am ".[6] Moira himself never, in any of his subsequent

[1] *Parl. Deb.* xxiii. 552-559, 606-626.

[2] *Ibid.* 453.

[3] *Ibid.* 456 : though its theatricality is no very good evidence against its genuineness.   [4] *Ibid.* 596-597.

[5] *Ibid.* 597. Holland states (*Further Memoirs*, p. 143) that Moira was careful to make it clear that it was he, and not the Prince, that had scruples about the Household at the meeting. But Moira would naturally keep the Prince out of it if he could.

[6] Cf. *Creevey Papers*, p. 162, for the current view of his devotion to

explanations of his own conduct and the Prince's, made any reference to the conversation that Canning described so circumstantially. Does it not seem at least possible that Canning's "authority" was anxious to establish the Prince's willingness to make concessions, and thus still further to put the Whigs in the wrong ? [1]

It is possible, therefore, that the circumstance to which Sheridan referred was the Regent's surrender upon the Household question. On this hypothesis, the Prince's friends tried to stop Sheridan's explanation because they were afraid that he would tell the House that he knew quite well that the Prince would never desert the Household. Such an admission would certainly have removed much of the odium from the shoulders of the Whigs, who had been represented to be demanding as a condition precedent a step which could have been easily and gracefully carried out after they had taken office. If Canning's story was an inspired one, it would fit in well with this explanation, as being an attempt to discount beforehand any revelations Sheridan might make. But other evidence makes it probable that the matter was more serious than that ; and the true explanation seems to be, that the contingency which Sheridan thought so improbable was the accession of Grey and Grenville to office. This is in any case a perfectly natural explanation. Yarmouth told Sheridan he would resign if the Whigs came in : Sheridan did not think the Whigs would come in, and therefore bet Tierney that the Household would not resign. But why was the Regent so anxious to prevent Sheridan from giving

his Household. Yarmouth avowed that the Prince had known of the Household's intention to resign, and had combated it. *Parl. Deb.* xxiii. 478.

[1] Moira too knew of Yarmouth's intention, but considered it as no more than an ebullition of ill-temper, of which it would not be fair to take advantage. His explanation on this point is not altogether satisfactory ; and it is hard to resist the conclusion that he was nearly in the same position as Sheridan. *Ibid.* 596.

this clear and simple explanation ? He was afraid that
Sheridan would reveal the fact that Moira had all along
contemplated making his Government on quite a different
basis, and that the negotiations with the Whigs had been
entered into without hope or expectation of success, in
order to remove from the Whigs the last possible excuse
in the eyes of the public.[1]

In the earlier stages of the Ministerial crisis there can
be little doubt that Moira was well disposed towards the
Whigs. But their rejection of Wellesley's offer—with its
insinuation that they could not regard Moira as a man to
be relied upon to support them—was certainly very disappointing to him. When he wrote to them on 3 June to
suggest a resumption of negotiations, they returned a
distant and evasive answer. Thereupon he seems to have
lost all confidence in their *bona fides*.

The Opposition are behaving as ill as possible. An unhandsome
impatience at not having everything at their own disposal makes

---

[1] Moore, *Life of Sheridan*, ii. 426, regards this episode as " the only
indefensible part of his whole public life ". Sichel, *Sheridan*, gives several
explanations of the " contingency ", each more difficult than the last.
Thus (ii. 360) : " Neither he nor Moira would make terms with them
[Grey and Grenville] ; the Household should not resign. . . . Meanwhile,
Lord Yarmouth . . . had planned things otherwise. He fancied he had
won over the Regent's acquiescence in the hard condition. But all along it
was only a condition precedent, nor was it to take effect till the two peda-
gogues should have come in." Did Yarmouth ever suggest that they
should retire *before* a Whig Government came in ? Is there any evidence
that he had acted in concert with the Regent ? Again (ii. 367) : " The
sum of Sheridan's transgression was not to have taken the Grey-Grenville group into his confidence, and to have stuck by Moira against the
cabals of Yarmouth ". What cabals were these ? How did Yarmouth
stand to gain by resignation ? Again (ii. 362) : " Sheridan had not
removed the false impression that Moira's party was in the ascendant
at Carlton House ". It is not easy to see the bearing of this remark. Mr.
Crompton Rhodes (*Harlequin Sheridan*, p. 225) thinks that the " contingency " was the substitution of Moira for Wellesley as negotiator.
But Moira was negotiator already.

them fight off upon petty distractions and little captious forms. I regard it as impossible to settle anything with them.[1]

Acting upon this conviction, he immediately set about the task of forming an Administration from which the Whigs should be excluded. Canning and Eldon were to be among its leading members, and it was hoped to secure the adhesion of Lord Wellesley.[2] Canning declared decidedly in favour of a union with Moira, and Huskisson was of the same opinion, for he drafted a little later a memorandum in which the bases for the projected Government were laid down, and its personnel more or less determined.[3] The Regent gave his support, and Whitbread and perhaps Erskine would have come in.[4] But before finally settling the composition of the Administration, Moira, with the Prince's consent, decided to make assurance doubly sure by taking away from the Whigs their last pretext for complaint. They should not say that he had never offered to them.[5] He expected the negotiation to fail, Canning expected it to fail,[6] and neither was surprised or concerned

---

[1] *Hastings Papers*, iii. 295, Moira to Sir C. Hastings, 4 June.

[2] Windsor Arch., George IV, Moira to McMahon, McMahon to Regent, 4 June. See Appendix B, Nos. IV and V.

[3] Add. MS. 38738, ff. 257-258. See Appendix B, No. XI.

[4] Windsor Arch., George IV, Moira to McMahon, 4 June [1812]: wrongly calendared under 1811. See Appendix B, No. III. Creevey, pp. 163-164, 156, for Whitbread, who knew and resented the fact that Grey and Grenville had contemplated leaving him out of their projected Government. Holland, *Further Memoirs*, p. 145, confirms this unlikely detail. It is perhaps worth noting that Colonel George Hanger, one of the Regent's boon companions, passed as a Burdettite : see *Adultery and Patriotism*, p. 32. Holland, *op. cit.* p. 144, seems to show that Erskine was not to be counted upon.

[5] Windsor Arch., George IV, Moira to McMahon, 4 June. See Appendix B, No. IV.

[6] Add. MS. 37297, f. 130 ; Windsor Arch., George IV, Moira to Regent, 5 June. See Appendix B, Nos. VI and VII. Romilly (*Memoirs*, iii. 42) narrates that Eldon seemed in no apprehension of being displaced, for he made no effort to clear off pending business in the Court of Chancery, but remained closeted all day with the Duke of Cumberland.

when it did fail, for all their Parliamentary protestations.
It is possible that Moira guessed that his well-known views
upon the Household question would provide the pretext
which he believed the Whigs to be seeking, for terminating
the affair. Or he may simply have gone to the meeting with
an inner conviction that a hitch would arise somewhere :
it is at all events certain that he felt that there was little
danger of his current schemes for a Ministry being interrupted. As soon as he returned from the interview, he
resumed his preparations for the formation of a Government with the Tories.[1] Thenceforward his activities emerged
into the light of day. On 7 June he secured the assurance of
Liverpool's cordial support, and the prospects looked very
promising.[2] But at the very last moment he lost his nerve.

If he had followed Mr. Pole's advice and boldly declared himself
Prime Minister in his place in the House of Lords, whilst Mr. Canning
and Mr. Pole moved for writs in the Commons for new elections in
consequence of their acceptance of office, I do believe he might have
formed a government: but his friend Sir Charles Hastings told me he
was a brave soldier, but the greatest political coward in the world.[3]

Moira himself had no doubt that he could have formed a
Government ; but, as he explained to Sir Charles Hastings,
that was not sufficient.

It was requisite that the Administration should be declared on
Monday last, or the loan would have fallen to the ground, entailing
infinite distress on every public branch. It was not till Saturday
night [6 June] that the Opposition declared off. Sunday was the
only day for looking to other arrangements, and on that day Erskine
and the Duke of Norfolk unexpectedly hung back, frightened by the
high language of some of the Oppositionists.[4]

[1] Add. MS. 38738, f. 245, Moira to Huskisson, 6 June. See Appendix
B, No. VIII.   [2] Add. MS. 38738, f. 247 ; Bathurst Papers, p. 177.
[3] Wellington, Supplementary Despatches, vii. 282. [In a memorandum
in the handwriting of Colonel Meyricke Shaw, dated January, 1814.]
[4] Hastings Papers, iii. 296. Erskine was disappointed because he was
not to have the Chancellorship ; Norfolk was alarmed at being the only
Whig. Holland, Further Memoirs, pp. 144, 146.

This would have entailed still further recourse to the Liverpool group, which Moira feared would not please the country. Nor did he wish to have it said, that he had protected the Hertfords for the sake of office.[1] So on Monday, 8 June, he laid down his commission; and the same day Lord Liverpool formed—or began to form—that Ministry which was to last for fifteen years.[2]

Moira's excuses are certainly feeble. Liverpool accepted office on 8 June with a Cabinet in a much less forward state than his. If the inclusion of two more of Liverpool's men would have made Moira's Government unpopular, would not a revival of the old Administration be more unpopular still ? Moira's friends were certainly bitterly chagrined at his conduct. Yet it is perhaps explicable by the attitude of the Regent. The Regent had got rid of the Whigs. He had put Wellesley personally out of the way. There stood now only Lord Moira between him and a return to the Perceval system, *minus* Perceval. He had no objection to Moira's forming a Government, since it was to contain a majority of old Pittites, and since it would be to a certain extent amenable to his control. But Moira, in his interview with Whitbread on 7 June, produced a plan " for revoking [the] Orders in Council, conciliating America by all manner of means, the most rigid Economical Reform, nay, Parliamentary Reform if it was wished for ".[3] Such a programme would not suit the Regent; and it is therefore hardly surprising that, when the Duke of Norfolk and Erskine deserted, and Moira grew discouraged, the Prince made no effort to induce him to persevere, but fell back with relief into the safer arms of Liverpool.

[1] *Hastings Papers*, iii. 295.

[2] Holland's account (*Further Memoirs*, p. 146) of Liverpool's being waiting in the adjoining room, when Moira abandoned his attempt, may be true in substance, but gives the misleading impression that it was the Regent, and not Moira, that put an end to his commission.

[3] Creevey, p. 165.

It is now possible to estimate the conduct of the Whigs in rejecting Moira's overture. They were, after all, justified in some degree by the insincerity of the men with whom they had to deal. They could not know the double game that Moira was playing; they could not perceive precisely how the Prince sought to discredit them; but they had an instinctive feeling that there was danger. Admittedly, they came to the interview with no great desire for office.[1] As it happened, if they had been less cautious they would have won their victory; for an acceptance of Moira's offer would have turned the tables upon him and given them all that they required. Moreover, the mass of the party again condemned the action of its leaders, and to all appearance had a good deal of justice on its side.[2] But the ordinary Whig of the rank and file did not know the Prince as his leaders did, and could therefore look at the situation with eyes unclouded by fears and suspicions. Nor was he so averse from the labours of office as his leaders were.[3] On the constitutional point, Grey and Grenville were of course on the side of posterity.

Sheridan's reputation, in the matter that so pained his first biographer, must be pronounced nearly rehabilitated.

[1] Holland, op. cit. p. 142. The question of the premiership troubled them.

[2] Sydney Smith (Letters, p. 94) wrote: " I dare say Lords Grey and Grenville meant extremely well, but they have bungled the matter so, as to put themselves in the wrong, both with the public and with their own troops. The bad faith of the Court is nothing. If they had suspected that bad faith, they should have put it to the proof, and made it clear to all the world that the Court did not mean them well; at present they have made the Court the subject of public love and compassion; made Lord Yarmouth appear like a virtuous man; given character to the Prince; and restored the dilapidation of Kingly power."

[3] E.g. Grey to Grenville, 15 May: " If we peremptorily reject a proposition made upon the ground of conceding the Catholic question, I am afraid most of our friends would think us in the wrong. Yet this is the course to which I most incline...." Dropmore Papers, x. 251; Court of Regency, i. 350; Supplementary Despatches, vii. 282.

Some faint odour of *suppressio veri* and *suggestio falsi* may perhaps still cling to him, but he is at least purged of deliberate falsehood. His conversation with Tierney took place on 5 June, at the very moment when Moira was forming his Government on a Tory basis.[1] It was strictly accurate to say that there was at that moment no prospect of the Household's resignation: the contingency upon which such a resignation depended was indeed farther off than ever. If he had reported Yarmouth's conversation, it would have made no difference; for the Whigs would still have found Moira quixotically defending Yarmouth's office and the Prince's feelings, so that unless they had maintained rigid silence upon the topic a clash could hardly have been avoided.

From 12 May to 8 June there had been a continuous Ministerial crisis. On 21 May Liverpool's attempt to carry on Perceval's Government had been damned by the House of Commons. On 8 June the same Government came quietly into office, and continued there undisturbed with a comfortable majority normally at its command.

Thus an address moved by a partisan of Mr. Canning, and carried by the assistance of the Whigs, for the purpose of forcing either or both into the Cabinet, terminated in riveting those against whom it was directed more securely than ever in power, and procuring a share in it to the only parliamentary faction [*sc.* the Sidmouths] which had concurred in resisting the motion.[2]

For this extraordinary result the Prince was directly responsible. He completely realized the objects with which he faced the situation. He pursued a policy of calculated inactivity to the brink of a financial crisis. He lured the Whigs into a false position, so that they seemed to be unwilling to abandon trivialities in a national emergency. He

---

[1] It is clear, from *Parl. Deb.* xxiii. 615 and from Grey Bennet's Diary (cited by Fitzgerald, *George IV*, ii. 103), that 5 June was the day of the bet, and not, as appears from Tierney's speech (*Parl. Deb.* xxiii. 456), 11 June.   [2] Holland, *Further Memoirs*, p. 147.

used Wellesley and Moira as his tools, and gently discarded
them when they no longer served him. And in the end he
retained a Government based upon his own *laissez-faire*
policy towards the Catholics, and upon a prosecution of the
war as vigorous as Wellesley's, and at least as successful.
Best of all, he drew from the unpopularity of the Whigs
with the country at large some of the support which the
Regency so sorely needed.[1] It was a piece of political
dexterity of which his father need not have been ashamed.

In three years the Whigs had had four offers of a
share in the Government. That of 1809 they should have
accepted ; that of February 1812 was an insult ; those of
June 1812 were dubious. The war and the Catholics provided them always with a solid background of principle
for their most unreasonable cavils, as well as for their
justifiable refusals. If the party had been less obviously in
a state of flux, their courage might have been equal to the
adventure of office. Their rivals were brave enough to act and
blunder, and to stand their punishment afterwards ; and
in Ministerial emoluments they reaped their reward. In
1812 the position of 1807 had come round again, with this
difference, that the Tories had not five, but fifteen years
of office before them. The heats and agitations of the
Commons and the Cabinet-makers had subsided, leaving
the surface of politics as though they had never been.
Henceforward,

> The ritual of each party is rehearsed,
> Dislodging not one vote or prejudice ;
> The Ministers their Ministries retain,
> And Ins as Ins, and Outs as Outs, remain.[2]

[1] Horner, ii. 113 ; *Court of Regency*, i. 380 ; *Bath Archives*, i. 386 ;
Letters to " Ivy ", p. 158 ; *Letter to Lords Grey and Grenville*, p. 24 :
" Like two spoiled children, you were fond of a certain rattle, and that
you must have before you could be pleased ".

> " You'ld save the nation if you could,
> But damn it if another should " (*ibid.* p. 18).

[2] Hardy, *The Dynasts*, I. 1. iv.

APPENDIX A

SIR ARTHUR WELLESLEY'S VIEWS ON THE VETO

[Add. MS. 38079.]

[This manuscript belonged to J. W. Croker, and seems to have been suggestions for a pamphlet to be written by him. It was probably produced in June 1808. On the fly-leaf is a pencil memorandum by Croker as follows : " This is a memorandum written for me by the Duke of Wellington when he was Secretary in Ireland about 1807 on the Catholic question. Some one for mere mischief or to get an autograph has torn away the first leaf."]

. . . The pamphlet should set out with the profession of stating facts and defining principles in answer to the torrent of falsehood and misrepresentation which have gone abroad upon this question.

The proposition of Grattan and of Lord Grenville as stated to the Houses of Lords and Commons should then be extracted from the parliamentary reporters [*sic*] of the day ; and in order to avoid to embarrass the subsequent discussion of the question by involving it in the *Milnerian* controversy it should be taken for granted and avowedly so for the purposes of argument that Lord Grenville and Grattan were authorized by Milner or other competent authority to state what they did. It must then be shewn that the proposition of Lord Grenville etc. could go to no more than to signify the assent of the Roman Catholics of Ireland to the adoption of the measure proposed, as far as they had any concern in or any power over it.

First neither the Roman Catholic clergy or laity had any right to grant to His Majesty this power of appointing or of negativing the appointment of Bishops. Admitting that there exists by law in Ireland such an office as that of Roman Catholic bishop, the appointment of the person to fill the office according to the known rules of the Roman Catholic church acknowledged by the Catholics themselves is in His Holiness the Pope. The arrangement then by which the power to be conferred on His Majesty must be carried into effect must be settled by the Pope, and can be settled by no other power whatever.

But secondly before His Majesty can take this power of appointing or of negativing the appointment by others of the Roman Catholic Bishops in Ireland it is necessary to give to the Bishops and to the Roman Catholic clergy in Ireland a legal establishment and legal powers. These powers ought to be technically defined ; and it ought to be shewn that although the exercise of the Roman Catholic religion is tolerated in Ireland, and the Bishops and clergy exercise a spiritual power, they have no power and no existence in the eye of the law. The first question therefore with His Majesty and his government would be not whether he should receive from the Pope a great additional patronage, not whether he should hold in his hands the " last symbol of the independence of Ireland " (in the words of Trotter's pamphlet) but whether he should give to the Roman Catholic religion in Ireland not only toleration but legal establishment.

It must be observed that if this question is not decided in the first instance, the power vested in the Crown in whatever manner obtained whether by concession from the Pope or by the consent of the Roman Catholics of Ireland themselves would be not only illegal, as it would be to appoint a person to fill an office, the existence of which the law did not recognize, but it would be nugatory.

This might be proved by showing that after three persons should have been presented to His Majesty of whom he should have chosen one to be the Bishop there would exist no power of compelling the people to submit to his spiritual jurisdiction, and indeed he could have no spiritual jurisdiction in the eye of the law, till the law should establish the Roman Catholic religion in Ireland ; and it might likewise be shewn from Mr. Trotter's own letter that till this legal establishment should be made the people might and would reject the Bishop selected by His Majesty and would submit themselves to the jurisdiction of one appointed by themselves.

From this reasoning it may be concluded that the first step towards the adoption of the measure proposed by Lord Grenville and Mr. Grattan must be to give a legal establishment to the Roman Catholic religion in Ireland, and the second to obtain the consent of the Pope to grant to His Majesty His heirs and successors the powers with which those who made the proposition deemed it expedient to invest him.

Lastly it must be concluded that the Roman Catholics of Ireland themselves can have nothing to say to this transfer of the power of appointment excepting so far as that any power of this description would be difficult to exercise in Ireland, unless transferred to His Majesty with the consent of those more immediately interested in its exercise.

This is the general reasoning upon which the question should be placed. It might probably be stated in a different manner and order with advantage, but of this the writer of the pamphlet would be the best judge.

From these facts and this reasoning the folly and wickedness might be shown of arguing this question as one of Irish independence. It might be stated that the liberties and independence of the people of Ireland depend upon the existence of similar checks and controls on the exercise of the executive power with those existing in Great Britain and other countries for the same purposes; and they do exist in Ireland in as strong a degree as in any other country.

It has been considered desirable in every country to free the executive power from the exercise of the power of the Pope; as the first step towards establishing the independence of that country from foreign domination, and the freedom of the people. But in Ireland it appears by this jumble of argument and sense that to free the country from all interference on the part of any foreign power, and to place all power which must be exercised by a Chief Magistrate, in the hands of the lawful King of the country, is an invasion of liberty and independence, and as such to be resisted; and this contrary to the example and practice of every other country in Europe.

The ordinary checks and controuls established in different countries upon the executive government with a view to the preservation of the independence of the country and the liberties of the people, should be enumerated; and their effect should be pointed out. It should be shewn that the continuance of the existence of an establishment not known to the law, the individuals comprising which are appointed by a foreign power, cannot tend to the preservation of the independence of the country or of the freedom of its inheritance.

The question whether His Majesty shall have any concern in the appointment of the Roman Catholic bishops and clergy is one of a spiritual nature as far as regards His Holiness the Pope, and as far as the Roman Catholics of Ireland can be supposed to have any particular concern in it; and it is one of a political nature to

His Majesty and the parliament of the United Kingdom. But it can never be stated to be one of independence to the Irish people for any purpose excepting that of exciting discontent, and clamour. In order to effect this object more completely, an attack is made upon the character of Dr. Milner, who is warned to keep clear of ecclesiastical questions affecting the Roman Catholics of Ireland. As a clergyman of that persuasion Dr. Milner may be supposed to be of the highest authority and as zealous in the cause as the most zealous would wish him to be. But as an Englishman suspicion must be cast upon his opinions and interference, and in order to diminish his authority upon the question, it must be stated not as one of an ecclesiastical nature, but as one of Irish independence.

APPENDIX B

DOCUMENTS RELATING TO THE NEGOTIATION OF LORD MOIRA, JUNE, 1812

I

SHERIDAN TO THE PRINCE REGENT, 1 JUNE. [EXTRACT]

I should think myself deficient in the respect and duty I owe to you were I to close this day without conveying to your Royal Highness in a few words my humble congratulations on the wisdom and magnanimity of the part you have taken in giving to Lord Wellesley the powers with which you have invested him this morning.—At the same time I should be insincere if I attempted to dissemble the deep regret I have felt at an apparent alteration in your manner towards me—produced solely I must believe by my expressing an opinion that a proscription of Lord Grey in the formation of a new administration would be a proceeding equally injurious to the estimation of your personal dignity and the maintenance of the public interests.

Long indulgence, Sir, on your part, in allowing me to speak the truth to you leads me not to hesitate, or consider it as presumptuous to say that you grievously wrong'd me if you supposed I ventured to press this my opinion on you from any undue partiality to the noble Lord in question or any of those with whom he is allied.—I have never profess'd or affected any such motive,—and with great submission I must express my surprise that your Royal Highness could for a moment have entertained this notion. My object was . . . founded on what I considered best for *your honor and your interest* and *the general good of the country.*

[Windsor Archives. George IV.] [1]

---

[1] Portions of this letter are printed in Moore, *Sheridan*, ii. 428. It is wrongly stated by Sichel (*Sheridan*, ii. 354) that no trace of the original remains.

II

ARBUTHNOT TO HUSKISSON [2 JUNE]

Confidential.

Dear H.——

  I don't call except when I see a chance of bringing old friends together.

  I wanted much to see you. This morning I was sent for to Carlton House, and was desired to communicate with Lord Moira as to the state of the House of Commons. I was shewn what had been received from Lord Wellesley, which the Prince looks upon as a refusal on the part of Opposition.

  The Prince intends now to give full authority to Lord Moira, and he was anxious that I should see you. The Prince feels that you and Canning will have been most anxious to protect him against the Opposition but of this and of other things we will talk. In the mean while consider this as confidential I pray of you.

[Add. MS. 38738, f. 236.]

III

LORD MOIRA TO McMAHON, 4 JUNE [1]

¼ past 11.

The Prince's injunction shall be strictly obeyed : and, indeed, all the steps which I am taking are calculated upon the decisive assumption that it is no longer of any use to look to the Opposition.

[Windsor Archives. George IV.]

IV

LORD MOIRA TO McMAHON, 4 JUNE

5 o'clock.

  I had not the good fortune to find the Chancellor at home, but I shall try to fix an interview with him.

  Enclosed, you have Lord Wellesley's final decision. I was with him this morning, and he was in good humour, tho' I could not gain

---

[1] Wrongly placed in 1811 at Windsor. This date is impossible because McMahon is addressed as " The Right Honourable ", and he was not made a Privy Councillor until 20 March 1812.

upon him. I have an answer from Lord Grey, resting entirely upon his former objections. It is clear that they do not mean to accept any terms whatever. The only point to be determined is, whether one should take from them the last shadow of excuse which they might attempt in saying that *I* had made no overture to them ; my letter being to be considered as an explanation of a matter already defunct. The expedience of this, as a ground for detaching many partisans of the Opposition, must be canvassed with Lord Melville and Canning. I shall see them immediately.

[Windsor Archives. George IV.]

V

McMahon to the Prince Regent, 4 June

½ past nine o'clock.

I have the honour to send Your Royal Highness, four distinct letters, which will better serve to explain, than anything I could otherwise detail, the political operations of this day. In suggesting to Lord Moira the essential propriety, and advantage of his *immediately* communicating with the Lord Chancellor, Your Royal Highness will find an answer in his Lordship's note to me of this evening, bearing date '5 o'clock', [*i.e.* No. IV, above] covering Lord Wellesley's final letter. Lord Wellesley had, however, at their meeting in the morning, when he equally declined any component part in the new administration, nevertheless, offered his best interposition with Mr. Canning to enter into office, but I own, I cannot with any share of confidence, subscribe to the sincerity of this profession, when I read Mr. Canning's letter of late this evening to Lord Moira, as written subsequent to his interview with Lord Wellesley, and his Lordship's proffered mediation being antecedent to such interview, for Canning's letter to Lord Moira, bears no evidence of any such disposition on the part of Lord Wellesley. Erskine's letter, goes certainly to establish, that Lord Moira's letter to Lord Grey of yesterday, was no *renewal* of overture to the opposition, and only a mere individual correspondence.

Mr. Ponsonby held to-day at one o'clock a numerous meeting of the Opposition, where I learn that nothing more passed than in reading them the correspondence between Lord Wellesley and the Lords Grey and Grenville, and without deciding on any specific course of proceeding.[1] The general and prevailing sentiment, I have understood everywhere today, is an abhorrence of the factious and intollerant views of an obnoxious Opposition.

[Windsor Archives. George IV.]

VI

LORD MOIRA TO THE PRINCE REGENT, 5 JUNE. [EXTRACT]

7 o'clock.

[Gives an account of Moira's speech in the Lords that afternoon.] The paper of which the enclosed is a copy was carried by the Duke of Bedford to Lord Grey, who told Lord Moira in the House that an answer should be immediately sent.[2] Lord Moira anticipates that they will decline the interview. In that event, Mr. Canning and Mr. Huskisson have professed their readiness to take office.

[Windsor Archives. George IV.]

VII

LORD MOIRA TO THE PRINCE REGENT, 5 JUNE. [EXTRACT]

Half past eleven P.M. [*i.e.* after receiving Grey and Grenville's refusal to participate in informal discussions].

Lord Moira, that nothing may be left indistinct, most respectfully entreats your Royal Highness's permission to propose a meeting with Lords Grey and Grenville, tho' their obvious endeavours to evade a conclusive discussion leaves scarcely a hope of any efficient result from the interview. [Windsor Archives. George IV.]

VIII

LORD MOIRA TO HUSKISSON, 6 JUNE

My dear Sir. ½ past 5.

The business is but just closed. They have broken off on the

---

[1] There was a similar conference of peers. Lord Byron, turning to the Duke of Grafton, enquired, " What is to be done next ? " " Wake the Duke of Norfolk ", said he, " I don't think the negotiators have left anything else for us to do this turn." Byron, *Letters and Journals*, i. 263.

[2] This answer is printed in *Parl. Deb.* xxiii. App. xxxix, No. XXVI.

Household. Can you and Mr. Canning call on me at ten this evening ?   [Add. MS. 38738, f. 245.]

IX

LORD MOIRA TO HUSKISSON, 7 JUNE. [EXTRACT]

Lord Eldon and Lord Liverpool complained to a friend that we had not had the politeness to ask for the support of their party tho' they were disposed to give it handsomely without sharing in government with us. This little point of honour must be gratified, and I said that Mr. Canning and I would call at Lord Liverpool's about half past nine tonight.   [Add. MS. 38738, f. 247.]

X

LORD MOIRA TO MCMAHON, 7 JUNE

3 o'clock.

Lord Liverpool, tho' he answers that he cannot come into office *at present* without fallaciously misconstruing the terms of our pledge for considering the Catholic Question, has promised his most zealous support. He is much flattered by the way in which we have addressed him.   [Windsor Archives. George IV.]

XI

MEMORANDUM INTENDED FOR LORD MOIRA, [8] JUNE 1812
[IN HUSKISSON'S HANDWRITING]

1. If the attempt to form an Administration is to be persevered in it is absolutely indispensable that the basis of it should be settled before the two Houses meet this day [*i.e.* Monday, 8 June].
2. The means of forming an administration are so circumscribed that there is no chance of success, if every part of those means is not distributed in the manner which, upon a first consideration, appears to be best calculated to afford solidity and efficiency to the whole frame.
3°. Lord Wellesley may be prevailed upon to go to Ireland ; but he will not accept any other situation and on his acceptance will depend the decision of Mr. W. Pole.

4°. Mr. Huskisson is not to be shaken from his resolution of not taking the Chancellorship of the Exchequer, from a firm conviction that the interests of the Government cannot be adequately maintained in the House of Commons, especially at this moment, unless this office, united to that of first Lord of the Treasury is held by the person who leads the House.

5°. In this state of things, will Lord Moira undertake the Home Department with the portefeuille and station of Premier, as explained and understood to be agreed to at a former interview ?—If he will the basis of an administration may be settled almost immediately.* If Lord Moira does not approve of this proposal for himself, and the outline of the Cabinet as sketched in the margin (or something not materially different), there is, in my opinion, no chance of forming an Administration.

6°. In that case not a moment should be lost in apprizing the Regent of the difficulties which have occurred to disappoint Lord Moira's hopes of success ; in order that H.R.H. may be enabled to decide upon the course to be taken to meet the difficulties of his situation and to direct some person to make a communication to the House in the course of the evening.

7°. If, on the other hand, what is here suggested should meet with Lord Moira's concurrence, and when submitted by him to the Regent, with H.R.H.'s approbation, I should feel a confident expectation that the new Administration would be enabled to struggle with the difficulties of the present moment ; to bring the present session successfully to a close ; and to acquire strength both in numbers and in accession of official talents, before the opening of the next.

8°. With a view to this latter object, the frame of the government would be such as to admit of such accessions without any dangerous dislocation of its most essential parts.

9°. It might be understood by Lord Eldon that some arrangement of his office would be made at the end of the session, so as to provide some means of getting rid of the arrears in the Court

* Lord Wellesley—Ireland ; Mr. Canning—Chancellor of Exchequer and First Lord, and the Lead in the House of Commons ; Lord Moira, Home Department, with Portefeuille, and to lead the House of Lords. Mr. W. Pole—War Department ; Lord G. Leveson Gower—Foreign ; Lord Eldon—to remain ? Lord Melville—Admiralty.

[Marginal note attached to Memorandum.]

of Chancery; and that this arrangement should if possible be such as to bring Sir W. Grant into the Cabinet with a seat in the House of Lords.

Lord Castlereagh to be proposed to go up to the Lords and to take office, not immediately but before the opening of next session.

I have not mentioned the President of the Council, and the Privy Seal. There can be no doubt that proper persons may be found to hold these offices; if the efficient offices can be arranged. Neither would there be any difficulty with respect to the Ordnance or the India Board, neither of which need be in the Cabinet.

[Add. MS. 38738, f. 257.]

XII

Lord Moira to McMahon, 14 June

All argument with Sheridan (and I have used to the utmost of his patience whatever could be urged) has been unavailing. This much, however, I have gained; that I have made him limit definitely the substance of what he is to address to the House. The amount is this. He will assert that he never gave to the Regent any secret council on the subject of the negotiation; and he will declare that what Lord Yarmouth said to him respecting the projected resignation of the Hertford family was not communicated in any manner which should make it incumbent on him (Sheridan) to impart the determination to Lords Grey and Grenville directly or thro' me. If he keep to this I think no harm will be done; and I think he will be precise to the point, as I understand Whitbread concurs with him and is keen to vindicate his own judgement by showing how the Opposition have erred in all their constructions. Do not think that I have pressed the Prince's wishes feebly. I insisted on them till Sheridan became absolutely violent. It is on Wednesday he is to make the motion, which will be in itself of some nugatory nature and only framed to let in the explanation. He means previously to ask an audience of the Prince. I do not think it will be possible for His Royal Highness to gain on Sheridan's resolution, and all that can be effected I apprehend, will be the binding him strictly to the line which I have described.

[Windsor Archives. George IV.]

XIII

Sheridan to McMahon [16 June]

My dear McMahon.

Unquestionably I shall obey the Prince's commands by waiting on him tomorrow at the time he is pleased to command—but I am really so ill that I have not left my bed today but to receive Ld. Yarmouth for an hour tonight—between whom and myself there remains, not a shade of difference[1] and further I do most humbly hope and implore that His Royal Highness would press no more that I should submit to the attacks so foully leveld at me and forfeit my pledge to vindicate myself. To act [so] would render me the most disgraced and dishonour'd man living and I could never show my face again. Surely surely my dear Friend I may be trusted with the discretion that my devotion to the Prince will guide me thro' the whole of the *very little* I shall have to state and that I shall not utter one word that will not be in maintenance of his honour.—I am aware of the points he dislikes my touching on and of my anticipating part of the Lords' debate, not one word that I shall utter can lead to any such result. Pray let me have another line. Upon my honor I can scarcely hold the pen I am scrawling with.

Ever faithfully yours

R. B. Sheridan.

I mean a line graciously dispensing with my attendance tomorrow.

[Windsor Archives. George IV.]

---

[1] H. G. Bennet, who had seen a correspondence between Sheridan and Yarmouth on this matter, confirms this statement. Cited by Fitzgerald, *Lives of the Sheridans*, ii. 178.

BIBLIOGRAPHY

A. *Manuscript Material*

(1) At Windsor :
    Correspondence of George III.
    Correspondence of George III (Private).
    Correspondence of the Prince of Wales.
    Correspondence of the Prince Regent.
    Correspondence of Queen Charlotte.
    Papers of Sir William Knighton.

(2) In the possession of Brig.-Gen. W. Madocks :
    The Papers of George Tierney (unfoliated).

(3) In the National Library of Wales, Aberystwyth :
    The Williams Wynn Papers. MS. 2791 (unfoliated).
                        MS. 4814.

(4) In the Dr. Williams Library, London :
    Reminiscences of Henry Crabb Robinson.
    Letters of Henry Crabb Robinson.
    Diary of Henry Crabb Robinson (in typescript).

(5) In the British Museum :

The Auckland Papers.	Add. MSS.	34457, 34458.
The Broughton Papers.	,,	36456.
The Hardwicke Papers.	,,	35394, 35646-9, 35424.
The Leigh Hunt Papers.	,,	38108-11, 38523.
The Huskisson Papers.	,,	38737-9, 38759-60, 39948.
The Liverpool Papers.	,,	38191-3, 38242-8, 38320-2, 38324, 38378, 38458, 38473.
The Place Papers.	,,	29475, 27839.
The Redesdale Papers.	,,	36650-1.
The Wellesley Papers.	,,	37286-8, 37295-7, 37309-10.
The Sir Robert Wilson Papers.	,,	30099, 30105-6, 30115, 30118-21, 30136-7.
The Windham Papers.	,,	37842, 37846-9, 37886-8, 37906-9.

    Miscellaneous Add. MSS. 34079 ; 34472 ; 34545 ; 36524 ; 38079 (Wellington's notes on the Veto). 38833 (Canning's correspondence with Frere).

Note.—Several important MS. collections were, it appeared, not open to inspection. Thus it was impossible to see the papers of Lord Grey, or of Lord Rosslyn, or the Holland House Papers in the possession of Lord Ilchester. It was, moreover, disappointing to find that no MSS. existed in many cases where a rich source might have been expected. Thus there are no Whitbread MSS., no Ponsonby MSS. and no Lansdowne MSS. bearing upon this period. Still more lamentable is the disappearance of the MS. Diary of Henry Grey Bennet, which was in existence towards the end of the last century, and was used by Torrens and Fitzgerald in their works. Careful enquiry among all known descendants of Bennet makes it probable that the Diary was not in the possession of the family when Torrens used it.

B. *Newspapers and Periodicals*

The following were used *in extenso* :

    The Annual Register.
    Cobbett's Political Register.
    The Examiner.
    The Reflector.
    The Edinburgh Review.
    The Morning Chronicle.
    The Independent Whig.

Occasional reference was made also to the following :

    The Alfred, or Westminster Gazette.
    The Day.
    The Morning Post.
    The Courier.
    The Quarterly.
    The Pamphleteer.
    The Statesman.
    The Sun.
    The Sunday Review.
    The Times.

C. *Printed Collections of Documents, and Works containing a High Proportion of Original Material*

ALTHORP. Memoirs of Lord Althorp. By Sir Denis Le Marchant. London, 1876.

AUCKLAND. The Journal and Correspondence of William, Lord Auckland. Vol. IV. London, 1862.

The Barnard Letters, 1778–1884. Edited by Anthony Powell. London, 1928.

BENTHAM, JEREMY. Works. Edited by John Bowring. Vols. III., V., X. Edinburgh, 1843.

The Berry Papers, *etc.* Edited by Lewis Melville. London, 1914.

BLAND BURGES. Selections from the Letters and Correspondence of Sir James Bland Burges, Bt., *etc.* Edited by James Hutton. London, 1885.

BROUGHAM, HENRY. Works. Edinburgh, 1872.

    The Life and Times of Henry Lord Brougham. Written by himself. Edinburgh, 1871.

    Brougham and his Early Friends. Letters . . . 1798–1809. Edited by R. H. M. B. Atkinson and G. A. Jackson. Privately printed. London, 1908.

BUCKINGHAM AND CHANDOS, DUKE OF. Memoirs of the Court and Cabinets of George III, from original family documents. Vol. IV. London, 1855.

Memoirs of the Court of England during the Regency. London, 1856.

BURGHERSH, LORD. Correspondence of Lord Burghersh . . . 1808–1840. Edited by Rachel Weigall. London, 1912.

BURY, LADY CHARLOTTE. The Diary of a Lady in Waiting, *etc.* Edited by A. F. Steuart. London, 1908.

BUTLER, CHARLES. Historical Memoirs respecting the English, Irish, and Scottish Catholics, from the Reformation to the Present Time. London, 1819.

Additions to the Historical Memoirs respecting the English, Irish, and Scottish Catholics. London, 1821.

BYRON, LORD. Letters and Journals of Lord Byron, *etc.* Edited by Thomas Moore. London, 1830.

Lord Byron's Correspondence. Edited by John Murray. London, 1922.

CAMPBELL, THOMAS. The Life and Letters of Thomas Campbell. Edited by W. Beattie. London, 1849.

CANNING, GEORGE. George Canning and his Friends, *etc.* Edited by J. Bagot. London, 1909.

CARTWRIGHT, MAJOR. Life and Correspondence. London, 1826.

CASTLEREAGH, LORD. Memoirs and Correspondence. Edited by Lord Londonderry. London, 1848–1853.

CLARKE, MARY ANNE. The Rival Princes, or a Faithful Narration of Facts. London, 1810.

COBBETT, WILLIAM. The Life and Letters of William Cobbett, *etc.* Edited by Lewis Melville. London, 1913.

COKE, THOMAS. Coke of Norfolk and his Friends. By A. M. W. Sterling. London, 1908.

COLCHESTER, LORD. The Diary and Correspondence of Charles Abbott, Lord Colchester. Edited by his son. London, 1861.

COLERIDGE, S. T. Essays on his own Times, *etc.* Edited by his daughter. London, 1850.

COMBERMERE, LORD. Memoirs and Correspondence of Field-Marshal Viscount Combermere. By Mary, Viscountess Combermere, and Capt. W. W. Knollys. London, 1866.

The Creevey Papers. Edited by Sir H. Maxwell. London, 1905. [One vol. edn.]

Creevey's Life and Times. Edited by John Gore. London, 1934.

CROKER, J. W. The Correspondence and Diaries of John William Croker, edited by L. J. Jennings. London, 1885.

DENMAN, LORD. Memoir of Thomas, first Lord Denman. London, 1873.

Diaries of a Lady of Quality from 1797 to 1844. Edited by A. Hayward. London, 1864.

DUDLEY, EARL OF. Letters of the Earl of Dudley to the Bishop of Llandaff. London, 1840.

DUNDONALD, THOMAS, 10TH EARL OF [*i.e.* Lord Cochrane]. The Autobiography of a Seaman. London, 1860.

ELDON, LORD. The Public and Private Life of Lord Chancellor Eldon, by H. Twiss. London, 1844.

The Farington Diary. Edited by J. Greig. Vol. VII. London, 1925.

FLETCHER, MRS. Autobiography. Edinburgh, 1875.

The Francis Letters. Edited by B. Francis and C. F. Keary. London, n.d.

GLENBERVIE, LORD. The Diaries of Lord Glenbervie. Edited by F. Bickley. London, 1928.

GORDON, PRYSE L. Personal Memoirs, *etc.* London, 1830.

GRANVILLE, COUNTESS. Letters of Harriet Countess Granville, 1810–1845. Edited by F. Leveson Gower. London, 1894.

GRATTAN, HENRY. Memoirs of the Life and Times of the Rt. Hon. Henry Grattan. By his son, Henry Grattan. Vol. V. London, 1849.

GREY, EARL. Life and Opinions of Charles, 2nd Earl Grey. By C. Grey. London, 1861.

The Hamwood Papers of the Ladies of Llangollen and of Caroline Hamilton. Edited by E. M. Bell. London, 1930.

The Harcourt Papers. Edited by E. W. Harcourt. Privately printed. Oxford, 1880–1905.

HAZLITT, W. Works. Edited by P. P. Howe. London, 1930–1934.

HERRIES, J. C. Memoir of the public life of the Rt. Hon. John Charles Herries. By E. Herries. Vol. I. London, 1880.

Historical Manuscripts Commission. Report on MSS. of Earl Bathurst, 1913.
J. B. Fortescue (Vols. IX. and X.), 1915.
R. R. Hastings (Vol. III.), 1934.
Laing (Vol. II.), 1925.
Lord Lonsdale, 1893.
Col. Milne Home, 1902.
C. Wykeham-Martin (in Various Collections, Vol. VI.), 1909.

HOLLAND, LADY. The Journals of Elizabeth Lady Holland. Edited by the Earl of Ilchester. London, 1908.

The Spanish Journals of Elizabeth Lady Holland. Edited by the Earl of Ilchester. London, 1910.

HOLLAND, LORD. Memoirs of the Whig Party during my Time. Edited by his son. Vol. II. London, 1854.

Further Memoirs of the Whig Party, 1807–1821, *etc.* Edited by Lord Stavordale. London, 1905.

HORNER, FRANCIS. Memoirs and Correspondence of Francis Horner. London, 1843.

HUNT, J. LEIGH. Autobiography. [Revised edition.] London, 1860.
Correspondence. Edited by his eldest son. London, 1862.

The Huskisson Papers. Edited by Lewis Melville. London, 1931.

JACKSON, SIR GEORGE. The Diaries and Letters of Sir George Jackson. Edited by Lady Jackson. London, 1872.

The Bath Archives. A further Selection from the Diaries and Letters of Sir George Jackson ... 1809 to 1816. Edited by Lady Jackson. London, 1873.

JEBB, JOHN. Thirty Years' Correspondence between John Jebb and Alexander Knox. Edited by the Rev. C. Forster. London, 1834.

JEFFREY, LORD. Life of Lord Jeffrey. By Lord Cockburn. Edinburgh, 1852.

JERNINGHAM, EDWARD. Edward Jerningham and his Friends. Edited by Lewis Bettany. London, 1919.

The Jerningham Letters, *etc.* Edited by Egerton Castle. London, 1896.

KNIGHT, CORNELIA. Autobiography, *etc.* London, 1861.

KNIGHTON, SIR WILLIAM. Memoirs. Edited by Lady Knighton. London, 1838.

LENNOX, LADY SARAH. The Life and Letters of Lady Sarah Lennox. Edited by the Countess of Ilchester and Lord Stavordale. London, 1901.

Letters of the Lake Poets . . . to Daniel Stuart. Privately printed. London, 1889.

LEVESON GOWER, LORD GRANVILLE. Private Correspondence, 1781–1821. Edited by Castalia Countess Granville. London, 1916.

LEWIS, M. G. Life and Correspondence. London, 1839.

LIVERPOOL, EARL OF. Memoirs of the Public Life and Administration of the Rt. Hon. the Earl of Liverpool. London, 1827.

Life of Lord Liverpool, by C. D. Yonge. London, 1868.

LYTTELTON, LADY. Correspondence of Sarah Spencer, Lady Lyttelton. Edited by the Hon. Mrs. Hugh Wyndham. London, 1912.

MACAULAY, ZACHARY. The Life and Letters of Zachary Macaulay. By his grand-daughter, Viscountess Knutsford. London, 1900.

MACKINTOSH, SIR JAMES. Memoirs of the Life of the Rt. Hon. Sir James Mackintosh. Edited by R. J. Mackintosh. Boston, 1853.

MALMESBURY, EARL OF. Diaries and Correspondence of James Harris, 1st Earl of Malmesbury. Edited by his grandson, the 3rd Earl. Vol. IV. London, 1844.

A Series of Letters of the 1st Earl of Malmesbury, his family, and friends, from 1745 to 1820. Edited by his grandson. Vol. II. London, 1870.

MELBOURNE, LORD. Memoirs of the Rt. Hon. William, 2nd Lord Melbourne. Edited by W. Torrens. London, 1878.

Lord Melbourne's Papers. Edited by L. C. Saunders. London, 1889.

MILES, W. A. Correspondence . . . 1789–1817. London, 1890.

MOORE, JAMES. A Narrative of the Campaign of the British Army in Spain. London, 1809.

MOORE, THOMAS. Memoirs, Journal and Correspondence. Edited by Lord John Russell. London, 1853–1854.

The Paget Papers. Diplomatic and other Correspondence of the Rt. Hon. Sir Arthur Paget, 1794–1807. Edited by Sir A. B. Paget. Vol. II. London 1896.

PALMERSTON, LORD. The Life of Henry John Temple, Viscount Palmerston. By Sir H. Lytton Bulwer. Vol. I. London, 1870.

The Parliamentary Debates ; first series. [Published until 1812 by Cobbett ; thereafter by Hansard.]

PEEL, SIR ROBERT. Sir Robert Peel . . . From his private correspondence. . . . Edited by C. S. Parker. London, 1891.

PEPYS, SIR W. W. A Later Pepys, etc. Edited by A. C. C. Gaussen. London, 1904.

PERCEVAL, SPENCER. The Life of the Rt. Hon. Spencer Perceval . . . by his grandson. London, 1874.

PLOWDEN, FRANCIS. The History of Ireland . . . 1801–1810. Vols. II and III. London, 1811.

PLUNKET, LORD. The Life, Letters and Speeches of Lord Plunket. By his grandson, the Hon. David Plunket. London, 1867.

ROBINSON, HENRY CRABB. Diary, Reminiscences and Correspondence. Edited by T. Sadler. London, 1869.

The Correspondence of Henry Crabb Robinson with the Wordsworth Circle, 1808–1866. Edited by E. J. Morley. Oxford, 1927.

ROGERS, J. T. Protests of the Lords. Vol. II. Oxford, 1875.

ROMILLY, SAMUEL. Memoirs of the Life of Sir Samuel Romilly, written by himself. . . . Edited by his sons. London, 1840.

Rose, George. The Diaries and Correspondence. Edited by L. V. Harcourt. London, 1860.

Russell, Lord John. Early Correspondence of Lord John Russell, 1805–1840. Edited by Rollo Russell. Vol. I. London, 1913.

Selections from Speeches of Earl Russell 1817–41 and Despatches 1859–69; with Introductions. London, 1870.

St. Vincent, Earl. Life and Correspondence of John, Earl of St. Vincent. By E. P. Brenton. London, 1838.

Saumarez, Lord de. Memoirs and Correspondence of Admiral Lord de Saumarez. Edited by Sir John Ross. London, 1838.

Scott, Sir Walter. The Letters of Sir Walter Scott. Edited by H. J. C. Grierson. London, 1932.

Shelley, P. B. Prose Works. Edited by H. Buxton Forman. London, n.d.

Sheridan, R. B. Memoirs of the Life of the Rt. Hon. Richard Brinsley Sheridan. By Thomas Moore. London, 1825.

Sidmouth, Lord. The Life and Correspondence of the Rt. Hon. Henry Addington, First Viscount Sidmouth. By G. Pellew. London, 1847.

Sinclair, Sir John. The Correspondence of the Rt. Hon. Sir John Sinclair. London, 1831.

Smith, Rev. Sydney.

Memoir of the Rev. Sydney Smith. By Lady Holland. With a selection from his letters, edited by Mrs. Austin. London, 1855.

The Letters of Peter Plymley. Edited by C. G. Heseltine. London, 1929.

Southey, R. Essays, Moral and Political. London, 1832.

Selections from the Letters. Edited by J. W. Warter. London, 1856.

Teignmouth, Lord. Memoir of the Life and Correspondence of John Lord Teignmouth. By Lord Teignmouth. London, 1843.

Ward, Bernard. The Eve of Catholic Emancipation. London, 1911.

Ward, J. W. Letters to Ivy from the First Earl of Dudley. Edited by S. H. Romilly. London, 1905.

Ward, R. Plumer. Memoirs. Edited by E. Phipps. London, 1850.

Warre, Sir W. Letters from the Peninsula, 1808–12. Edited by E. Warre. London, 1909.

Wellesley, Marquess. Memoirs and Correspondence of . . . Richard . . . Marquess of Wellesley. Edited by R. R. Pearce. London, 1846.

The Wellesley Papers. London, 1914.

The Marquess Wellesley. By W. M. Torrens. London, 1880.

Wellington, Duke of. Civil Correspondence and Memoranda. Ireland. Edited by his son. London, 1860. (Vol. V of Supplementary Despatches; see below.)

The Despatches . . . during his Various Campaigns. Edited by Lieut.-Col. Gurwood. Vols. IV-VII. London, 1835–1837.

Supplementary Despatches, Correspondence and Memoranda. Edited by his son. Vols. V-VII. London, 1840.

Whishaw, John. The " Pope " of Holland House. Selections from the Correspondence of John Whishaw and his Friends. 1813–1840. Edited and annotated by Lady Seymour. London, 1906.

Whittingham, Sir " Samford ". A Memoir of the Services of Lieut.-Gen. Sir Samuel Ford Whittingham. Edited by Major-Gen. Ferdinand Whittingham. London, 1868.

WILBERFORCE, WILLIAM. The Life of William Wilberforce. By his sons, R. I. and S. Wilberforce. London, 1838.

Private Papers of William Wilberforce. Collected and edited by A. M. Wilberforce. London, 1897.

The Correspondence of William Wilberforce. Edited by R. I. and S. Wilberforce. London, 1840.

WILLIAMS WYNN, LADY. Correspondence of Charlotte Grenville, Lady Williams Wynn. Edited by Rachel Leighton. London, 1920.

WILSON, SIR R. Private Diary . . . of . . . Sir Robert Wilson. Edited by H. Randolph. London, 1861.

WINDHAM, W. Diary of the Rt. Hon. William Windham. Edited by Mrs. H. Baring. London, 1866.

The Windham Papers; with an Introduction by the Rt. Hon. the Earl of Rosebery. London, 1913.

WORDSWORTH, W. Prose Works. Edited by A. B. Grosart. London, 1876.

Tract on the Convention of Cintra. Edited by A. V. Dicey. Oxford, 1915.

Letters of the Wordsworth Family. Edited by W. A Knight. Boston, 1907.

WYSE, THOMAS. Historical Sketch of the late Catholic Association of Ireland. London, 1829.

D. *Pamphlets*

"A.B." Six Letters on the Subject of Dr. Milner's Explanation. London, 1809.

An Account of the Proceedings of the Electors of . . . Southwark. On Wednesday the 12th April, 1809. London, 1809.

Adultery and Patriotism. By an Elector of Westminster. London, 1811.

[ALLEN, JOHN.] Letters of Scaevola. 2 vols. London, 1807.

All the Talents in Ireland ! A satirical poem, with notes. By Scrutator. London, 1807.

An Answer to " A Roman Catholic Bishop's Caveat against the Methodists ". By a Protestant. London, 1810.

An Answer to Lord Grenville's Letter to the Earl of Fingall . . . by a Fingalian. London, 1810.

An Answer to the Rt. Hon. P. Duigenan's two great arguments against full enfranchisement of the Irish Roman Catholics, by a member of the Establishment. Dublin, 1810.

An Appeal to the Nation by the Union for Parliamentary Reform according to the Constitution. London, 1812.

[BARNES, THOMAS.] Parliamentary Portraits. London, 1814.

BOWLES, JOHN. A Letter to Samuel Whitbread, Esq., M.P., in consequence of the Unqualified Approbation expressed by him, in the House of Commons, of Mr. Lancaster's system of education [etc.]. London, 1808.

" BRITANNICUS." Letter to Samuel Whitbread, upon the military conduct of Lord Wellington, etc. London, 1810.

BROUGHAM, HENRY. Speeches . . . together with an impartial account of the election. . . . Liverpool, 1813.

BURDETT, SIR F. A letter addressed to Sir Francis Burdett, by Crito the Euclidean. London, [1807].

BURDETT, SIR F. (contd.)—

An Exposition of the Circumstances which gave rise to the Election of Sir Francis Burdett, Bart., for the City of Westminster, etc. [By Francis Place.] London, 1807.

Speech . . . at the Crown and Anchor Tavern, July 31, 1810. London, 1810.

The Political Principles of Sir Francis Burdett exposed. London, 1810.

Speech . . . on 28 March, 1811. [On] the Practice of Ex-Officio Informations . . . in Cases of Libel. London, 1811.

[A Letter from Oxford.] Sir Francis Burdett to his constituents. An Address to the Electors of the City of Westminster. Oxford, 1812.

A Letter to Sir Francis Burdett, Bart., with a Criterion proposed to ascertain his Patriotism, and some Reflections on the Subject of Reform ; by a Country Gentleman. London, 1810.

The Plan of Reform proposed by Sir Francis Burdett. London, 1809.

Account of the Proceedings of the Electors of Westminster, on the Commitment of their Representative, Sir Francis Burdett, to the Tower, April 17, 1810. London, 1810.

The Red Book ; or the Government of Francis the First. By Cassandra Non-Reveur. London, 1807.

BURGOYNE, M. The Speech of M. B., Esq., of Mark Hall, to the freeholders of Essex. On Monday the 19th of October, 1812. Chelmsford, etc., 1811 [sic].

BURTON, MONTAGU. Letters by " Anglicus ". London, 1811.

BUTLER, CHARLES. Miscellaneous Tracts. London, 1812.

CARTWRIGHT, J. Address to the Freeholders of Lincolnshire. Boston, [Lincs], 1807.

Reasons for Reformation. London, 1809.

The Comparison : in which Mock Reform, Half Reform, and Constitutional Reform are considered, etc. London, 1810.

Six Letters to the Marquis of Tavistock on a Reform of the Commons House of Parliament, etc. London, 1812.

CHARMILLY, V. DE. Narrative of his Transactions in Spain. London, 1810.

CLINCH, J. BERNARD. An Inquiry, Legal and Political, into the Consequences of giving His Majesty a Negative. Dublin, 1808.

COBBETT, W. Elements of Reform, etc. London, 1809.

COKER, JOHN. Some Reflections on the Late Election of a Chancellor of the University of Oxford. Maidstone, 1809.

Letter to the Hon. Thomas Brand, upon the subject of Parliamentary Reform. London, 1811.

[COOKE, E.] Letters addressed to Lord Grenville and Lord Howick, etc. London, 1807.

A Correspondence between Richard Wilson, Esq. . . . the Rt. Hon. William Elliot, . . . and the Rt. Hon. George Ponsonby. Dublin, 1806.

CURWEN, J. C. Observations on the State of Ireland, etc. London, 1818.

DUIGENAN, P. The Nature and Extent of the Demands of the Irish Roman Catholics fully explained, etc. London, 1810.

ELRINGTON, REV. THOS. Reflections on the Appointment of Dr. Milner as the Political Agent of the Roman Catholic Clergy of Ireland. Dublin, 1809.

The Faction Detected and Despised. London, 1810.

FLECKIE, A. An Answer to the Argument of Sir Francis Burdett relative to the Power of the House of Commons to commit Persons not Members. London, 1810.

The French Spy : or, Five Original Letters found in the Bureau of a Foreigner. London, 1808.

GREEN, W. Portraits of Mr. Pitt and Mr. Fox, *etc*. London, 1808.

Portraits of the Late and Present Administration, *etc*. London, 1807.

GRENVILLE, LORD. Substance of the Speech delivered in the House of Lords, March 26, 1807, on the change of Ministry. London, 1807.

The State of the Case. Addressed to Lord Grenville and Lord Howick. London, 1807.

Letter from . . . Lord Grenville to the Earl of Fingall. London, 1810.

Letter to the Lords Grey and Grenville on their late conduct, *etc.* ; by a Plain Englishman. London, 1812.

Hints to J. Nollekens, Esq., R.A., on his modelling a Bust of Lord G*******e. London, 1808. [A political satire in verse. By J. Sayers.]

HAGUE, THOMAS. A Letter to the Duke of York on recent events, *etc*. London, 1808.

HIPPISLEY, SIR J. C. The Substance of Additional Observations, intended to have been delivered in the House of Commons in the Debate on the Petition of the Roman Catholics of Ireland, on the 13th and 14th of May, 1805. London, 1806.

Substance of the Speech of Sir John Coxe Hippisley, on seconding the Motion of the Rt. Hon. H. Grattan . . . Friday, 18th May, 1810. London, 1810.

HOGAN, MAJOR DENIS. An Appeal to the Public and a Farewell Address to the Army. London, 1808.

HUNT, LEIGH. The Reformist's Answer to the Article entitled " State of Parties " in the last " Edinburgh Review ". London, 1810.

HUNTER, W. Thoughts on the Present Political State of Affairs in a letter. London, [1811].

Institution and Early Proceedings of the Union for Parliamentary Reform, according to the Constitution. London, 1812.

JONES, J. GALE. Five Letters to the Rt. Hon. G. Tierney, Esq. London, [1806].

KENYON, LORD. Observations on the Roman Catholic Question. London, 1810.

KEOGH, CORNELIUS. The Veto. A Commentary on the Grenville Manifesto, by Cornelius Keogh, Esq. (late of Mount Jerome in Ireland), a Catholic, and a Member of some Literary Societies. London, 1810.

The King, on the prosecution of G. L. Wardle, Esq., M.P., against F. Wright, D. Wright, and M. A. Clarke, for a Conspiracy, *etc*. London, 1809.

" LAICUS." The Fourth Letter of Laicus in Answer to Dr. Milner's Appeal, *etc*. Dublin, [1809].

LECKIE, G. F. An Historical Survey of the Foreign Affairs of Great Britain ; Parts I and II. London, 1808.

An Essay on the Practice of the British Government ; distinguished from the Abstract Theory upon which it is supposed to be founded. London, 1817. [1st edition, 1812.] [In *The Pamphleteer*, Vol. XI.]

A Letter to His Majesty. The Bandogs ; or Remarks on the Managers against W. Hastings, Esq., and Lord Melville. London, 1808.

Letter on the Catholic Claims, written to the late Rt. Hon. Edmund Burke in the year 1795. London, 1808.

A Letter, stating the Connection which the Presbyterians, Dissenters, and

Catholics, had with the Recent Event, which has agitated, and still agitates, the British Empire. Glasgow, 1807.

Letter to the Duke of Sussex on a Dinner of the Self-misnamed Friends of Civil and Religious Liberty. By an Orangeman. London, 1813.

McCALLUM, P. F. Le Livre rouge ; or, a new and extraordinary Red-Book. London, 1810. [3rd edition.]

McKENNA, T. Views of the Catholic Question, submitted to the Good Sense of the People of England. London, 1808.

MEADLEY, G. W. A Sketch of the Various Proposals for Constitutional Reform in the Representation of the People. [In Bentham's *Works*, Vol. III. London, 1843.]

" MENTOR." The Dangers of the " Edinburgh Review " ; or a brief Exposure of its Principles in Religion, Morals, and Politics. London, 1808.

MILBURNE, H. A Narrative of the Circumstances attending the Retreat of the British Army under the Command of the late Lieut.-Gen. Sir John Moore. London, 1809.

MILNER, J. The Case of Conscience solved ; or the Catholic Claims proved to be compatible with the Coronation Oath. London, 1807.

An Inquiry into certain Vulgar Opinions concerning the Catholic Inhabitants and the Antiquities of Ireland. London, 1808.

Dr. Milner's Appeal to the Catholics of Ireland. Dublin, 1809.

Supplement to a Pastoral Letter. London, 1809.

An Elucidation of the Veto. London, 1810.

Letters from the Rev. Dr. Milner (which appeared in the *Statesman*). London, 1810.

Letters to a Roman Catholic Prelate of Ireland. Dublin, 1811.

An Explanation with the R. Rev. Dr. Poynter. Wolverhampton, [1812].

MOORE, THOMAS. Letter to the Roman Catholics of Dublin. Dublin, 1810. [2nd edition.]

Notice of the Evidence given in the Committee of the House of Commons, during the Inquiry into the Conduct and Policy of the late Expedition to the River Scheldt ; with Observations. London, 1810. [A judicious and successful defence of Government.]

Observations on (what is called) the Catholic Bill lately introduced into Parliament by Lord Howick. With a Copy of the Bill. By an Eminent Lawyer. Dublin, 1808.

Observations on the System of War of the Allies in the Spanish Peninsula. London, 1811.

O'CONOR, C. Columbanus ad Hibernos. Buckingham, 1810.

Columbanus ad Hibernos, No. 2. Buckingham, 1810.

Columbanus' Third Letter, on the Liberties of the Irish Church. London, 1810.

An Historical Address on the Calamities occasioned by Foreign Influence, in the Nomination of Bishops to Irish Sees. Buckingham, 1812.

Operations of the British Army in Spain, involving Broad Hints to the Commissariat ; by an Officer of the Staff. London, 1809.

The Parliament of Ispahan, an Oriental Eclogue. London, 1810.

PASLEY, C. W. Essay on the Military Policy and Institutions of the British Empire. London, 1811. [3rd edition ; 1st edition, 1810.]

The Patriots and the Whigs the most Dangerous Enemies of the State. [Perhaps by I. Brock.] London, 1810.

Peace with France! Ships, Colonies, and Commerce ; Bankruptcies considered ; Sir Francis Burdett ; some Light thrown on the Causes of the Riots, April, 1810 ; Bullion Report ; Circulating Medium ; Peninsula ; Prophecies. London, 1812.

Mr. Pitt, the grand Political Delinquent. London, 1812.

PLOWDEN, F. An Historical Reply to the Rev. Dr. Charles O'Conor's " Columbanus No. IV ". London, 1813.

POLE, W. W. Substance of the Speech of . . . 8th March, 1811, upon a Motion of the Rt. Hon. George Ponsonby, *etc*. London, 1811.

Proceedings of the First Anniversary Meeting of the Triumph of Westminster, May 23, 1808, at the Crown and Anchor Tavern. London, n.d.

" PUBLICOLA." Letter to the Freeholders of the County of Middlesex. *In* Six Letters of Publicola on the liberty of the subject, and, the privileges of the House of Commons, originally published in *The Times*. London, 1810.

RANBY, JOHN. An Inquiry into the supposed Increase of the Influence of the Crown. London, 1811.

First Report of the Select Committee on Sinecure Offices. London, 1810.

A Full Report of the Proceedings of the Electors of Westminster on the 29th of March, 1809. London, 1809.

Report of the Proceedings at the Meeting at the Crown and Anchor Tavern, May 1, 1809. London, 1809.

A Report of the Trial of Thomas Kirwan, Merchant, for a Misdemeanour. By Wm. Ridgeway. Dublin, 1812.

ROMILLY, S. Memoirs of the Life of that Illustrious Patriot Sir Samuel Romilly. London, [1818].

ROSCOE, W. Considerations on the Causes, Objects, and Consequences of the Present War ; and on the Expediency, or the Danger of Peace with France. London, 1808.

Brief Observations on the Address to His Majesty proposed by Earl Grey . . . June 13, 1810. Liverpool, 1810.

Letter to William Roscoe, Esq., containing strictures on his late publication, *etc*. Liverpool and New York, 1808.

Letter to Henry Brougham, Esq., M.P., on the subject of reform in the representation, *etc*. Liverpool, 1811.

ROSE, GEORGE. Observations respecting the Public Expenditure and the Influence of the Crown. London, 1810.

Royal Veto considered ; in reply to Dr. Milner's Letter to a Parish Priest. By an Irish Catholic Clergyman. London, 1809.

R——l Consistency. A Poetical Parody on an Original Letter extracted from the " British Press " of March 7, 1812. [By Tom Moore.] London, 1812.

RYAN, E. Strictures on Dr. Milner's Tour. Dublin, 1809.

SELKIRK, EARL OF. A Letter to John Cartwright, Esq.

A Short Account of a Late Short Administration. London, 1807. [This rare pamphlet is by F. Horner and H. G. Bennet. There is no copy either in the British Museum or the Bodleian. The writer was so fortunate as to find one in the library of Princeton, N.J.]

A Short Answer to a Long Irish Story. 3rd edition, London, 1808.

Short Remarks on the State of Parties at the close of the year 1809. London, 1809.

SIDMOUTH, LORD. Speech . . . on April 13, 1807. London, 1807.

A Sketch of the State of Ireland, Past and Present. London, 1808.

" SYDNEY." Letters on the Affairs of Spain. London, 1809.

TARLETON, B. Substance of a Speech intended for the Vote of Credit Bill for 1810. London, 1810.

TOMLINE, G. A Charge delivered to the Clergy of the Diocese of Lincoln, *etc.* London, 1812.

TOOKE, HORNE. A Letter to the Editor of " The Times ". London, 1807.

A Warning to the Electors of Westminster. London, 1807.

Trial of Thirty-eight Men on a Charge of administering an Unlawful Oath . . . at Lancaster, August 27, 1812. With an Introductory Narrative by John Knight, one of the Defendants. Manchester, 1812.

TROTTER, J. B. A Letter to Lord Grenville, controverting his Lordship's Propositions on the Veto. Dublin, 1810.

The True Briton, by way of reply to Sir Francis Burdett's Letter ; wherein the Rights of the House of Commons are clearly enunciated. (Earnestly recommended to be read by every friend and lover of his country.) London, 1810.

" VETUS." The Letters of Vetus [*i.e.* E. Sterling]. London, 1812.

A Vindication of the Conduct of the Irish Catholics during the late Administration. By a Protestant Barrister. Dublin, 1807.

WADDINGTON, S. F. Three Letters to that greatest of Political Apostates, George Tierney . . . together with a Correct State of the Imperfect Representation of the Commons of the United Kingdom. London, 1806.

Authentic Correspondence and Documents, explaining the Proceedings of the Marquess Wellesley, and of the Earl of Moira. London, 1812.

WHITBREAD, S. Substance of a Speech delivered in the House of Commons, on Monday, January 5, 1807. London, 1807.

An authentic Account of the late Mr. Whitbread, *etc.* By F. Phippen. London, 1815.

WYNN, C. W. W. Argument upon the Jurisdiction of the House of Commons to commit in Cases of Breach of Privilege. London, 1810.

WYVILLE, REV. C. A more extended Discussion in favour of Liberty of Conscience recommended. London, 1808.

YATE, W. H. Political and Historical Arguments proving the necessity of a Parliamentary Reform, *etc.* London, 1812.

A Candid Address. London, 1812.

E. *General Works*

AIRLIE, MABELL COUNTESS. In Whig Society. London, 1921.

" ALFRED." The History of the Factory Movement from the year 1802, *etc.* [By Sam Kydd.] London, 1857.

AMYOT, THOMAS. Some Account of the Life of the Right Honourable William Windham. London, 1812.

[ANONYMOUS.] The Life of . . . Sir David Baird. [By T. E. Hook.] London, 1832.

[ANONYMOUS.] Personal Recollections of the Life and Times . . . of Lord Cloncurry. Dublin, 1849.

ASHTON, JOHN. The Dawn of the 19th Century in England. London, 1886.
Social England under the Regency. London, 1899.

ASPINALL, A. Lord Brougham and the Whig Party. Manchester, 1927.
The Canningite Party (in " Transactions of the Royal Historical Society ",
Vol. XVII, IV Series, 1934, at p. 117).

BAIN, ALEXANDER. James Mill. A Biography. London, 1882.

BARRINGTON, SIR JONAH. Personal Sketches of his own Times. Edited by
Townsend Young. 3rd edition. London, 1869.

BLEASE, W. L. A Short History of English Liberalism. London, 1913.

BLUNDEN, E. C. Leigh Hunt. London, 1930.
Leigh Hunt's " Examiner " Examined, etc. London, 1928.

BOURNE, H. FOX. English Newspapers. Chapters in the History of Journalism.
London, 1887.

BRAILSFORD, H. N. Shelley, Godwin, and their Circle. [Home University
Library.] 1913.

BRIDGES, J. H. Part III, " From the Union to Catholic Emancipation ", in
Two Centuries of Irish History, 1691–1870. London, 1888.

BRINTON, CRANE. The Political Ideas of the English Romanticists. London, 1926.

BROUGHAM, HENRY. Historical Sketches of Statesmen . . . of the Time of
George III. I and II Series. London, 1839.

BROUGHTON, LORD. Recollections of a Long Life. Edited by Lady Dorchester.
London, 1909.

The Cambridge History of English Literature. Vol. XI. The Period of the
French Revolution. Vol. XII. The Nineteenth Century, I. Cambridge, 1932.

CARLYLE, E. I. William Cobbett. A Study of His Life as shown in his
Writings. London, 1904.

CHESTERTON, G. K. William Cobbett. London, n.d.

CLARKE, W. The Authentic and Impartial Life of Mrs. Clarke, etc. London,
1809.

CLAYDEN, P. W. Rogers and his Contemporaries. London, 1889.

COBBAN, A. Edmund Burke and the Revolt against the Eighteenth Century.
London, 1929.

COBBETT, W. Rural Rides ; edited by G. D. H. and M. Cole. London, 1930.
[Has a valuable, though imperfect, biographical index to Vol. III.]

COCKBURN, LORD. Memorials of his Time. Edinburgh, 1856.

COLE, G. D. H. Robert Owen. London, 1925.
The Life of William Cobbett. London, 1924.

COOKE, G. W. The History of Party. London, 1836–1837.

COPINGER, W. A. On the Authorship of the first Hundred Numbers of the
" Edinburgh Review ". Privately printed. Manchester, 1895.

COQUELLE, P. Napoleon and England, 1803–1813. A Study from unprinted
documents. Translated by Gordon D. Knox. London, 1904.

CORTI, COUNT. Huset Rothschild. Stockholm, 1928.

COTTLE, JOSEPH. Reminiscences of S. T. Coleridge and R. Southey. London,
1847.

COUPLAND, R. Wilberforce. A Narrative. Oxford, 1923.

CUNNINGHAM, AUDREY. British Credit in the Last Napoleonic War, etc. Cambridge, 1910.

CUNNINGTON, B. H. Some Annals of the Borough of Devizes, 1791–1835.
Devizes, 1925.

DAVIES, GODFREY. The Whigs and the Peninsular War. In " Transactions of the Royal Historical Society ", Vol. II (IV Series), London, 1919, at p. 113. [Of very slight value.]

DAVIS, H. W. C. The Age of Grey and Peel. Oxford, 1929.

DICEY, A. V. The Statesmanship of Wordsworth. Oxford, 1917.

DUNDONALD, T. B., 11th EARL OF, and BOURNE, H. R. F. The Life of Thos., Lord Cochrane, etc. London, 1869.

DUNLOP, R. Daniel O'Connell. [Heroes of the Nations.]

EMDEN, C. S. The People and the Constitution. Oxford, 1933.

FAGAN, W. The Life and Times of Daniel O'Connell, Esq. Cork, 1847–48.

FALKINER, C. LITTON. Studies in Irish History and Biography, mainly of the 18th Century. London, 1902.

FESTING, GABRIELLE. John Hookham Frere and his Friends. London, 1899.

FITZGERALD, PERCY H. The Life of George IV, etc. London, 1881.
The Lives of the Sheridans. London, 1886.

FITZPATRICK, W. J. The Life, Times, and Contemporaries of Lord Cloncurry. Dublin, 1855.

FORTESCUE, SIR JOHN W. Dundonald. [English Men of Action.] London, 1895.
The County Lieutenancies and the Army, 1803–14. London, 1909.
British Statesmen of the Great War, 1793–1814. Oxford, 1911.
History of the British Army, London, 1899–1930.

FRANCIS, SIR PHILIP. Memoirs. Edited by J. Parkes and H. Merivale. London, 1867.

FREMANTLE, A. F. England in the Nineteenth Century. Vols. I. and II. London, 1929–1930.

FRERE, JOHN HOOKHAM. Works. [Vol. I. has a Memoir by Sir Bartle Frere.] London, 1874.

FULFORD, ROGER. Royal Dukes. London, 1933.

FURBER, HOLDEN. Henry Dundas, first Viscount Melville. Oxford, 1931.
New York, 1925.

GALPIN, W. F. The Grain Supply of England during the Napoleonic Period.

GREGO, J. History of Parliamentary Elections. London, 1886.

HALÉVY, E. A History of the English People in 1815. London, 1924.
La Formation du radicalisme philosophique. II. L'Évolution de la doctrine utilitaire, de 1789 à 1815. Paris, 1901.

HAMMOND, J. L. and B. The Skilled Labourer, 1760–1832. London, 1919.
The Village Labourer, 1760–1832. London, 1911.
The Town Labourer, 1760–1832. London, 1917.

HARPER, G. M. William Wordsworth. His Life, Works and Influence. London, 1916.

HARRIS, W. History of the Radical Party in Parliament. London, 1885.

HAYDON, B. R. Autobiography, etc. Edited by Tom Taylor. Introduction by Aldous Huxley. London, 1926.

HECKSHER, ELI. The Continental System. An economic interpretation. Oxford, 1922.

HOVELL, MARK. The Chartist Movement. Manchester, 1925.

HOWE, P. P. The Life of William Hazlitt. London, 1928.

HUISH, R. Memoirs of George IV. London, 1830.
The Memoirs, Private and Political, of Daniel O'Connell, Esq., etc. London 1836.

HUNT, F. K. The Fourth Estate. A Contribution towards the history of Newspapers, etc. London, 1850.

HUSENBETH, F. C. The Life of the Rt. Rev. John Milner, D.D. Dublin, 1862.

KEBBEL, T. A History of Toryism, etc. London, 1886.

KEIR, D. L. Economical Reform, 1779–1787 ; in " The Law Quarterly Review ", No. CXCIX.

LONSDALE, H. The Worthies of Cumberland. Vol. I. John Christian Curwen. London, 1867.

MacCARTHY, J. G. Henry Grattan. Dublin, 1886.

MacCUNN, F. J. The Contemporary English View of Napoleon. London, 1914.

MANCHESTER, A. K. British Pre-eminence in Brazil, its Rise and Decline. Chapel Hill (University of North Carolina), 1933.

MATHESON, C. The Life of Henry Dundas, first Viscount Melville. London, 1933.

MEIKLE, H. W. Scotland and the French Revolution. Glasgow, 1912.

MOORE, J. C. The Life of Lieut.-Gen. Sir John Moore, K.B. London, 1834.

MOORE, THOMAS. The Memoirs of Lord Edward Fitzgerald. London, 1897.

MUNK, W. The Life of Sir Henry Halford, Bart. London, 1895.

"A MUNSTER FARMER." Reminiscences of Daniel O'Connell, Esq. Dublin, 1847.

NEALE, E. The Life of Field-Marshal H.R.H. Edward, Duke of Kent, etc. London, 1850.

NEWENHAM, THOMAS. A View of the Natural, Political, and Commercial Circumstances of Ireland. London, 1809.

O'CONNELL, J. The Life and Speeches of Daniel O'Connell. Edited by his son. Dublin, 1846.

O'CONNOR, SIR JAMES. History of Ireland, 1798–1924. London, 1926.

O'FLANAGAN, J. R. The Lives of the Lord Chancellors and Keepers of the Great Seal of Ireland. London, 1870.

OLDFIELD, T. H. B. The Representative History of Great Britain and Ireland, etc. 2nd edition. London, 1816.

OMAN, SIR CHARLES W. C. A History of the Peninsular War. Oxford, 1902–1930. Wellington's Army, 1809–1814. London, 1912.

PATTERSON, M. W. Sir Francis Burdett and his Times. London, 1930.

PAUL, ALEXANDER. Short Parliaments. A History of the National Demand for frequent General Elections. London, 1883.

PAUL, C. KEGAN. William Godwin, his Friends and Contemporaries. London, 1876.

PEEL, FRANK. The Risings of the Luddites, Chartists and Plugdrawers. Heckmondwike, 1888.

PHILLIPS, CHARLES. Recollections of Curran, and some of his Contemporaries. London, 1818.

[PHILLIPS, SIR RICHARD.] Public Characters. [An annual volume. The issues for 1806, 1807, 1809, and 1810 contain useful matter.]

PONSONBY, ARTHUR, LORD. English Diaries. London, 1923.
More English Diaries, etc. London, 1927.
Scottish and Irish Diaries, etc. London, 1927.

PORRITT, E. The Unreformed House of Commons. Cambridge, 1909.

PORTER, G. R. The Progress of the Nation. 2nd edition. London, 1851.

PRENTICE, ARCHIBALD. Historical Sketches and Personal Recollections of Manchester. London and Manchester, 1851.

REDDING, CYRUS. Yesterday and Today. London, 1863.

RHODES, R. CROMPTON. Harlequin Sheridan. The Man and the Legends. Oxford, 1933.

ROSCOE, HENRY. The Life of William Roscoe. London, 1833.

ROSE, J. HOLLAND. Napoleonic Studies. London, 1904.

The Rise of Democracy. London, 1912.

SCARLETT, Hon. P. C. A Memoir of the Rt. Hon. James, first Lord Abinger, etc. London, 1877.

SHEIL, R. LALOR. Sketches, Legal and Political, etc. London, 1855.

SICHEL, W. Sheridan. London, 1909.

STANHOPE, G., and GOOCH, G. P. The Life of Charles, third Earl Stanhope. London, 1914.

STAPLETON, A. G. George Canning and his Times. London, 1859.

STEPHEN, SIR LESLIE. The English Utilitarians. Vol. I. Jeremy Bentham. London, 1900.

STEPHENS, ALEXANDER. Memoirs of J. Horne Tooke. London, 1813.

TEMPERLEY, H. M. V. Life of Canning. London, 1905.

Thelwall, J. By C. Cestre. London, 1906.

TIMBS, J. Club Life of London, etc. London, 1866.

TOYNBEE, W. Vignettes of the Regency, etc. London, 1907.

TREVELYAN, G. M. Lord Grey of the Reform Bill. London, 1920.

TUCKER, J. S. Memoirs of Admiral the Rt. Hon. the Earl of St. Vincent. London, 1844.

VEITCH, G. S. The Genesis of Parliamentary Reform. London, 1913.

WAKEFIELD, EDWARD. An account of Ireland, Statistical and Political. London, 1812.

WALLAS, GRAHAM. The Life of Francis Place. New York, 1919.

WARD, BERNARD. Catholic London a Century Ago. London, 1905.

WEBSTER, C. K. The Foreign Policy of Castlereagh, 1812–1815. London, 1931.

White, J. Blanco, The Life of. Edited by J. H. Thom. London, 1845.

WICKWAR, W. H. The Struggle for the Freedom of the Press, 1819–1832. London, 1928.

WILKIN, W. H. The Life of Sir David Baird. London, 1912.

Wilson, Sir Robert T., The Life of. Edited by H. Randolph. London, 1862.

WRIGHT, THOMAS. Caricature History of the Georges, etc. London, 1867.

INDEX